MARGARET
Queen of Sicily

By the Same Author

Queens of Sicily 1061-1266

Sicilian Queenship

Kingdom of Sicily 1130-1266

Women of Sicily

The Peoples of Sicily

The Ferraris Chronicle

Sicilian Studies

Sicilian Court Culture 1061-1266

Sicilian Food and Wine

Sicily: The Time Traveler's Guide

Norman-Arab-Byzantine
Palermo, Monreale and Cefalù

MARGARET
Queen of Sicily

Jacqueline Alio

Copyright © 2016 Calogera Jacqueline Alio. All rights reserved.

Published by Trinacria Editions, New York.

This book may not be reproduced by any means whatsoever, in whole or in part, including illustrations, photographs and maps, in any form beyond the fair-use copying permitted by the United States Copyright Law and the Berne Convention, except by reviewers for the public press (magazines, newspapers and their websites), without written permission from the copyright holder.

The right of Calogera Jacqueline Alio to be identified as the author of this work has been asserted by her in accordance with the Copyright, Design and Patents Act, 1988 (UK).

Legal Deposit: Library of Congress, British Library (and Bodleian Libraries, Cambridge University Library, Trinity College Library, National Libraries of Scotland and Wales, under ALDL number 1.3475044), Italian National Libraries (Rome, Florence).

The title of this book was assigned a Library of Congress Control Number on 13 November 2014. Copyright of this work was pre-registered with the United States Copyright Office on 13 November 2015 under number PRE000008358 in the class "Literary Work in Book Form." Identifying information was registered by the British Library through Bibliographic Data Services on 27 April 2016.

Except where otherwise indicated, all translations contained herein are by Calogera Jacqueline Alio. Illustrations, photographs, maps and cover design by Louis Mendola. Additional credits in Acknowledgments. The text of this monograph was double-blind peer-reviewed.

ORCID identifier of Calogera Jacqueline Alio: 0000-0003-1134-1217

Printed on acid-free paper.

ISBN 9780991588657 (print)
ISBN 9781943639076 (ebook)

Library of Congress Control Number 2014956863

A CIP catalogue record for this book is available from the British Library.

IN MEMORIAM

Vincenzo Alio

1920 - 2012

The loving father who taught me,
when I was just five years old,
how to use a dictionary
to find answers

MARGARET'S BIOGRAPHER

Jacqueline Alio is an accomplished medievalist, having published original, scholarly research as well as books and articles for a general readership. She is a popular lecturer.

Consulted over the years by The History Channel, The Discovery Channel and other media, she was the first Sicilian woman living in Sicily to write books on her island's ancient and medieval history in English, rather than Italian, for readers around the world.

This book is the lengthiest scholarly, peer-reviewed monograph ever published that was written in English, as its original language, by a historian based in Sicily.

Read by millions over the last decade, Jackie Alio's online articles have made her one of the most popular Sicilian historians internationally.

In 2012 she contributed a chapter on the Jews of Palermo to *Sicilian Genealogy and Heraldry,* a book that established a new Dewey catalogue subject category in the British Library and in the New York Public Library.

The following year, she co-authored *The Peoples of Sicily: A Multicultural Legacy,* a sophisticated ethnography that surveys the island's complex ancient and medieval history, proposing pluralistic, twelfth-century Sicily as a model of social diversity and an inspiration for the modern world.

Her *Women of Sicily: Saints, Queens and Rebels* was published to critical acclaim in 2014. In addition to its profiles of seventeen historical figures, it presents a chronology of dates and events into the twenty-first century, and a concise overview of the status of Sicilian women today.

In 2015 she ventured into the realm of culinary history, co-authoring *Sicilian Food and Wine: The Cognoscente's Guide*.

Perfectly suited to our times, Jackie Alio's work is multidisciplinary and multifaceted. As this book was going to press, she was writing the first compendium of biographies of the queens of the Kingdom of Sicily.

She resides in Palermo in what used to be the Genoard Park known to Queen Margaret, in the shadow of Monreale.

PROLOGUE

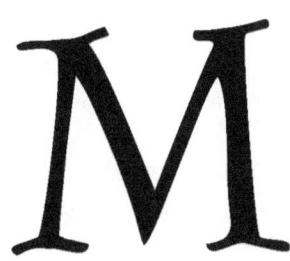

"Being a princess isn't all it's cracked up to be."

— Diana, Princess of Wales

Unprompted by her tutor, a thirtyish lady-in-waiting fluent in half a dozen languages, the girl rose from her throne-like chair and went to close the thick shutters. The winds of the snow-capped Pyrenees were not always kind to Pamplona this time of year, and a sudden gust from them rustled the sheet of parchment on the stout oaken table, depositing a dried leaf on an unscrolled map held in place by two stone paper weights.

The flames of the fireplace made up for the absence of what little daylight penetrated this part of the castle from the grayish sky beyond the window. The flickering light of the table lamp, a rare luxury, shone upon the map.

Margaret returned to her seat to find the leaf concealing part of a jagged, triangular outline near an edge of the vast drawing.

Sicily.

Brushing back long, brownish hair, the teenager gazed at

the map for a long moment and then asked the tutor how long the voyage would take.

"Two months," came the reply.

"By land?"

"Yes. At least from Iruña to Marseille. Then we'll take a ship to Sicily."

"And you'll go with me? All the way?"

"Of course."

"You'll stay with me in Palermo?"

"As long as you wish, Lady Margaret."

"You said Sicily is much like Navarre and Aragon."

"Very much."

"And there are Muslims and Jews, like at Tudela?"

"Of course," said the tutor. "And Greeks."

"And the Hautevilles are Norman, like my mother's family?"

"So it is said."

But here true curiosity intervened. It was the natural, unfettered curiosity of a girl's fourteen years.

"I hope William isn't too ugly. Or too stupid. Well, especially not too ugly."

"Let's get back to studying," said the tutor, continuing the morning's lesson in a distinctive mixture of Euskara and Latin. "Ni amo, zu amas, hura amat, gu amamus —"

"Why must it be *that* word?" Margaret interrupted.

"Because *love* is the most important verb for you to know."

"Let's just hope his French is better than my Latin."

"Don't worry, Margaret. I'm sure he'll make himself understood. Just try to be a good wife."

Now the rhythmic sound of heavy raindrops could be heard pelting the shutters.

Followed by a burst of thunder.

PREFACE

"Never cease to act because you fear you may fail."

— Queen Liliuokalani of Hawaii

As Queen Regent of Sicily, Margaret Jiménez of Navarre was the most powerful woman in Europe for five eventful years. She was the most important woman of medieval Sicily. If only for that simple reason, her story is worthy of our interest. But there are other reasons to consider her life and times.

Margaret of Navarre represents the dynastic and social bridge between Sicily and the northeastern Iberian lands. This began with the marriage of Roger II, Sicily's first king, to Elvira of Castile, Margaret's cousin. It was destined to reach a fuller fruition with the marriage of Frederick II to Constance of Aragon in 1209 and, of course, the crowning of Peter III of Aragon as King of Sicily in 1282. Coming on the heels of the bloody War of the Vespers, this last development led to Sicily finding herself in the Iberian political orbit for the next few centuries, first as a jewel in the "Crown of Aragon" ruled from Barcelona, and then as a cornerstone of the Spanish Empire.

Margaret's relationships with Thomas Becket and her Navarrese countryman, the rabbi Benjamin of Tudela, say as much about each of these two men as they do about her and her adopted people, the polyglot Sicilians.

"You have gained praise among your countrymen, and glory among posterity, and made us your debtors," wrote Thomas Becket to Margaret in a letter thanking her for extending hospitality to his family when they were exiled from England by King Henry II, whose daughter ended up marrying Margaret's son.

Like most past ages, Europe's High Middle Ages were not a great era for women. They were benighted times that witnessed very few females groomed to lead nations, or indeed anything more grandiose than a convent or a kitchen. Yet the first century of Sicily's life as a kingdom saw two intrepid women pilot the realm through perilous waters. Margaret of Navarre, as we shall see, became queen regent; a few decades later, Constance of Hauteville, who inherited the Kingdom of Sicily, was queen regnant. They knew each other, and young Constance may even have patterned part of her "leadership style" after Margaret's. A sisterhood, though tenuous, probably existed.

Both were the daughters of kings, the sisters of kings, the mothers of kings. In youth, neither seemed destined for greatness, or even queenship. It was widowhood that prompted their ascents to power. Their lives deserve to be studied, or at least noted, for there is something to be learned from them. Our focus, of course, is Margaret, who arrived in Sicily at the end of her girlhood. Indeed, it was the arrival itself that brought her girlhood to an end.

Inevitably, Margaret's story, like those of the queens who were her contemporaries, is to some degree defined dialectically by the entrenched patriarchy. In her time there were kingdoms but no true European queendoms. Chroniclers recounted more tales of heroes than heroines.

It is inescapable — a formless subtext lurking in the shadows cast by the long march of centuries. Sooner or later, any biography of a female leader must confront the thorny question of gender. Therein lies a latent sexism, a lingering vestige of the infamous double standard that colors the ages, for nobody writing about a man is expected to address the subject's masculinity as if it were a barrier to be overcome. We need not dwell on this tired topos, nor make it the object of arcane debates, but we cannot ignore it.

Women are different from their brothers, and those differences were far more acute in the twelfth century — an epoch of absolute monarchies, absolute roles and absolute power — than in our time. In practice, the act of ruling was essentially the same regardless of the sex of the ruler; it was the ubiquitous misogynists who created most of the obstacles facing those few queens who found themselves actually governing kingdoms.

During the Middle Ages, Sicily was one of the few places where a woman ruled a population that included many Muslims. Yet the more outspoken men who challenged Margaret's authority were not the kingdom's Muslims, but rather its Christians, including two of her kinsmen.

Anybody familiar with chess, a game introduced in Sicily by the Arabs, knows that the queen is the most versatile piece on the board. She can defend her king or attack opponents. Margaret proved adept at both tactics. Checkmating foes was part of the job.

Medieval queenhood was more grit than glitter. Despite good meals, comfortable beds and occasional pageantry, ruling a kingdom was a burdensome task.

Twelfth-century queens regent and regnant assumed the

duties usually reserved to men. Thus we find Constance of France, the widow of Bohemond of Antioch, a monarch of Sicily's House of Hauteville, acting as her son's regent and knighting the boy herself.

The historiography and method that led to this biography are considered at some length in the following pages. For the moment, let it suffice to say that sound epistemology is key, and if our quest for accuracy is essential so is the balanced presentation of history. Historical biography must never wander into the domain of historical fiction.

Margaret's travels took her from her native Navarre to Sicily, a tortuous path followed, very literally, by the author, albeit using slightly more modern means than horse and galley. From Pamplona to Palermo, across seas and mountains, Margaret edged her way to greatness, step by step, out of simple necessity. It was not an easy road, nor even an expected one.

The lessons learned are general, perhaps abstract. Chief among them is the very simple idea that strength springs forth from our response to adversity. This is something embodied not only by "leaders" but by women who face challenges in their daily lives; the single mother and the businesswoman have much in common with Margaret of Navarre.

Because our journey follows Margaret's, we'll cast an eye over the social environment she found in the Kingdom of Sicily, which included the islands of Sicily and Malta, and most of the Italian peninsula south of Rome. The realm, the *Regnum Siciliae,* boasted a prosperous, multicultural population, a fair degree of independence from the Papacy, a reasonably efficient feudal system of land ownership and, not leastly, a solid legal code, the Assizes of Ariano, inspired by the Code of Justinian. The middle years of the twelfth century found the kingdom with one of the wealthiest economies in Europe and the Mediterranean, having a population distinguished by its ethno-religious and intellectual diversitude.

We shall, of course, glance over the reigns of three kings Margaret knew, the men who shaped her life. These were her father García Ramírez, her father-in-law Roger II, and her husband William I. Then there was the reign of her son, William II, for whom she was regent. However, ours will not be an exhaustive study of those kingly reigns, to which entire volumes have been dedicated. Nor will it focus exclusively on chronicles and charters, although such sources shall be considered extensively.

Island kingdoms seem to enjoy a special niche in history, and certainly in literature. Tragically, one finds few obvious traces of Liliuokalani's noble legacy in Hawaii. More celebrated are the signs that Margaret left in Sicily, among them the magnificent cathedral at Monreale, which her son built and where she rests.

The name *Margaret* is thought to derive from ancient Persian or Greek words for pearls, clusters of pearls, or blossoms. Saint Margaret of Antioch was a Christian virgin martyred in 304. Queen Margaret's death at forty-eight years was a natural one, though far too premature.

This book is not an encomium. In life, Queen Margaret was loved and despised, praised and disparaged. Such is the fate of queens. Among sage historians her detractors are few, her legacy assured. But nobody has ever seen fit to write a book about her, until now.

The story of Europe's eventful twelfth century is now one step closer to completeness.

Fortitude, thy name is woman.

Margaret's Journey to Palermo

ACKNOWLEDGMENTS

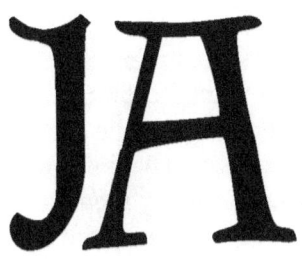

"In youth we learn. In age we understand."

— Marie von Ebner-Eschenbach

The road to knowledge can be as difficult as the road to greatness, and often the two cross paths. However, tracing Margaret's footsteps was not nearly so challenging as the queen's personal journey must have been during what we now call the *High Middle Ages*. The author did not risk assassination in La Guardia, Nájera, Pamplona, Logroño, Zaragoza or Barcelona, nor public humiliation in Palermo, Monreale, Canterbury or Maniace. At Tudela, the gentle storks nesting in church towers posed no threat. In New York, where the reliquary shown on this book's cover is housed in serene dignity in Upper Manhattan, the only mild annoyance was the January snow.

The archival sources were readily available and easily consulted, the chronicles published centuries ago.

Nevertheless, a book of this kind cannot be written in a vacuum.

Thanks are expressed to Professor Gwenyth Hood of Marshall University, West Virginia, for making available her cogent commentary regarding authorship of the chronicle of "Hugh Falcandus."

The author wishes to thank the cooperative staffs at state archives and public libraries here in southern Italy, as well as the archdioceses of Palermo, Monreale and Messina, for granting access to manuscripts in their chartularies. She expresses her gratitude to Paolo Vian, the director of the manuscript department of the Vatican Apostolic Library, and the staff of the Vatican Secret Archives. Thanks also to the accommodating staff of the Archivo Real y General de Navarra in Pamplona, housed in the last vestige of the royal palace, where the author was permitted to consult records even on a Saturday morning in winter. Thanks to the diligent archivists of the Hospital de Tavera (de San Juan Bautista) in Toledo.

Special thanks to the Metropolitan Museum of Art (New York) for permission to reproduce an image of the reliquary shown on this book's cover, licensed through the OASC (Open Access for Scholarly Content) program under accession number 63.160. Thanks to the British Library for permission to use the image of the page from the Harley Trilingual Psalter, catalogued as Harley MS 5786, folio 106v.

A number of readers have lent their encouragement over the last few years. They are too many to name, but their support is very much appreciated. I thank my editor, a frenetic New Yorker, for his patience. Last but not least, heartfelt thanks to the two colleagues who very kindly found time in their busy schedules to undertake a diligent peer review of the text.

The author alone assumes responsibility for what is presented in these pages.

— C. Jacqueline Alio

Palermo, December 2016

CONTENTS

Prologue ix
Preface xi
Acknowledgments xvii
Introduction 1
Maps and Imprints 11
Photographs 37
1. Identity 59
2. Kingdom 67
3. Princess 75
4. Betrothal 91
5. Polyglot Realm 99
6. Motherhood 111
7. Queen Consort 119
8. Tragedy 129
9. Estrangement 143
10. Queen Regent 153
11. Power 173
12. Justice 185
13. Sovereignty 203
14. Palimpsest 221

15. Leadership	241
16. Thomas Becket	251
17. Transition	261
18. Benjamin of Tudela	267
19. Monreale	271
20. Queen Mother	289
21. Mother-in-Law	301
22. Patroness	309
23. Quietus	315
Epilogue	325
Chronology	329
Genealogical Tables	339
Appendix 1: bin Jubayr	345
Appendix 2: Chroniclers and Visitors	347
Appendix 3: Hugh Falcandus	353
Appendix 4: Romuald of Salerno	357
Appendix 5: Letters	359
Appendix 6: The Pendant	365
Appendix 7: Assizes of Ariano	369
Appendix 8: Chronicon Excerpts	387
Appendix 9: Joanna's Betrothal	399
Appendix 10: Margaret's Decrees	409
Notes	417
Sources and Bibliography	457
Index	475

INTRODUCTION

"Facts can obscure truth."

— Maya Angelou

Writing a biography is an exercise in responsibility and humility, especially when it happens to be the *first* biography of an important historical figure. Some exceptional royal biographies have been written in recent decades, though very few of these deal with the lives of medieval Sicilian queens. So little has been published about Margaret's *sui generis* reign that platitudes are easily avoided.

Discovering the essential facts of Margaret's life was only the beginning. The most difficult task was unearthing Margaret's "self," the *spirit* that made her what she was, and what, in historical memory, she still is. That is an underlying challenge facing any biographer seeking to reveal the details, but also the personality, of a subject who lived so long ago, in a time long before printing, photography, fast travel and faster communication.

But there exists a particular danger, a potential obstacle that dwells in the depths of the mind. This is the very real risk of presumption and preconception. Seeking facts, the historian must never fall prey to the temptation to embellish or invent details in order to make the object of her study more appealing to the reader, for no historical figure was ever perfect, or perfectly known.

In other words, the biographer must seek to present a universal truth, not a personal one. Psychoanalysis has no place in medieval biography. We cannot presume to know every thought that ever crossed our subject's mind. At best, we can apply the principles of prosopography to our study.

Context, the omnipresent barometer, helps us to ascertain accuracy. While Margaret probably would have agreed that La Rioja and the Nebrodian Mountains are splendid regions, the social milieux of Navarre and Sicily present their own complexities. These were prosperous, multicultural kingdoms of Christians, Muslims and Jews.

Subtext of that kind must never be overlooked. We must seek to know how and why certain things happened. Rarely is it sufficient, or even very satisfying, simply to know that they occurred. History is more than names, places and a few quasi-significant dates.

Then there are the political realities of an age when every kingdom, even powerful Sicily, lived under the constant threat of invasion. As an island and half a peninsula washed by warm waters, the Kingdom of Sicily was especially vulnerable.

In modern fiction, the Middle Ages are much romanticized. In reality, life brought with it daily challenges, even for royalty. Apart from outright regicide, infant mortality was a constant, merciless menace, making a child's survival to the age of three or four seem miraculous indeed. Bishops prayed for young princes to reach adulthood, although the same clerics seemed less concerned with the fate of young princesses.

Disease was rife. Malaria and dysentery were widespread

and homicidal. Plagues did not deign to distinguish between aristocrats and peasants.

Travel was perilous at best. In 1271, a pregnant Queen Isabella of France died when she fell from her horse while fording a stream in Calabria.

Childbirth was blindly femicidal, claiming the lives of mothers in every social class.

Questions of bias and perspective dominate historiography. Every historian, and indeed every thinking adult, should entertain something of a "world view" or philosophy, however rudimentary. Unlike some historical biographies, however, this one has no social or political "agenda" rooted in feminism, Italianism, Sicilianism or revisionism. Its objective is to inform the reader, perhaps offering a few insights garnered from Margaret's life and times. In doing so, the author hopes to shed some light on the experience of a woman too often considered little more than a footnote to history.

True, we must, in a sense, "transport" ourselves to Margaret's times if we are to understand her world. Empathy is not out of place in the field of historical biography. Yet, while we may look to the lives of people who lived in centuries past to inspire us, it is unhealthy when either the biographer or the reader assumes the role of idolater, identifying too closely with a deceased person, as if assuming the personality of a medieval woman. (Fear not: Jackie Alio does not think herself to be Margaret of Navarre.)

More generally, the last few decades have seen a resurgence of interest in Sicily's multicultural "golden age," a trend reflected in academic studies, museum exhibits, books, websites and tourism. That is generally a good thing. So much the better if the women of history are included.

Unfortunately, the annals of medieval history focus on men, not women, so Margaret's early life in Navarre is not documented as well or as fully as one might wish. Obviously, we know more about her life in Sicily.

We know that she spent more years in Pamplona and Palermo than elsewhere. Knowing something about these cities as they existed during the twelfth century tells us something about the woman who lived in them. Both are magnificent cities where, fortunately, much of the medieval past survives.

That a detailed biography of Margaret Jiménez of Navarre, Queen of Sicily, was not written until 2016 may strike the historian as peculiar, even bizarre, because more is known about her quinquennial regency than the reign of any other Sicilian queen of her century. By way of comparison, far less is known about the brief reign of Constance of Hauteville from 1194 to 1198.

There is an implicit risk when the history of the most consequential years in the life of a woman like Margaret is based on the words of just one or two chroniclers, and especially one so cynical as "Hugh Falcandus." Here there is no perfect remedy, no ideal solution. We have to use context and information from other sources to ascertain the difference between fact and opinion. It is important to recognize that *all* chronicles are biased to some degree. What distinguishes that of Falcandus is that its chronicler was most likely at the court when certain events transpired. For that reason he cannot be ignored, and for that reason his chronicle, with its descriptions of events until 1169, is one of our chief sources for Margaret's regency. One of the shortcomings of Falcandus is a slight ambiguity in the sequence of certain episodes he describes.

William, Margaret's son, reached the age of majority in the second half of 1171. A younger son, Henry, died the following year, leaving the king as her only surviving child.

Another contemporary chronicle pertinent to the reigns of Sicily's two Williams is the *Chronicon sive Annales* of Romuald Guarna of Salerno, who spent some time at the court of

INTRODUCTION

William I and crowned William II. We know that eloquent Bishop Romuald lived in Palermo during the years that Margaret served as her son's regent. As a high-ranking prelate, his perspective bore with it a certain intrinsic bias that favored the Papacy. Romuald's chronicle, which recounts far fewer events than that of Falcandus, takes us to 1179. Margaret died four years later.

Several other chronicles and annals were consulted, some written by chroniclers who lived further afield. In England, Ralph of Diceto and Roger of Howden wrote about Joanna, Margaret's daughter-in-law, who was the daughter of Henry II "Plantagenet," and recorded letters the English king received from William II.

At all events, precedence was given to "primary" sources, that is to say contemporary (or near-contemporary) records, be they chronicles, charters or letters. Some of these were transcribed and published long ago, but several extracts from royal charters, and a few excerpts from the *Chronicon,* appear in this monograph for the first time in English.

The few accounts published at the beginning of the age of printing were carefully considered as they reflect a late-medieval historiographical tradition. Here one *opus* stands out.

Thomas Fazello's post-incunable *De Rebus Siculis* was published in installments beginning in 1558, initially in Latin. At nearly seven hundred pages, this tome was the first major general history of Sicily to see print. Although it is not necessary that we consult Fazello's work for essential facts, it does tell us something about how the Norman kings and their consorts were viewed by historians writing in the sixteenth century, with William I accorded the epithet "the Bad" and William II "the Good." Margaret is mentioned only perfunctorily, in such fleeting passages as *Margaritam Reginam eius uxorem voluit totius regni administratricem,* in this case stating simply that she undertook royal administration. A few lines later the source is revealed. *Quod aliquot post annos sub nomine Hugonis Falcandi dum pararem haec edere.*[1] Tellingly, Fazello does not grant Margaret so much as the dignity of an entry in his book's index.

It is precisely because the important role of women, even queens, is typically overlooked in secondary works like Fazello's that we must look to primary (contemporary) sources for reliable information.

A number of Spanish sources were consulted in order that this volume's first chapters might present a succinct yet accurate profile of Margaret's Jiménez dynasty. These include several chronicles which mention the reign of García Ramírez or his immediate predecessors. Of note are the *Crónica Nájerense* and the *Crónica Navarro-Aragonesa*. Various charters from the reign of García Ramírez were studied, such as those by which he and his wife, Margaret's mother, endowed Pamplona Cathedral.

Rather little has been published in English on young Margaret's parents or their Kingdom of Navarre (Pamplona). Written by Henry Chaytor in 1933, *A History of Aragon and Catalonia* stands the test of time as a good general framework for studying the region during the period considered, and indeed into the era of the "Crown of Aragon," a thalassocracy that included Sicily after 1282.

In the popular mind, for better or worse, perceptions of Margaret's homeland are sometimes inspired by modern writings, such as Ernest Hemingway's enchanting descriptions of Pamplona. An obvious influence on many people of a certain age is *El Cid,* the 1961 motion picture starring Charlton Heston, on which the distinguished scholar Ramón Menéndez Pidal was the historical advisor. Unlike the great majority of cinematic portrayals of famous medieval figures, this one is reasonably accurate.

Although Margaret is *per forza* mentioned in histories dealing with the reigns of William I and William II, there exists no scholarly consensus of opinion about her regency. It is the author's conviction, based on the available evidence, that Queen Margaret was competent, courageous and decisive.

As medieval biographies go, this book follows a slightly unconventional path. Most readers, understandably, cultivate a "generalist" interest in history, yet the information in these pages reflects the author's original "academic" research, some of it yielding facts published here for the first time. Because it is the first biography of Queen Margaret, this book necessarily follows a prescribed format. The alternative to this would have been a superficial narrative that insults your intelligence.

Apologies are in order to those who may find this endeavour to straddle two worlds, the popular and the scholarly, a distraction. Here the author begs the reader's indulgence.

The translations of excerpts from the charters and the two Sicilian chronicles are the author's, and by intent these are more literal than literary. For the benefit of jurists and scholars, both surviving texts of the Assizes of Ariano, the legal code in force in Sicily during Margaret's lifetime, are presented in their original Latin.

There is no extant proof that Middle Sicilian, reflected in the poetry composed at the court of Frederick II by Giacomo of Lentini and Ciullo of Alcamo, was very widely spoken until the thirteenth century, but it seemed appropriate to dedicate a few words to it, as well as Basque (Euskara), Siculo Arabic, Judeo Arabic and Norman French, *pro forma*. The languages spoken in Navarre and Sicily during the twelfth century are largely extinct.

The appendices present information intended to facilitate a greater knowledge of the topics mentioned in the main text. It was deemed appropriate to include such background details in this monograph because, quite simply, they are difficult to obtain elsewhere, even on the internet.

This book reflects the most meticulous research ever conducted into the life of Margaret of Navarre. Some of the information presented in these pages may differ, if only slightly, from what is published elsewhere. Though corrective in some respects, this biography need not be seen as a rebuttal or revision of the work of other authors, nor the catalyst for esoteric debates. It is hardly academic iconoclasm to conclude that Margaret was married in 1149 instead of 1150, or that she appointed Stephen of Perche her chancellor in 1167 rather than the previous year. The reasoning for such conclusions is explained in the endnotes.

The reader is warned that certain details reported elsewhere are simply incorrect. For example, the statement that a Greek Orthodox chapel once stood on the site where Monreale Abbey was erected is based on the imprecise translation of a phrase in a charter issued in 1176 (see note 346).

More serious misperceptions among otherwise erudite scholars are sometimes rooted in such phenomena as a lack of understanding of the theology and culture of the Roman Catholic and Greek Orthodox churches so influential in Sicily during Margaret's lifetime, and even the influence of Islam. This concerns questions regarding the nature of kingship and queenship, the significance of coronations and anointings, and of course such topics as ecclesiastical authority, ecclesial architecture, iconography and, most importantly, the role of religion in the Kingdom of Sicily.

We are not interested in etiology or prolix analyses for their own sake.

While every effort has been made to avoid what the author has sometimes described as "the pedantic and the semantic," the reader's prior familiarity with Navarre and Sicily cannot be presumed, hence the details presented here through maps, photographs, genealogical tables and the introductory chapters, as well as the chronology, appendices and notes.

One rejoices that heaven has seen fit to bestow upon us

enough raw information to write a biography of a very special woman. Even so, an analysis of Margaret's regency beyond what is presented in this volume would be inordinately tedious, adding more verbiage than gravitas.

The author lives in Sicily, of course, but she does not have any personal or professional affiliations which might cast her perspective into the murky waters that lead to historiographical bias.

Our journey, like Margaret's, begins in northeastern Spain.

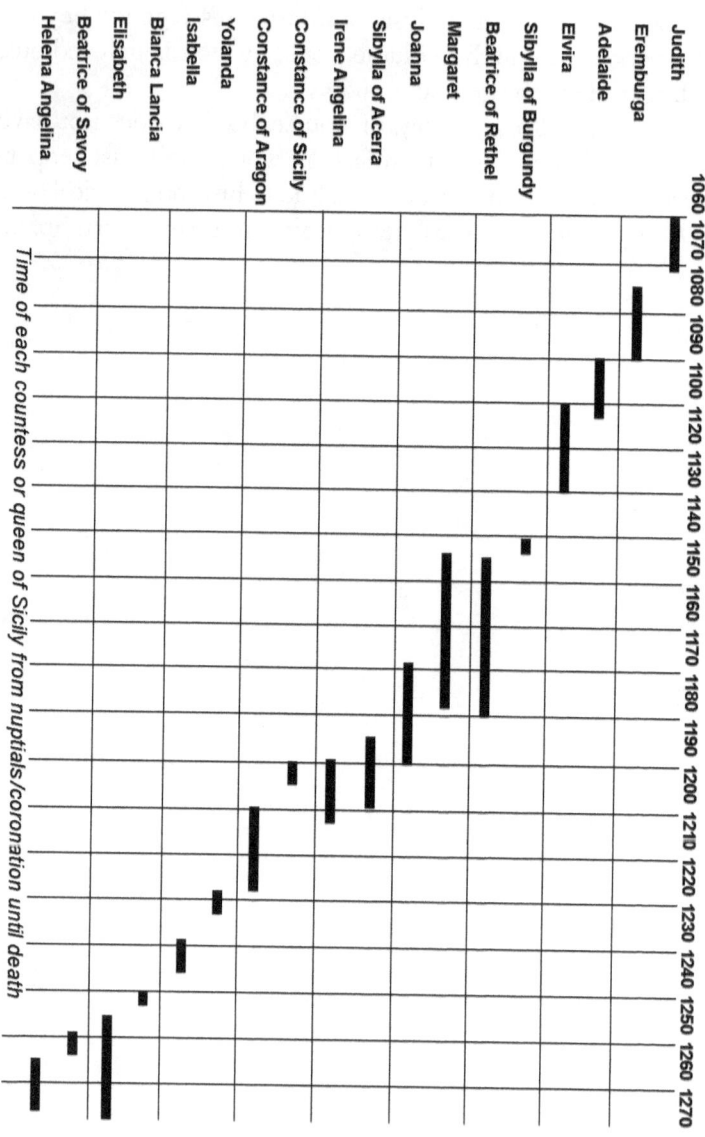

MAPS
and
IMPRINTS

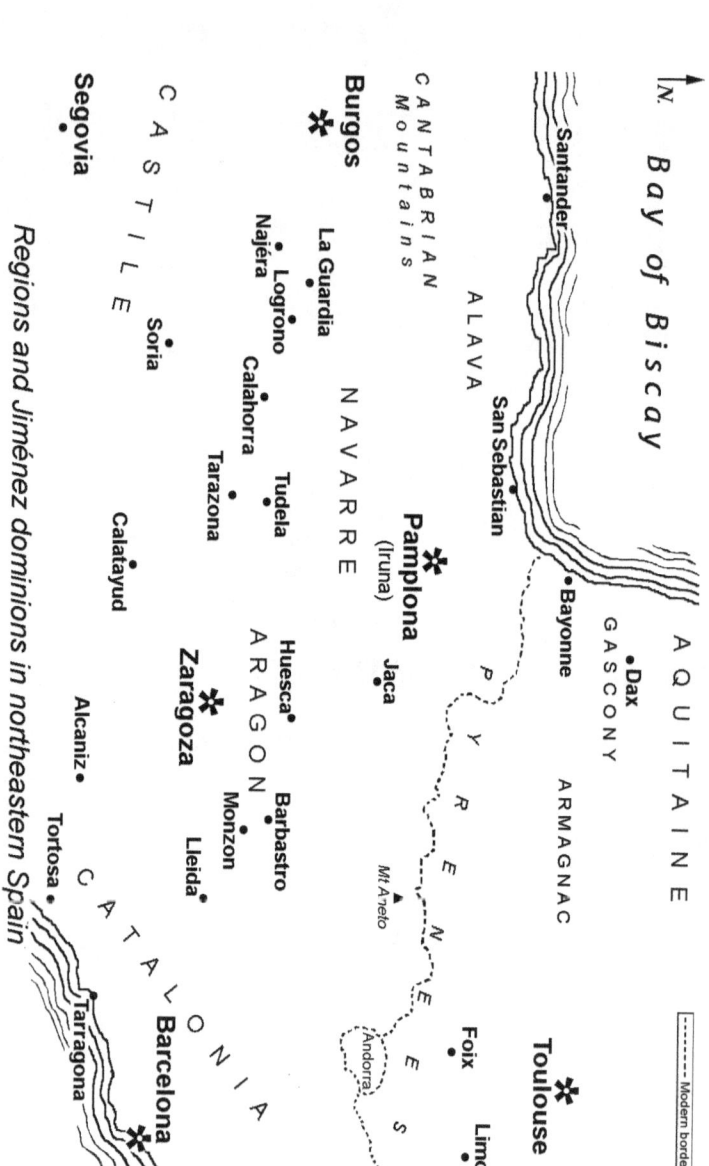

Regions and Jiménez dominions in northeastern Spain

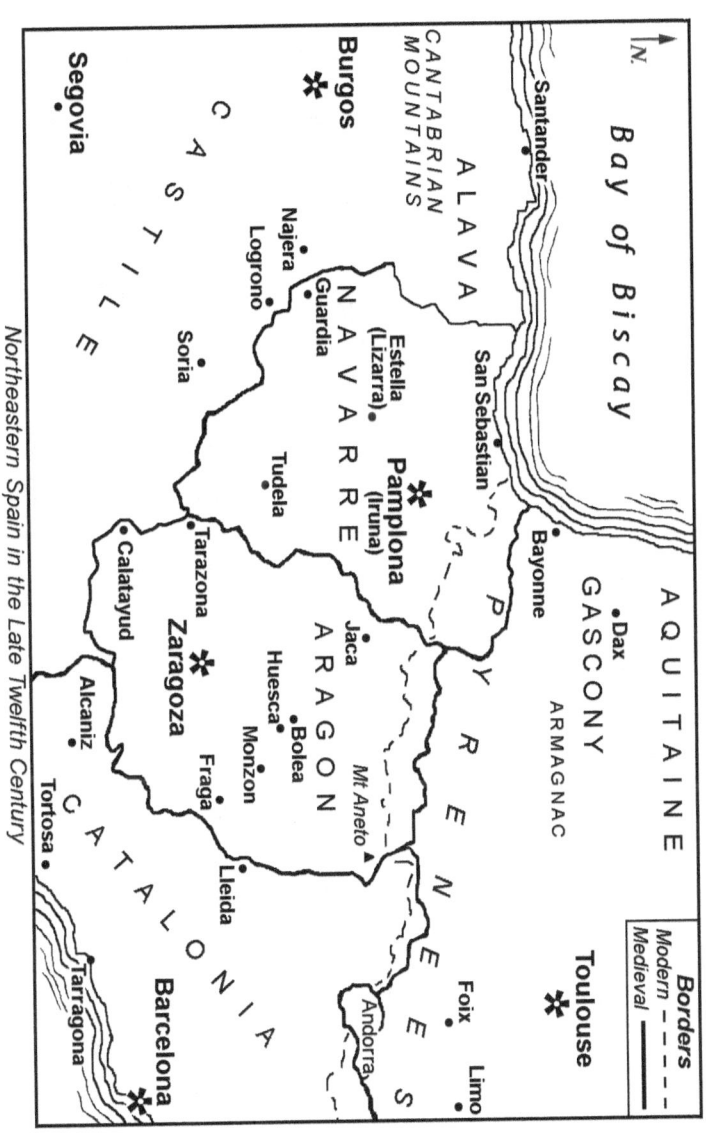

Northeastern Spain in the Late Twelfth Century

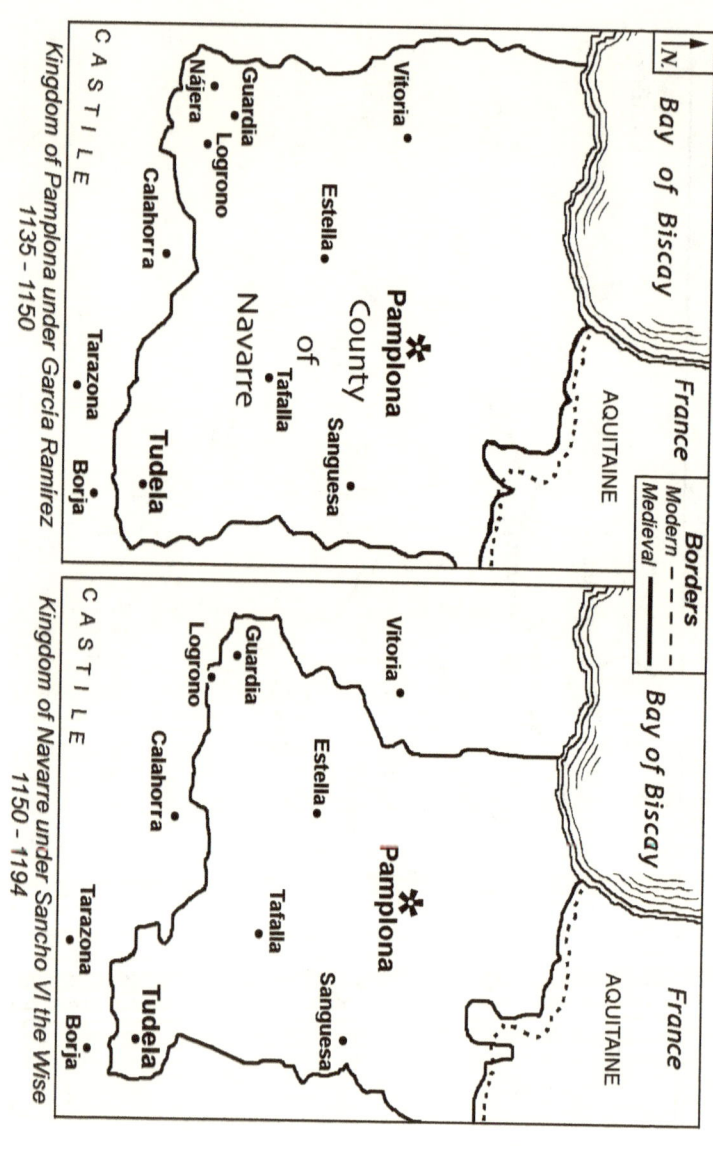

MAPS AND IMPRINTS

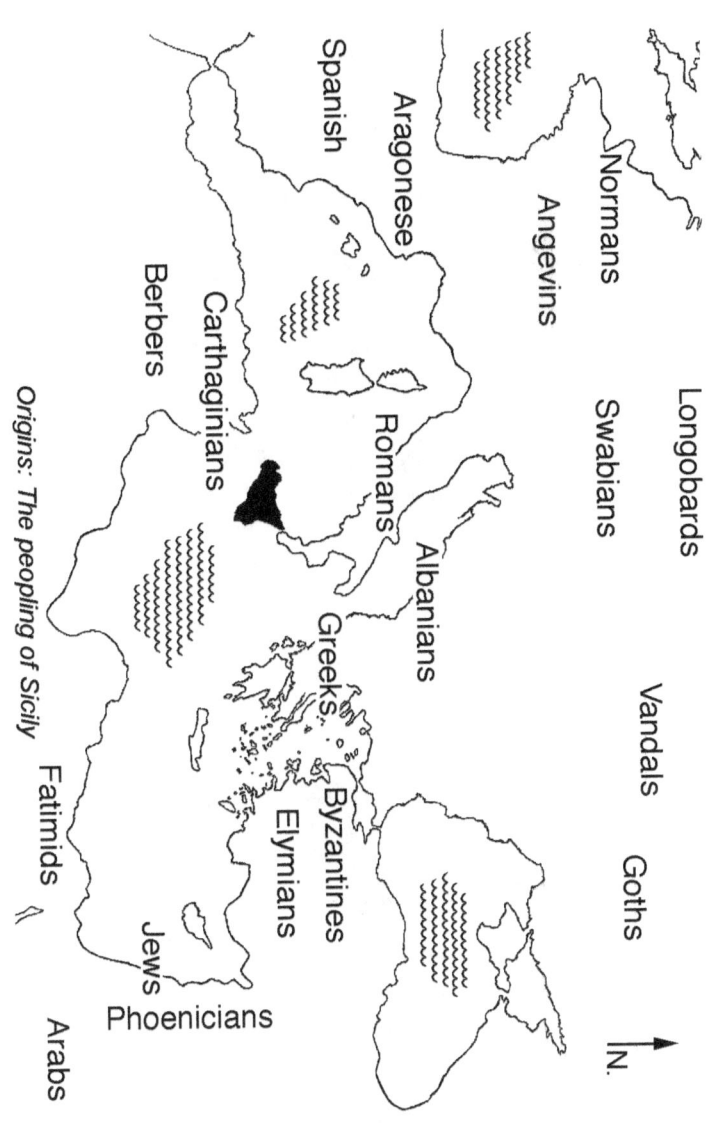

Origins: The peopling of Sicily

Regnum Siciliae: The Norman Kingdom of Sicily

MARGARET, QUEEN OF SICILY

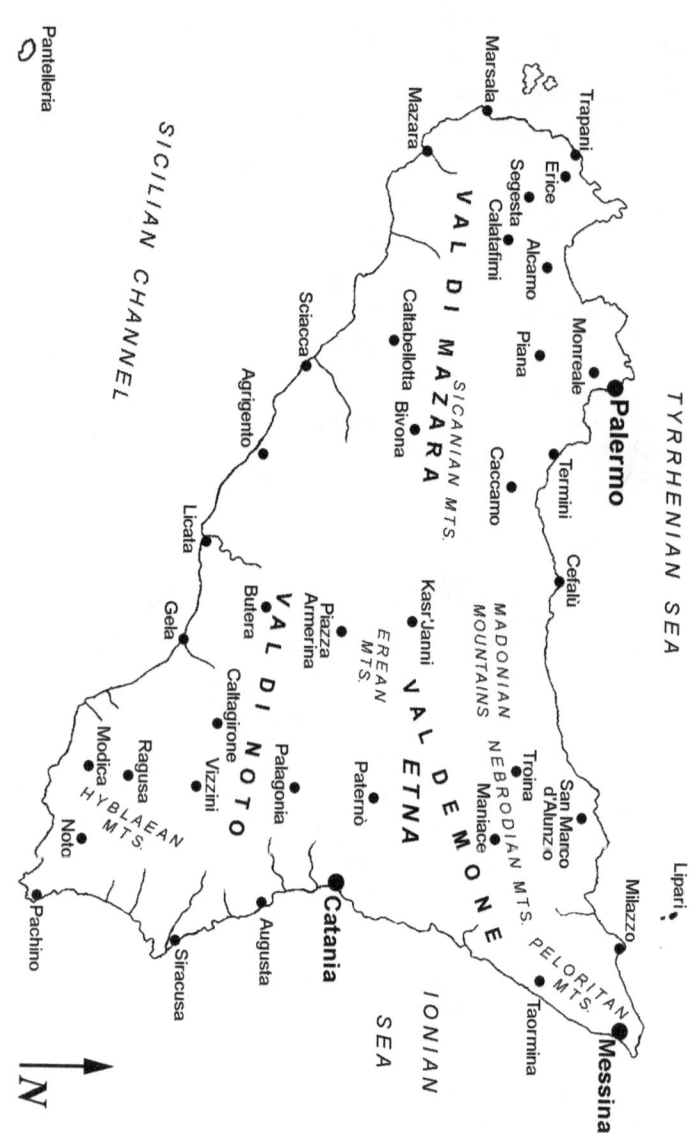

MAPS AND IMPRINTS

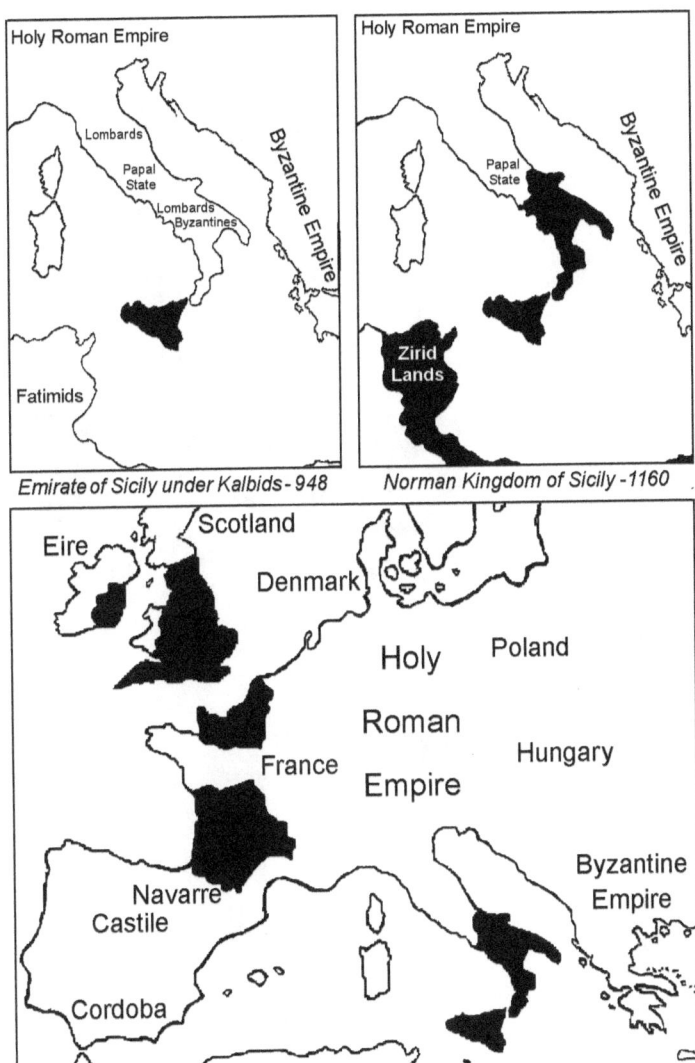

Emirate of Sicily under Kalbids - 948

Norman Kingdom of Sicily - 1160

Norman control in 1171: Normandy, Sicily, England, Ireland, Aquitaine, Malta

Shifting Borders: Principal European and Mediterranean states and regions in 1200

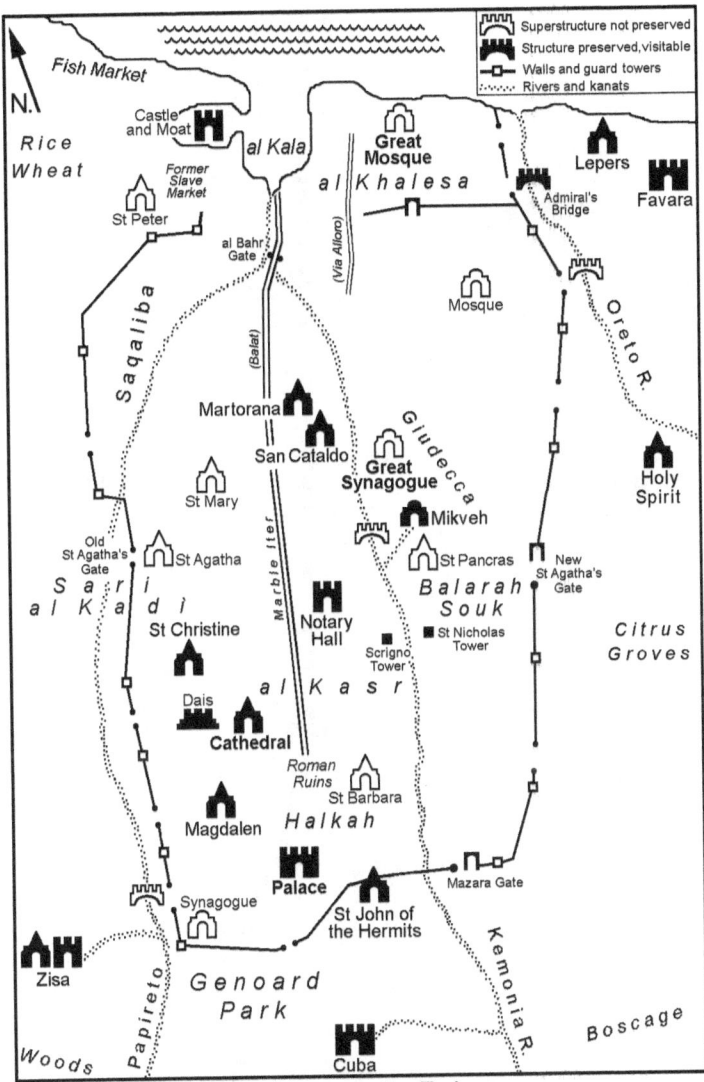

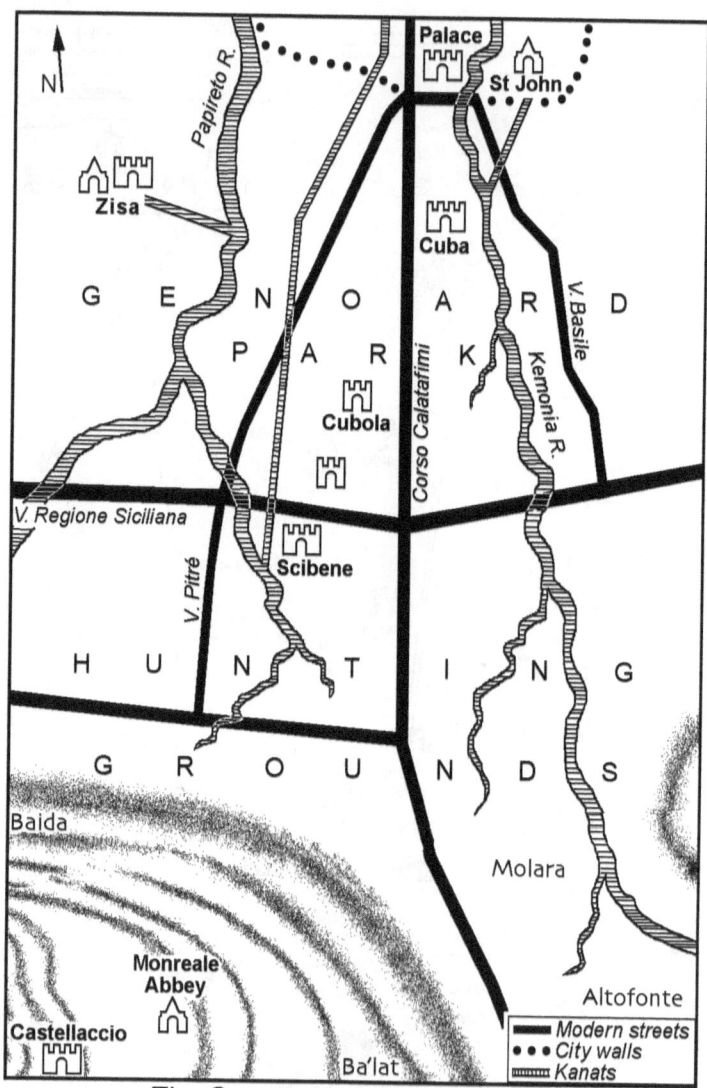

The Genoard in Margaret's time

MAPS AND IMPRINTS

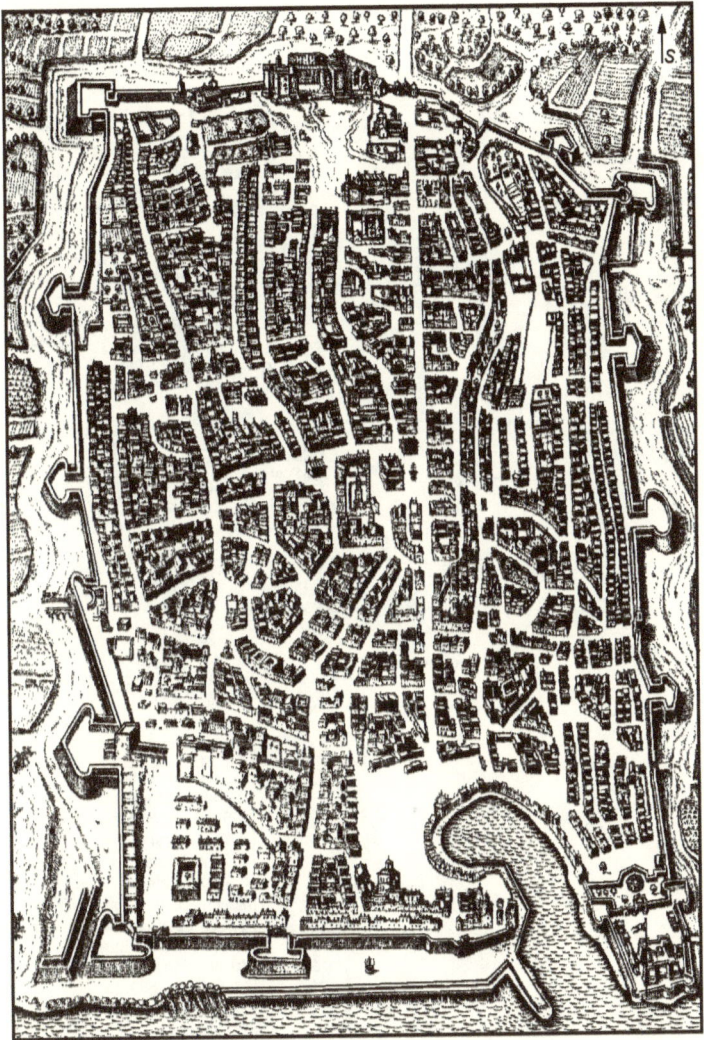

This map dated 1570 shows some streets that existed in Palermo in Margaret's time. The city wall seen here was erected in 1536.

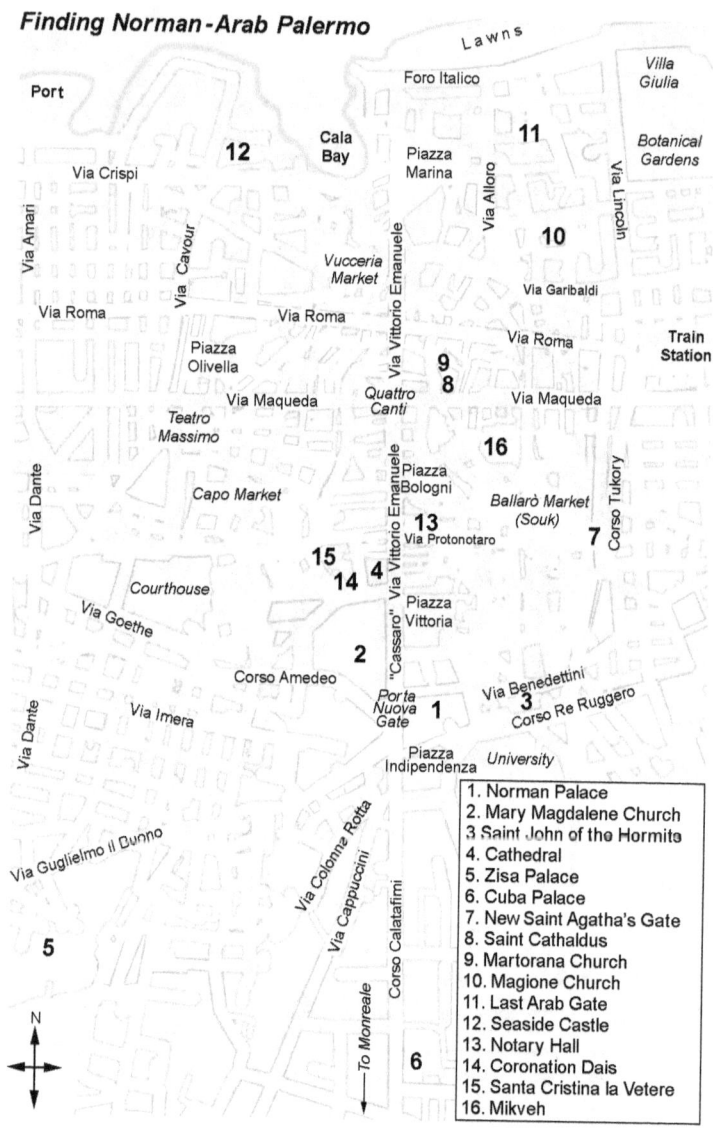

Jewish Districts of Syracuse and Palermo

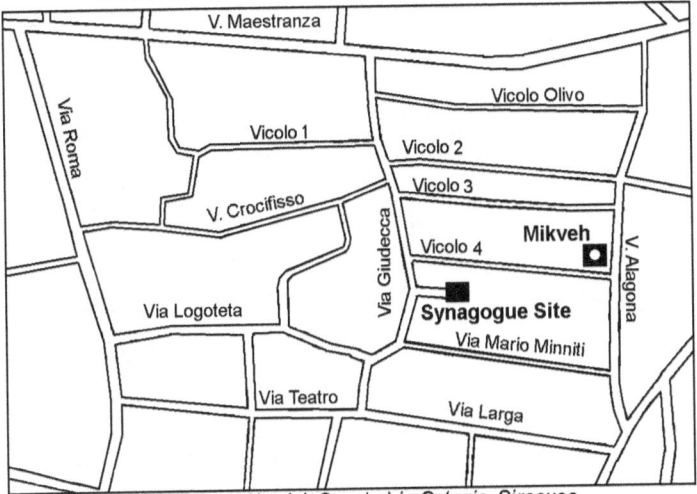

Giudecca (Jewish Quarter) in Ortygia, Siracusa
Great synagogue site is St John's Church. Mikveh at Via Alagona 52.

Palermo's Jewish Quarter, Souk (now Ballarò Market) and Kemonia Spring
Great synagogue site is San Nicolò da Tolentino Church. Mikveh under Jesuit cloister.

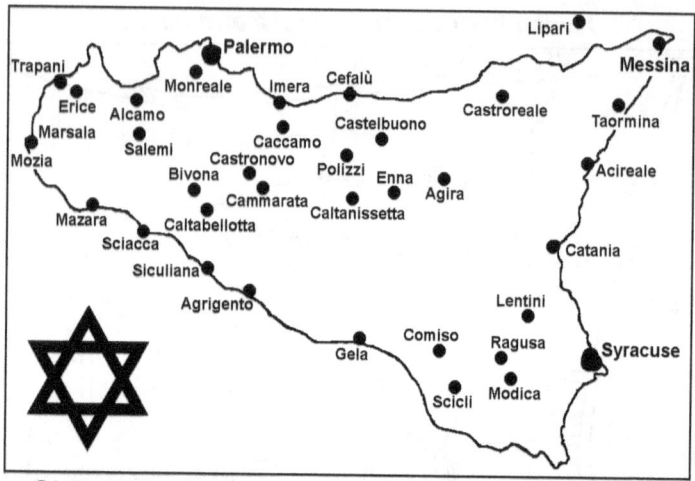

Sicily's Jewish communities in Margaret's time

Trilingual street sign at the site where Palermo's chief synagogue stood until 1493 (off Via Calderai)

Sicilian tombstone dated 1148 inscribed in Latin, Hebrew, Greek and Arabic. Like Navarre, Sicily was a multicultural society.

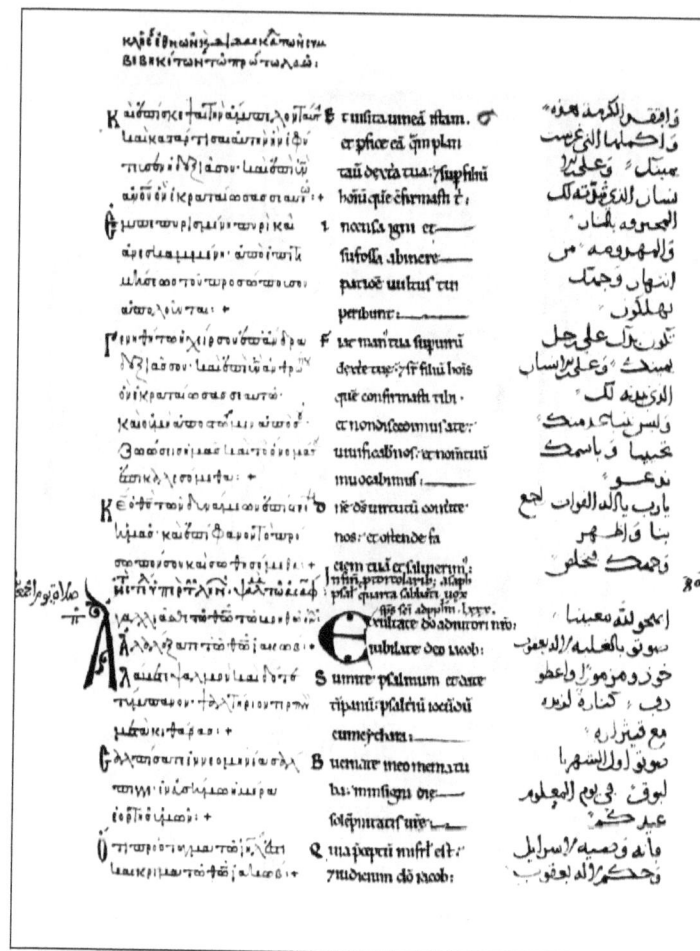

The Harley Psalter, composed in Palermo before 1153 in Greek, Latin and Arabic. Margaret may have used this book, or one similar to it, during services in the Palatine Chapel.

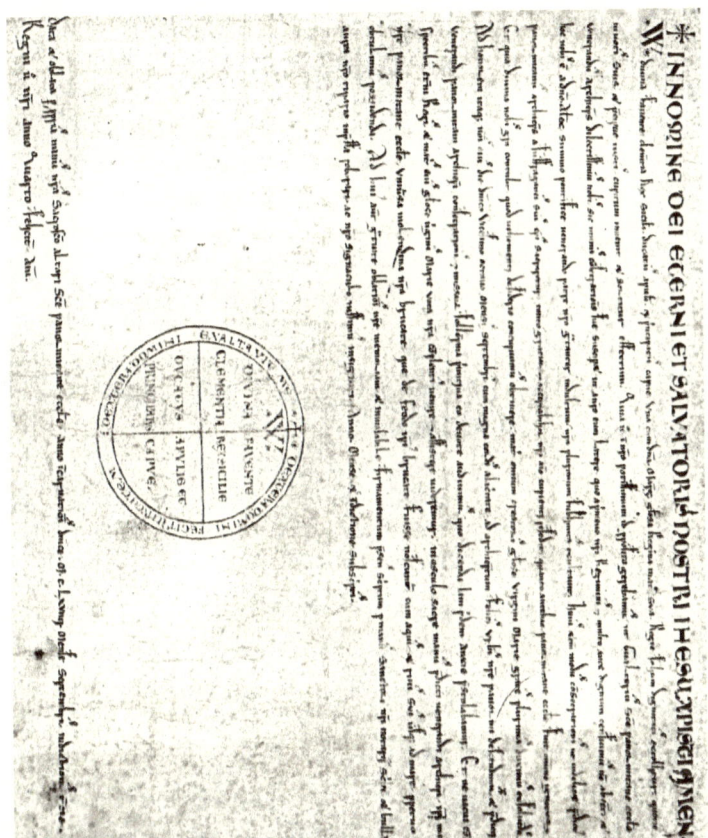

Feudal charter issued by Margaret to Walter, Archbishop of Palermo, in the name of her son, King William II, in 1169, a rarity as very few charters issued during her regency survive. The seal was designed in deep red ink, a common practice in Sicily during this period. The charter on the following page appears to be granted in the queen's name.

Margaret's charter of November 1171 in Latin and Greek confirming privileges granted by Roger II to abbeys in the Nebrodian Mountains

MAPS AND IMPRINTS

From emirate to kingdom: Census of serfs in a feudal manor in 1141, recorded in Arabic and signed in Greek by King Roger II of Sicily

HISTORIA HV-
GONIS FALCANDI SICVLI DE
rebus gestis in Siciliæ regno, iam primùm typis
excusa, studio & beneficio Reuerendi D. Domini
Matthæi Longogęi Suefsionũ pontificıs & regni
Galliæ ab interiore ac penitiore consilio.

Huc accefsit in librum præfatio, & historicæ lectionis Encomi
um per Geruasium Tornacæum Suefsionensem.

PARISIIS

Apud Mathurinum Dupuys via Iacobea,
sub insigni Hominis sylueſtris, & Frobenij.
M. D. L.

CVM PRIVILEGIO REGIS.

Editio princeps of the chronicle of Hugh Falcandus, 1550

CHRONICON
ROMUALDI II.
ARCHIEPISCOPI SALERNITANI.
In Christi nomine incipit Chronica.

DE ÆTATIBUS.

Rima mundi ætas est ab Adam usque ad diluvium, côtinens annos, juxta Hebraicam veritatem mille sexcentos quinquaginta sex, juxta septuaginta verò Interpretes duo millia ducentos quadraginta duos; generationes verò juxta utramque editionem numero decem, quæ universali est deleta diluvio, sicut primam cujusque hominis oblivio demergere consuevit ætatem. Fuerunt Noë filii tres, ex quibus ita sunt ortæ gentes. De Japhet quindecim. De Cham triginta. De Sem XXVII. Sem annos duos post diluvium genuit Salem: à quo Samaritæ & Indi. Sale genuit Heber: à quo Hebræi. Heber genuit Falech, cujus tempore turris ædificatur, & linguarum divisio fit. In solo Heber prisca remansit lingua, quia in ea conspiratione non fuit. Turris verò duo millia CLXXIV. dicitur passuum. Hanc Nembroth gigas construxit. Hac ætate Scitharum regnum oritur, ubi primus regnavit Ihannus. Tunc & regnum Ægyptiorum ubi primus regnavit Thoës. Dehinc regnum Assiriorum, ubi primus regnavit Belus, quem dicunt Saturnum quidam: deinde Ninus, qui condidit Ninivem. Hoc tempore Abraham nascitur: & post mortem Nini à Semiramide Regina reædificata est Babylonia, ubi regnavit annos quadraginta.

Secunda ætas à Noë usque ad Abraham generationes juxta Hebraicam veritatem complexa decem, annos autem ducentos nonaginta duos; porrò juxta septuaginta Interpretes anni MLXXII. Generationes verò XI. hæc verò quasi pueritia fuit generationis populi Dei, & ideo in lingua inventa est Hebræa, à pueritia namque homo incipit noscere loqui, quæ idcirco appellata est, quòd fari non potest. Ab Adam itaque usque ad Abraham juxta Hebraicam veritatem computantur anni mille nongenti quadraginta octo, secundùm septuaginta Interpretes sunt anni tria millia trecenti quatuordecim.

Tertia ab Abraham usque ad David generationes juxta utramque auctoritatem XIV. annos verò, secundùm Hebræorum auctoritatem nongentos quadraginta duos complectens; juxta septuaginta verò Interpretes anni tria millia CXXXVII. hæc velut quædam adolescentia fuit populi Dei, à qua ætate incipit homo posse generare, propterea Matthæus Evangelista generationum ab Abraham sumpsit exordium, qui etiam pater multarum gentium constitutus est, quando mutatum nomen accepit. Ab Adam verò juxta Hebræorum auctoritatem usque ad David sunt anni duo millia octingenti nonaginta, secundùm septuaginta Interpretes tria millia CV. Cur autem annorum hæc diversitas sit, in sequentibus ostendetur.

Quarta à David usque ad transmigrationem

1725 edition of Romuald's chronicle of Norman Sicily

ITINERARIVM BENIAMINI TVDELENSIS;

IN QVO

RES MEMORABILES, QVAS

ANTE QVADRINGENTOS
annos totum ferè terrarum orbem notatis itineribus dimensus vel ipse vidit vel à fide dignis suæ ætatis hominibus accepit, breuiter atque dilucidè describuntur;

Ex Hebraico Latinum factum
BENED. ARIA MONTANO
INTERPRETE.

ANTVERPIÆ,
Ex officina Christophori Plantini,
Architypographi regij.
M. D. LXXV.

Early edition of the Itinerary of Benjamin of Tudela, from Navarre, who visited Norman Sicily and wrote about its Jewish communities.

Roger II, depicted as a Byzantine basileus, crowned by Christ in engraving based on mosaic in Palermo's Martorana church

F. THOMÆ FAZELLI.
SICVLI OR. PRÆDICA-
TORVM.

DE REBVS SICVLIS DECADES DVAE, NVNC
PRIMVM IN LVCEM EDITAE.

HIS ACCESSIT TOTIVS OPERIS IN-
DEX LOCVPLETISSIMVS.

CAVTVM EST PHILIPPI ANGLIAE, HISPANIAE,
Siciliæq; Regis, Pauli. IIII. Pont. Max. ac Venetæ Reip. priuilegio, ne
cui has Decades de Siculis rebus ad decennium in eorum di-
tione vel imprimere, vel alibi impressas venales
habere, neue in sermone Italicũ iniuſ-
ſu authoris vertere sub mul-
cta liceat.

First published history of Sicily, by Thomas Fazello, in 1558

PHOTOGRAPHS

The author at the site of La Guardia Castle, where very little remains of the fortress known to young Margaret. This tower became part of an abbey.

Pamplona Cathedral: Margaret's father and brother rest in the royal crypt in the center of the nave. The figure to its right is the author.

Except for this wall and crypt, little remains of the royal palace built by Margaret's brother near Pamplona's cathedral. The site now houses the Archivo Real y General de Navarra.

Santa María la Real at Nájera, resting place of Blanca of Navarre and the kingdom's earliest monarchs.

Blanca's sarcophagus at Nájera (top) depicts her death in childbirth. The sobbing female figure on the left may be Margaret.

Tudela (now Tudela de Navarra), town of Benjamin who visited the court of King William II near the end of Queen Margaret's regency.

Cuisine of northeastern Spain: Mushrooms and snails in Barcelona's Boqueria market, which inspired the Vucceria of Palermo. Much of the agriculture of Navarre was similar to Sicily's.

View from the walls of Pamplona looking northward beyond the Arga River toward the foothills of the western Pyrenees. Most of the landscape of Navarre and La Rioja is very similar to that of Sicily.

Barcelona's Sant Pau del Camp, a typical church of northern Spain when young Margaret lived there.

Zaragoza's Aljaferia Palace in Aragon, the region bordering Navarre and Rioja. The Mudéjar style, like Sicilian architecture, had Islamic influences.

Facade, muqarnas and mosaics of Palermo's Zisa.

Canterbury Cathedral: Margaret gave hospitality to Thomas Becket's kin, and he is depicted on the reliquary shown on this book's cover.

The author in a Romanesque corner of the abbey at Canterbury little changed since the days when Thomas Becket lived there.

Cefalù Cathedral viewed from the fortress overlooking it. The style of the church is Norman Romanesque with a few Byzantine details.

Apse and cupola of the Palatine Chapel

Pisan Tower of Palermo's Norman Palace.

Benedictine cloister of Saint John of the Hermits.

PHOTOGRAPHS

Palermo Cathedral much as it appeared originally, long before the unsightly Baroque dome was added.

Martorana tower and Saint Cathaldus

Saint Cathaldus nave and apse

Bell tower of the Martorana church, Palermo

The Cubola, one of the few pavilions in the vast Genoard park to survive from the Norman era until our times, is a sight with which Margaret was familiar.

Crown of Queen Constance, consort of Frederick II. The crown worn by Margaret was of similar Byzantine design.

Sicilian Coinage in Margaret's Time
(See note 61)

"Scyphate" ducat of Roger II

"Lion's face" follaris of William II

Fatimid tarì   *Tarì of Roger II*

Chapter 1
IDENTITY

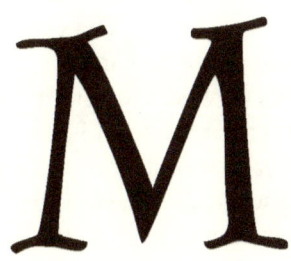

"They do not see beyond the superficial to a man's spirit, nor do they regard his virtue, but stand in awe only of his physical presence, his daring, his virility, his agility and his size, and these they judge make him worthy of the purple robe and the crown."

— Anna Comnena

Perched upon a plateau surrounded by plains and gently rolling hills of endless vineyards, La Guardia, as its name implies, stands guard over what is now La Rioja, a region known today for its robust red wine and reddish soil. In the twelfth century, the high town was the perfect place to erect a compact castle for the safety of a warring, wandering nobleman's family, and that is precisely what García Ramírez, Lord of Monzón and Logroño, did some time after his marriage to Margaret of Aigle in 1130.

A small garrison of knights was sufficient to protect the castle and the tiny village, where the Templars had a church and perhaps a small preceptory.

Viticulture was not as widespread in La Rioja in the twelfth century as it is today, and the valleys below La Guardia were covered with woods punctuated by the occasional field, the region populated by an abundance of deer, boar and chamois. Graceful storks nested in the higher trees. The climate was cooler then, with a generous dose of annual snowfall, but artichokes and olives grew in the valleys, where the ground did not freeze.

By the time a daughter named Margaret was born here in 1135, García Ramírez "the Restorer" was about to be crowned King of Navarre[2] and he was already the father of two children. Sancho, an heir, was born in 1132, and Blanca was born two years later.[3]

House of Jiménez

García Ramírez was born to a distinguished family, and some of his kin rest in the stately Gothic church in the charming village of Nájera, the dynasty's effective capital for generations. However, as a solitary sprig of the family tree, he was not born to be king. That was something he would have to fight for.

His destiny was intricately woven into the land of his forefathers, so intricately that it was difficult to discern in the complex tapestry of northeastern Spain at the beginning of the twelfth century when García was born.

La familia meant as much to Spaniards as *la famiglia* did to Italians, and in Navarre the word belied as much complexity as it did in Sicily. García Ramírez's extended family, the House of Jiménez, was full of cousins and siblings who despised each other, often to the point of homicide.

Like the Jiménez themselves, the lands they ruled were steeped in colorful history. As a kingdom, Navarre began its life some distance north of La Rioja near the foothills of the Pyrenees.

Pamplona

Set upon high ground, the city of Pamplona, or Iruña, traces its remote origins to the Vascones who inhabited the region in Roman times, their dominion stretching northward across the Pyrenees into what is now Gascony, where they had contact with the Gauls. Philologists debate the origins of the Vascones' language, thought to be an early precursor of Basque, or Euskara.

To the south were Celtic peoples, to the east Iberians. Such was the cultural landscape encountered by the Phoenicians around 900 BC (BCE).

The arrival of the Phoenicians' descendants, the Carthaginians, brought colonization, and Barcino, now Barcelona, is said to have been named for their leader Hamilcar Barca. The Punic Wars saw the Carthaginians' defeat in 209 BC by the Romans led by Scipio Africanus.

The Romans founded great urban centers like Caesarea Augustus, from which the name *Zaragoza*, sometimes *Saragossa*, which later became the capital of Aragon to the east of Navarre. Except for occasional, isolated rebellions by the indigenous tribes, the following centuries were generally peaceful in the place the Romans called *Hispania*, where Christianity was introduced with the Edict of Milan of 313.

As Rome's vast empire dissolved, the invading Visigoths settled the northeastern part of what is now Spain, *España*, gradually amalgamating with the existing populations while establishing the region's earliest medieval aristocracy.

Having occupied Catalonia, a territory reaching eastward from Aragon to the Mediterranean, the Visigoths entered into a truce with Rome and, ostensibly on her behalf, expelled the other "barbarian" invaders, most notably the Vandals and the Alans. The fall of the Western Roman Empire in 476 found the Visigoths in control of much of Spain and the western coastal region that became Portugal.

They spent the next century consolidating their power on the peninsula. The Visigoths preferred "heretical" Arianism to the more orthodox Christianity espoused in Rome and Constantinople, and this fostered occasional conflicts. These ended with the conversion of Reccared in 587.

Around this time, the Vascones and their society were described by Reccared's contemporary, the Visigothic chronicler John of Biclaro, who was bishop of the diocese of Girona.

In 711, the Moors — Arabs and Berbers — crossed the Strait of Gibraltar into the Iberian Peninsula, bringing Islam with them. Within a decade, their leader, intrepid Tariq ibn Ziyad, had conquered most of Spain. These Umayyads were Sunnis.

Led by the emir Abdul Rahman al Ghafiqi Abd al Rahman, the Muslims made a major military incursion into what is now France in 732, to be fought back by Charles Martel at the Battle of Tours. This came in the wake of earlier confrontations at Toulouse in 721 and Autun in 725. For the next two centuries the focus of Muslim-Arab expansionism into Europe would not reach far beyond the Iberian lands and Sicily, where the populations increased while science and literature flourished.

Internecine conflicts were not unknown in the Moors' Iberian dominions. The Berbers revolted against the Arabs for several years beginning in 739. Eventually, the Muslims of Spain, united by faith and by the Andalusian dialect of Arabic, made common cause with each other. In future centuries the conflicts among the Spanish Muslim population were many, but they were more political than cultural or ethnic.

By 750, the European part of the Umayyad Caliphate included most of Spain but only part of Navarre. Prosperous Pamplona sometimes attracted the interest of potential suitors from the other side of the Pyrenees. It emerged as an important county during the reign of Charlemagne, the Holy Roman Emperor, as a "buffer" region to protect his Frankish dominions north of the Pyrenees from the expanding Muslim empire. Yet it wasn't long before the fiercely independent Pamplonans subtly but effectively rebelled against Charlemagne's authority.

This reflected a trend, as the era found much of northeastern Spain being divided into a patchwork of tiny emirates, such as prosperous Tudela, with its multicultural population of Christians, Muslims and Jews. At times there was a tenuous peace.

The lines were not always very clearly drawn, and not every political conflict could be attributed solely to religious differences. Theoretically united in their opposition to Muslim hegemony, the Christians often warred with each other. The Basques' adamant sense of independence sometimes transcended religious ideologies, pitting them against whichever leader, Christian or Muslim, they viewed as an aggressor or oppressor at some particular moment. Although it dwelled just beyond the fringe of Muslim expansion, Pamplona boasted a few mosques.

In early 778, Charlemagne, allied with a Muslim leader, Sulaiman ibn al-Arabi, who predicted a facile triumph in the region, took Pamplona. Encouraged by this, and seeking a more extensive conquest of the wealthy Iberian lands, he then lay siege to the city of Zaragoza in Aragon.

What happened next was unexpected in view of wily al-Arabi having promised an easy victory. Hussain ibn al-Ansari, Zaragoza's governor, defiantly refused to surrender the city. Finally, in return for Charlemagne lifting the futile siege, al-Ansari remitted a payment in gold and freed some prisoners. This was expedient, for the Christian invader wished to return with alacrity to his own dominions, where some rebellious Saxons were threatening the peace. Havering over details was not in his nature. On the way home in August, he decided to destroy Pamplona's city walls to rein in the rebellious Basques, effectively "teaching them a lesson." In retaliation, a Basque army ambushed and defeated Charlemagne's arrogant Franks at the Roncevaux Pass in the Pyrenees. Immortalized in the *Song of Roland*, this battle was Charlemagne's only significant military defeat.

As fate would have it, the same pass was to be the site of a later battle, this time against Charlemagne's son. In 824, Iñigo Arista, a Basque leader with Moorish ties, established himself as King of Pamplona after defeating a Carolingian army led by Louis the Pious.

Initially, the Kingdom of Pamplona was, in essence, the northern half of Navarre. Basque culture might extend across the Pyrenees, but Pamplona's territories ended there.

Before long, life in northern Navarre generally conformed to what existed across the mountains in southwestern France. Just as Christianity differed from Islam, European manorialism (feudalism) differed from the traditional Arab system of smallholding.

Knighthood was, in its essence, a contract guaranteeing military service to the king in exchange for feudal tenure, the knight's right to hold land. This arrangement, with its tangible links between the mounted warrior and the king he served, brought a personal sense of duty to the military force that defended the realm, for knighthood, first and foremost, was an obligation.

Navarre

As kingdoms go, nascent Pamplona was small but promising, her borders ever shifting as towns in adjoining regions were acquired, lost, and reacquired.

A Christian nobility was emerging, if slowly, one generation at a time. Its bloodlines reflected an eclectic admixture, but in northeastern Spain a subtle racism prevailed, with Visigothic ancestry, either real or imagined, prized by the new knightly class. The idea that a nobleman had blue blood, *sangre azul*, probably originated in the ever more frequent act of a knight holding up his clenched fist to reveal a forearm full of blue veins set starkly against pale white skin.

Often, the knight's hand bore a sword.

It was through warfare that the Kingdom of Pamplona expanded, at times reaching the Atlantic coast. Iñigo Arista's dynasty was overthrown by Sancho Garcés, a neighboring ruler, in 905. His dynasty has come to be known as the House of Jiménez, or *Ximenez*.

This was the ancestral family of Margaret of Navarre through her father, and in the two centuries prior to her birth we encounter a bewildering array of Sanchos, Garcías, Ramiros and Alfonsos. (Kinship among the panoply of Jiménez rulers is illustrated in this volume's first genealogical table.)

With the conquest of Moorish lands, Sancho Garcés extended his realm southward to Nájera, in the County of Navarre, a development outlined in the *Chronicle of Albelda* completed around 976. Here we see the seeds of what, over the next centuries, came to be known as the *Reconquista*, which culminated in the conquest of Granada, the last Muslim state, in the southern tip of the peninsula, in 1492.

The Moorish dynasties, like those of the Christian states, changed from time to time, indeed rather frequently. Like the Christian monarchies, these were, in principle, based on male primogeniture; in practice, however, an emir might choose a successor from among many sons. Disputes between brothers or cousins were almost as commonplace among minor Muslim dynasties as among Christians.

In some instances, changes in regional power reflected

more general political trends elsewhere in the growing Muslim world. The gradual decline of the Umayyads in Spain and Morocco resulted from their being deposed by the rising Abbasids in Damascus in the middle of the eighth century, even if they were succeeded by a new dynasty in Spain only much later, in 929. This led to the establishment of the ephemeral Caliphate of Cordoba, which controlled the southern two-thirds of the Iberian peninsula, developing into a *de facto* sovereign Muslim state under the nominal suzerainty of the Islamic rulers of northern Africa. Spain was not unique in Muslim Europe, and we see a parallel development in Sicily where, beginning in 948, the Kalbid emirs ruled independently despite owing fealty to the Fatimids of Cairo. Spanning parts of three continents, from Portugal to Pakistan, the Umayyad Caliphate was the last unified Muslim empire to encompass the entire Islamic world of its era. In its wake, the Muslim nations constituted a loose federation rather than an empire based on something vaguely resembling the Roman model.

By the end of the tenth century, it was no longer possible for Spain's Christians to view their Abrahamic brethren the Muslims as an altogether "foreign" element. The Jews, likewise, were part of the fabric of Spanish society. "Spain," of course, was a geographical expression rather than a political or social reality.

Nevertheless, the restless Christian nobles were no longer content to submit to Muslim rule, even if it meant little more than paying tribute and other sundry taxes.

Chapter 2
KINGDOM

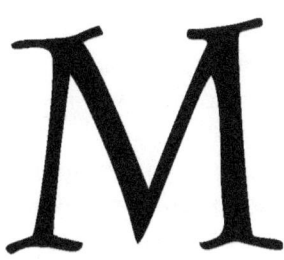

"I was born dreaming of monarchies. I want to die that way."

— Letitia Baldrige

The Kingdom of Pamplona reached its greatest extent under Sancho III "the Great" and his successors in the first half of the eleventh century. This they owed to a Christian coalition defeating and killing Al Mansur ibn Abi Aamir, or *Almanzor,* in 1002, an event that freed most of Navarre and Catalonia, and parts of Aragon and Castile, from Muslim dominance.

Expansion

In the remaining Moorish territories civil war ensued as rival claimants sought Almanzor's place as ruler. This internal dissension, more than any Christian effort, divided the Muslim states of the erstwhile Caliphate of Cordoba into a loose network of *taifa* emirates which, over the next few centuries, the Christian kings would defeat one by one. Subdued but not eliminated, the Moors in the taifas of northeastern Spain would challenge Christian authority from time to time. In 1018, Zaragoza, in what is now Aragon, became the capital of an important taifa.

To meet the Moorish threat while facilitating close administration of his various dominions, Sancho III established his effective capital at Nájera, on a low hill along the Nájerilla River. Its name derives from an Arabic phrase meaning "place between the rocks."

In addition to being King of Pamplona (Navarre), Sancho III was Count of Aragon, which one of his sons inherited. By marriage to the heiress Muniadona Mayor, Sancho was also Count of Castile. He exercised control over Gascony, possibly as its suzerain, and he seized the Kingdom of León. Control of these contiguous dominions made him one of the most powerful rulers in northern Spain. But where did his family of intrepid warriors come from?

The precise geographical origin of the Jiménez dynasty of Sancho III, himself a direct ancestor of García Ramírez, Margaret's father, is unknown, although Sancho was raised in Leyre. A possible ancestor worth mentioning is a certain García Jiménez, sometimes *Garcí Ximénez*, believed to have been Count of Sobrarbe from 724 until 758.

The Sancho Garcés we met earlier, who ruled Pamplona beginning in 905, was probably the son of another García Jiménez, about whom precious little is known.[4]

All we know with reasonable certainty is that the founder of the family (the grandfather of Sancho Garcés) was most likely named *Jimeno,* and he seems to have ruled the County of Alava. A certain Vela Jiménez is mentioned as Count of Alava in the *Codex Vigilanus* compiled around 882.[5]

Whatever their ancestral provenance, by 1000, the Kings of Pamplona were spending more time at Nájera and other localities in La Rioja, in the County of Navarre, than in Pamplona itself. Like most medieval rulers, they travelled constantly, their realms perpetually under threat.

Out of the northern Iberian morass there emerged several feudal states besides Pamplona-Navarre. Posing the most immediate threat to Navarre were Aragon to the east and Castile to the south.

The County of Aragon, once a vassal state of Pamplona ruled (as we have seen) by Sancho III, became a kingdom in 1035, the year Sancho was assassinated. Until 1097 its capital was Jaca. The Kingdom of Castile was founded in 1065; its first capital was Burgos. Catalonia, a county since 988, was governed from Barcelona.[6]

These states were sometimes united through dynastic marriages, but even during the long union between, for example, Aragon and Catalonia, the inhabitants felt a strong sense of what might be termed "nationalism." Indeed, each of these regions had their own vernacular language, even though Latin was the written one. The Basque[7] and Catalan tongues survive to this day, while Castilian became Spanish just as Tuscan became Italian. Navarro-Aragonese, the mother tongue of the Jiménez for several generations, vanished by the sixteenth century.

As one might imagine, Castile, the southernmost of these kingdoms, came into the most frequent, most direct conflict with the Moors. Here the most celebrated knight of his age was a grandfather of García Ramírez, and therefore a great-grandfather to Margaret.

El Cid

In 1052, García Sánchez III of Pamplona and Navarre, the eldest legitimate son of the empire-building Sancho III, founded the Church of Santa María la Real at Nájera, and this sanctuary became an important pilgrimage stop on the Way of Saint James. The present Gothic structure replaced a Romanesque church, but its pantheon of royal tombs survives from the crypt of the original edifice. A small castle stood nearby. So closely is he associated with this place that García Sánchez III is sometimes referred to as "García of Nájera."

Fernando, another son of Sancho III, became the ruler of Castile and León to the south of Navarre.

Ramiro, the illegitimate son of Sancho III, ruled Aragon to the east of Navarre.

Before long, sibling rivalries eroded any trace of fraternal affection that ever existed among these three sons of Sancho III.

At Fernando's court was a young esquire, a nobleman from Vivar, a village near the Castilian capital of Burgos. Born around 1040, Rodrigo Díaz de Vivar became a knight in the service of Fernando's eldest son, King Sancho II, nicknamed "the Strong," who was crowned King of Castile in 1065. His wife, Alberta, is said to have been a daughter of William the Conqueror, King of England, but Sancho's immediate interests were to be found in his native Spain.[8]

Sancho II of Castile emerged marginally victorious in the War of the Three Sanchos which broke out in 1065 between the three Jiménez cousins who ruled Navarre, Aragon and Castile, each king named Sancho for the same grandfather, namely Sancho III "the Great" of Pamplona. This bizarre conflict was rooted in disputes over the empire left by Sancho III to his sons upon his death three decades earlier.

Most of the battles took place in La Rioja and around Burgos. During one campaign, Rodrigo Díaz de Vivar, the Castilian standard bearer, is said to have defeated his Navarrese counterpart, Jimeno Garcés, thereby earning the nickname *campi doctor*, literally "master of the field," which in literature became *el Campeador*.

This familial war ended in 1067 in what was essentially a stalemate, albeit with the shifting of a few borders. The military conflict might well have continued, but Sancho II of Castile, generally viewed as the instigator, now turned his attention to his brothers. The death of Sancha, the widow of King Fernando, opened the way for her quarrelsome sons to wage war on each other.

By now, Sancho II had garnered plenty of experience fighting kin, and he seized León and Galicia from his younger brothers. Rodrigo Díaz de Vivar, who the Moors nicknamed *el Cid*, from their word *sayyid* (lord), led these campaigns, as well as some against the region's Muslims.[9]

In 1072, nasty Sancho II, who seemed to be hated by almost everybody, met his end in a regicide at the hands of a pack of conspirators. His only heir was his younger brother, deposed Alfonso, formerly the King of León, who had been dethroned through the Cid's military prowess. Now, at the restored court of Alfonso VI of León and Castile, the Cid was divested of his rank as a military leader and treated with suspicion, to be exiled in 1081.

He soon found work in the service of the Moors who now ruled the taifa of Zaragoza. A mercenary in everything but name, he fought the Christians of Aragon and Barcelona who were constantly at war with Zaragoza. Over the next few years, the Cid found himself fighting both Christians and Muslims in the complex, interminable wars that plagued the peninsula.

In 1086, an Almoravid force sent from Morocco inflicted a crippling defeat on Alfonso VI, compelling him to make peace with the man he had banished from his court five years earlier. The Cid had ambitions of his own, and while supporting those native Spanish Moors who opposed the invading Almoravids he sought influence at Valencia, which he conquered in 1094. This became a sovereign principality with a mixed population of Muslims and Christians. When the Cid died in 1099, his widow, Jimena (Ximena) of Oviedo, became the city's ruler, but she was forced to surrender it to the Almoravids three years later.

Cristina, one of the daughters of Rodrigo and Jimena, wed Ramiro, Lord of Monzón, a descendant of Sancho III "the Great" of Pamplona, who we met earlier. García Ramírez, the father of Margaret of Navarre, was Cristina's son. It is through García Ramírez that most of the Cid's myriad descendants claim their kinship from him.

Elvira, a daughter of Alfonso VI of León and Castile by his fourth wife, Isabella, wed Roger II of Sicily, becoming the island's first queen.

Ambitions

The ancestry of García Ramírez was nothing if not distinguished. One could be forgiven for expecting great things from a man of his pedigree, and he was not prone to disappoint. García Ramírez was born around 1100 to Ramiro Sánchez, Lord of the Aragonese town of Monzón, and Cristina, daughter of the Cid.

Ramiro Sánchez, who lived from 1070 to 1116, was the son of Sancho Garcés, Lord of Uncastillo, who was born around 1038 outside marriage to a concubine of García Sánchez III of Pamplona and Navarre, the monarch who established the royal seat of power at Nájera.

In 1076, after the War of the Three Sanchos, the reigning King of Navarre, Sancho IV, eldest son and heir of García Sánchez III, was killed in Peñalén by his siblings. Ramiro's father, Sancho Garcés (the illegitimate half-brother of Sancho IV), was not embroiled in this murder plot.

The death of Ramiro's uncle Sancho IV led to a period of instability in Navarre, which was ultimately invaded by the greedy Jiménez kinsmen who ruled neighboring Castile and Aragon. The Kingdom of Navarre was thus divided between these two kingdoms. Along the Ebro River, La Rioja, the coveted region that included Nájera, was annexed to Castile.

In eleventh-century Spain, as elsewhere in Europe, the evolving concept of the state was fluid, based more on the ambitions of feudal families than on any sense of nationhood. Countries were defined by kings. True, the Basques might regard themselves as a people, but whether their rulers shared that view was open to question. Nevertheless, language and customs identified the region and its population.

By 1100, the Jiménez cousins ruled the better part of the northern third of Spain, but not as anything resembling what most of us might regard as a united family. Indeed, there were frequent quarrels among them.

Where was Navarre? Subsumed, is the simple answer. Like Poland in 1939, partitioned Navarre knew who she was, yet to the rest of the world she was a veiled mistress, present but largely hidden.

Geography complicates matters as often as it simplifies them. Islands like Sicily and Ireland, with their natural frontiers, make "nationality," or ethnicity, a more facile achievement than it might otherwise be, but even islands can be divided by stark differences in culture, religion, and of course language. For centuries, Sicily was divided by Carthaginians and Greeks and their chronic conflicts.

Where the borders separating Navarre from Castile and Aragon were rivers, bridges sufficed to extend the frontier beyond the next hill to the next valley to the next river. That is what happened in La Rioja, where the land is shared by seven rivers.

In the end, identity dwells in hearts, not valleys.

If only for the prestige of his family, young García Ramírez was entitled to the life of a powerful feudal lord. From his father, he stood to inherit the revenues of the town and environs of Monzón, in Aragon. García had a sister, Elvira, but no brothers to contest his inheritance. His patrimony, it seemed, would make for an ample sinecure.

The reality was to prove far more complicated.

Young García Ramírez knew not his destiny, but he knew his family's roots. The origins of the Jiménez tree were unabashedly Navarrese. One branch would seek to become so again.

Chapter 3
PRINCESS

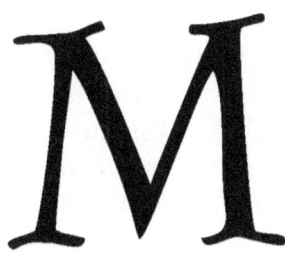

"You may be a princess or the richest woman in the world, but you cannot be more than a lady."

— Lady Randolph Churchill

Margaret of Navarre was born a princess, but barely. In fact, her father had only recently become a king, to be crowned shortly after her birth. The girl was not, strictly speaking, Basque, but Pamplona's Basque culture had an early influence on her and her siblings. Margaret's childhood was shaped by the violent vicissitudes of her times. Her social status, indeed her very destiny, was the direct result of her father's adventures as a warrior king.

Knight Errant

García Ramírez, as we have seen, was descended from a long line of rulers, but not every generation of his ancestral lineage was legitimate. It was because his father's father, Sancho Garcés of Uncastillo, was born *outside* marriage to García

Sánchez III that young García Ramírez ended up a feudal lord and not a royal heir, a baron rather than a prince.

If he wanted Navarre, García would have to carve it himself from the rocky, unforgiving soil of northeastern Spain.

Ramiro Sánchez of Monzón, Sancho's son (who eventually sired García Ramírez), wed Cristina Rodríguez de Vivar around 1098. However humble the status of Sancho of Uncastillo himself, the betrothal of his son to a daughter of the celebrated Cid spoke volumes about the prestige he enjoyed. Cristina's social position is not easily defined. Although the Cid had ruled Valencia, his was not a royal dynasty in the literal sense even if his wife, Jimena, was a cousin of King Alfonso VI of León and Castile (a Jiménez). Cristina was a quasi-princess, part of the high nobility. Certain it is that she brought some lustre to her husband's illegitimate lineage.

García Ramírez was born a year or two following his parents' marriage. His childhood seems to have been tranquil enough, but his father, Ramiro, had trouble holding Monzón, whether it was the Moors or his fellow Christians who were trying to take it from him.

Raised on tales about his mother's father, García Ramírez never had any reason to doubt what his own career would be.

His father, Ramiro Sánchez, died in 1116 at the age of forty-six. As his heir and successor, García Ramírez was probably knighted at this time, slightly earlier than the usual eighteen or twenty years. Such a milestone would have signalled his coming of age. As the daughter of so great a knight as the Cid, García's mother, the widowed Cristina, understood the significance of this rite of passage.[10]

She also understood the importance of finding her son a suitable bride, a maiden of blue blood.[11] Ancestry aside, it would not be a bad thing if García's wife happened to be the heiress to a prosperous estate or two. Here fate intervened in the person of a Norman crusader.

76

Rotrou of Perche

In 1104, when García Ramírez was still a child, his cousin, Alfonso I, who earned the appropriate nickname "the Battler," became King of Aragon and Navarre.[12] Among the Norman mercenaries in Alfonso's service was a knight distinguished for fighting Muslims in the Holy Land. This was none other than Rotrou III of Perche.[13] Like Alfonso, Rotrou came to be known by a flattering appellation, although its resonance was slightly more generic. To history, he is very simply "Rotrou the Great." To comrades who found French pronunciation challenging he was known by the more Germanic *Rothrud*.

Intrepid if hardly unique, Rotrou was part of a swashbuckling trend that had become something of a tradition among the Normans. During the First Crusade, he served in the army of Robert "Curthose," Duke of Normandy. The Siege of Antioch found him fighting alongside another Norman warrior, Bohemond Hauteville, Prince of Taranto, whose ambitious family ruled Sicily and most of southern Italy. Bohemond himself established a monarchy that gave rise to the Principality of Antioch.[14]

Rotrou's rights to the counties of Perche and Mortagne obligated him to protect a border territory in Normandy, but he enjoyed close familial connections to royalty. Matilda, his wife, was an illegitimate daughter of Henry I of England. Rotrou was a first cousin to King Alfonso, whose mother, Felicia, was a sister of Rotrou's mother, Beatrice; both sisters were daughters of Hilduin of Montdidier (see genealogical table 3).

Tales abound of how Rotrou introduced the Arabian horse in his native Perche, fostering development of the sturdy Percheron breed, and how he founded an abbey at La Trappe that became the cornerstone of the Trappist religious order. The story about the equines may be true; the one about the Trappists certainly is. But there is much more to Rotrou's legacy than destriers and monks.

In northern Spain, where he fought against the Almoravids, he gained a few small estates and, eventually, one of importance, namely Tudela, a prosperous center of learning in Navarre populated by Jewish and Muslim intellectuals. King Alfonso had seized this jewel from Moorish control in 1119. Despite his battles in Spain, Rotrou still spent enough time in Normandy to offer his sister's young daughter in betrothal to García Ramírez.

Sealed in 1121, the marriage contract between Margaret of Aigle and García Ramírez included a large dowry.[15] Contrary to popular belief, however, Tudela was not initially part of it, for Rotrou did not come into possession of the city until two years later, in 1123, and a decade would pass before he was free to give it to his niece, although he eventually did.[16]

Auspicious though the betrothal was for García and his mother, the wedding ceremony was years away. For now, the fatherless young knight had more pedestrian matters to address, like claiming his birthright and forging an identity of his own. He may also have forged the occasional liaison with one or another pretty maiden he found on his own, without the need for a matchmaker.

In Royal Service

For the next few years García Ramírez travelled constantly around his dominions, trying to enlarge his territory as opportunity was wont to allow. On one side his cousin Alfonso might thwart his ambitions; on the other an emir might encroach upon his territory. Most of the time, García scarcely managed to retain the lands he already possessed.

In 1126, the Almoravids seized Monzón and the surrounding territories. A series of power shifts followed. The chronicles and charters of these years tell us that towns and valleys in this part of Spain changed hands frequently, sometimes from one month to the next. In 1130 García Ramírez led some of the Christian forces that occupied Monzón, but that did not make the city his, even though he had inherited the rights to it from his father.

Most of the time, García Ramírez found himself under the authority of his cousin, Alfonso. In effect, Alfonso was the younger cousin's suzerain. This was an anomalous situation for a man of Alfonso's own dynasty, a junior prince who, understandably, might presume a greater place at court. By inviting foreign nobles like Rotrou of Perche into his realm and endowing them with lucrative estates, Alfonso probably hoped to marginalize the native nobility. Added to this tactic was the relegation of his Jiménez kinsmen to secondary, even tertiary, roles in the Kingdom of Aragon.

King Alfonso's only surviving brother, Ramiro, was a Benedictine monk. To curtail this sibling's potential influence, the monarch impeded the cleric's episcopal appointment to the sees of Burgos and Pamplona. This ran counter to custom as most royal princes in holy orders could expect to become bishops. Ramiro could do little to resolve his predicament so long as Alfonso reigned.

True, Rotrou of Perche was Alfonso's cousin, but he was not a Jiménez. In Normandy and England, Rotrou found himself at the center of political intrigues; in the Iberian lands he was a warrior serving a king intent on prosecuting a "holy war" to oust the Muslims from control. Rotrou posed no threat to Alfonso's authority.

The chief problem that Alfonso would be forced to confront eventually was that he lacked sons who might succeed him as king. His relationship with his wife, ambitious Urraca "the Reckless" of León, with whom he had a politically expedient but loveless marriage, was stormy at best; in what must be the epitome of spousal conflict, he once besieged her at one of her castles.[17] Alfonso's expansion of his territory and influence was far more successful than his marriage, which was eventually annulled, but who would inherit this burgeoning empire?

Margaret of Aigle

Cristina de Vivar, García's mother, died in 1130. We do not know if she ever met her future daughter-in-law. The next year, her son wed Margaret of Aigle (l'Aigle), the niece of Rotrou of Perche.

Margaret was the daughter of Gilbert of Aigle, a powerful Norman lord, and Juliana of Perche. Her father's family was nothing if not influential.[18] In England, where they were known as *Laigle,* they had been present since the Conquest in 1066. Margaret's elder brother, Richard (Richer), succeeded to estates on both sides of the Channel.

Most of Navarre was in Alfonso's hands, and he had erected a splendid cathedral at Pamplona, seat of a diocese, the region's most important city.

García Ramírez was intent on building a family. He housed Margaret in the castle at La Guardia, a town in his possession. By 1132, he held Logroño on the Ebro River nearby, along with Bolea, near Huesca to the east.[19]

In April of that year Margaret bore a son, Sancho.[20]

Meanwhile, García's sphere of influence was increasing. It may be that his marriage reflected a degree of seriousness that impressed Alfonso and Rotrou to entrust him with more responsibility. Whatever the case, he spent ever more time in Nájera, the historical town of the Jiménez family, and Pamplona to the north. But for now he kept his wife and child at La Guardia, out of harm's way.

Margaret gave birth to Blanca in 1134 while her husband was off campaigning with Alfonso's forces in eastern Aragon.[21]

The Leader

Monzón served as a springboard from which Alfonso's army launched an attack on the Almoravids at Fraga, near what is now the border of Aragon and Catalonia, during the summer. An unexpectedly lengthy siege ensued. Here Alfonso suffered one of his few military defeats when reinforcements arrived to relieve the city, and he was wounded in combat.[22] With what remained of his decimated army, the king, now in the throes of death, retreated to Zaragoza, the capital of Aragon.

García Ramírez was one of just ten knights with him when Alfonso died at the Monastery of San Juan de la Peña in September.[23] The Battler had fought his last battle.

With Aragon and Navarre poorly-defended and lacking a king, or even an obvious successor, the victorious Almoravids wasted no time occupying as much territory as they could. This was not mere religious zeal, but the desire to obtain the greenest, most fertile part of Spain.

But Aragon was more than that. As luck would have it, this happened to be a strategic region that might serve as a convenient gateway to the French territories to the north. Through vassalage, Alfonso had controlled some French regions, such as Toulouse, which might make an enticing objective for the Almoravids.

In life, Alfonso had done much to foster the idea of the *Reconquista,* and future kings would be inspired by his efforts, but now, in the aftermath of his death, his mini-empire began to crumble. In a bizarre twist, the childless king had left his kingdom to the crusading Hospitallers and Templars, with some estates willed to the Knights of the Holy Sepulchre.[24] Unwilling to let the realm fall to the control of the knightly orders, the baronage cast an eye around the kingdom for a suitable heir. There were two obvious candidates.

Alfonso's brother, Ramiro, the Benedictine monk, was supported by a vocal faction that was predominantly Aragonese. García Ramírez gained the support of some Navarrese barons.

The clergy seemed divided, but the bishop of Navarre's most important city lent his unequivocal support, both moral and financial, to García.[25] This was a propitious gesture.

Nevertheless, until a choice could be confirmed, a power vacuum remained. Exploiting this, Alfonso VII of Castile arrived at Zaragoza with a formidable army and asserted his own claim to Aragon on the basis of his mother, Urraca, having once been married to the late king.[26] This did not set well with the ecclesiastics and nobles opposed to the crown falling upon the head of a man who already ruled a sizeable chunk of Spain. Seeking to make his candidature more palatable, Ramiro shed his monk's robes and made known his intention to take a wife.[27]

With Alfonso of Castile excluded from serious consideration, a choice had to be made between a soldier and a friar.

Restoration

In late 1134 the Navarrese nobles and bishops elected García Ramírez their king, while the Aragonese elected Ramiro. The difference was that the Navarrese were only really interested in Navarre, whilst the Aragonese wanted their king to be the ruler of both realms.

The twin kingdoms divided from each other and Navarre was "restored." A reconciliation with Ramiro was attempted but failed. García formed an alliance with Castile while Ramiro established one with the Count of Barcelona, who ruled Catalonia to the east. A war between Navarre and Aragon was averted through this balance of power, forming a delicate detente.

By the time Margaret was born at La Guardia in 1135, her

parents were doubtless preparing to move to Pamplona, but both late pregnancy and early infancy argued for a delay.[28]

Because medieval chroniclers paid little heed to the births of daughters, we know little of the earliest years of Blanca and Margaret of the House of Jiménez. Even their first home offers precious few clues. Virtually nothing remains of La Guardia Castle, their presumed birthplace, where a school now stands.

Some nine centuries later, La Guardia is a charming town of reddish stone full of winding, narrow streets, but its churches and ring walls were erected long after the Jiménez family had departed for their new home, Pamplona, within a year of Margaret's birth.

García Ramírez was not present when Margaret was born. Most of 1135 saw him tending to administrative matters beyond Navarre. In that year, he received Zaragoza as a fief from his ally Alfonso VII of Castile, whose troops still occupied it. This meant that Ramiro, who the Aragonese had elected as their sovereign, did not control his own capital city, whose fortress, the Aljafería, was virtually impregnable to attack. But García did not wish to keep Zaragoza, either for himself or for Alfonso. It was Pamplona and Navarre that interested him.

In late 1135, García Ramírez was crowned King of Pamplona in that city's newly-constructed Romanesque cathedral.[29] Margaret of Aigle was now a queen. The children, Sancho, Blanca and little Margaret, were now part of a truly royal family.

More importantly, Navarre was again a sovereign country, even if, for now, it was called the "Kingdom of Pamplona" for its splendid capital city.

The following year, Alfonso of Castile recognized Ramiro, the former monk, as Aragon's ruler. By that time, García Ramírez had renounced his claim to Zaragoza and most of his lordships beyond Navarre's shifting borders. Rooted firmly in Navarran soil, Tudela was his *jure uxoris,* by right of his wife.

Royal Childhood

Hilltop Pamplona was full of gently-curving streets that branched out from its cathedral and castle. The new cathedral was built just in time for García's coronation by Sancho de Rosas, the Bishop of Pamplona.

The castle[30] was little more than a shadow of its former self. Not much remained of its walls. The city had not been the seat of royal power for some sixty years, and it was too far out of the way to draw much attention from the Almoravids who occupied nearly half of Iberia. Pamplona had defensive walls, but a large, imposing fortress seemed unnecessary. The old one had fallen into crumbling decay, used in recent times to house nothing more illustrious than a few notaries and their horses.

Zaragoza was far away, beyond hills and forests and valleys and rivers. Over the course of nearly six long decades, the Aragonese branch of the House of Jiménez had paid little attention to Pamplona except when it was time to collect taxes. Pamplona had a small Jewish community and a smaller Muslim one. A good part of the Christian population was Basque. Royal governors arrived from time to time, but it was the local bishop who held the reins of true leadership.

Poised at the frontier leading to the Pyrenees and Gascony, Pamplona's identity, however one describes it, was barely Spanish at all, not that a gentilic like *Spanish* had much significance in 1135.

Having spent his entire adult life as a warring knight, García Ramírez was looking forward to a less hectic pace. There would always be battles to fight. But if he could never retreat into leisure and luxury, García might still dedicate more of his time to constructive pursuits like raising his children and founding monasteries. And rebuilding Pamplona's castle.

Ruling a small kingdom entailed a fair degree of day-to-day

administration. The monarch and his family might enjoy a closer familiarity with their subjects, their people, than what could be presumed by the sovereigns of larger kingdoms. In our times, the Netherlands and Denmark are good examples of this. They epitomize what most European monarchies were in the Middle Ages, many of their names now little more than those of regions: Swabia, Aquitaine, Bavaria, Connacht, Hessen, Tolouse, Savoy, Anjou.

Little Margaret's Navarre had a very special status. As a kingdom restored, it had a long history yet a very new sense of sovereignty and what today would be called *identity*. It was almost as if her father, the king, were its founder. This brought with it a certain prestige.

Queen Margaret of Pamplona was accorded an uncommon deference. This may be attributed to the importance of her Aigle family. For evidence of this one need only have considered that Tudela, one of the realm's most prosperous towns, was readily integrated into the reconstituted kingdom through the auspices of Margaret's uncle, Rotrou.

Yet that is not sufficient to explain the presence of her name alongside her husband's on several surviving charters, for Margaret was not a queen in her own right or even a regent. Her position derived solely from that of her husband, who had literally fought for it.

It is most likely that García Ramírez, who in 1135 found himself with but a single male heir, and no Jiménez kinsmen to whom his reborn kingdom could be entrusted in the event of his own early demise, wished to ensure that his wife, the mother of his children, would be viewed as a suitable regent. Several charters issued over the course of just a few years are scarcely enough to form a solid hypothesis, but they lead one to connote Margaret's role as something more than passive, as if she were García's advisor as well as his consort.

Despite having what, for a man of thirty-five, had been a

long military career, García Ramírez may not have had many close confidants. Over the years, the first fealty of many of the knights and nobles who served with him was pledged to his cousin, Alfonso of Aragon. Others were, firstly, the friends of Rotrou of Perche or other nobles, including many from north of the Pyrenees. García does not seem to have cultivated especially close friendships with the clergy or the commanders of knightly orders like the Templars and Hospitallers. He had no brothers.

It was difficult to know who to trust, especially now that he was king. Could he trust his wife?

Many of his first acts as king involved the Catholic Church. In Navarre, as in many western European kingdoms, the Church was the single largest landholder after the sovereign himself. In this region, the constant Almoravid threat increased the importance of the Church in secular affairs because religious institutions such as monasteries were seen as an ideological bulwark against Islam's influence on the established order. Whereas the rulers of kingdoms like England or Denmark might challenge ecclesiastical authority from time to time, a ruler like García Ramírez was more likely to embrace it.

This was equally advantageous for the Church because whilst a Christian king would support the Christian hierarchy a Muslim emir would merely tolerate it.

A number of surviving charters reflect the new king's amicable rapport with Bishop Sancho of Pamplona, who had supported him against Ramiro in 1134, and a few of these very prominently include Margaret's name.

As early as 1135, we find a royal decree confirming the privileges previously granted to Pamplona's diocese by Alfonso I of Aragon, stating that the new sovereign is acting *cum consilio et auctoritate uxoris mee Margarite regine,* "on the advice and with the consent of my wife Queen Margaret."[31]

A similar formula appears in several subsequent decrees.

Of particular note is a charter relative to the city of Tudela, which had come into the actual possession of Margaret and her husband around the time García Ramírez was elected king.[32] Issued in 1138, this charter assigns to the Bishop of Pamplona the Church of Saint Mary at Tudela, "with all the assets therein appertaining to Moors and Christians."[33]

In these years, the children of García Ramírez and his queen enjoyed a playful, pleasant life in a serene city far beyond the turmoil of the constant conflicts between Christians and Moors that so often plagued the other kingdoms of Spain. Their education by monks and nuns was a steady process of tutoring. Blanca and Margaret may have been tutored together. One imagines private lessons in the mornings, with afternoons and Sundays free.

It seems that their mother, the queen, found ways to pass the time while García was making the rounds of Navarre's towns.

Around 1139, she gave birth to a son christened *Rodrigo* in honour of García's grandfather, the intrepid Cid. But, despite his name, baby Rodrigo was not descended from the Cid, for the infant was not the son of King García Ramírez.

Writing about him at the Sicilian court a few decades later, the chronicler Romuald of Salerno described Rodrigo, who the Sicilians took to calling "Henry," simply as *Henricus naturalis frater*, "Henry the natural brother" of Margaret of Navarre.

The words of Hugh Falcandus were more venomous: *Rex navarrorum nunquam filium suum vel esse credidit vel dici voluit, indignum existimans eum quem mater multorum patens libidini vulgo concepisset, regis filium appellari*. "The King of Navarre never considered him his son, nor did he wish him to be called such, for it would be disgraceful if this boy conceived by a woman notorious for her sexual liaisons with various men were identified as the son of a king."

To justify this unflattering comment, Falcandus further explains that the information was provided by the Navarrese who accompanied Rodrigo to Sicily.³⁴ Of Rodrigo's name, Falcandus reports that *Roderic* was "abhorrent, derided by the Sicilians as unknown and barbaric, so the queen decided that he should be called Henry."³⁵

Although Margaret of Aigle has been tainted by her reputation as a harlot, the number of her lovers is probably exaggerated. Nevertheless, her husband seems not to have been deceived. It is most likely that García Ramírez, who frequently travelled around his kingdom, was not present with Margaret in Pamplona during the period when Rodrigo was conceived, so he knew that the child could not be his.³⁶

Margaret of Aigle did not have to bear her disgrace for very long. She died in May 1141.³⁷ Whatever her foibles may have been in life, in death her funeral in Pamplona's splendid cathedral was one befitting a queen. The celebrant was Bishop Sancho, the same man who had crowned Margaret six years earlier. God might forgive, but posterity never forgot.

Education of a Queen

However inherently stoic her character, a girl of six faces her mother's death only with the greatest unwillingness. A parent who was there one moment is gone the next. Margaret of Aigle may not have been an exemplary wife, but there is nothing to suggest that she was anything but a caring mother.

Blanca and Margaret were too young to understand the harsh words murmured about their mother at court, if, as young children, they ever even heard these rumours. How much of their mother's Norman French tongue would they remember? And her love?

We cannot fathom the sorrow in young Margaret's tears as they cascaded onto the harsh stone floor of a cold cathedral. So frequently were people of her time visited by death that this may not have been the first funeral the girl ever attended, but it was certainly the one she would live to remember most vividly throughout her youth. Here her childhood had suddenly taken a bad turn.

Time may heal many wounds, but it cannot nullify their memory.

Both sisters were destined to become queens, but neither could know it in 1141. Nobody knew it, for the sisters' betrothals were years away. Nevertheless, their education would be suitable to girls for whom queenhood was a realistic expectation, even a birthright.

Many aristocratic households were full of siblings and aunts and cousins, and perhaps even a grandparent or two. Even the castle of a petty baron might assume the character of a royal court in miniature. But García Ramírez and his wife did not live among an extended family. At the most, a French cousin might pass through Pamplona on his way to Santiago de Compostela on pilgrimage.[38]

Sancho, Blanca, Margaret and Rodrigo had playmates, of course, children chosen from among the nobility. Compared to most children their age, they spent more time around adults, especially their guardians and tutors. With their mother gone, and no aunt to serve as a maternal surrogate, the duty of raising the children fell to monks, nuns and the few women at court who had been the late queen's friends.

Aristocratic girls were educated, for the most part, in convents. Living with the nuns, they learned piety and devotion. Blanca and Margaret lived in a convent just outside Pamplona, and this allowed for frequent visits to the family home near the cathedral. Boys might spend a few formative years at the castle of a neighboring baron.

Many noblewomen were better-educated than their brothers.

Lessons included languages, especially Latin, and simple arithmetic, along with penmanship. The rudiments of botany and agriculture were studied. Poetry and theology were important. Parts of the Bible were studied, perhaps memorized. Some sense of canon law was inculcated into the children's minds. There might be a touch of music, and such studies as alchemy.

The children learned how to play chess, and the girls were taught to let the boys win.

Queens were inevitably sacrificed to kings, but there was a healthy respect for unpredictable knights, avaricious bishops and ambitious pawns. Royalty, the highest aristocracy, was mindful of the potential power of the nobility, the clergy and the common folk. The children were taught to appreciate the complexities of human nature as these were perceived in the medieval mind.

Horsemanship was important, even for a princess. This began with ponies and ended with palfreys. A knowledge of history, geography, genealogy, architecture, iconography and coinage was part of a young aristocrat's education.

The girls were taught how to recognize good fruit and luxurious fabric, and how to cook and weave. Even if a princess never had to butcher a goat or shear a sheep, her place as the directress of a noble household made it necessary for her to be able to oversee those who did.

For the boys, swordplay, archery and hunting were important. These skills they learned from the king's most trusted men-at-arms. A prince need not be the ablest knight at a tournament or on the battlefield, but he had to be able to defend himself. More importantly, he had to inspire courage, even audacity, in those who looked to him as their leader. His travels might take him to remote regions where the ability to down a stag or boar, and then roast it, would be more necessity than sport.

Chapter 4
BETROTHAL

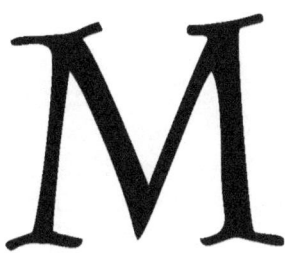

"I feel sure that no woman would go to the altar if she knew all."

— Queen Victoria

An unspoken but very real part of the education of a young princess involved learning about responsibility. As she became a woman, she came to understand what was expected of her, something she must accept without question or complaint. The most important part of her role was easily summed up in two words. Marriage and motherhood.

Coming of Age

Adulthood came quickly, especially for royalty, typically seventeen for a boy and fourteen for a girl.

Some girls were betrothed at an even younger age, and in June 1144 García Ramírez took as his second wife Urraca, who was only twelve. She was the illegitimate daughter of his ally King Alfonso VII of Castile. This union was meant to resolve a short-lived but potentially catastrophic conflict with Alfonso.

The marriage, happy or not, would strengthen the bonds between Navarre and Castile.[39]

Urraca[40] was about the same age as Blanca, so the young bride was hardly a "stepmother" to the daughters of King García Ramírez. They may not have been too accepting of a very young woman who they probably perceived more as a sister than their father's wife. Some semblance of such attitudes existed even in the twelfth century.

Another complexity was Urraca's social, and even dynastic, position. Because she was now Queen of Pamplona, Blanca and Margaret had to defer to her rank and status. Much had changed since the death of the mother of the two young sisters just a few years earlier.

For Sancho, as heir apparent, the new situation was less severe. Whatever he thought of Urraca, or she of him, his dynastic position was assured. At this point in his young life, he was already being taught about geography and politics, as well as the importance of dynastic marriages arranged with both in mind.[41]

In truth, we know virtually nothing about the intricacies of the relationship of Blanca and Margaret with their father's second wife, who eventually gave birth to a daughter.

Though remarried, García Ramírez had not put his first wife completely out of his mind. In August 1145, he seized a synagogue at Estella (Lizarra) which was to be converted into a church that would be ceded to Pamplona's diocese in memory of the late queen, *pro anima uxoris Margarite regine,* as well as the souls of himself and his entire family.[42]

Blanca and Margaret saw their father only rarely during these years. Ever the warrior king, he occupied Tauste in 1146. Though located very near the border, it was claimed by Aragon, and García's father-in-law, Alfonso of Castile, intervened to negotiate an immediate end to what might have sparked a war between Navarre and Aragon.

A few towns in La Rioja, on the southern fringe of Navarre, had already been lost to Castile. Although none were very important economically, at least two had sentimental value. The Jiménez kings rested at Nájera, and García's daughters were born at La Guardia. Nevertheless, García Ramírez had consolidated his power and re-established a kingdom. Navarre was finally at peace with her neighbors, at least for now.

Crowned in a Far Country

The Kingdom of Pamplona, as it was still known officially, was beginning to attract the attention of kings further afield, and it was time to find suitable husbands for the Jiménez sisters.

Here age conferred precedence. Negotiations began for Blanca to marry into the family that ruled Catalonia from Barcelona on the other side of Aragon, a dynastic union meant to neutralize the more zealous machinations that emanated from Zaragoza every now and then.[43]

Late in 1148 there arrived at Pamplona several noblemen and a bishop sent from Palermo by Roger II, the King of Sicily.

Established just eighteen years earlier, the Kingdom of Sicily encompassed the southern half of the Italian peninsula, and its sovereign also controlled part of the African coast. It was ruled by the Hauteville dynasty, which, like the Aigle and Perche ancestors of Margaret's mother, had roots in Normandy. It was through an informal network of such families that the Hautevilles were familiar with Norman activities in the Iberian lands, such as the adventures of Rotrou of Perche.

In the chess board of Norman society, which was a patchwork of kingdoms and counties, there was a great deal of kinship and camaraderie going back several generations. Some of the same Norman knights present at the Battle of Messina in 1061 fought at Hastings five years later. In 1097, Odo of Bayeux, half-brother of William the Conqueror, died at Palermo, where he rests in the crypt of that city's cathedral.[44]

The Sicilian ambassadors were seeking the betrothal of Margaret to King Roger's son. One imagines the heart of the young princess being filled by equal parts of exhilaration and apprehension.

Rotrou of Perche had died too soon to be involved in the marriage negotiations, although he may have spoken to García Ramírez about the possibility of one of the girls marrying into a Norman family, but his son, Margaret's cousin, was to play a role in Sicilian history.[45]

From England to Spain to Constantinople to Antioch to Tunisia, the Normans had made their influence felt, and no family was more successful than the Hautevilles. It will be remembered that Rotrou himself went on crusade with Bohemond of Hauteville, who established a monarchy at Antioch.

The twelfth century was the Normans' century.

But the Sicilian ambassadors did not bring with them just a marriage proposal. Margaret was being offered queenship. All that was needed was her father's approval. Despite his frequent absences, García Ramírez was probably present in Pamplona on this occasion to receive the Sicilians.

In reality, of course, Margaret had little say in the matter, nay none at all. The decision would be her father's.

It was proposed that Margaret marry William, King Roger's only legitimate, surviving son, who was fourteen years her senior. There was a certain urgency in the wedding arrangements because by late 1148 the Sicilian royal family found itself, rather unexpectedly, with a dearth of heirs to the throne.

Roger's wife, William's mother Elvira, had died the same year Margaret was born, leaving behind four healthy sons. The king loved Elvira so profoundly that he was reluctant to remarry after her death. Indeed, when she died he went into seclusion, leading many of his subjects to think he too was dead. Roger mourned Elvira for years. When his sons were all alive, the widower saw no reason to take another wife simply for the purpose of producing more heirs. But with the recent death of William's elder brother the situation had grown dire. Roger now had only one legitimate son and no grandsons.[46]

The ambassadors wanted to see the girl, and perhaps even speak with her. Was she reasonably intelligent and well-educated? Was she pretty enough to become their queen? Most importantly in view of the dynasty's present predicament, was Margaret of childbearing age?

In the case of Sicily, as opposed to a kingdom like England, there was an additional consideration, and it was almost as pragmatic as the others. Could Margaret, devoutly Catholic though she may be, accept the presence of people of other religions and cultures in her own kingdom, perhaps even in her own household?

Palermo had a large Muslim population and a fair number of Jews. It was full of mosques and synagogues. Margaret need not be a theologian, but it was important for her to understand something of Islam and Judaism, and to understand that in Sicily the people of these faiths enjoyed the same rights as Christians. Many held positions in government, and some served in the royal bodyguard.

This matter was not an obstacle, as Margaret was familiar with the Muslims and Jews of her native land. In Pamplona, as in Palermo, there were mosques and synagogues just down the street from the cathedral. Spain's Muslims and Christians had their differences, but the experience of cities like Tudela had shown that peaceful coexistence, even brotherhood, was possible.

Margaret had a tenuous dynastic connection to the man she was expected to wed. Through his mother, William was Margaret's third cousin once removed. King Roger's first wife, the much beloved Elvira of Castile, was a Jiménez.[47]

The precise details of Margaret's betrothal and dower are not known to us, but we do have a well-documented example that offers us some insight into what it was. This is the betrothal of Joanna of England to Margaret's son in 1176.[48] By then, such things had changed, but not very much.

With her father's consent, Margaret was betrothed to William and given a few months to prepare for her voyage to Sicily.

In the late spring of 1149, she said good-bye to her father, brother and sister. She would never see them again. Parting from her sister, Blanca, was especially trying, but Margaret gathered up all the courage her tender years allowed.

Setting off for Sicily, Margaret was accompanied by a few ladies-in-waiting, a few barons, a bishop or two, a small company of knights and around twenty servants and other retainers. In all, there were at least sixty people traveling in Margaret's entourage. A dozen or so would remain with her in Sicily.

Undertaken in early summer, the first leg of the journey would take them across Aragon and Catalonia to Barcelona, through lands ruled by Christians or friendly Moors. From there, they would follow the coast from Girona, passing Perpignan, Marseille, Toulon and other cities along the French coast. Around Nice, they would board a flotilla of galleys sent by the King of Sicily, for Navarre had no fleet to speak of.

The ships would follow the Italian coast to Naples or Salerno, and thence to Messina and finally Palermo. This maritime route along the coasts ensured that the travelers were always in friendly waters.

A faster, direct route from Barcelona to Majorca to Sardinia and then Sicily would have entailed a far greater risk of the flotilla encountering pirates. The ships of the Sicilian navy could very effectively respond to such a threat, but there was always the danger of a galley or two being lost. Natural hazards posed another danger. Whilst the Mediterranean was usually serene by May, storms were unpredictable, so it was better to stay fairly near the coast.

At Palermo, where she was acclaimed by ecstatic crowds, Margaret met the man she was to marry. William had medium brown hair and brown eyes, essentially the same coloring as Margaret.

The wedding was celebrated in the Palatine Chapel of the opulent royal palace, where the couple took up residence. The setting was nothing if not romantic, but were Margaret and William in love?

Fatimid fountain in Monreale's cloister

Chapter 5
POLYGLOT REALM

"How do we create a harmonious society out of so many kinds of people? The key is tolerance."

— Barbara Jordan

The island that greeted Margaret in the summer of 1149 was a cacophony of cultures. George Bernard Shaw famously observed that, "England and America are two countries divided by a common language." What would he have made of Norman Sicily, a place strangely united despite several languages being spoken there?

Languages and Peoples

When the Normans arrived in 1061, they encountered people they generically described as "Greeks" and "Saracens."[49] Devoid of nuance, these descriptions were based on the languages spoken by the majority of Sicilians at that time.

The "Greeks" were the corpus of "indigenous" Sicilians descended from those inhabitants who lived on the island when it was part of the Byzantine Empire. Their ancestors were the native Sicanians, Elymians and Sikels, and then the Greeks, Punics, Romans, Vandals and Ostrogoths. In 535, at the dawn of the Middle Ages, and with the Vandals and Ostrogoths defeated, Sicily became the western frontier of Constantinople's dominion. Among the Sicilians, Greek had long been the chief spoken language, with Latin a distant second, and many islanders were bilingual. The population's ecclesial orientation vacillated between Latin Rome and Greek Constantinople, eventually favoring the latter, from whence the vestiges of Rome's crumbling empire were governed.

In 827 Tunisia's Aghlabids landed in Sicily with a large invasion force. Arabic, the language of the Prophet, united them. Yet, like the Sicilians they subjugated, these invaders were, in reality, a diverse group: Arabs, Berbers, even some Persians. In the veins of a few flowed the blood of the erstwhile Vandals, whose ephemeral mini-empire based in northern Africa was now all but forgotten, and the Carthaginians, who once challenged the Romans for control of Sicily and the western Mediterranean.

It was during the Roman era that the first Jews are known to have settled in Sicily in significant numbers, although some Samaritans probably lived in Syracuse in earlier times. The Jews living in Sicily in the ninth century had close ties to their brethren in Tunisia and spoke Judeo Arabic.[50]

The Latin Vulgate had emerged as a convenient means of communication in peninsular Italy south of Rome, where Byzantines and Lombards vied for power. The Norman mercenaries who arrived in this part of Italy during the early decades of the eleventh century spoke their own brand of French among themselves.

By then, nearly half the Sicilian population spoke Greek and the other half Arabic. As in earlier times, many Sicilians were bilingual. The Jews' Judeo Arabic was easily understood by the Arabs, whose Siculo Arabic survives as Maltese.[51] The baronage spoke Norman French. As we shall see, some of these barons recognized the merits of their fellow Sicilians, and especially the Muslims, only grudgingly, but their resentment was not rooted in linguistic differences.

Not surprisingly, the royal family, the Hautevilles, spoke Norman French among themselves, and this was the language used at court, but by necessity they were at least marginally proficient in other tongues.

Latin was widely re-introduced with the Latin liturgy and religious orders like the ubiquitous Benedictines. The aftermath of the Great Schism of 1054 led to the Christians of southern Italy assimilating with either the Roman "Catholic" West or the Greek "Orthodox" East.[52] Here there were no traumatic conversions, just the insidious substitution of one rite and language by another. Muslims were encouraged, but rarely coerced, to convert to Catholicism.[53]

Sicily's Norman rulers enjoyed what was generally a good rapport with the Papacy. In 1098, Pope Urban II granted them the "apostolic legateship," the right to approve episcopal appointments in Sicily, a privilege all but unknown elsewhere in Europe.

The realm's transition to Catholicism, however subtle, did not go unnoticed. Nilos Doxopatrios, an Orthodox cleric who arrived at Palermo about 1142, wrote a theological treatise expounding upon the traditions of the Orthodox Church at a time when Rome's influence was becoming dominant in Sicily.[54] Around the same time, Palermo's Martorana Church was built for the Orthodox community by George of Antioch. The Arabic inscription around its dome reflects a multicultural zeitgeist, but a few years later a Catholic church was built next to it, dedicated to Saint Cathaldus, an Irish monk (known as *San Cataldo* to Italians) who became Bishop of Taranto.

In Margaret's time conversion was encouraged gently, and

here the written word lends us a few clues about the form it took.

The *Harley Trilingual Psalter* (shown in this book), with its text in Greek, Latin and Arabic, was composed in Palermo between 1130 and 1153. It is thought that this psalter was used at services in the royal presence in the Palatine Chapel. Most of the Greek text is drawn from the Septuagint, an early translation of the scriptures from Hebrew into Koine Greek. The Latin text is Saint Jerome's Gallican revision, completed around 384, itself formulated with an eye to the Greek texts. The Arabic is the eleventh-century translation *ex novo* by Abu'l-Fath Abdallah ibn al-Fadl ibn Abdallah al-Mutran al-Antaki.[55]

The quadrilingual tombstone preserved in Palermo (and shown in this book) was inscribed in 1148 in Latin, Greek, Arabic, and Judeo Arabic written in Hebrew.

These languages were written as well as spoken. The growing influence of Latin and, to a much lesser extent, Norman French, led to a Romance vernacular sometimes referred to as "Middle Sicilian" that flowered after 1200. The earliest surviving poetry composed in this tongue, the predecessor of modern Sicilian, dates from the early decades of the thirteenth century.[56] The oldest known work of narrative prose written in Middle Sicilian was composed toward the end of the same century.[57]

Certain Gallo-Italic elements in the dialects of some towns in eastern Sicily reflect the influence of Lombard vassals who arrived with the Normans.

The Queen's Tongue

Margaret's first language, which her mother spoke to her, was Norman French. The l'Aigle lands of her mother's father (Gilbert) were in lower Normandy, and the Perche family of her mother's mother (Juliana) held lands in a county that straddled the regions of Normandy and Maine.

But Margaret's mother, as we have seen, died when her younger daughter was only six years old. To the local aristocrats, the princess most often spoke Navarro-Aragonese. Like Norman French, it is now "extinct." Navarro-Aragonese was subsumed in Castilian.

As a girl in Pamplona, Margaret learned Basque, for there would be virtually no other way to communicate with most of the local people.

Basque, which seems to have been spoken in some form before the ancient Romans conquered Spain, is not closely related to the Iberian and Romance languages. It may not be related to them at all.

Like Sicilian, these languages were written rather rarely in Margaret's girlhood, when Latin was the formal and uniting language of western Europe. Except for Basque, which existed in a category of its own, the Iberian vernacular tongues, being based on Latin, were somewhat similar to each other yet quite different.

Apropos similarities, the common noun *woman* was *muyller* or *muger* in Navarro-Aragonese and *mujer* in Castilian. In Middle Sicilian *mugleri* was *wife*.

Of course, Catalan and Arabic were also spoken in northeastern Spain.

Provençal, an Occitan language, was developing as the courtly vernacular of poets and troubadours. This was the first medieval literature written in a vernacular Romance language, and its popularity probably inspired those who heard it, including the Sicilian courtiers, to write poetry in their own languages.[58]

Margaret, like most royalty, studied Latin, even if she may not have mastered this inflective language to the point of writing it very well. Reading it was a necessity because Latin was the language of books, charters, correspondence and the Bible.

She probably learned some Arabic. New languages were not the only thing in Sicily waiting to test Margaret's tongue.

Tasting Sicily

Unlike the common women of her era, Margaret, as royalty, enjoyed the privilege of spending more time tasting food than cooking it. Medieval Sicilian cuisine reflected the diversity of Sicily's population. Southern Europe, with its two annual harvests and Mediterranean flora, offered much more than cooler climates in the way of culinary delights. Olives, almonds, figs, artichokes and, naturally, grapes, were part of this bounty. This wasn't very different from what Margaret knew in Navarre.

Precious few recipes survive from the twelfth century. Abdullah al Idrisi, the court geographer, wrote that the people of Trabia, east of Palermo, made what today would be called *spaghetti*.

The Arabs introduced sugar cane and mulberries, the latter for silk making. Their irrigation systems permitted the cultivation of rice. The *arancina*, the rice ball, may have come to us from this tradition. In any case, we know that rice flavored with saffron was an Arab dish. Candied fruits seem to be a holdover from the Fatimid era. *Caponata*, a salad made with eggplants (aubergines), capers and olives, may be a modern recipe, but its ingredients were certainly available in Sicily during the days of Norman rule. The *Kitab al-Tabikh* of the thirteenth century alludes to aubergine salad recipes in the Muslim world.[59] *Panelle* (chickpea fritters) may be Arab in origin.

Stemperata, a delicious fish recipe based on an *agrodolce* (sweet and sour) sauce made from white wine vinegar, sugar and onions, is thought to have originated in Arab times. Couscous, once a mainstay of the Berber diet, is still popular in Trapani, Marsala and Erice.

Granita (flavored ices) and ice cream may have been known

during the Greek era, but sorbet seems to have been re-introduced by the Arabs, who cultivated sugarcane in Sicily.

Sicily's forests were full of deer and boar. Goat meat and mutton were popular. The Arabs probably introduced the Girgentan goat, whose spiralled horns give it the appearance of a markhor.

Palermo boasted several large souks. Ballarò, a popular street market, stands on the site of one of them, present here for centuries. Margaret probably made occasional forays into this market district.

The king's cooks were Arabs. So were the women in his harem.

Normans, Arabs, Greeks, Jews

Details of such practices are elusive, sometimes expressed in a manner that lends itself to euphemism. The women in King Roger's "harem" were, according to some descriptions, responsible for weaving silk — when they weren't tending to more important matters. There was no way for Margaret not to have known of the presence in the palace of these women, who were guarded by eunuchs.

Most of the institutions inherited from the Aghlabids, Fatimids and Kalbids were far more significant than this in the day-to-day operation of the *Regnum Siciliae*. Among these was the *diwan*, the royal treasury, from which the Italian *dogana* and French *douane*, which nowadays refers to a custom house or duty.[60]

Palermo's diversity, perhaps paradoxically, was its greatest strength, and at the middle of the twelfth century the Muslims still comprised the greater part of the city's population.

Some of the most important positions in the kingdom were based on Arab traditions. The rank of admiral probably derived from the Arabic *amir al-bahr*, literally "commander of the sea," akin to the title of emir.

Even some of the coinage of the Kingdom of Sicily was Arab in origin. The gold *tarì*, for example, was patterned after the Muslims' *ruba'i*, the popular quarter-dinar.[61]

The royal bodyguard consisted largely of Muslim Arabs who, unlike many of the greedy Norman barons, were steadfastly loyal to the king and not easily swayed by zealous Catholic prelates. Many of the kingdom's longbow archers, thought to be the finest in Europe, were Muslims.[62]

Signs of Muslim-Arab culture were everywhere. Just beyond the royal palace, Margaret could walk through the *Genoard*, the Arabs' *Jannàt al-àrd*, their "Paradise on Earth." This was the name of the extensive park and hunting ground that King Roger had Arab architects create for him. Extending across the capital's vast fluvial valley and beyond Monreale, Baida, Molara and Altofonte to the rugged mountains encircling the city, it was a marvel of Europe.

Long before the park existed, the countryside in the Valley of Palermo, surrounded by its natural amphitheatre made up of hills and mountains, was a miracle of flora and fauna, thanks to its fertile soil, rivers and springs. Beginning in the ninth century, long before the Norman conquest, the Arabs introduced new irrigational and agricultural techniques here, where they planted citrus groves of oranges, lemons and citrons, earning the valley its nickname *Conca d'Oro*, meaning "Golden Conch." Indigo and henna were cultivated.

There were canals and *norias*, water wheels, nourishing both common and exotic plants, bushes, and trees such as palms, plane trees (sycamores), almond, pistachio, chestnuts and walnuts, wild olive and fig trees, medlar trees, myrtle and laurel. There was also papyrus and sugarcane growing along the streams and the two rivers, the *Kemonia* and the suitably-named *Papyrus* or *Papireto*. The scent of jasmine and orange blossoms was everywhere.

While the precise extent of the Genoard park is unknown today, we do know that it embraced a series of streams and *kanats* (man-made water channels) linked to the palaces built in the valley for both emirs and kings, a territory extending to the base of the mountain crowned by Monreale and beyond.[63]

Though the oldest of the Fatimid palaces was several miles east of the Genoard, it is worth mentioning because it was the inspiration for palaces constructed later. The *Favara,* also known as *Maredolce,* in what is now the tarnished Brancaccio district of Palermo, was built by Ja'far, the Emir of Bal'harm, at the end of the tenth century. Its name derives from the two freshwater springs, *fawwàra* in Arabic, that supplied water to the area, flowing down from nearby Mount Grifone into the Oreto River. These natural springs permitted the emir's guests to luxuriate in a verdant park and bathe in a small lake.

The "Admiral's Bridge" nearby now spans dry ground, the course of the Oreto having been diverted long ago. But this isn't the only vestige of the Norman era to be found in Palermo.

Norman-Arab Architecture

Although the Genoard's lakes and rivers are gone, along with its woods, a few of its palaces and pavilions survive amidst Palermo's modern urban sprawl. These included the Zisa and the Cubola (photographs of these appear in this book), as well as the Cuba palace and part of the Scibene. Their architectural style was, to say the least, unusual.

The beautiful Romanesque architectural style of Normandy so important in changing the face of Saxon England was accommodated in Sicily, but it merely embellished what the Byzantines and Arabs were already doing. The syncretic "Norman-Arab" style of art and architecture was unique, perhaps even a new expression of aesthetics. The Martorana and Saint

Cathaldus are examples of this movement.

Monreale Abbey (which deserves its own chapter) and the Palatine Chapel represent the epitome of this style.

The baths at Cefalà Diana are the most complete building of the Arab period still standing in Sicily designed in a purely Arab architectural style, and the oldest part of Taormina's Palazzo Corvaja was a Fatimid edifice.

Tangible evidence of Sicily's medieval mosques is scant at best. In a corner of the interior of Palermo Cathedral, near the stairs leading to the crypt, is a piece of the muqarnas ceiling from a mihrab of the Great Friday Mosque, itself built upon a Paleo-Christian basilica in the ninth century. Outside, a pillar that was once part of another mosque supports the portico. Beneath the watchful gaze of a gargoyle shaped as a boar, it is inscribed in relief with an Arabic verse from the Koran.

Concealed beneath the cloister of Palermo's largest Jesuit monastery is what may be Europe's oldest surviving mikveh, once fed by waters from an underground *kanat*. Another subterranean mikveh is preserved at Syracuse.

Margaret's adopted country was very prosperous. It was said that the tax revenue of Palermo exceeded that of the entire Kingdom of England. The law favored commerce, trade and productivity, and even a certain degree of personal freedom.

Historical serendipity forged Sicily's multicultural society. Inspired government permitted kings to rule it.

Law

If Margaret found an orderly *Regnum,* one of the reasons for this was the uniform legal code that brought a sense of justice to what began as an eclectic potpourri.

For many decades, indeed since the Normans' arrival, Sicily's legal system was essentially a patchwork of disparate codes, ranging from the feudal to the religious. Justice was uneven, if not arbitrary. Each citizen was judged by her own religion: Canon law, Maliki law, Halakha law. For the barons, there was Justinian's *Codex Juris Civilis* but also the Lombards' *Codex Legum Longobardorum*. What was needed was a legal code that could be applied universally without undue complexity or subjectivity, in the process bolstering centralized government. For everybody.

This arrived during the reign of Roger II in the form of the Assizes of Ariano.[64] Apart from the legal principles themselves, clearly inspired by the Code of Justinian, this code asserted the new king's role as lawgiver.

All subjects were equal in the eyes of the law, even if a few were "more equal than others." This was a European kingdom, after all, so justice was weighted in favour of the nobility and the Catholic Church. Barons and bishops could still mistreat almost everybody else, usually with impunity, but even *they* might be called to account for their actions every now and then.

Various offenses were addressed, particularly violent ones. Arming a mob, thereby inciting riots, was a grave act. Bishops, like nobles, were accorded certain privileges. Among Christians, apostates and heretics lost their rights of citizenship.

Rape was outlawed.[65] Treason was made a capital offense, Jews were forbidden the holding of Christian serfs, jesters were prohibited from blaspheming, simony was made illegal, fugitives were permitted asylum in churches. Sentences for crimes against public officials were to be taken seriously, taking into account that these acts were, in effect, affronts to the monarch himself.

The forgery and theft of documents were unequivocally capital crimes. Counterfeiting or clipping coins was outlawed. Royal approval was required for men born outside the nobility to become knights, judges and notaries. Infringement of royal estates was outlawed. Marriage was required as the basis for legitimacy of heirs. Adultery and prostitution were addressed, likewise kidnapping and robbery. Licensing of physicians was established. Overt corruption was not tolerated; judges who accepted bribes could be executed.

Many of these principles were already known, some from the time of Justinian, but Roger made them the law of the land. (The two known codices of the Assizes are presented in an appendix of this volume.)

As a further sign of royal authority, at Ariano Roger decreed the issuance of his *ducalis,* or ducat, the silver coin's name based on his *duchy* of Apulia.[66]

We also find among the Arabs of Norman Sicily the application of an early form of common law, which soon vanished in Italy but survived in England. This reflects Muslim influences.[67]

A great deal was written about the Kingdom of Sicily, and much of this has been preserved for us, but the greater part of what we know about the realm, and especially the prosperous island of Sicily where half its population lived, is drawn from our knowledge of the places Margaret herself knew.

Chapter 6
MOTHERHOOD

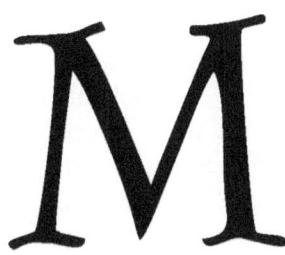

"If you bungle raising your children, I don't think whatever else you do matters very much."

— Jacqueline Bouvier Kennedy

Margaret's new home was a palace set on high ground between the city of Palermo to the north and the vast Genoard park to the south. She could see both from the arched windows of her residence on the top floor of one of the stout, square towers. Beyond a cityscape of golden limestone buildings, where the cupolas of churches and mosques looked like the bulbous caps of freshly-sprouted mushrooms, was the blue Tyrrhenian. On the other side, looking past the green Genoard, with its trees and streams, she could see rocky mountains.[68] And beyond the mountains were more mountains.

Life in Palermo

Crowning a hill in the Halkah district, the palace was fortified, its massive crenelated walls built to withstand an attack from any direction, yet its interior was far more luxurious than any castle Margaret or her Navarrese companions had ever seen.

There were walls covered with ornate mosaics depicting the peacocks and palm trees of the Genoard. The designs themselves were simple yet sophisticated, combining traditional Byzantine workmanship with Islamic symmetry, so one encountered such elements as twin leopards rendered in profile, facing each other. The usual background of the mosaic designs was a field of gold tiles. One wall of a room used as a kind of throne chamber and office by Margaret's father-in-law was covered in these tiny golden tiles of uniform lustre.[69]

The capitals of the stone columns were carved into ornate Fatimid motifs inspired by local creatures and plants. Here a Sicilian lizard creeping across an acanthus leaf could wind his tail into a knot.

The walls of some rooms, including the sleeping quarters, were covered by tapestries of velvet in colors ranging from the deepest crimson to a light pastel green. Silk drapes concealed some of the windows. Oil lamps were suspended from the ceilings by endless chains.

Margaret was accustomed to tables made of wood. In Palermo's palace the top of every table was a polychrome plain of pieces of inlayed marble formed into unidentifiable yet pleasing motifs. These too were Arab. The floors bore some of the same geometrical designs, only larger.

She had never seen Baghdad, but the Muslims at court told Margaret that its palaces and mosques were similar to Palermo's.

The palace had two chapels. The older one, constructed during the previous century, served as the crypt of a newer one built by Margaret's father-in-law, King Roger.

The newer chapel, where Margaret and William were wed, had a wooden muqarnas ceiling replete with painted designs and figures of such things as people playing chess. Spreading his arms across the apse was an imposing icon of Christ Pantocrator rendered in mosaic, similar to another at Cefalù's cathedral up the coast. Here the Byzantine and Fatimid traditions met.[70]

Margaret was not the only bride living in the palace. Around the same time William married Margaret, King Roger, following fourteen years as a widower, wed his second wife, Sibylla of Burgundy, who was about ten years older than Margaret. Roger and Sibylla lived in another tower, but they were rarely in Palermo, so Margaret and William never had a chance to get to know Sibylla very well.

Sibylla had given birth to a son who died in infancy. Before long, she was said to be pregnant with another child.

When Roger travelled, he sometimes took Sibylla with him, usually leaving William in charge in Palermo. Although William seemed to enjoy conjugal life, or at least accept it, he also enjoyed hawking in the Genoard and the hills beyond, leading the life of a wayward knight.

In youth, as the youngest of the king's legitimate sons to reach adolescence, William never had to entertain serious thoughts of ever sitting on the throne and assuming the awesome responsibility kingship entailed. By the time his last full brother died in May 1148, William was long accustomed to the unencumbered lifestyle of a royal prince unlikely ever to be called upon to rule. The *Regnum* was full of pretty girls willing to fulfill his prurient desires. Marriage does not seem to have diminished William's zeal in these hedonistic pursuits.

Some courtiers and barons thought William less intelligent than his brothers. It is quite possible that Roger himself was not entirely convinced of his youngest son's capacity to rule.[71] But William had better produce some heirs.

In late September 1150, news arrived at court that Sibylla had died while giving birth in Salerno. She was buried at the

Benedictine monastery of Cava nearby. King Roger had lost a wife and child in a single moment.

Margaret's father died two months later. Her brother, Sancho, was now king, but not yet married.

Except for such sad news as the death of García Ramírez, Margaret usually enjoyed receiving letters from her sister.

Blanca's Catalonian marriage did not materialize. In January 1151 she wed Sancho, the son and heir apparent of Alfonso VII of Castile, at Calahorra near Logroño in La Rioja's fertile Ebro Valley, not far from La Guardia, her birthplace. In order to ensure the succession, Sancho of Castile had already been crowned, and by 1149 he was styled "King of Nájera." Neither Calahorra or Nájera could compare to Palermo, but they were not without their charm.

Although Blanca got married after her younger sister, she was already a queen. Margaret's turn would come soon. Indeed, 1151 was to prove an eventful year.

Queen Margaret

William was now thirty years old[72] and Roger had not sired any other surviving sons, at least not by his wives.[73] Whatever reservations he may have entertained about William's abilities, he had already declared him to be his successor. With Sibylla's death there was, for the moment, no Queen of Sicily.

Margaret filled those shoes when William was crowned on Easter, which fell on the fifteenth of April in 1151. Her sister, Blanca, had beaten her by only three months.

Attended by numerous barons, this coronation followed the practice of a king crowning his son as *rex filius* to avoid the possibility of later contestations. Though favored by the Normans, it was not an exclusively Norman custom. As we have seen, Alfonso VII of Castile did something similar when he crowned his son, Sancho, who wed Margaret's sister. An heir who became *rex filius* wore a crown but did not sit on a throne.

It is likely that Margaret was crowned with William, but the fact is not mentioned explicitly in the surviving accounts of the event, which are not highly detailed.

Margaret's monopoly on Sicilian queenhood was not to last. Her father-in-law had not resigned himself to living without a wife, and in the same year that he personally crowned William, Roger wed Beatrice, daughter of Gunther of Rethel, a powerful German count.

This left the Kingdom of Sicily with a queen consort, Beatrice, who was two or three years older than Margaret, and Margaret herself, a kind of "queen designate" as the crowned consort of the heir apparent.[74]

But questions of court precedence were the least important matters confronting Margaret in 1151. By the end of the year she was pregnant with her first child.

The healthy boy born in 1152 was christened Roger.

Producing an heir enhanced Margaret's prestige at court and throughout the *Regnum*. The birth confirmed her fertility, and a male child, naturally, was seen as the better result. Sicily needed future kings more than it needed royal princesses. William and his father had good reason to be happy.

In the eyes of her father-in-law and her subjects, who were granted two days of celebration to mark the prince's's birth, Margaret, at seventeen, had proven her worth. With luck, she would bear more sons. Queen Beatrice, on the other hand, had better get busy.

Did the birth of a grandson encourage King Roger to view William in a better light? Perhaps not. At the very least, though, the child filled a void in the succession.

The kingdom found itself in a rare period of peace. In 1147 and 1148, using the Second Crusade as a pretext, Roger had sent his admiral, George of Antioch, on a campaign to take control of some Greek lands; although most of these territories were soon lost, the invasion brought an influx of wealth to Sicily. During the same years, Roger obtained a part of the African coast that included Tripoli and the area around Cape Bon; unlike the Greek territory, when Margaret arrived this was still under the control of the Kingdom of Sicily, which had emerged as the chief maritime power of the Mediterranean. Palermo, whose population numbered at least a hundred thousand, was the jewel in the crown.[75]

The Sicilian court boasted some great minds. Maio of Bari, who succeeded the Englishman Robert of Selby, was an efficient chancellor, effectively the kingdom's "prime minister." English-born Thomas le Brun managed the royal treasury using Hindu-Arabic numerals. Abdullah al Idrisi was busy mapping Sicily and other territories and constructing a planisphere of a round Earth. It is clear that Roger was able and willing to delegate a great deal of the realm's daily administration to trusted officials.[76]

Although William assisted his father in the running of the *Regnum,* we have only vague impressions of what his precise responsibilities were. Despite his saturnine temperament, he was not remiss in his conjugal duties, and in 1153 Margaret gave birth to a second son, who was named Robert.

Did Margaret and William have any daughters? We know of none, but it is a distinct possibility.

In truth, we don't even know the names of all the daughters of Roger II.[77] That is hardly surprising since chroniclers usually noted the existence of a royal daughter only when she was betrothed to an important king or prince. Likewise, the birth of a child of either sex who died in infancy was rarely recorded. There were only two chroniclers present in Sicily who were close enough to the court to even learn of such events, and neither Hugh Falcandus nor Romuald of Salerno mention a daughter of Margaret and William.[78]

Margaret may have wished for a daughter or two, but her

husband desired sons. So did her father-in-law.

On the twenty-seventh of February 1154 King Roger II died in Palermo of natural causes at the age of fifty-eight.[79] He was survived by his pregnant wife, Beatrice of Rethel.

William automatically became regnant King of Sicily and Margaret became the realm's unequivocal queen consort.

This royal succession, as it happened, was painless and uncomplicated, but it belied great challenges. Compared to what was to come, the last few years had been a honeymoon.

The chronicle of Peter of Eboli shows Elvira, Sibylla, Beatrice and Constance wearing the same type of Byzantine crown

Chapter 7
QUEEN CONSORT

"I work hard in social work, public relations, and raising the Grimaldi heirs."

— Princess Grace of Monaco

Roger had wished to be buried at the cathedral in Cefalù, a splendid church that he founded. Instead, his porphyry sarcophagus was placed in Palermo's cathedral. His successor's decision was challenged but never changed.[80]

Roger had proven himself a remarkable ruler. Not without reason, Sicily's first king is cited by historians as a paragon of intellect, one of the greatest rulers of Europe's High Middle Ages. He united southern Italy into a cohesive state while forming Sicily's diversity of peoples into something resembling a single nation. The Kingdom of Sicily would survive, in one form or another, until the nineteenth century.

First, however, it had to survive William's reign.

The Reign of William I

William I was crowned, or re-crowned, and anointed in

Palermo on Easter, which fell on the eleventh of April, in the presence of hundreds of barons and ecclesiastics. The same public ceremony saw Margaret crowned and anointed with her husband.

Could William be a good king?

It was true enough that Roger had defined the *Regnum* on his own terms. That was necessary considering its multicultural roots. The Greek, Arab and Norman populations each had their own concepts of kingship. A mosaic in Palermo's Martorana Church depicts him garbed in Byzantine robes, receiving the crown from Christ Himself. Although its implications have been debated for centuries, this image seems to reflect the notion that, at its root, the authority of the King of Sicily derived directly from God, and not necessarily through the auspices of the Pope.

The first King of Sicily had to bring his people together while defending his territory. It would be prudent for William to continue the policies of his father.

But even in death Roger himself cast a very long shadow. He was an intellectual, a humanist whose court cultivated intellect, even brilliance. What is more, he was able to inspire the people he led. Any heir, however competent, would encounter great difficulty in succeeding so great a figure. Those at court understood this.[81]

So did Margaret. She would have to be much more than William's wife. Necessity made her his advisor. But whether he would accept her advice was another matter altogether.

In early November Beatrice, Roger's widow and now "queen dowager," gave birth to a daughter christened Constance.[82] The birth of a boy would have bolstered Beatrice's importance and perhaps even attenuated Margaret's prominence as the mother of the reigning king's heir.

By now, William had more urgent duties to address than celebrating the birth of a half-sister. Encouraged by the new

Pope, Adrian IV, the recently-crowned Holy Roman Emperor, Frederick I "Barbarossa" was planning an invasion of the Kingdom of Sicily.[83] Manuel Comnenus of Constantinople, whose Byzantine Empire had been invaded by King Roger, was willing to cooperate in this effort, perhaps by attacking Apulia (Puglia) by sea while Barbarossa attacked the northern part of the *Regnum* by land. A major war was very possible, and for William it would be a defensive conflict.

Yet he seemed prepared for it. With the baronage united in Palermo at his coronation, William had appointed Maio of Bari his privileged *amiratus,* the "emir of emirs," naming a new chancellor.[84] He also used the occasion to grant Loritello to Robert of Bassonville, a cousin who had been divested of other feudal lands by King Roger.[85] Maio was reasonably loyal, at least for now; Robert was to prove much less so.

At the head of an army of some five hundred knights, Robert of Loritello[86] exploited the prospect of Barbarossa's planned invasion to lead a rebellious faction of the baronage against William.

The Italians have an old saying rooted in the Middle Ages: *Parenti serpenti!* "Relatives are snakes." Robert was a good example of this. He seems to have wanted the throne for himself.[87]

The fighting began with William's unsuccessful siege of Benevento, an enclave of the Pope within the territory of the *Regnum*. This was led by Asclettin, who was a trusted general as well as chancellor, while William himself returned to Palermo in April 1155 to his family.

This included a third son, William's namesake.[88]

King William now made his firstborn son, Roger, the Duke of Apulia, a title reserved to the heir apparent.

Meanwhile, unable to take Benevento but hoping to intimidate Pope Adrian, Asclettin attacked a number of towns on the southern fringe of the Papal State. This gave Pope Adrian a pretext for excommunicating King William. Margaret was happy that her husband, excommunicated or not, was back in Palermo to spend time with her and the children.

By June, when Barbarossa was crowned Holy Roman Emperor, his German knights and barons were beginning to make it clear to their leader that they had no intention of participating in his plan to march southward into the Kingdom of Sicily in the middle of the summer. This did not entirely discourage Robert of Loritello, William's disloyal kinsman, who soon began receiving troops and gold from Manuel of Constantinople. Robert began to use Apulia as a base from which to launch occasional attacks northward and westward into other regions of the peninsular part of the *Regnum*.

William wanted to respond to these attacks but he fell ill late in 1155. Margaret and the court physicians cared for him. What struck William was probably a very debilitating, viral pneumonia. His absence from public life led many to think he had died.

By spring of the following year, he was strong enough to ride to the Sicilian town of Butera to quash a revolt there. Then he headed for Messina, where a large army and navy were waiting for him.

Asclettin was chastised for his poor tactics against the rebels. William had never been very enthusiastic about this former cleric, who he now ordered jailed.

With the imposing force assembled in Sicily, William himself would go to Apulia to excise the cancer infecting his kingdom.

The royal army, with its knights and archers, made its way across Calabria to Taranto, along the way gaining strength through the support of loyal barons and eliminating token resistance. The navy reached the port city of Brindisi, whose coastal fortress had been resisting a long siege by the rebels.

The warrior king had returned.

Victory came easily. The traitors were punished, some put to death. Bari, which had fallen to Byzantine control with the collusion of its citizens, many of whom were Greek, was largely destroyed, although its major churches were left unscathed.

William then led his army westward to Salerno and other cities in the Campania region around Naples. Robert of Loritello was not beheaded but exiled; he found refuge at the court of Frederick Barbarossa, whose aborted invasion of the *Regnum* he had supported.

Clearly, anybody who ever thought William incompetent or weak had underestimated him.

Margaret was not one of the doubters. Yet she understood that her husband was inclined to delegate authority whenever he could. This was shown by his appointment of Maio as a kind of "super minister" and his reliance on Asclettin to fight battles that he, as king, should have prosecuted himself. It was good to have competent ministers, but relying on them completely was ill-advised.

Peace Restored

Lacking support in view of humiliating military defeats, zealous Pope Adrian was chased out of Rome by an angry populace. He took refuge at Benevento, which William besieged. In June 1156, with this Papal city on the verge of starvation, Adrian negotiated a truce. Here William was represented by Maio of Bari, and Adrian by Roland of Siena, a learned cardinal fated to become Pope Alexander III. Archbishop Hugh of Palermo was also present, accompanied by Romuald of Salerno. The young scribe who composed the text of the Treaty of Benevento[89] was Matthew of Aiello, a notary destined to play a greater role at court.

The Sicilian monarch remunerated to the Pope a tribute

pledged by his late father, and the Papacy finally, unequivocally recognized William as King of Sicily. The apostolic legateship, the right of the sovereign to approve the appointment of bishops, was confirmed on the island of Sicily.

William's excommunication was lifted. In Sicily, Palermo was erected to a metropolitan see, with other bishops on the island suffragan to it. Archbishop Hugh became the Primate of Sicily.[90] That is to say, he was the most senior prelate of the entire Kingdom of Sicily, outranking the bishops of Salerno, Bari, Capua, Syracuse and Messina.

Frederick Barbarossa regarded the treaty as an affront because it effectively nullified his own, prior alliance with Pope Adrian, but for now the Holy Roman Emperor was not in a position to invade the *Regnum* as he had hoped. William's ministers also concluded a treaty with Genoa, one of the kingdom's most important trade partners.

Barbarossa was soon facing his own rebellion by the vassals and cities of northern Italy.[91] William, on the other hand, found himself at peace with the Papacy and most of the northern Italian communes.

Margaret's inner peace was shattered late in 1156 when news arrived that her sister, Blanca, had died in August while giving birth to a second child, who died with her. Naturally, Margaret had longed to see her beloved sister again someday, if only one last time, even if she knew that a journey back to Spain was unlikely. Sicily was where she belonged, and she had better make the best of it.

Blanca was buried at Santa María la Real in Nájera. Her sarcophagus, regarded as a supreme twelfth-century European expression of emotions in sculpture, depicts a mourning female figure. It has been suggested that the woman represented is Blanca's sister-in-law, Sancha, but it may be her sister. If the weeping figure is not Margaret, it could just as easily have been. The following year, Sancha also became Margaret's sister-in-law, and Queen of Navarre, when she wed her brother, Sancho "the Wise."

In 1158, Margaret gave birth to a fourth son, Henry. The same year, the King of Sicily named his secondborn son, Robert, Prince of Capua, a title reserved to the prince who was second in line to the throne. Roger, the eldest son of William and Margaret, was already Duke of Apulia.

William had every reason to be content. His family was growing, and following some raids in what is now Greece a treaty was negotiated with the Byzantine Empire.

For Margaret, tranquility was a luxury. With four young children to raise, advising her husband on matters of government was not her only job. But during the long absences of William and Maio, the Palermitans looked to their queen for leadership.

This was Margaret's last taste of serene motherhood — if raising four young boys was ever very "serene."

By the end of 1159, it seemed clear that William was about to lose his last outposts in northern Africa. That was an economic misfortune.

Whether for lack of inspiration in Sicily or for greater opportunities abroad, the court's greatest minds had left; Thomas le Brun went to England, where he ended up as the almoner for King Henry II. Idrisi left for his native land.[92]

It would happen that most of the challenges confronting Margaret and William over the next few years were to come from domestic quarters.

The Barons

Court intrigues were no novelty, either in Italy or anyplace else. But in Sicily they bore the mark of peculiar conditions. The Bariots and other Greeks in Apulia might rebel if instigated by forces in the Byzantine Empire. The Arabs in northern Africa may have decided against Norman rule. It was disquieting whenever any group in the kingdom's multicultural mosaic thought itself mistreated.

But the real problem came from the baronage, itself a privileged, even overprivileged, feudal class woven from ever-fraying threads into a coarse piece of fabric that could rarely decide whether it was linen or silk. The rebellion led by Robert of Loritello had shown that even a richly-enfeoffed royal cousin could not be trusted to uphold his oath of fealty. The barons' faux obeisance to the king fooled nobody.

Unlike their brethren in England, the first Norman barons of Italy were, for the most part, mercenaries born into Normandy's minor families. Generations after their arrival in Italy, some families still harbored resentment that the Hautevilles, once ordinary knights errant like themselves, had become kings.

In 1159, Margaret welcomed at court her young cousin, Gilbert. She saw to it that he was invested with the wealthy county of Gravina near Bari. Gilbert's father, Bertrand, was an illegitimate son of Margaret's generous great-uncle, Rotrou of Perche. At first, Gilbert seemed to be trustworthy, aloof of local politics, but before long the words of the native barons began to cloud his judgment.

Sicily's barons were an untamed lot. Even as they acquired manors and serfs, there were those among their number who rarely seemed content with the great wealth the conquest of southern Italy had brought them and their families. Now, a century after the Battle of Messina, they were little more than a noisy pack of hungry hounds, and there is evidence to suggest that they were envious of the island's mercantile classes, especially the Muslims of Palermo.

Here the flower of chivalry bore the malicious spore of bigotry, if not racism.

Most barons were wealthier than most merchants. The difference was that while a baron's wealth, based on agriculture, was difficult to conceal, a trader could hide his coins in a purse buried in a shallow hole beneath the floor of his house.

The Hautevilles had given a great number of manors, or fiefs, to the knights who accompanied them to Sicily in 1061. During the last years of his reign, King Roger sought, with the help of the treasurers of the royal diwan, to make the heirs of these barons accountable for their feudal duties. Usually this meant military service, and a large barony might be expected to provide several knights. Training and outfitting a knight was costly, but scutage, the payment of money in lieu of military service, was still unknown in southern Italy.

Although a baron or enfeoffed knight could elevate an esquire to knighthood, he could not do so merely at whim. Apart from the many years of martial training required, the postulant had to meet certain conditions set forth in the statute *De Nova Militia,* "Dubbing Knights," of the Assizes of Ariano. Most notably, the young man had to be born into a family of knightly status. Only an act of royal grace could supersede this prerequisite.

In the Kingdom of Sicily the record of the barons, not only their names and manors but their feudal obligations, was compiled in a roll analogous to England's *Domesday Book,* the *Catalogus Baronum.*[93]

Here such terms as *baronage* and *baronial* refer to the landed nobility generically, but there existed a feudal hierarchy in the Kingdom of Sicily by 1160. In Margaret's time, there was little distinction between princedoms (like Taranto) and dukedoms (Apulia), each of which might consist of several large counties (Mandra). A county comprised a number of baronies; within a barony there were usually a few manors (fiefs). Naturally, the actual size and wealth of such territories varied greatly.

The manorial system was held together through vassalage. The knight enfeoffed with a manor swore fealty to the baron from whom he held it. The baron, in turn, swore fealty to the count, and so forth. Ultimately, every vassal of the *Regnum Siciliae* owed fealty and homage to the king, who held some lands directly (see note 184).

Despite feudal bonds, baronial revolts were disturbingly frequent. Sometimes they arose when a renegade in a place like Loritello or Butera incited some of his neighboring barons to challenge royal authority. It was never too hard to concoct an unfounded justification as a pretext for open conflict. The instigators knew that loyalty was the foundation of the barons' relationship to the crown. They also knew that loyalty could often be purchased.

Some grievances with the crown were motivated by little more than personal grudges, and the resulting violence spelled the difference between life and death.

Margaret was too busy raising her children and thinking about the greater challenges facing her husband's realm to worry about the barons' vexing quibbles, be they real or imaginary.

Chapter 8
TRAGEDY

"Grief is not too different from illness. In its flames it does not recognize lords nor fear its own peers. It does not respect or fear anybody, not even itself."

— Eleanor of Aquitaine

In the last days of 1159 Margaret's son Robert, the Prince of Capua, died during one of those illnesses that claims the lives of young children. The boy was entombed in the Church of Mary Magdalene attached to the cathedral, within sight of the palace.[94] Grief-stricken by the death of a son who was not yet seven years old, Margaret was unaware of the plotting of a growing number of dissentients beyond the Strait of Messina.

The unruly barons could hardly be trusted under the best of circumstances. By 1160, their cauldron of discontent was boiling over. Here their scapegoat was not the king but his chief minister.

If not overtly arrogant, Maio of Bari was certainly confident in his own abilities. He exercised great control not only in the daily function of government but over policy, and despite successes like the Treaty of Benevento he was blamed for obvious failures like the recent loss of Mahdia, Sicily's last African stronghold, to the Almohads.[95]

Perhaps it was Maio's privileged position at court that rankled some of the barons.[96] Much of the venom directed at him grew out of envy. Not surprisingly, exiled Robert of Loritello was a leading detractor.

Nevertheless, it seems that at least a few baronial grievances were justified. If even a fraction of what nasty Hugh Falcandus wrote about him is true, Maio was avaricious, lecherous, publicly disdainful of William, and guilty of torturing and blinding some of the rebels taken prisoner in Apulia following the revolts a few years earlier. Romuald of Salerno is kinder, or at least less strident.

There seems to have been a nugget or two of truth to some of the allegations against Maio, yet William trusted him. So did Margaret.

Of course, an attack on Maio was an *ipso facto* attack on William, and even on Margaret. The barons knew this.

They also knew that King Roger had died leaving the coffers of the treasury full. Land was nice but gold was better. There was enough gold and silver in Sicily's treasury to buy a small country or two, perhaps even three or four. Or to equip a navy to invade Africa and take back Mahdia.

For one of the barons the grievance with Maio of Bari was to become violently personal.

Matthew Bonello

Matthew Bonello held lands around Caccamo and Prizzi, as well as some estates in Calabria. Overlooking a fertile valley to the east of Palermo, Caccamo was dominated by a large castle built during Arab rule and expanded by the Normans. Bonello, who was not yet forty, was engaged to marry the young daughter of Maio of Bari.

Bonello's future father-in-law trusted him enough to send him to mainland Italy to assuage the doubts of some barons who were sufficiently disgruntled with Maio to have sent missives to the king requesting the minister's removal. Here Bonello began to wander astray, first by courting a beautiful heiress[97] and then by heeding the words of Roger of Martorano, one of Maio's most vocal detractors.[98] Among the malcontents was Gilbert of Gravina, Margaret's cousin.[99]

All kinds of things were being said. The campaign against Maio was a dirty one. It was even alleged that he had tried to kill Archbishop Hugh of Palermo by poisoning, and that Matthew of Aiello, Maio's protégé, had attempted to bribe the newly-elected Pontiff, Alexander III, into deposing King William.[100]

Margaret herself was not immune to vicious rumours. According to Falcandus: "Voices flew around Sicily, one sometimes contradicting the other, saying that Maio had shown some of his confederates several crowns and other regalia, insinuating that the queen herself had sent him these objects from the palace. It was believed, in fact, that everything took place with her consent, linked as she was to Maio by bonds of undignified familiarity. However, many people thought these rumours false."[101]

The power of innuendo to shape public opinion cannot be underestimated, and this inexpungible passage is the source of a persistent perception about Margaret's moral character that has survived eight centuries, painting her as unfaithful.[102] Yet there is no evidence to implicate her in Maio's actions, and Falcandus himself tells us that the rumour's veracity was sometimes questioned. Indeed, the allegation about the crowns being purloined from the royal treasury was later debunked.[103]

Why would a bereaving queen, who at twenty-five years of age had just lost a child and still had three others to raise, cultivate "undignified familiarity" with Maio of Bari?[104]

Maio was warned that a conspiracy was afoot and that Bonello might be involved. However, he found himself reassured by the denial of his future son-in-law, who went so far as to request that the wedding be celebrated even sooner than had originally been planned. This led him to set aside any lingering doubts.

The baronial conspirators planned the assassination fastidiously. As they saw it, the killer had to be somebody who could get close to Maio without arousing suspicion. Bonello was the ideal candidate.

Saint Martin's Day, the feast on the eleventh of November that marked the end of autumn, was approaching.[105] The days were getting ever shorter, the nights ever cooler. It was as good a time as any to commit a murder. But Bonello would not act alone.

Street Crime

The day before Martinmas fell on a Thursday. Around dusk, not long after the sun had descended behind the mountains surrounding the city, Maio of Bari and a small entourage paid a visit to Archbishop Hugh[106] at Palermo's archiepiscopal palace, which was located near the cathedral. In the group was Matthew of Aiello.

After some time, the group left the archbishop's residence. By now it was completely dark and a bit chilly. For some, it would get colder still.

Maio and his cortege had made their way to Old Saint Agatha's Gate, where there was an imposing wall, beyond which the ground sloped toward the bed of the Papyrus River, whose waters had been diverted through a subterranean *kanat*.

Here the ambush took place. Bonello sprang upon Maio, slaying him with a sword. At the same time, his squad of knights attacked Maio's companions. One of them, Matthew of Aiello, was wounded but managed to escape with the others.

Matthew Bonello and his company of rogues immediately fled the city, riding at full gallop to the castle at Caccamo in the dead of night. Back in Palermo, a crowd of exultant citizens dragged Maio's corpse along the streets. The vigil of Martinmas had just become more festive than usual.

So great was the tumult that it could be heard from the palace. The festivities seemed to be getting out of hand, and William demanded to know what was happening. It wasn't long before he was informed. The king immediately sent guards into the labyrinth of streets and squares to prevent a general insurrection. He had the presence of mind to dispatch some men to protect Maio's home to ensure that the dead man's family was not harmed.

If William was angry, Margaret was livid, expressing her rage in no uncertain terms. Her worst wrath was directed at Bonello and his accomplices, who by now were well on their way up the coast.[107]

Margaret's reaction was crystal clear. Beyond his initial response, however, William felt a twinge of uncertainty, perhaps for the first time in his life. From the comfort of his window in a high tower of the palace, he could see the jubilant behavior of the Palermitans.

The scene was disturbing. William's subjects seemed happy to be rid of Maio. The people who had lit bonfires for the vigil of Martinmas were now dancing around the flames to celebrate the death of a tyrant. This suggested to the king that the man he so long defended was indeed despised by many.

How should William act? Matthew Bonello, though a fugitive, had popular support. In the present climate, arresting the defiant baron would be an operation fraught with peril. Where there was one rebellious vassal there were usually others as well.

Margaret entertained no such doubts. She wanted the perpetrators punished. What, she wondered, was keeping her husband from ordering their immediate arrest?

Court Intrigues

The true extent of Maio's guilt will never be known. At first, William was reluctant to accept the tales of corruption he heard about the dead man. This changed with the discovery of royal crowns in a chest found in Maio's possession; did Maio's delusions of grandeur lead him to think he could wear them himself?

In truth, the crowns were not royal property but gifts Maio was planning to give the sovereign.[108]

As inquiries were made, it became clear that some of the accusations made against Maio had been based on exaggerations while others were rooted in reality. Damning revelations came from those in his family who worked as his assistants; his son and brother confessed to Maio's explicit acts of wrongdoing, such as the payment of bribes to ecclesiastics with money pilfered from the royal treasury. A Calabrian bishop[109] confirmed this by reimbursing money received from Maio.

Matthew Bonello was granted clemency for the murder on the pretext of Maio having deceived the king. With this, the baron returned to Palermo, where he was received at the palace by William and acclaimed by the people. If unpersuaded by Bonello's feigned sincerity, the king did not have to be convinced of his influence among both the baronage and the populace.

Margaret entertained suspicions about Bonello. As if her own doubts were not enough, the palace eunuchs warned her of his amoral ambition.[110]

Some eunuchs were servants, scribes and cooks, and a few were advisors. One of their chief duties at the palace was guarding and managing the harem.

Matthew Bonello was dangerous, and his audacity increased with each passing day.

Unbeknownst to the king, the late Maio had permitted his

intended son-in-law to defer payment of a debt due the crown of sixty thousand gold tarì, an extremely large sum.[111] Advised of this, the king now demanded remittance of these monies from Bonello and his guarantors.

As the months passed, Bonello found himself invited to court rather infrequently. This implicit admonition he blamed on Adenolf, the chamberlain, who had been a friend of Maio.[112] With the recent death of his ally Archbishop Hugh, Bonello's own friends at the royal court were ever fewer.[113] The arrogant baron correctly inferred that the king, supported by Margaret, was trying to marginalize him.

Not willing to accept his diminished position, Bonello began to conspire with other barons. There were always a few malcontents about, but this time he didn't have to look beyond the putrid fruit of the Hauteville family tree, where covetous serpents concealed themselves among the leaves.

It was easy to enlist the support of one man who had a particularly large axe to grind with the King of Sicily. He was Simon, William's half-brother. This illegitimate son of King Roger harbored a grudge against William for divesting him of Taranto some years earlier.

Another conspirator was Tancred, Count of Lecce, a wealthy city in Apulia.[114] Young Tancred was the king's nephew, being the illegitimate son of William's elder brother, Roger, who died in 1148.

Being born outside marriage may have made Simon and Tancred dynastically illegitimate, but in the eyes of many their role in the conspiracy legitimized the plot against King William I, for here were two of the king's nearest blood relatives acting against him.

For good measure, Gilbert, Margaret's cousin, joined the plot.

Whatever one could say of Bonello, he was not lacking in ambition. Now his target was not an emir of emirs but the man on the throne. In early March Bonello convened a secret meeting at his castle in Caccamo to finalize his plans.[115]

What followed was an object lesson in how to execute the overthrow of a medieval monarch in his own household.[116]

Because the royal palace was heavily guarded, it was necessary to enlist the cooperation of two key figures if the plot were to have any hope of success. The palace castellan, the chief saboteur recruited, controlled the entrances. The guards' captain commanded some three hundred men and oversaw the jail. Enticed by coin, both were convinced to betray their king, leaving no more obstacles to the plan being set in motion.

Every step of the plan was worked out in detail, calling upon the knowledge and expertise of each player. For example, Simon, who had spent his childhood in the palace, was familiar with its corridors and chambers, as well as the maze of passages known only to those who lived there. This meant that he could help the others find the king. The possibility that the rebels' plan may have already been revealed to William forced Simon and Tancred to act prematurely, without waiting for Bonello to arrive from eastern Sicily.

Since the murder of Maio of Bari, Margaret saw that her husband was unmotivated to do much except meet with his ministers. He rarely found time for her or the children. Indeed, he was growing apathetic, if not despondent.

Margaret had a growing sense of foreboding.

Palace Coup

Thursday, the ninth of March, probably seemed like any other day in late winter. There was still a trace of snow on the rugged summits of the mountains visible from the towers of the palace, but wild asparagus was sprouting in the countryside, where the almonds were blossoming in shades of pink and white. Easter was around the corner, less than a month away, and William spent an early hour of daylight at liturgy in the chapel, where he was joined by Margaret and the children.[117]

The conspirators took advantage of this time to enter the palace and free all of its prisoners. By the time the royal family left the chapel, the rebels were already on their way to the Pisan Tower, the king's inner sanctum. Margaret and the children went to the royal apartments to begin the day's lessons, while William headed toward his chamber accompanied by Henry Aristippo, the archdeacon of Catania, who had replaced Maio of Bari. An intellectual, Henry was one of the few advisors the king still trusted.[118]

Nearing the chamber he used as an office, William was walking down a narrow corridor with Henry when the pair saw half a dozen men striding toward them, brusquely and unannounced. It was unusual to see soldiers carrying swords and daggers in this part of the palace. The king did not yet know what had transpired whilst he was at holy mass. Who were these men?

Either William's eyes deceived him, or it was Tancred of Lecce and Simon of Taranto. The king's first reaction was instinctive anger that these two undesirable kinsmen had been granted entry into the palace. What were they even doing in Palermo? This dastardly duo couldn't have overpowered the palace guards by themselves.

But William quickly realized that his immediate problem was far worse than the arrival of uninvited guests within the castle walls. With the two princes were irate nobles who, until a few minutes earlier, had been imprisoned in the palace dungeon. The mere fact of this confrontation meant that William's predicament was dire indeed.

Unarmed, and unaccompanied by a military escort, William glanced down the corridor behind him, thinking he might find a guard or two at the other end of the hall. If he acted quickly enough he might even slip into a secret passage to his tiny armory, where he kept swords and daggers. Outnumbered, he and Henry considered running but thought better of it.[119] They were seized by the intruders. After haranguing the king, the rebels suggested his abdication.

But now the group turned from regnal politics to unbridled thievery. Leaving the king under guard in one of the tower's rooms, the men, led by Simon, made their way into those chambers where money, regalia, rings, precious gemstones and silver vases were kept. Joined by the castellan and other traitors, they looted the premises. Some stole royal robes. Others hurled handfuls of glittering gold tarì coins out the windows to a boisterous crowd that was gathering below, seeking in this way to buy the Palermitans' loyalty.[120]

Some preferred the pleasures of the concubines in the harem to material wealth.[121] Each rebel plundered according to his own taste. Here was the epitome of rape and pillage.

Henry Aristippo, though an ordained deacon, worshipped at the same altar of debauchery as the others. He abducted a few girls for himself and kept them at his house, where he set up his own little harem.

Margaret and a few servants were in a room with the children. It wasn't long before some rebels arrived to ensure that they didn't leave.[122]

Confined to a chamber on the fourth floor of the Pisan Tower, William was left alone to think about a course of action. The rebel cabal posted a guard outside the door but the room had a window from which the king could shout down onto the square for help. If anybody heard, nobody responded.[123]

Meanwhile, the knights of Bonello's beastly cohort gave chase to the eunuchs, most of whom had fled the palace at the first sign of danger.[124] As part of their plan, the revolt's ringleaders had already found sympathizers beyond the palace district to join the riot, and a number of knights, swords in hand, left the seaside castle to murder some escaped eunuchs they found in the streets.[125]

The violence didn't end with the eunuchs and concubines. A great number of Muslim shopkeepers, along with those collecting taxes in the building that housed the diwan, or those walking along the streets, were killed by the same knights who had massacred the eunuchs.

When many of these Muslims, who Maio of Bari had disarmed the previous year, realized the extent of the knights' assault, they made for the part of the Sari al Kadi district outside the city wall, beyond the Papyrus River. They were pursued by the Christians, but the fighting reached a stalemate because the aggressors had trouble attacking the defenders in the narrow alleys. In this way, the knights were repelled and the butchery minimized.[126]

Not content with the mayhem they had wrought, the leaders of the revolt incited the citizens to build a bonfire into which they tossed a great number of records. Not surprisingly, this included the tax rolls listing the barons' feudal obligations.

The queen and her ladies-in-waiting could see the smoke and chaos from a palace window, even if they couldn't make out every skirmish taking place in the streets below. It was one thing to observe an isolated riot, but here was the better part of one of Europe's largest cities in utter turmoil. Margaret was frightened, and she kept her sons away from the window. She didn't want the boys to witness this ugly scene. Where was her husband? Was he safe? Terrible thoughts ran through the queen's mind, but for now she had to think about protecting her children.

Violent as the revolt was, regicide was not precisely what Simon and Tancred had in mind. What they wanted most was a friendly monarch they and Bonello could control. A puppet king.

Early in the afternoon, the two princes entered the chamber where Margaret and her three sons were sequestered. The rebels demanded that her eldest son, Roger, Duke of Apulia, who was then nine years old, don some regal robes and then go with them to the stables. Seeing that she had no choice, Margaret complied with this request.

In late afternoon, the two renegade princes set young Roger upon a pony and led the boy around the streets of Palermo, presenting him as the new king to the cheering crowds.[127] Walter, Roger's tutor, addressed the people, holding forth on how King William was a tyrant that now had to be replaced.[128] Young Roger was proclaimed king.[129]

That night, the rebels secured the palace, allowing nobody to enter. The next day, Friday, they repeated Thursday's spectacle, again parading Roger around the city. This failed to placate everybody, and there were isolated skirmishes between Muslims and Christians which led to a number of Arabs being killed, their shops looted.

By Saturday, Matthew Bonello still had not arrived at Palermo. There were those in the populace who began to question recent events, wondering why the crowned King of Sicily, whatever anybody thought of him, was still being held prisoner, and why the rebels' killing and pillaging should be justified. And anyway, who had appointed Simon and Tancred to act as kingmakers?

Increasingly worried about the atmosphere in Palermo, Tancred rode with several other rebels to Mistretta, in the Nebrodian Mountains, to confer with Bonello. Simon, meanwhile, was beginning to entertain serious thoughts of having himself crowned.

Goaded by several clerics, a large group of local men took up arms and stormed the palace, threatening to besiege it with ladders and towers unless the rebels freed King William.[130] Simon and the other conspirators held out initially but finally complied. They went to William, who promised to grant them safe conduct if he were freed. Once released, the king spoke to the populace from a tower window.

When the crowd demanded that the rebels be executed, William announced to his subjects that their loyalty to him was more than sufficient to satisfy any need for justice or reprisal. With entente thus achieved, Simon and his henchmen rode off to Bonello's castle at Caccamo.

Margaret was relieved that the crisis was over. But in the commotion a stray arrow hit young Roger, who was standing near a window, mortally wounding him. He was dead within hours.[131]

Condolences were expressed by many who had once despised the king, but Margaret was inconsolable. Her sorrow was limitless. Her tears flowed like the rains of March. She had lost her second child.[132]

Site where Maio of Bari was murdered in 1160

Chapter 9
ESTRANGEMENT

"I do not want a husband who honours me as a queen if he does not love me as a woman."

— Elizabeth I of England

It was almost impossible for things to return to normal, whatever normal was. Following a period of mourning, William met with local leaders to reassure them.

Bonello had not given up his ambition to unseat the king. Having assembled a rebel force, he marched toward Palermo from Caccamo, but he retreated as some of the king's galleys arrived from Messina with reinforcements.

The defiant baron was coaxed to the palace, where he was arrested. Some Palermitans protested this, but Bonello died in a dungeon within the palace walls late in 1161. Sporadic revolts around Sicily were suppressed.

If the king could not tolerate open rebellion, he could make a sincere effort to mend his tattered ties with the barons by addressing their grievances. One of his measures in this direction was the restoration of the right of feudal inheritance to the sons of vassals killed in royal service.[133]

Eliminating Opponents

William exiled Tancred and Simon, who went to the eastern Mediterranean, where they could go on pilgrimage in the Holy Land or render service as mercenaries in Constantinople. Gilbert of Gravina, the queen's cousin, was pardoned at Margaret's urging even though he had participated in the hellish folly that cost her the life of her son. William ordered him back to Apulia to respond to some raids by Robert of Loritello.[134]

This accounted for some of the extended family, but where was Beatrice with Constance, the young daughter of King Roger? Mother and child were out of harm's way, living undisturbed at San Marco d'Alunzio, the Hautevilles' familial castle (of which little remains standing) set upon a rocky summit near a convent in the Nebrodian Mountains. Constance, a pretty princess with blondish red locks, was now seven years old. Margaret came to envy Beatrice's uncomplicated existence beyond the world of court intrigues. Unlike Margaret's sons, Constance, being a girl, was not likely to be manipulated by plotters seeking to crown their own puppet king.

In the aftermath of recent events, William was left with very few people he could trust. He pardoned the notary Matthew of Aiello, who set about compiling a feudal tax roll to replace the *Catalogus Baronum* destroyed by the rebels. The king was suspicious of the intellectual deacon Henry Aristippo, who had raided the harem, although he chose not to punish him.

He could trust Margaret. With the loyalty of the realm's highest officers left in a nebula of doubt, William more frequently turned to his wife for counsel, even reassurance.

But not for love. The emotional distance between the queen and king was wider than ever.

The physical distance between the two grew after a sullen Christmas when the king swept through eastern Sicily and onto the mainland with a large army to quell some isolated disturbances that could not be left to the limited military resources of Gilbert of Gravina. William left Margaret in Palermo as his effective surrogate until he returned in the summer of 1162.

She was assisted by an Arab eunuch named Martin, a convert to Catholicism who undertook retaliations against people thought to be the king's adversaries. Caïd Martin was especially hostile to Christians.[135] Henry Aristippo, the lecherous deacon, was apprehended, deprived of his mini-harem, and cast into a dark dungeon to die.

We do not know how influential Margaret was in these bloody reprisals. Did she instigate them? Had she, like her sister queens confronted by adversity, become a she-wolf? Having seen a son killed in connection with the revolt of the previous year, she was embittered. Whilst the king was away, she and Martin did what her husband was unwilling, or at least less willing, to do. If Margaret did not personally order the reprisals, she certainly knew of them. Perhaps she relished them. Here was the dark side of her personality. Dark but perhaps understandable.

Ruling the Kingdom

When he returned to Palermo, William fell into his old habits. He still preferred passing his time in the Genoard to the pleasure of Margaret's company. A new coterie of concubines was lured, or coerced, to serve in the harem. The Christian king seemed to enjoy the life of a baptized sultan.[136]

But the status of Palermo's Muslim Arab population had

suffered in the recent riots. For the first time since the Normans took the city in 1071, its Muslims had been attacked in large numbers by Christian knights. This doubtless prompted many to consider abandoning Islam.

Religious freedom, women's rights, prostitution, slavery, forced castration. All were important issues. Of course, in the twelfth century none of these things were viewed from the same perspectives as the sensibilities that color our times. Even if it were argued that the presence of eunuchs and harems reflected what were essentially Muslim practices inherited from the emirs who once ruled Sicily, William was unwilling to alter this aspect of the society over which he reigned.

By the end of 1162, the king was again ceding day-to-day administration to others. Martin was joined by Richard Palmer and Matthew of Aiello.

An event the next year reminded Margaret of the dangers still lurking around every corner, even within the palace walls.

Following the revolt led by Simon, Tancred and Bonello, the king had transferred important prisoners to a jail outside the palace.[137] However, a few were still in the palace dungeon enclosed by thick Phoenician walls.[138] It was only a matter of time before these men were moved to another jail, such as the round tower of Palermo's seaside castle.

Lacking any hope for being released, several prisoners convinced the guards to free them. With this accomplished, they made for a gate leading out of the palace. Their escape was foiled by the castellan, who quickly went through the gate, closing it from the outside and trapping the fugitives within the palace's curtain wall.

Next they entered the base of one of the towers, thinking they might find the king on one of the upper floors. Instead, they ended up in the room where young William and his brother, Henry, usually met for their lessons. Fortunately, the boys' tutor, Walter, had whisked the two to the safety of the bell tower as soon as he heard the commotion. Margaret was in a chamber upstairs and unaware of what was happening.

Martin managed to lock the escapees in a large room, where they were all killed. The knaves' lifeless bodies were literally thrown to the dogs, and the corpses were forbidden a burial.[139]

Margaret was annoyed that she and her family were placed at such risk in their own home. Perhaps at her urging, William ensured that henceforth no prisoners were ever to be jailed in the palace, even temporarily.

Overlooking the Kala harbor and protected by a moat, the sea castle was far more secure than the palace dungeon. Its master, sadistic Robert of Calatabiano, had made the fortress infamous for torturing the prisoners kept there.

His fief was on the other side of Sicily, near Catania, but Robert used his position to accrue wealth through corrupt means everyplace on the island. With the collusion of Caïd Martin, several avaricious justiciars[140] would bring fraudulent charges against men whose estates they desired. The accused would be released only upon paying substantial bribes, or ceding a manor or two. This extortion seems to have touched many innocent Sicilians, but William was probably unaware of it.

Apart from these chronic abuses, the *Regnum* was peaceful. Indeed, the king had told his three chief counsellors to avoid disturbing him unless it was absolutely necessary.[141]

For her part, Margaret was occupied with raising her two sons. By now, she gave little thought to her husband's habits and whims. Martin and his ilk, like Maio of Bari years earlier, concealed their corruption.

Building Bridges

Whilst an effort was undertaken to build bridges with the Muslims, the construction of churches and palaces continued in earnest. By 1164, new monasteries and castles were springing up around Sicily in an unprecedented number.[142]

In the capital a few noteworthy edifices besides the royal palace and its chapel were already standing. (Here it may be best to focus on those which have survived until the present day.)

The "admiral's bridge" over the Oreto was built on the orders of George of Antioch, who also built the Martorana Church. San Cataldo was erected under the auspices of Maio of Bari. The original Saint Mary Magdalene, built by Elvira of Castile, was already standing; it is where Margaret's sons were buried.

Beyond the Genoard, in the vast hunting grounds in the mountains, a chapel dedicated to Saint Michael the Archangel was erected at what is now the town of Altofonte; next to it was a royal hunting lodge. This meant that William could spend a few days at a time hunting in the woodlands without having to return to Palermo to attend mass.

In the former slave district was a church dedicated to Saint Peter. This was destroyed during the bombings of the Second World War, but a stone bearing the Greek inscription marking its foundation by Robert "Guiscard" of Hauteville and his wife, Sichelgaita, in 1081 is preserved in a museum in Palermo. One wonders whether the congregants of Saint Peter's ever heard an occasional scream from a prisoner being tortured by Robert of Calatabiano in the sea castle nearby.

To the east, beyond the Oreto, was Saint John of the Lepers, erected during the same period as Saint Peter's.

That should not be confused with Saint John of the Hermits, a Benedictine monastery near the royal palace. This stood on the site of a mosque which had been a church before the ninth century.

At least two of the emir's palaces were still standing. Located in the Genoard, the Scibene[143] was expanded following

William's reign. The Favara, in what is now the Brancaccio district, was a favorite place for William, Margaret and the children to pass the torrid days of summer. Both had tiny lakes fed by springs.

Old Saint Agatha's Gate, where Maio of Bari was killed, no longer exists. It took its name from the nearby church, still standing though greatly altered over time.

Several segments of Palermo's Punic walls remain intact; these were known to Margaret. Part of the wall protecting the Khalesa district when the Normans arrived can be seen along Vicolo della Salvezza (off Via Alloro), and a gate from that era is preserved within the Oratory of the Bianchi nearby, at the corner of Via dello Spasimo. A segment of the city's Norman wall erected before 1164 can be seen running from Saint John of the Hermits along a line parallel to Corso Tukory down to Via Maqueda. Here one finds New Saint Agatha's Gate.

A few parts of the cathedral remain from William's reign, but most of what we see today was constructed later. Down the street, a curious structure is the "Notary's Hall" in what is now Via Protonotaro. This dates from the Norman era, if not earlier. Overlooking its ground floor are Fatimid loopholes.

In Messina, the Church of the Annunciation dates from the middle of the twelfth century. In Syracuse, the cathedral had stood for many centuries, built around an ancient Greek temple whose columns form part of the church's walls; here is a textbook example of the transition from mythology to early Christianity.

Transition was the last thing on Margaret's mind. However distant her husband seemed, her greatest concern was preserving the *status quo* for her two sons, William and Henry.

Roger and Robert, the two who had died, were never far out of her mind, and she often went to pray at the Magdalene church where they were entombed.

Their deaths reminded her, as if any medieval queen need be reminded, of how tenuous was life, easily claimed by a sudden illness or a stray arrow. Blanca, her sister, had died giving birth to a son who died with her, leaving behind another son who at that time was less than a year old.[144]

The House of Hauteville was like a castle built of sand. A single wave of discontent could carry it away. If that happened, the monarchy would endure, but under the crown and aegis of another family. By now, the dynasty into which Margaret had married had ruled Sicily for a century, and as kings for just thirty-four years. Margaret herself was not quite thirty.

Legacy of William I

In 1165, the king ordered his architects to draw up plans for a new palace to be erected in the Genoard. The Zisa[145] took its name from the Arabic *aziz*, "splendid" or "beautiful," a word that survives in the Sicilian language as *azzizare*, "to make attractive." It was William's wish that this palace set amidst lakes and greenery might surpass the splendour of those of his father.[146]

But William's father had built more than palaces. Roger founded a kingdom; William was little more than its caretaker.

The greater part of the Zisa was built in a short time. Margaret was not involved in this project. Her concerns were more domestic, even prosaic. She was beginning to think about her place in the world she knew. It was impossible to avoid thinking of the family into which she was born. At the age of ten, Margaret's nephew, Blanca's son Alfonso, was already the King of Castile.[147]

The chief duty of a queen was to produce a future king, even if she died doing it. Any other responsibility was secondary. Ruling kingdoms was the job of kings, not queens. Most of the time.

The year 1166 began well enough, but in March the king was struck by a terrible bout of dysentery. This illness seemed to have passed when a relapse made William suspect that his end was near. Seeking to settle his affairs to avoid contestations should he die, he formally decreed his elder son as his heir. He took the step of appointing Richard Palmer and Matthew of Aiello as *familiares,* trusted counsellors, to assist in governing the *Regnum*.[148] The *familiares* would become a leitmotif in the government of the Sicilian kingdom.

Significantly, the moribund monarch named Margaret "keeper of the entire realm." Regent.[149]

King William I of Sicily expired in May at the age of forty-six.[150] He was buried in the palace chapel.[151]

At the age of twelve, Margaret's son was now King William II of Sicily. He was crowned by Romuald of Salerno in Palermo's cathedral.[152]

Viva lu re! Long live the king!

The girl born in Navarre had endured adversity after adversity to become, in her thirty-first year, Queen Regent of one of Europe's most important kingdoms. She was now the most powerful woman in Europe and the Mediterranean.[153]

Viva la regina!

Margaret's life until this point had been little more than a haphazard apprenticeship for what lay ahead of her.

In nomine sci individue & trinitatis patris & filij & sps sci. Ego Sichelgaita ducissa volens obsequi meis diebus uiuens districti iudicij iudices rerum dicentes. fides n' absque operibus opera quæ possidere n' potest nisi esse discipulæ & diligenti uniuersi illud. qd' uni ex meis fecistis & michi fecistis. memor cuiusdem illius. quicumque sua voluntate pars mea qm odis e mee sui fr. soror. & uxor e. Jnme uita noftri ducis. & quoruncium spiritui parentum remedio & p' me meorumque negotij felices dies. necnon uestri iam gaudentis cum corpore cum animaru salute. uestique eius & pi negocij fidele conuite faluere concesso. & firmo. & firmus inconcussu dono ecclesiæ beate dei genitricis marie que panormi e. & loci illius uenerabili archiepo domno petro huiusque partem de riddanusi itudemque panormæ communitante.

Pot decessu uero mi. cum eodem beate trinitatis ur ipsa & marito meo & me. & filiis meis & contra uestra ficti meretrice futurum chrn xpm. xpm. concedo omnes fui dictos. deosque robustis & irrevocato mea possestoides. Doc confirmationis donu sue fecti. anno ab incarnatione diu nri xpi. xpi. millesimo octogesimo nono Indictione duodecima que regnante sedis splica urbani sedi regnante regem uolui ducis fitio. apud calabriæ & siciliæ duce. hanc elemosinam quia psentiste mea & sup scriptos falue. leue marce & canonicas feruentibus accerboru siquis diabolicæ ductus mundia auferre temptauerit. aut fraudulenti aliquo raptoris euommicati. & a die ihu confectio siquidem patri cui dampnat & alicuiusmodi quod unum eius absoluent. & ei nisi potuerit quod suspendat eripere necus. & in sitti inferiori carnis supplicia patiat. nisi confessante ab emendationis accerent mercaturumque auferre mihit seboq uincit; Gunsto filio meus ceff. (Guaferius maximonis espo ceff. Vgo de aueta ceff. Iustino hargone ceff. Goffrido de unuttanutta ceff. Pandulfus de ruudio. ceff;

Courtesy Archdiocese of Palermo

Margaret inherited the prerogative of protection and taxation of Palermo's Jews established in 1089 by Sichelgaita of Salerno, widow of Robert Guiscard Hauteville

152

Chapter 10
QUEEN REGENT

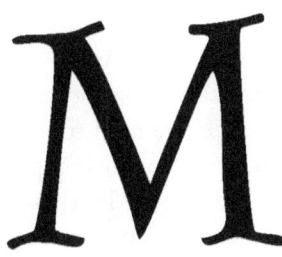

"A woman is like a tea bag. You never know how strong she is until she gets in hot water."

— Eleanor Roosevelt

In the spring of 1166, the path before Margaret was obscured by a fog of incertitude. She did not know exactly what to do, but she had very definite ideas about what *not* to do, and she wished to avoid what she and others regarded as the mistakes of her late husband.[154]

Benevolent Rule

William was as prepared for the transition to kingship as a boy of his age could be. Was Margaret ready for regency?

Every scrap of information known to us suggests that she was. When her husband was absent from the capital, Margaret, the progenitrix of the next monarch, was the political point of reference for a city wealthier and more influential than most European kingdoms. During one of these absences, she probably colluded with Caïd Martin to eliminate some of the king's opponents. For the final years of her husband's reign, she had a say in certain aspects of royal government.[155] It is abundantly clear that William I, particularly during his last few years on the throne, did not care very much for "hands-on" administration of the *Regnum*. His complacency was disturbing.

Margaret spent very little time mourning the death of her husband, if she was even inclined to shed more than a few tears for him. Instead, she immediately plunged into the business of running the kingdom. In this she really had little choice, for the appearance of a power vacuum would be even worse than the effect of poor decisions. It was usually better to act than not to.

Her initial actions, though not unheard of in the annals of European medieval history, were unusual enough to make people stand up and notice her. Margaret's intent, of course, was that the subjects should ascribe these sage decisions to their sovereign, William II.

There was no model, no guide to follow except perhaps some of the policies of her father-in-law, the fondly-remembered Roger II. The royal sisterhood, such as it was, found itself with a dearth of sisters. In England, headstrong Eleanor of Aquitaine, wife of Henry II, was influential but wielded little power of her own; in Normandy the decisions of Eleanor's mother-in-law, Maude, reflected the policies of Henry II. Margaret had very little contact with such female contemporaries during her regency, certainly none that would permit her to garner any advice from them.[156] In the event, the social fabric of the Kingdom of Sicily was far more complex than what one encountered in these other regions.

Some of her husband's unfinished undertakings had to be completed. For the most part, that meant wrapping up construction of the Zisa and similar projects.

Building a solid foundation for her son's power was a far

greater challenge, and there was no time to lose. Margaret needed a base of support and she needed it now. In an absolute monarchy the sagacious use of power was absolutely necessary.

If there was a framework for Margaret's authority, it was millennial tradition and the kingdom's Assizes of Ariano.

Using Power

The queen could not afford to be indifferent. Reasoning that bloody revolts were the progeny of dissent, she sought to eliminate their root cause. She beguiled the restless baronage by redressing their unvoiced grievances. Her stratagems were simple.

The first decrees Margaret issued in the name of her son were intended to still troubled waters and to encourage loyalty toward the new monarch. These took several forms, all quite pragmatic.[157]

The justiciars seem to have applied the law arbitrarily, meting out justice as they saw fit but ever influenced by the king's mentality. This sometimes resulted in overzealous prosecution and excessively harsh sentences even for minor transgressions. A disturbing degree of corruption permeated officialdom.

To reconcile such matters, Margaret released a great number of prisoners from the kingdom's jails, including those on islands such as Lipari. Mostly men, some were barons to whom she restored lands that had been confiscated by William I, albeit usually with good cause when this was a punishment for treason. She forgave the debts of most of the prisoners she released.

Through a further act of clemency, the queen repealed the exile imposed on a number of barons who had openly rebelled. They were permitted to return to the *Regnum* and claim their former lands, which in most cases had been confiscated.

She began to grant property to nobles but especially to the

monastic orders. As we shall see, her granting of lands to monasteries increased over time.

Margaret abolished certain taxes that had been levied in recent years, particularly the "redemption fees" which had become a burden in Apulia and in the area around Salerno and Naples.[158] She made it clear that such taxes were not to be collected in the future.

The queen was not seeking the subjects' unctuous obedience; their compliance with the law and a smidgen of loyalty to the crown would be sufficient.

Her sobriety of thought distinguished her. Presented in a velvet glove, Margaret's policy concealed an iron fist.

Familiarity

She appointed the eunuch Caïd Peter, the head of the royal diwan, as her chief *familiare,* telling Richard Palmer and Matthew of Aiello that henceforth they had to answer to him. Neither Richard nor Matthew accepted this blissfully, but for now there was nothing they could do about it.

In appointing her own team, Margaret was choosing her own approach to government. But the ubiquitous court intrigues did not cease just because the queen was asserting her authority.

It didn't take long for some bishops to begin trying to convince Peter that Richard Palmer was planning to kill him. Yet Peter was reluctant to act against Richard despite the insistence of the bishops that he do something.

Obviously, the intended target of this episcopal scheming was Richard Palmer.

With him removed, Gentile Tuscus of Agrigento or one of the other bishops could take his place. Gentile, in particular, was unabashedly ambitious; he had always behaved as a sycophant around William I but grew disillusioned when Richard, who was closer to the king, thwarted his proposals for various projects. According to Falcandus, one of the plotters was Romuald of Salerno. Matthew of Aiello, who also began to believe that Richard should perhaps be removed from power but still respected him as a colleague and peer, preferred to use his own methods to achieve the task.

According to Falcandus, one of the pretexts for the antipathy towards Richard Palmer was his Anglo-Norman origin. Gentile and his unsavory ilk probably inferred that as an "outsider" Richard would never be easily manipulated. As the last Englishman at court, he was the only obvious obstacle to them taking control.

Caïd Peter, they thought, could be dominated more easily. An Arab convert to Catholicism, he had once served as a naval commander.

Margaret herself did not cultivate a great liking for Richard Palmer, but she refused to dismiss him.

There was a reason for her resentment. When her husband was alive, the queen had sought support from Richard for some of her proposals, only to receive from the pompous cleric cynical and condescending missives.[159] His arrogant comportment led Margaret to believe that he hated her, and she was probably right. But for now she preferred marginalizing Richard to removing him altogether.[160]

Meanwhile, Gilbert of Gravina, Margaret's cousin, having been advised of young William's accession to the throne, and Margaret's regency, made his way to Palermo. Couriers arrived at Palermo with this news when Gilbert was still at Messina, a few days away.

Gilbert was already the acting governor of the mainland part of the *Regnum*. Now he sought to displace Caïd Peter, the chief *familiare*. He may have thought his cousin weak, yet her word alone had saved his hide from serious punishment for conspiring with Bonello a few years earlier. Arrogant Gilbert came to believe that he had been rewarded for his own merits; in reality, his "success" was little more than the product of nepotism. Quite simply, he was the queen's cousin. If King William I exiled his own kinsmen, Simon and Tancred, he certainly would have had Gilbert exiled or killed.

The arrival of Gilbert imposed a temporary delay on the plans of the bishops to remove Richard Palmer from power.

The company of knights traveling with Gilbert was not sufficient to attack Palermo, but it made an impression on Gentile of Agrigento and the other plotters. Richard Palmer also took note, and warned Gilbert about the conspirators. The queen's cousin reassured Richard of his support.

Caïd Peter's faction, being loyal to Margaret, was not closely allied to any of the others. These men publicly commended Gilbert for having raced to Palermo to support his kinswoman. In private, however, they sought to convince the queen of her cousin's ambition to rule the kingdom. Their caveats were unnecessary, as Margaret already knew enough about Gilbert's character, or lack of it, to ascertain his objectives.

One day, Gilbert spoke to her in private audience, though in the presence of Caïd Peter. Here Gilbert defended Richard Palmer, spoke against the court eunuchs, and suggested that changes be made at court.

Margaret affirmed her faith in the people at court and her general agreement with the organization her late husband had put in place. She offered her cousin a place as *familiare* under Peter. This enraged Gilbert, who found it offensive to be offered a position beneath that of a palace eunuch. He launched into a diatribe, ranting that Margaret's prestige in Apulia was abysmal, and before long his utterances degenerated into a series of vicious personal insults against his cousin.

Tears of disillusion gathered in the eyes of the woman who had done so much to help a wayward kinsman of low birth. But the queen stood her ground throughout the tirade.[161]

Having thoroughly berated his cousin, Gilbert stormed out of the palace but he did not leave Palermo. He began to contemplate ways of eliminating the chief *familiare*.

Peter surmised that Gilbert's knights could be divided into two groups.

The enfeoffed knights were landed barons of the peninsular part of the *Regnum* who served Gilbert and the crown as part of their military obligation. Looking toward their own interests, these barons preferred to see Gilbert appointed chief *familiare* in Peter's stead.

Most of the mercenary knights, on the other hand, were indifferent about such matters. Led by a salaried constable, Richard of Mandra, they need only be paid for their service; it was not a feudal obligation on their part. Before long, they would return home, which for many of them was someplace beyond the Alps.

At Caïd Peter's suggestion, the queen enfeoffed Richard of Mandra with the County of Molise, which included wealthy baronies like Boiano and Venafro.[162]

Not only did Margaret know how to sew together a patchwork of supporters, she knew how to sow the seeds of dissent among those who chose to oppose her. Woe betide her antagonists.

The formal investiture of Richard with his prosperous county was an ostentatious event, and the first public occasion of its kind over which Queen Margaret presided. Here the entire nobility could see the use of royal power.

Gilbert and his followers were rankled by the elevation of Richard of Mandra, now Count Richard of Molise. There was nothing they could do to stop a feudal investiture, which was a royal prerogative, but they now conspired in earnest to kill Peter.

Thinking his position untenable and his life endangered, Caïd Peter departed Palermo under cover of night, taking a chest of gold tarì with him. He sailed to Africa, where he renounced Christianity, to which he had converted in youth, to embrace Islam anew under his original name, *Ahmed*.

It was rumoured that Peter had taken some crowns and other regalia with him. The queen refuted this nonsense but to clear the air she summoned the barons, bishops and court officers present in northwestern Sicily to an audience at the palace.

It wasn't long before the meeting degenerated into a heated exchange, with Gilbert of Gravina insulting Peter and Richard of Molise defending him. In defense of Peter's honour, Richard challenged to trial by combat any baron present who persisted in defaming the absent *familiare*.

The argument descended to the level of personal insults, with Richard calling Gilbert a coward unworthy to lead royal troops.

These fighting words were precisely the kind of opening Gilbert was waiting for, and the two men squared off, swords drawn. Fortunately, some knights intervened to separate them before anybody was hurt.

Margaret ordered the two counts to desist, and they retracted the stream of invective they had unleashed upon each other. But their mutual acrimony remained, and Gilbert began a covert campaign to sully Richard's reputation.

Realpolitik

Now, only a few months into her regency, Margaret found herself confronted by a stark choice. Either she could somehow marginalize her cousin or she could have him arrested and possibly killed.

Gilbert's altercation with Richard of Molise had shown just how difficult it would be to subdue him. The queen wished to do so without her actions appearing to be motivated by hatred for her cousin. How could she accomplish such a feat?

The *familiare* Matthew of Aiello was responsible for reading correspondence that arrived at court from around the *Regnum*. Seizing on rumours that Frederick Barbarossa was again planning an invasion of southern Italy, Matthew had such a letter forged stating that the threat was imminent.[163] He read this message to an assembly of barons.

This gave Margaret a credible pretext for sending Gilbert back to Apulia.[164] She flattered her cousin by telling him he was the best man to raise an army and defend that part of the kingdom. To reinforce his authority in the region, she made him governor of Apulia and Campania. Gilbert suspected there may be trickery behind his appointment to this mission, but open insubordination would make him an enemy of the court. Besides, he had already come to understand that, realistically, there was little more he could do to facilitate his ambitions in Palermo. Mollified, he departed for Apulia with his son, Bertrand.

Gilbert's audacious pretensions to influence at court were yet another confirmation that royal authority was likely to be challenged, especially when it was vested in a woman, and that the instigators would make use of any means at their disposal to tip the balance of power in their favour.

Although the actions of Gilbert and the bishops were not aimed solely at the Arabs, be they Muslim or Christian, the tenor of the insults directed against Peter reflected a subtle religious bigotry.

In place of Caïd Peter, Margaret promoted Richard of Molise to *familiare*. Unlike his predecessor, Richard was a decisive man who commanded his own little army. This struck fear into his opponents.

With Gilbert gone, the bishops resumed their efforts to subvert the position of Richard Palmer. This movement was led by Cardinal John of Naples, the Pope's envoy.[165]

It was not with unbridled enthusiasm that Margaret countenanced the obnoxious, condescending Richard Palmer as a *familiare* at court. Apprised of this, John suggested to the queen a plan not unlike the strategy that was so effective in prompting Gilbert's recent *exeunt*.

Richard Palmer was bishop-elect of Syracuse. During Margaret's regency this episcopal see was vacant and therefore depended directly from the Holy See.[166] It will be remembered that episcopal appointments in Sicily had to be confirmed by the monarch as the Pope's apostolic legate, but here there was no hindrance as Margaret wholeheartedly supported Richard's consecration.

If he were summoned to Rome to be consecrated, Richard would consequently have to assume his duties in Syracuse, his designated diocese, on the other side of Sicily. Naturally, this meant he could spend less time at court in Palermo. Margaret liked this idea as much as she disliked Richard.[167]

The plan was set in motion, and before long[168] John was at the palace standing before Margaret, young King William, the *familiares*, several bishops and sundry barons reading the Papal command to all of Sicily's bishops-elect to present themselves in Rome for consecration so as to regularize their positions. As a separate announcement, John added his own condition that the bishops-elect must comply with the Papal directive within a certain date.

Richard Palmer craftily agreed to the Papal order to be consecrated while refusing to accept any separate, additional conditions imposed by John of Naples. The aspiring prelate thus rejected the deadline. This abnegation was debated at length but resulted in an impasse.

Whilst Richard Palmer's obvious reason for the delay was to avoid abandoning the seat of power at court, he may have harbored an ulterior motive as well. Syracuse enjoyed great prestige as the oldest diocese of the *Regnum*, and arguably the oldest in western Europe, but Richard aspired to more. If he could swap his appointment to Syracuse for Palermo, he would emerge as the most powerful person in the kingdom after the regent herself.

Margaret would have to devise another way to distance Richard Palmer from her inner circle. Word had reached the court that he was beginning to speak against her openly in public. That was something she could not tolerate, for a lack of respect of the regent's decisions might weaken the subjects' loyalty to their queen.

Cardinal John of Naples did not give up trying to get Richard to Rome, and the latter knew he could not forestall consecration forever. So Richard Palmer appealed to another Richard, namely his fellow *familiare* Richard of Molise, who enjoyed the queen's confidence, to aid his cause.

There was no way to force a change in policy, but the Pope's envoy might be tricked into providing Molise a platform from which to defend Palmer. This tactic was to prove effective. At a subsequent audience at court, John of Naples responded negatively to requests that he delay the consecration deadline, prompting Richard of Molise to reproach him for threatening to enforce an order that would absent an important counsellor from royal service.

The cardinal responded that Richard Palmer would be free to return to Palermo following his consecration by Pope Alexander. But now John's resolve offended the queen's sense of authority.

Annoyed that a Papal prelate presumed to challenge her prerogative by ordering a *familiare* away from Palermo, Margaret stood up and declared that, "The presence of the archbishop-elect is needed at court, so for now he cannot leave. He can depart in another moment when circumstances permit."[169]

What persuaded the queen to change her mind? Perhaps Margaret was made privy to the tactic of Richard of Molise before the gathering took place, and had reason to think she should make a point of her own by reminding those present that she was in charge. Her decision had the additional benefit of placing Richard Palmer in her debt, in the eyes of others if not his own. Henceforth his public criticism of her would ring hollow. Whatever motivated Margaret, people would remember her willingness to take a decision long after they had forgotten its rationale or even what the decision was about.

The extemporaneous pronouncement had the desired effect of imparting to her subjects the notion that the queen was to be respected.

Divorce Court

Because the monarch was the judge of final appeal, all kinds of cases came before Margaret. Some were rooted in personal dilemmas.

Not long after the incident involving Richard Palmer, a man named Richard of Sai arrived at court accompanied by his wife, who he wished to divorce in order to marry Theodora, a girl who happened to be the niece of Alfano, archbishop of the important diocese of Capua, north of Naples.

Descended from a Norman family, Richard of Sai was captain and master constable of Apulia. His deeds over the last decade had shown him to be steadfastly loyal, even more faithful than Margaret's cousin Gilbert who held authority in the same region. Richard's wife was a noblewoman, sister of Bartholomew of Parisio.

Margaret's first decision was to reward Richard by enfeoffing him with Fondi, a county that had belonged to a deceitful vassal who was now exiled.[170] That was the simpler task, but it showed the queen's willingness to enforce her authority even in unpleasant matters.

A divorce could be just as bitter, and embittering, as the attainder of a disloyal baron. The crown permitted divorce, but because the couple seeking legal separation was Christian, rather than Muslim or Jewish, their case had to be referred to the ecclesiastical authorities.[171] The queen instructed the *familiares* to ask the prelates to convene a hearing so that both husband and wife could present their cases. Indeed, the cardinals present at court were accustomed to adjudicating divorces.[172]

Beyond purely legal questions, these matters bore with them all kinds of wickedness. Despite her uncle being a high prelate, Theodora was regarded as a sexual libertine, whether she actually was or not. The mere fact of a woman taking up with a married man was sufficient "justification" for her to be branded a whore.

For her part, Margaret did not hold an opinion of this case strong enough to dissuade her from giving a prosperous town to a loyal subject like Richard of Sai. In a stance redolent of modern sentiments, she was more concerned about Richard's professional life than his adultery.

Like many divorces, this one engendered certain complexities, and perhaps a touch of dishonesty. As the ecclesiastical council would not be satisfied with a vague lament such as adultery to justify dissolving a marriage, Richard of Sai had to come up with a convincing legal argument.

His chief witnesses were two knights who claimed to have seen Richard, some time before his marriage, conducting a romantic affair with a pretty cousin of the woman he eventually married. This would seem to violate the law regarding affinity, a legal form of kinship acquired through marriage "in law," which defined such relationships as a brother-in-law or sister-in-law.[173]

Witnesses for Richard's wife accused the two knights of perjury, claiming they could demonstrate that the two men had lied. Some of these witnesses, being cousins of Richard's estranged wife, felt their kinswoman had been maliciously slandered by her husband's very allegations. But their chief legal argument was that the statute regarding affinity simply did not apply to this case because Richard of Sai had never actually been married to his wife's cousin, with whom he claimed to have had sexual relations.

In this last affirmation they were correct. In strictest terms, the prohibition of affinity should only be applied if a man were actually married to a woman and later sought to wed her sister or cousin.

Cardinal John of Naples wanted to bring the case to a rapid conclusion. At the same time, he hoped to curry favour with Richard of Sai. He made the witnesses swear an oath on their words, he granted the divorce and, as was normal in such settlements, he made the ex-spouses vow not to engage in sexual relations with each other henceforth.

Not every prelate was happy with the decision rendered by John of Naples, for it did not conform to canon law. Ubaldo of Ostia, one of the men who negotiated the Treaty of Benevento a decade earlier, felt that his fellow cardinal had been compromised ethically through bribery. Other prelates also criticized John. When they asked him if they could apply a similar sentence in like cases, he arrogantly responded that his decision did not establish a legal precedent, and that anyway it was his personal perquisite to do what they could not.

Nobody ever accused John of Naples of lacking an ego. In any case, Richard of Sai was now free to wed Theodora.

Marriage Proposal

Divorces were not the only conjugal questions arising at court. When Manuel Comnenus, the Byzantine Emperor, learned about the death of the Sicilian monarch, he reasoned that the regent would be easier to deal with than the late king. Perhaps an actual alliance could be arranged.

Along with his condolences, he sent ambassadors from Constantinople bearing his proposal that young William II marry his daughter, Maria, who, as Manuel's only child, stood to inherit an empire that included part of Asia Minor and the Balkans.

After consulting with her son, the court prelates and the *familiares*, Margaret decided to delay responding to this seductive offer whilst confirming the peace treaty her husband had negotiated with Manuel some years earlier.

Although she did not refuse the betrothal proposal altogether, Margaret needed time to consider its complex stipulations. Having wed at so young an age herself, she saw no reason for her son to marry too soon.[174]

This would not be the only decision the queen was obliged to make regarding members of her immediate family and their marriages.

Arrival of Rodrigo, Margaret's Brother

Having heard that Margaret was regent, her half-brother, Rodrigo (who we met earlier), arrived at Palermo with a large contingent of Navarrese knights. She probably summoned him for additional protection at court, but his knights errant were little more than opportunists. Margaret encouraged Rodrigo to change his name to *Henry*, which the Sicilians found more acceptable and pronounceable.[175]

Falcandus describes him as rather fat and ugly, of dark complexion, prone to gambling and lacking in eloquence; boorish, even vulgar.

Margaret had not seen Rodrigo/Henry since he was a child. She did not know him, or his personality, very well, but she may have been warned about his habits.

As her experience with Gilbert had proven, kinsmen could be troublesome, especially male kin. These men were best kept at a distance, and Margaret knew a good place for her wayward brother.

The queen enfeoffed her younger brother with the prosperous County of Montescaglioso, near Taranto, and several towns in Sicily, namely Noto, Sclafani and Caltanissetta. She also provided him with enough coin to support himself in a dignified manner during his initial travels.

First he spent some time in Palermo, entranced by its souks and atmosphere. Never had he or his knights seen such a magnificent metropolis.

Then, having squandered most of the money his sister gave him, Henry of Montescaglioso (as he shall now be called) made his way to his new county on the mainland, stopping first to inspect his Sicilian manors.

Along the way to Montescaglioso, he had to pass through Messina. This port city, a springboard for European merchants, pilgrims, knights and pirates on their way to and from the eastern Mediterranean, was infamous for its vice and debauchery, attracting charlatans, beggars and prostitutes. To an inveterate gambler like Henry, the attractions of this place, a kind of medieval "Las Vegas on the Ionian," were irresistible.[176] If Palermo was a city of arrant luxury, Messina was an urban jungle of shameless sin.

News of Henry's impromptu sojourn got back to Margaret, who ordered him, as his sovereign and his older sister, to cross the Strait of Messina and make his way to Montescaglioso. It was summer and he had best reach his estates in time for the harvests.

Almost as an afterthought, Margaret arranged for her brother to marry Adelaide, one of the daughters of King Roger.

Arrival of Stephen of Perche, Margaret's Cousin

The government was served well enough by the *familiares* Richard Palmer, Matthew of Aiello and Richard of Molise, with the treasury overseen by Caïd Martin and the palace by its chamberlain Caïd Richard. Of course, these were not the only important courtiers; archdeacon Walter, the tutor of Margaret's sons, was considered important enough to witness royal charters.[177]

But personal ambitions threatened to create fissures in this façade. Matthew wanted to become grand chancellor of the realm, while Richard Palmer envisaged himself as Archbishop of Palermo. Richard of Molise was the most trusted of the *familiares*, and the one most likely to receive the political favours he requested.

Beyond the complexities engendered in the personalities of these men, Margaret saw potential problems in the existing organization of the *Regnum*. No longer a neophyte, she decided, as a matter of policy, to appoint councils of ecclesiastics to manage diocesan lands where there were no serving bishops, thus removing this power from the authority of bailiffs, who were easily corrupted.

The queen felt that she needed intelligent, trustworthy counsellors at her court. She knew that some of her kinsmen were more reliable than Gilbert and Henry, but there were too few of them she had ever had occasion to meet.

At this point she sent a letter to her cousin, Rotrou, who had recently been made Archbishop of Rouen.[178] There was a precedent in presuming to ask such a favour of him. Some years earlier, as Bishop of Evreux, Rotrou had sent Walter to Palermo to serve as the tutor of Margaret's sons. This was the same Walter who sheltered the children in the bell tower when some prisoners escaped the palace dungeon, the same Walter who served as a deacon of Cefalù. It was Walter who she sent to Rouen bearing her letter to Rotrou.

Margaret requested that her cousin might send to Palermo either Stephen of Perche or Robert of Neubourg, intellectuals known for their integrity.

It so happened that Stephen was already in Italy, where he was visiting Gilbert of Gravina, the son of his brother. Stephen and his company intended to go to the Holy Land, but made their way to Palermo when summoned.

In September, Stephen of Perche arrived in Palermo accompanied by the theologian Peter of Blois and thirty-six knights, esquires and friars. Here he was greeted by the Sicilian *familiares,* barons, knights and bishops, who escorted him to the palace to meet his cousin.

Margaret greeted him warmly, receiving him in audience in the crowded presence of her courtiers. Here, invoking memories of her childhood and the kinsman who gave the town of Tudela to her parents, she made a portentous pronouncement that she wanted heard by the entire court:

"Here I see myself finally achieving what I have ardently desired. To the sons of the Count of Perche I owe the same honour one accords a brother. The work of their father, in truth, gave my own father his kingdom. It was the Count of Perche who granted to my mother as his niece, and thereby to my father, a dowry of vast lands conquered in the face of great dangers and prolonged effort from the Muslims of Spain. You need not be surprised that I regard his son, Stephen, my mother's kinsman, as if he were my brother, welcoming him with joy the moment he arrives here from faraway lands. I desire and command that all who declare good wishes to me and my son will sincerely respect and honour Stephen. From your kind treatment of him, I will infer the depth of your fealty and affection toward us."[179]

These were royal words, regally spoken in Norman French, which Falcandus tells us was *quae maxime necessaria esset in curia,* "necessary for those at court to know."

What Margaret needed as much as fealty and good wishes

was a loyal advisor and confidant who answered directly to her. At this point, she was not contemplating the replacement of any of the *familiares,* but simply adding Stephen to their number. This, of course, presumed that Stephen himself wished to remain in the Kingdom of Sicily.

The riches they saw in Palermo were beginning to make some of his knights think that settling here might not be such a bad thing. Normandy and England were austere by comparison, and with the onset of winter the men began to cultivate an appreciation of Sicily's climate and delights that transcended olives, dates and artichokes.

As 1166 drew to an end, it was clear that Queen Margaret had shown her mettle to all and sundry.

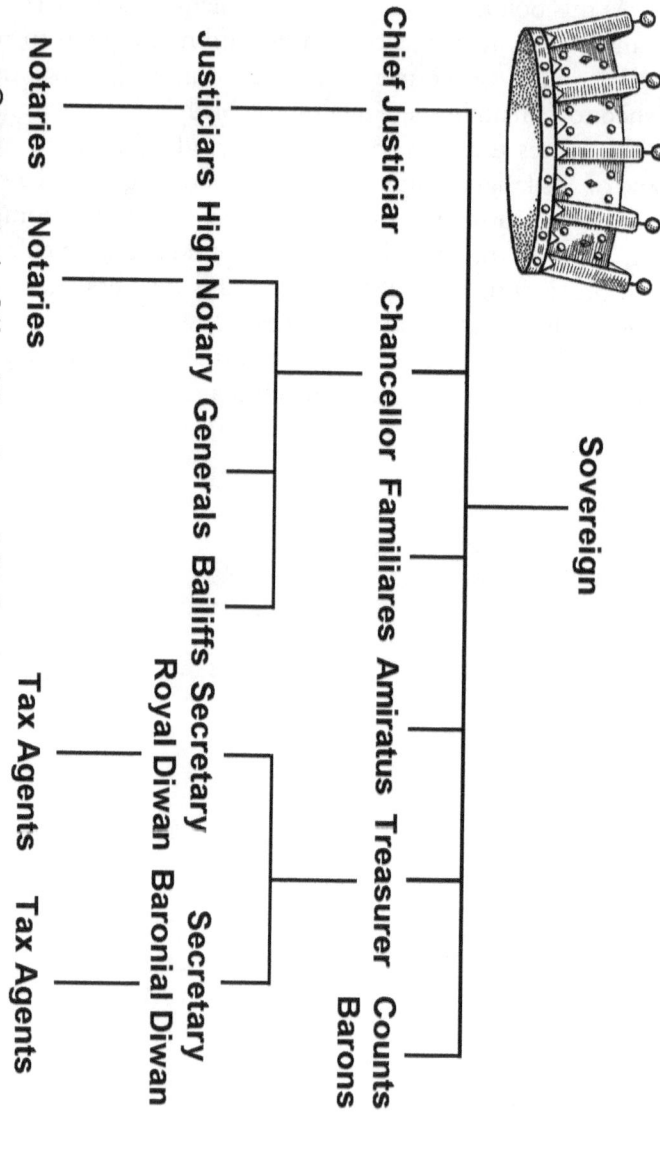

Government of the Kingdom of Sicily during Margaret's regency

Chapter 11
POWER

"The question isn't who is going to let me, it's who is going to stop me."

— Ayn Rand

The barons, ecclesiastics and courtiers promised to accord Stephen of Perche the reverence he deserved, even if, in the deepest depths of their hearts, some of them harbored resentment toward a visitor they viewed as an interloper. Despite the warm reception at court, Stephen expressed a certain reluctance to linger in the *Regnum* very long.

The attractions of Palermo were plainly evident. Anybody arriving from elsewhere in Europe was struck not only by its size but by its cosmopolitan ambience. If Messina was Las Vegas, here was New York or Tokyo.

The queen was too busy with the work of ruling the kingdom to partake in Palermo's pleasures. Most of her routine duties were indeed rather banal; a charter of March 1167 finds her acting in the transfer of ecclesiastical property in Palermo.[180]

Speaking to her newly-arrived cousin, Margaret made the point that he would prosper here, where his companions could expect wealth and opportunities far greater than what awaited them beyond the Alps.[181] Peter of Blois, for example, could presume an appointment as the young king's tutor, a position which would permit him plenty of time for his writings.

Stephen discussed the queen's proposal with the companions who had accompanied him to Italy with the intention of thence proceeding to the Holy Land. Not all of them need remain, but it was hoped that some would choose to stay. Among those persuaded to live in Sicily, at least for a few years, were Odo Quarrel, a canon of Chartres, and erudite Peter of Blois.

Grand Chancellor

It wasn't long before Stephen of Perche told his cousin, the queen, that he and most of the men in his company had decided to remain in the Kingdom of Sicily. Wasting no time, Margaret announced that she had appointed Stephen as her grand chancellor, with authority over the *familiares* and the rest of the court.[182] He would be the queen's sword and shield.

Not all at court were enthralled by this appointment, but it was supported by an important cardinal who happened to be in Sicily on his way to France. This was William of Pavia, a Papal diplomat whose presence was urgently required in England, where a dispute had broken out between King Henry II and the Archbishop of Canterbury, a London-born prelate of Norman lineage named Thomas Becket. Cardinal William would first stop in France, where Becket was living in self-imposed exile.

The intrigues at the Sicilian court were tame compared to the storm raging beyond the English Channel.

The Queen of Sicily had too many problems of her own

to find much time to contemplate the implications of this foreign dispute at any great length, but she knew that familial connections were intertwined across the Norman realms. One of Margaret's kinsmen, Richard of Aigle, held lands in Sussex, where in happier times he went hawking with Thomas Becket.

At an audience with Margaret, Cardinal William expressed how worried he was about two of the exiled archbishop's nephews who had been expelled from England. Could they, he wondered aloud, stay in Sicily until Henry permitted them to return to their homeland?

Yes, said the queen.[183]

Meanwhile, Stephen, as grand chancellor, set about governing the kingdom on his cousin's behalf. Margaret made it clear that all matters concerning administration should be submitted to him. Naturally, the other *familiares* were displeased by this, for it had the intended effect of restricting their access to the queen and their influence in the kingdom.

Outwardly, the prelates seemed to like Stephen. Before long, Romuald of Salerno, who had been Archbishop of Palermo for five years, ordained him a subdeacon. Soon the other bishops, acting on Romuald's suggestion, unanimously supported a decision to consecrate Stephen as Archbishop of Palermo and therefore Primate of Sicily, the first among equals in the island's ecclesiastical hierarchy.

This permitted Romuald, who was also Archbishop of Salerno, to focus on his duties as a Papal diplomat. However, as Romuald surely knew, Stephen's imminent consecration, which could be years away, created new complexities in the power structure.

At least two clerics at court were eyeing the appointment. Walter, a deacon of Cefalù and the royal tutor, may have seemed the more likely candidate, but Richard Palmer, the bishop-elect of Syracuse, was equally ambitious. Romuald's manoeuvre thwarted their ambitions.

To Romuald — and perhaps even to Margaret — naming the same man to the highest civil and ecclesiastical offices of the realm may have seemed like a good idea.

One of Stephen's first acts as chancellor was to appoint his friend Odo Quarrel as the master of his household. Just as it was necessary to go through Stephen to get to the queen, anybody seeking to reach Stephen needed Odo's consent and cooperation. The problem with this was that Odo's temperament was ill-suited to a secular environment beyond the walls of a monastery. Instead, Odo was given to greed, even extortion. He was easily bought, if for a high price.

Stephen's generosity, on the other hand, was beyond question and he was inclined to treat people fairly. Until Stephen's appointment as chancellor, Richard Palmer drew a hefty salary for his services at court. As these duties diminished, so did his salary. In practice, this money was paid from the taxes levied upon a number of hamlets which belonged to the crown rather than a baron or abbot.[184] Stephen permitted the *familiare* to exchange these small settlements for two wealthier villages, not only compensating Richard's loss of remuneration but actually increasing his earnings. One town would be held by Richard *ex officio* only during his tenure as *familiare*, whilst the other was his to keep and someday hand down to his heirs.[185]

Margaret voiced no objection to this *quid pro quo*. Indeed, it reflected her policy of granting counties and baronies to loyal subjects.

Although Romuald himself was instrumental in bringing about Stephen's eventual consecration, if only to foil the ambitions of other likely candidates, before very long he began to entertain grave misgivings about his decision.[186] He had sought to acquiesce to Margaret's desire to spare her court the constant intrigues of the *familiares* and prelates, but the concentration of so much power in one man was risky.

Appointing Stephen chancellor was at least rational. Conversely, electing him archbishop was part of an attempt to attenuate the power of the omnipresent prelates. This annoying problem need not have existed. The cardinals and bishops should have been tending to matters elsewhere instead of conniving in the capital. Once appointed to a diocese, a bishop belonged in his bishopric serving the needs of his flock, not in Palermo stirring up trouble.[187]

Corruption

Avarice was ubiquitous, but many of the grievances against the chancellor were petty complaints rather than affairs of state. Some of the resulting incidents were nothing short of bizarre, and it is fortunate that Margaret didn't have to deal with them herself.

Many nobles and prelates from other parts of the *Regnum*, even distant regions bordering the Papal lands, had to make their way to the court to have important charters notarized, or witnessed. It was customary to pay for this service, although the payment was in the nature of an honorarium or gratuity rather than a fixed fee. There was no schedule of fees, the clients paying what they thought was commensurate with the service rendered.[188]

Notaries did not simply witness documents; some were officers akin to what we now call a *barrister* or *attorney*, empowered to draft charters, contracts and treaties, and even to defend legal cases before a justiciar.[189]

A Palermitan notary named Peter, a kinsman of the *familiare* Matthew of Aiello, was rarely content with what was offered him and asked for much more. Such avarice was not aberrant, but the norm.

Refusing to pay the honorarium Peter demanded, several clients went together to Stephen, complaining not only about the high fee requested by Peter but the time the greedy notary required to seal a document.[190] Stephen immediately referred the drafting and notarization of the documents in question to another notary present at court, who completed the work that same day.

It didn't take long for Peter to realize that people who habitually requested his services in the past were no longer doing so. He inferred that his regular clients were going to another notary. If he couldn't entice them to be his clients he would coerce them into it.

Of course, he wasn't the only greedy notary in the capital. Accompanied by some like-minded colleagues, he undertook surveillance of the streets his former clients had to traverse when leaving the offices of the competing notaries who charged lower fees. One day the angry notaries and a squad of thugs violently confronted the clients, beating and insulting them, and confiscated their notarized documents, tearing the charters to shreds and smashing the wax seals affixed to them.[191]

Apprised of the incident, Stephen summoned the perpetrators to court. Among those ordered to appear was Peter, the instigator, who was thrown in jail following a perfunctory but fair hearing during which he readily admitted his guilt.

Richard Palmer took the occasion to denounce Peter's arrest as illegal and unreasonable. He scornfully affirmed, as if it were true, that in Stephen's native France the law might be enforced in this manner but not here in Sicily. According to Richard, the notaries, having great influence at court, did not deserve to be punished so harshly.

The chancellor was more than a little irritated by the belligerent tone of this criticism, especially coming from somebody for whom, just three days earlier, he had guaranteed the income of two wealthy villages. He was especially annoyed that Richard voiced his vociferous criticism in public instead of speaking to Stephen privately.

Rather than respond to this public insult, embittering as it was, the chancellor ordered that Peter be immured in a dungeon until a suitable sentence could be considered against a man capable of threatening the peace of the realm and thereby offending the dignity of the sovereign. But a few days later, acting on the request of the *familiares,* Stephen freed Peter, punishing him by rescinding his right to exercise the profession of notary.

To discourage future incidents of this kind, the chancellor fixed a limit on what notaries could charge for specific services.[192] Finding the profession a closed caste, he permitted the licensing of a number of new notaries, opening the ranks of this profession to many qualified men who, until now, had been unjustly excluded.

The notaries weren't the only officials adept at the unchecked abuse of power. The provincial and civic bailiffs[193] were likewise out of control, inclined to impose illegal fines on the people under their authority. Most of these monies found their way into the bailiffs' own coffers. This occurred in cities and other territories under royal jurisdiction, as opposed to the feudal lands held by barons.

Stephen's success in curtailing this profusion of abuses earned him the respect of the common folk. He instituted what today would be called an "open-door" policy. This meant that ordinary people could ask for justice. Men and women arrived at court in droves from every part of the *Regnum* seeking writs against their oppressors. So great was their number that there were scarcely enough notaries to draft their complaints or justiciars to hear their cases.

Some viewed Stephen as an angel sent by God, whilst others extolled the kingdom's new golden age.[194] There were still others, however, who saw in the chancellor a perpetual nemesis.

The Calatabiano Case

It was becoming apparent that, as grand chancellor, Stephen could not be corrupted. Besides this, he was now designated to become the premier ecclesiastic of the realm, something that only enhanced his moral authority. Indeed, it made him something of a "super enforcer" of the law, both religious and secular.

Aware of his power, some Palermitans prevailed upon the chancellor to rule on the position of Christians who had apostatised and embraced Islam, perhaps covertly. It was claimed that the deception perpetrated by these converts was encouraged by the eunuchs, many of whom were themselves christianized Arabs of dubious religious conviction.

But the reality was rarely so simple. Some of the alleged "apostates" had begun their lives as Muslims, converted to Christianity as young adults, and then, after much contemplation and soul-searching, returned to the Islam of their parents.[195] This was not exactly the same thing as a person raised as a Christian abruptly becoming a Muslim.

This nuance seemed to escape Stephen, who began to prosecute the "apostates" zealously. Such a policy did not endear him to Sicily's Muslims.[196] Only judiciously should modern ideas be applied to medieval circumstances, but there was a perceptible conflict between Stephen's position as chancellor, from whence he represented all the subjects of the realm, and his status as a prelate who spoke only for its Catholics.[197]

If Margaret was not yet *au courant* of Stephen's "apostate policy," she learned of it with the emergence of a specific case.

This involved Robert of Calatabiano. When we last encountered him, he was ensconced in Palermo's seaside castle, where he tortured prisoners and exacted bribes. His proclivity for violence and bribery had gone unpunished because the palace eunuchs concealed his misdeeds from royal eyes.

When it became obvious that Stephen's religious zeal was more than a mere gesture, a number of people took advantage of the situation to step forward to accuse Robert of Calatabiano of being a closet Muslim, a secret apostate. And that was only the tip of the iceberg.

Now Robert stood accused of everything from extortion to theft to murder. His accusers even claimed that he had forced Christian women and boys into prostitution at a private brothel frequented by Muslims. There was no telling where delusion ended and truth began, but the veracity of the allegations was presumed by many, including Stephen and the Pope.[198] The people clamored for justice.

Unlike most of the other cases brought before Stephen and his justiciars, this one involved a high official, a great number of alleged victims and monstrous sums of money. Moreover, Robert was well-connected. In former times he was protected by Caïd Peter, who had fled the court and gone to Africa. He now enjoyed the friendship of the influential palace eunuchs. This helped him at the royal court but hurt him in the court of public opinion, for most of the eunuchs were christianized Arabs whose alleged collusion lent credibility to the hypothesis of the private brothel and sexual abuse by Muslims.

The case against Robert of Calatabiano ended up before Margaret.

Here the eunuchs begged the queen to grant clemency to the accused, who they declared to be the victim of malicious slander. They further claimed that the fugitive Caïd Peter was the culpable party because it was he who had ordered, even coerced, Robert to steal and kill.

Stephen saw how difficult the case was, effectively pitting the populace and the public interest against the eunuchs and even the *familiares.*

Margaret likewise found herself in a trying predicament. She wanted to support the majority of her subjects without alienating her government. Attempting to appease both sides was like walking a tightrope without falling into the abyss.

Without actually defending Robert, she asked her chancellor to reduce the number and severity of the charges being brought against the murderous sadist. When Stephen balked at this, she used her authority to overrule him, and ordered him to desist in prosecuting Robert for allegations lodged against him by individuals.[199] This did not exclude crimes against the crown and the Catholic Church.

Margaret made it understood that she wanted an example made of Robert. She did not, and could not, condone his ungodly behavior. Yet her stance implied that, despite the gravity of his crimes, she did not wish to see him become a symbolic "martyr" for the *familiares,* eunuchs, bailiffs and barons.

Without contradicting the queen directly, the chancellor responded that the best he could do was to suspend prosecution of Robert for civil charges. This would exclude offenses that might result in capital punishment. It seemed like a pragmatic compromise.

Privately, Stephen told his royal cousin that he would resign from his positions if she ever again undermined him as she had during this legal case.

He made it clear that for crimes in ecclesiastical jurisdiction Robert would be tried by a jury of bishops. This addressed perjury firstly, followed by incest and adultery, leaving aside larceny, robbery, murder, rape and corruption.[200]

It could be argued that this legal remedy was slightly flawed because, according to the Assizes of Ariano[201] enacted by King Roger, perjury and adultery were civil crimes. One presumes that, in the first instance, they would be prosecuted by justiciars rather than bishops, even though they were also ecclesiastical offenses in the Roman Church.

The verdict was announced at a later audience. To the extent that it did not mete out a death sentence, the *familiares* and eunuchs were satisfied, if not entirely content.

Robert of Calatabiano was flogged before a jeering crowd. His property was seized, and he was sentenced to a prison term in the same castle where he had tortured so many innocent men.

On the way to the seaside fortress, the condemned man was to be paraded along Palermo's main streets as his crimes were announced to the multitude, but the bishops thought better of this plan when they saw how many angry people were gathered in narrow passages from which to pelt Robert with stones. Things were getting out of hand. The sword-bearing knights guarding the prisoner on all sides could barely restrain the relentless crowd, intent as it was on stoning the man to death.

At that point a more circumspect approach was suggested. It was decided to hold Robert behind a wall of the cathedral until the crowd dispersed. A few days later he was taken to the jail in the seaside castle. By then, it had become clear that the rumours of the prisoner bribing his way out of confinement were greatly exaggerated.

He died following some sporadic bouts of torture.

The common folk were happy to learn of the tyrant's fate, but others were less pleased by it. Robert's trial and punishment had the effect of cautioning the great of the realm that they too could be penalized for their crimes. This only exacerbated their dislike of Stephen of Perche.

In central Italy, meanwhile, Pope Alexander III was defending Papal territory against a major incursion by Frederick Barbarossa. Margaret sent funds to assist the besieged Pontiff, who was forced to leave Rome. In the event, it was not Papal military might but an epidemic among his Imperial troops that drove Frederick out of Italy. This eliminated any foreign threat to Margaret during the regency. Most of her detractors were in the *Regnum* itself.

Charter of Margaret in her own name in 1176 (top) and as regent with William II, her son, in 1168

Chapter 12
JUSTICE

"The day will come when man will recognize woman not only as his peer at the fireside but in councils of the nation."

— Susan B. Anthony

Until now, the magnates were reluctant to speak ill of the queen except perhaps through whispers about her poor choice of a chancellor. Whilst Margaret, in the interest of keeping the peace, might attenuate the prosecution of a corrupt castellan like Robert of Calatabiano, she was far less likely to tolerate overt treason against her son or herself.

Margaret's rule as regent was absolute. The occasional *curiae generales,* such as the meeting of barons summoned by King Roger on the eve of his coronation, was not a parliament and the baronage had no official say in royal decisions.[202]

Defamation

If it were difficult to find fault with Stephen of Perche, his detractors might invent flaws they could easily attribute to him and perhaps even the regent. Like most malicious rumours, these attacks were difficult to impute to specific persons; in effect, they were anonymous, emanating from the thin Mediterranean air. There was nothing novel in this form of defamation, even if the Sicilians were unusually proficient at it.

Certain conditions favored the wide and rapid diffusion of hearsay. Palermo was a very populous city, with a constant flow of people arriving and departing for other places in the *Regnum* and abroad. Of Europe's major capitals, Sicily's was the city nearest Papal power even if, for the moment, Pope Alexander was busy contending with the pretensions of Frederick Barbarossa in Italy. Unlike other royal capitals, Palermo was the home of an uninvited cabal of cardinals and bishops who spent most of their time scheming and gossiping. The city was a rumour mill.

Margaret knew this as well as anybody. A revolt fomented by rumours had claimed the life of one of her sons. However majestic its wonders, Palermo's vicissitudes had shown that the city was no magical Camelot on the Tyrrhenian.

Although the kingdom's magnates did not savor the idea of taking orders from a woman, something to which they were unaccustomed, they knew that it was only a matter of a few years before William reached the age of majority. In the meantime, however, the chancellor could do much to delimit the scope of their power. He had already shown what he could achieve in the space of just one year.

It was easy enough to contrive rumours about "corruption" at court, and the agitators knew that vague allegations of wrongdoing, however outlandish, were difficult to refute very convincingly. Simple reasoning would dictate that the burden of proof lies with the person asserting a claim, for it is easier to show that something happened than to prove that it did not, but by Margaret's time the epistemology enshrined in the Socratic method was all but forgotten. Facts were whatever the hate mongers wanted them to be.

Besmirching the queen's name would not be a very simple matter. There was nothing in Margaret's conduct that was anything less than proper. Well, almost nothing.

Somebody at court — so it was said — noticed the queen smile at the chancellor in a way that "somebody" deemed to reflect undue familiarity, even intimacy. "She devoured him with her eyes, and it was feared that an illicit love was hidden behind the guise of kinship," wrote Falcandus.[203]

Lacking any legitimate grievance against the regent, some men resorted to the centuries-old practice of what in our era is sometimes called "slut shaming."[204]

This technique for attacking medieval queens was not terribly original, nor even too unusual. In Margaret's time, accusing a queen of having a sexual affair with a highly-placed courtier was something of a cliché.[205] The path before many a woman was strewn with such innuendo.

The attacks directed at Stephen emanated from several quarters. The eunuchs despised him for imprisoning their ally Robert of Calatabiano. The barons resented him because most of the largesse and influence they monopolized in the past were now going to Stephen's friends. Sicily's most prominent Muslim, Abu'l Kasim, disliked the fact that his rival, Caïd Siddiq, Palermo's wealthiest Muslim, had become one of Stephen's advisors.

Little could be done to pacify those bemoaning the lust they thought revealed itself in Margaret's eyes, but Stephen sought to allay the laments that reached his ears.

Injury

Although his efforts were earnest, Stephen's reputation was not helped by an incident that seemed to reflect an overzealous surveillance of his adversaries.

One of the men suspected of stirring up dissent was

Matthew of Aiello, the *familiare*. When it was observed that he was sending more letters than usual across Sicily to his brother, John, an influential prelate in Catania, an attempt was made to intercept some of the couriers carrying these documents.[206] This mission was entrusted to Robert of Bellisina, whose men attempted to apprehend a messenger who was returning to Palermo.[207] While the courier bearing a letter from John got away, his colleague was caught. This man resisted arrest and was wounded.

Matthew soon learned of the incident. Finding himself under suspicion, he decided to act.

Not long after the incident involving Matthew's courier, Robert of Bellisina fell ill with a grave fever. A physician named Salernus[208] was recommended to administer a cure. Knowing Salernus to be a close acquaintance of Matthew, who had undertaken to get him appointed as a judge in the city of Salerno, Stephen sagely refused sending him to Robert. Instead, he ordered another doctor to treat him.

Concealing his movements from the chancellor, Salernus visited Robert several times. Nevertheless, the sick man failed to recover and soon died. Stephen was sad to learn of Robert's death.

The condition of the corpse was disturbing. Robert's hair fell out and patches of his skin separated from his muscle tissue. This suggested to some that poisoning had killed him, but to be certain the chancellor asked a team of physicians led by Romuald of Salerno[209] to begin a medical investigation.

Those who had been close to Robert of Bellisina confirmed that Salernus had offered him a liquid, but what was in the potion?

It so happened there was living proof of its toxicity. A friend of Robert's showed the investigators a hand bearing a wound from a haemorrhage that erupted when, out of view of Robert and the servants, this man had poured the same liquid on his own palm, thinking to test it in this way before ingesting it.

Another witness, a notary named William, informed the investigators that a man in the employ of Matthew of Aiello often approached him to ask about Robert.

Thus informed, Stephen of Perche met with the *familiares,* Romuald and others, who agreed that the chancellor should summon Salernus for questioning.

Initially, the man denied ever administering a medicinal syrup to Robert of Bellisina but recanted this mendacious testimony when confronted by witnesses. Then he claimed to have given Robert innocuous rose water made by Justus, a local druggist. However, when interrogated, this apothecary swore that he had sold nothing to Salernus during the four weeks prior to Robert's death. It was clear that Salernus was not telling the truth.

The next day, the high justiciars of the court convened an audience. Under interrogation, Salernus responded to their queries in a desultory way, offering no exculpatory evidence.

He was found guilty of murder, the justiciars ordering his death and the confiscation of his property. Had Salernus decided to cooperate with the investigation by divulging the name of his fellow conspirator, the justiciars might have been inclined to grant him clemency, commuting his sentence to prison time and sparing his life. However, he could not be persuaded to disclose this information.

Margaret was advised of the trial and sentence but played no part in it. If Matthew of Aiello were involved in some way, the incident was indeed disconcerting.

The fate of Salernus, unlike that of Robert of Calatabiano a few weeks earlier, was not important enough politically to warrant royal intervention. What is more, the evidence against Salernus was overwhelming.

As the weeks passed, there would be greater challenges to face.

Margaret's Brother Returns

It will be recalled that for his steadfast loyalty Richard of Molise (Mandra) was granted a large county and made a *familiare*. This irritated his Apulian peers, who managed to turn Margaret's brother, Henry (Rodrigo) of Montescaglioso against this man he barely knew. The pretext was that Richard was abusing his power, while Henry, as the regent's brother and the young monarch's uncle, deserved a lofty position at court.

Henry's arrogance was nourished by the support of the company of Spanish knights who came to Italy with him, their number augmented by others who had recently arrived from Navarre. With these knights and several influential barons[210] allied with him, he crossed from the mainland to Sicily with the intention of intimidating Margaret, Stephen and the *familiares* into acceding to his demands. If he knew that Gilbert of Gravina, who was his second cousin, had already failed in trying to achieve the same thing, it made no difference to him.

Advised of Henry's arrival at Messina, the *familiare* Richard of Molise met with Stephen of Perche to warn the chancellor that these interlopers must not be granted any standing at court, even if it were necessary to subdue them through armed confrontation.

Stephen was no great admirer of Richard of Molise, but the last thing he wanted was to see blood spilled in the city. Acting prudently, he sent to Henry a letter written on the queen's authority ordering him to come to the capital but without his confederates, who were to remain at Termini Imerese, about midway between Palermo and Cefalù.

Meeting with Henry, Stephen was able to convince him to ignore the complaints of the Apulian barons. As the queen's brother, he had obtained much and might be further rewarded if he were loyal to her. Henry made peace with Richard of Molise, who he had been led to view as a rival.

Margaret was angry about her brother's insubordination on the mainland, where for months he had failed to follow her orders, but the chancellor managed to broker a reconciliation between the siblings. Henry went so far as to promise obedience in the future.

With this familial truce achieved, Stephen summoned the vassals who had come to Sicily with Henry and were waiting at Termini up the coast. At court, they reaffirmed their fealty once they realized that their plan had failed. One amongst them, Bohemond of Manopello, who was distinguished for his exceptional intelligence, established a sincere friendship with the chancellor.

Henry also became very friendly with Stephen. This displeased those who were conspiring to obtain power.

Having failed to achieve their ends through force of arms, these malcontents now sought to dissuade Henry's friendship with Stephen through words. They strove to convince his most trusted Spanish knights that befriending the chancellor was not in their noble lord's interest. Here they resorted to what they thought were effective methods, telling the knights that Stephen was having an incestuous relationship with the queen.[211] They went further, implying that Henry was naive, seeing as he was the only person at court unaware of this (alleged) liaison between Stephen and Margaret.

Henry was not wise. Indeed, he was credulous and rather easily duped. Nevertheless, at first he was disinclined to believe what he heard about the affable chancellor and the queen, people he knew and respected.

He changed his mind when the rumour's imagined veracity was reinforced by the very people who, unbeknownst to Henry, had hatched it in the first place.[212] This led him to forswear his loyalty to Stephen of Perche, believing the worst about his own sister. With this, the queen's brother joined the plotters.

Ubiquitous Disloyalty

Henry of Montescaglioso was not alone. Within the palace walls, Caïd Richard, the chamberlain, who despised Stephen, was convincing ever more men-at-arms, from knights to archers, to join the plot against the chancellor.[213] Most of this he achieved through simple bribery.

Stephen was vaguely aware of this. He organized a fifty-man bodyguard that included many French knights, never going anywhere in Palermo without a company of at least twenty or thirty armed men.

One may argue the degree to which the hatred directed at the chancellor also reflected baronial resentment of the queen he served but, in the worst scenario, Stephen's death would certainly weaken Margaret's position. It would also spawn chaos at court. The *familiares* might remain loyal, but there was no way to tell where the unrest would end.

Margaret had already seen violence aplenty.

Stephen reasoned that confronting the conspirators at this point might be preferable to waiting for them to make the first move. For now, he lacked much evidence against any of them, yet he didn't want to give them more time to prepare a rebellion that could lead to a civil war.

If, as he had been informed, there were plotters like Caïd Richard within the palace walls, that made the capital itself potentially dangerous.[214]

Disturbing as this was, expediency alone suggested that it may be best to address the problems growing outside the confines of Palermo. Whatever they were doing on the island, the more egregious offenders garnered their most effective support in Apulia, where royal authority was entrusted to a cadre of men whose loyalty sometimes seemed dubious, among them Margaret's kinsmen Gilbert of Gravina and Henry of Montescaglioso. The queen therefore contemplated an inspection tour of the mainland during the spring. If nothing else, her appearance would remind any doubters of her authority throughout the realm, not only on the island of Sicily.

The strategic key to the kingdom was Messina, whose harbor was at least as important, both commercially and militarily, as the port of Palermo. From there, it was easy to follow Calabria's Ionian coast by land or sea to Taranto and then Bari.

With this in mind, Stephen proposed that the queen spend the approaching winter at Messina. The city wasn't really very far from the capital. A relay of couriers on fast steeds made it possible to get a letter to or from Palermo in three full days.

Margaret liked the idea of spending some time at Messina, where there was a fortified royal palace near the coast.[215] Her extended presence might even discourage some of the city's infamous vices.

Regardless of whether the queen ultimately decided to travel to Apulia, bringing the court to Messina from time to time was rooted in geographical reality. More than half the *Regnum* was in peninsular Italy, and for anybody coming from Apulia, Calabria, Campania, or even more distant Abruzzi, a journey to Messina was far more convenient than riding another four or five days to reach Palermo after crossing into Sicily.

In September, Stephen summoned his kinsman Gilbert of Gravina to Messina, explaining that the court planned on passing the winter there.

The October of 1167 was rainier than usual, and the *familiares* used this as an excuse to try to dissuade the queen's departure during this season. Stephen was undeterred, ordering that the coastal roads to Messina be prepared for the arrival of young King William and the royal family.

In early November, word was received that the Pope had ratified the nomination of Stephen as Archbishop of Palermo. The prelates of the kingdom swore their fealty to him as their primate, and Romuald intended to consecrate him in a solemn ceremony in the capital's cathedral. Yet Stephen was never actually consecrated as planned.[216]

Stephen, like the queen, often tended to minutiae, such as confirming the privileges of the Benedictine monastery of Saint John of the Hermits near the palace.[217]

The weather improved by Martinmas, and on the morning of Wednesday, the fifteenth of November, the royal party set out for Messina. The chancellor left an army of knights behind to guard the capital; these men were loyal to Stephen.

Caïd Richard, as the chamberlain, was left in charge of the palace, but couriers seeking to consign letters to the queen and chancellor knew where to find them.

Accompanied by the chancellor, high justiciars and some notaries, along with a large company of knights, the queen visited a number of towns *en route* to Messina. This included the fortress of San Marco d'Alunzio, where Beatrice, the widow of King Roger II, was living with her young daughter Constance. Although young King William was about the same age as Constance, the girl was his aunt.

The journey afforded Margaret an opportunity to appreciate the beauty of the forested Nebrodian Mountains, which took their name from the Greek *nebros* for their abundance of deer.

The queen and her family finally arrived in Messina at the very end of November during the beginning of the Christmas season.

Reginal Wisdom

A number of nobles were waiting for Margaret at Messina. One of them was Robert of Caserta.[218] This loyal count had heard that his cousin, William of San Severino, whose exile had recently been lifted, had convinced Margaret to restore his former lands to his possession.

Accompanied by several advocates, Robert petitioned the court requesting a revision of this decree on the basis that, in fact, certain lands now held by William legally belonged to the former. The reasoning for this was that in an earlier time William's father had come to possess them illegally through the use of force. In other words, these lands had never belonged to William by law.

Margaret wanted to rule justly. Although she understood Robert's complaint, the queen did not wish to alienate William by diminishing his property and wealth.

William had earned Stephen's trust; the chancellor considered him loyal. On the other hand, there were doubts in Stephen's mind about Robert's fealty. Nevertheless, there was no point in offending this man to the point that he might be encouraged to join the kingdom's malcontents.

Acting on Stephen's advice, the queen gave Robert of Caserta, who seemed to have the stronger case, the lands he requested, compensating William of San Severino with other manors. She imposed the condition that this decision was final, and therefore the matter would never again be brought before the court.

The ecclesiastical sphere, as always, was full of complexities, even conflict. Margaret granted a charter to Nicholas, the Archbishop of Messina, confirming his episcopal rights following a local dispute in which the prelate's authority had been challenged.[219]

The next matter brought before the queen involved local taxes. King Roger had given the city certain privileges and tax exemptions, only to rescind these measures later. The rights later confirmed by his son seemed insufficient compensation for those that had been revoked.[220] Seeking to encourage Stephen to reinstitute these rights, the Messinians offered him bribes. The chancellor categorically rejected the gifts proffered him but convinced Margaret to bestow anew the rights once granted by her father-in-law. This seemed like a good way to earn some respect from the local people.

Stephen's strategy was effective. By December, there was always a crowd of subjects at court seeking justice. The people came from Calabria, eastern Sicily and elsewhere in the *Regnum*. The scene was not unlike what had occurred a few months earlier in Palermo, when the chancellor instituted his "open door" policy and began to assail corruption. The queen herself addressed very few cases, usually those involving important prelates and nobles, but every decision was rendered in the name of her son, King William II.

Richard of Aversa

Seeing that the queen and chancellor were just, a delegation of Messinians, came forth to denounce the abuses of Richard of Aversa, their city's governor.[221] Here the long litany of accusations was similar to that advanced against Robert of Calatabiano. Richard was said to have committed every kind of crime, often through accomplices acting as his proxies. The jeremiad included murder, robbery, thievery, even arson. It was said that the governor had illegally confiscated houses and vineyards. The people claimed that he excelled at bribing justiciars. Debauchery and adultery were not overlooked. If even a fraction of the allegations were true, Richard was the busiest man in the kingdom.

Stephen of Perche suspected that a few of the accusations might well be true, but he sought to control the governor rather than subject him to the rigors of a formal trial.

Having believed that the queen's presence augured well for them, the Messinians resented this procrastination, offended that everybody else in the kingdom obtained justice whilst the crimes perpetrated in their loyal city were neglected. Some leaders wrote out the grievances against the governor on signs they attached to long poles, displaying these during a raucous protest in front of the palace.

The Christmas season had already begun, but the clamoring crowd convinced Margaret that she had to resolve this matter here and now. Without hesitation, she commanded Stephen to accept the Messinians' petitions. He referred the case to the high justiciars, ordering them to begin an inquest, specifying that a hearing be held during the next few days.

The subsequent trial revealed that Richard of Aversa was unambiguously guilty of a great many offenses. He was imprisoned and his property was confiscated. Having left the trial to the justiciars, Margaret and Stephen now remonstrated with Richard, and there was no vocal opposition to the verdict except perhaps from the condemned man and his family.

To say that this decision bolstered local esteem for Stephen would be an understatement. The people loved him. Just as importantly, the subjects sang the incessant praises of their queen. Margaret felt that, at long last, she was paving the way to a peaceful kingdom for her son.

It was finally time to celebrate Christmas. These festivities, with their endless liturgies, extended into early January, culminating with the Epiphany.

Management Style

The subtle contours of Margaret's policy were being shaped by pragmatism. She was not rewriting her late husband's script, merely editing it into a form resilient enough to survive into the first few years of her son's majority. She wanted to hand him a kingdom as free of disquietude as a medieval realm could be. In this she was selfless.

What emerges from a sober analysis of the first phase of the regency is an approach to governing that was meant to eliminate abuses whilst maintaining the essential organization of the monarchy. The three *familiares* represented the feudal (Richard of Molise), bureaucratic (Matthew of Aiello) and ecclesiastical (Richard Palmer) spheres.[222] The high justiciars were a kind of "supreme court," whilst the other justiciars were, essentially, district judges. Constables, bailiffs (governors), ecclesiastics (bishops and abbots), and vassals (counts and barons) administered specific territories. All reported to the regent and chancellor, although prelates answered to the Pope for strictly ecclesiastical matters. The legal code, the Assizes of Ariano, provided a juridical, and even social, framework for the Kingdom of Sicily, and the rights of religious minorities were guaranteed.

The sovereign was the defender of the three faiths — a reminder that what united the Sicilians was far greater than whatever might divide them.

In contrast to the smaller, less important realm of her brother, Sancho "the Wise" of Navarre, Margaret's *Regnum Siciliae* placed her on an economic and political parity with Henry II of England and Frederick Barbarossa.

However, whereas Henry and Frederick were waging their own jurisdictional or territorial battles with the Papacy, Margaret was friendly with Pope Alexander III. Her "foreign policy" (to use a modern term) was solid, and solidly beneficial to her subjects.

At home, the treasury was administered well, and the greater number of subjects were happy to see corrupt men removed from power. Serfdom was not as widespread here as it was in many other parts of Europe.

The three "feminine estates" were virgin, wife and widow, defining women by their relationship to men. The most influential Christian women were abbesses; these nuns were well-educated. The Muslim and Jewish women of the *Regnum* were, for the most part, just as literate as the nuns.[223]

Rare indeed was the woman who managed a small manor, let alone a barony, rarer still the woman who practiced medicine.[224]

Margaret was resolute in her conviction that the kingdom should be ruled a certain way, but her approach was much more than an instinctive reaction to the way her husband had ruled.

At a formative stage in his life, young William was learning by example as he attended royal audiences. Procedures and principles were explained to him. Unlike most young European monarchs, he was being taught not only by male tutors but by the woman who ruled in his name. This was highly exceptional in 1167, and it was one of the things that made William II an exceptional monarch.

There is nothing to suggest that Margaret was unduly harsh, but there can be no doubt that she was unafraid to wield the absolute royal authority she held in her slender hands. At least a few criminals and traitors reluctant to live righteously under her rule died by it.[225] Anybody who presumed to break the law with impunity simply because there was a woman on the throne had best think again.

Falcandus tells us that there were subjects who resented the "Spanish woman," but there is no evidence to suggest that Margaret ever attracted much opprobrium from the common folk who, on the contrary, literally cheered when oppressive tyrants like Robert of Calatabiano and Richard of Aversa were tried and punished. The most obstreperous naysayers were to be found among the aristocracy.

By the beginning of 1168 Margaret knew this. She was no dilettante.

Catholicism

Whatever the caprices of individual bishops might be, the queen's relationship with the Catholic Church as an institution was solid.

As ever more Muslims converted to Christianity, and as the

Greek Christians of the *Regnum* became latinized, Papal influence was increasingly felt in matters of faith. The most recent general pronouncement from the Papacy came with the thirty canons, or "articles," issued at the Second Lateran Council (in 1139) under Pope Innocent II. Some of these rules reiterated prior declarations, and of course the Papacy continually issued bulls and other decrees. However, several canons were especially relevant to the Kingdom of Sicily during Margaret's regency, and a few discouraged the abuse of power by the clergy. Whether or not these directives were applied in practice, they indicate that the Pope was aware of the problems that prompted their issuance. It is worth casting a glance over some of the situations addressed.

Priests or deacons who have taken wives or concubines are strongly condemned, and constrained to be removed from their ecclesiastical offices. Monks are prohibited from working as lawyers for pay in the civil (secular) sphere. Nuns are forbidden the foundation of convents outside the established religious orders.[226]

Use of the crossbow against Christians is prohibited, although it certainly continued. Jousts in tournaments are condemned, yet these continued unabated.

Churches are considered a sanctuary for fugitives. Arsonists are denied Christian burial.

Children born of incest are banned from inheriting property, while the children and other kin of priests are forbidden the inheritance of church property. The sons of priests may serve as clergy only in monasteries, not in diocesan churches.

The laity has no power over ecclesiastical estates. That is to say, neither a baron nor the son of a priest can claim church land.

Bishoprics are not to be left vacant for more than three months. This provides for the speedy election of bishops without inordinate delay.

JUSTICE

What of Margaret's faith?

The queen was very devout, even if she cultivated a healthy suspicion of certain Catholic prelates. As the number of Greek Christians diminished, with ever more of their monasteries in Calabria and northeastern Sicily being abandoned, Margaret encouraged the Latin religious orders to take their place. Initially, these were the Benedictines and Cistercians.

The Jews were largely undisturbed, while the Muslims gradually converted in large numbers.

In Margaret's time there were not overwhelming cultural differences among the majority of Sicilian women, and bin Jubayr tells us that the Christian women dressed similarly to their Muslim sisters.[227] This was something of a Mediterranean norm. One imagines the queen herself wearing a long silk headscarf in public, and certainly in church.

Faith as power: Mosaic icon of Christ Pantocrator at Monreale (chapter 19)

Chapter 13
SOVEREIGNTY

"If you want something said, ask a man. If you want something done, ask a woman."

— Margaret Thatcher

By the middle of January in 1168, the majority of Messinians seemed content. Unbeknownst to the queen, however, Henry of Montescaglioso, her troublesome half-brother, was up to his old tricks. In this he was abetted by Bartholomew of Parisio, whose sister, it may be recalled, was once married to Richard of Sai, the man granted a divorce on questionable grounds in order to wed a woman reputed to be a harlot. Bartholomew's conniving may have had less to do with the perceived slight against his sister than with his own maneuvering to achieve greater power for himself through his close alliance with Henry. Not only did Bartholomew exercise a certain influence over some Messinians, a number of Calabrians present in the city to greet the young king were party to his covert machinations.

Bad Blood

No attempt at rioting was made during the Christmas season that had just ended, but it would transpire that Henry was contemplating a more specific operation, for which public disorder was merely a diversionary tactic.

Bartholomew was to some degree discouraged by the arrival of Gilbert of Gravina, Margaret's cousin, with a formidable company of a hundred well-armed knights. It was precisely to avoid potential dissension that Stephen of Perche had summoned Gilbert to Messina. Gilbert, of course, was Stephen's nephew.

Both were Norman to the core, and here was the root of yet another potential problem, for in recent weeks the French knights present in unruly Messina had taken to treating the local people[228] with contempt, frequently insulting them.

Bartholomew wanted more than an insurrection. He and his minions incited Henry to plan the assassination of Stephen, thinking that the chancellor's death might pave the way for the queen's half-brother to seize power. To that end, Henry solicited a certain Roger, a local justiciar, to join the plot. Roger feigned collaboration but secretly advised the chancellor of Henry's homicidal plan a day before it was to be set in motion.

Stephen instructed Roger the justiciar to behave with Henry and Bartholomew as if nothing had changed; in the meantime he informed the queen of the situation, advising her to act without delay.

News of the murder conspiracy upset Margaret greatly. Its implications were myriad. Here was gross disrespect by a man toward his own sister, who had helped him in every conceivable way. Beyond that, he was a traitor to the kingdom she ruled in the name of her son.

The queen knew she had to act if this kind of thing were

to be discouraged throughout the *Regnum,* but she found it, at the very least, distasteful to mete out justice to her own brother. More immediately, Henry had to be punished to dissuade others who might still attempt to carry out the assassination even after its chief plotter and beneficiary was unmasked.

The more she thought about it, the angrier she became, her fair complexion reddening with rage. Margaret Jiménez might consider clemency for her stupid brother, but Margaret, Queen Regent of Sicily, enjoyed no such prerogative.

How dare that insolent bastard seek to undermine royal authority!

Henry's Trial

The queen needed a strategy. First, she would convene a formal trial. Either Henry would be found guilty, or he would admit to his crimes of his own volition. Either way, he would then be expected to cooperate by identifying the other conspirators. If he were reluctant to name them, some time in a castle jail might loosen his traitorous tongue. Dungeons were cold this time of year.[229]

Margaret had Henry arrested, and ordered Stephen to summon the high justiciars, *familiares,* bishops and nobles who were to hear the case. The hearing took place ten days later under heavy guard.

Even though Henry himself was in custody, most of his co-conspirators were still at large; they posed a very real risk. In his opening statement, the accused man decried the value of his "paltry" income from the County of Montescaglioso. An aggrieved Henry wanted Taranto, even though that strategic port city was traditionally reserved to a member of the royal family. At the very least, he felt entitled to some wealthy lands in eastern Sicily.

Ridiculous as this demand was, it did not lack for a pretext. If refused these prosperous lands, Henry hoped to more plausibly justify his hatred of Stephen of Perche for forcing the queen's half-brother into penury.

In response, Gilbert of Gravina thundered that Henry had tried to use the implicit threat of military force to coerce the queen into giving him lands which, had he behaved better in the first place, might have already been in his possession. He accused the queen's half-brother of deception, stating that the man should not, by right, hold any lands in the kingdom. He then excoriated him for being a spendthrift whilst oppressing the peasants on his estates. Gilbert went on to cite Henry's foolish suggestion that Margaret fortify castles in his manors and hide money there against the future possibility that William II might not always be loyal to his own mother. He spoke of how Henry tried to manipulate young William into thinking that Margaret was somehow damaging the king and the kingdom, and how the boy responded (to Henry) that in distrusting his own mother he would also have to distrust her brother. Gilbert spoke of how Henry accused him, Gilbert, of disloyalty. He asked Henry what fault he found in Stephen so grave that it justified assassination.

Gilbert concluded by saying that Henry, despite his maudlin appeal, deserved no lands in the Kingdom of Sicily. As a traitor, he deserved to be deprived of his property, along with his very life.

When Henry vehemently denied organizing any conspiracy to kill the chancellor, Roger the justiciar was brought in to testify, affirming the details of the plot. Henry's testimony became even more unseemly as he lost his temper and accused Roger of betraying a promise to collaborate in the conspiracy. Here the accused man contradicted himself, for just a few minutes earlier he had adamantly denied plotting to kill the chancellor.

In this way Henry condemned himself with his own words. He was ordered detained in the palace, where the trial had taken place.

Before long, word reached Stephen that Henry's company of knights was assembling at the condemned man's residence in the city, and that many Messinians were taking up arms in expectation of a riot, or even a battle. The chancellor ordered his own knights, and those of Gilbert of Gravina, to guard the palace. Armed men were dispatched into the streets to restore order by assuring the populace that there was no need for alarm.

Whilst Henry languished in jail, his knights[230] were ordered to surrender their weapons and immediately cross into Calabria, with the caveat that any men who failed to comply with this royal command would be imprisoned immediately. Deprived of their swords, daggers and shields, the downtrodden knights made their way to the port and traversed the strait.

Having heard about what had occurred over in Sicily, the local Greeks[231] saw the opportunity for plunder and a touch of vengeance. An angry mob assaulted the disarmed men, leaving them with little more than the clothes they were wearing. The beaten knights made their way northward but many died in the frozen forests of the Sila Mountains.

Back in Messina, an attempt was made to identify Henry's most pernicious partisans. One who approached the chancellor and voluntarily confessed was temporarily exiled whilst his lands were entrusted to an abbot friendly to the queen.[232] Another, conversely, was imprisoned because he came forward only after the identities of the chief conspirators had already been divulged by Margaret's incarcerated half-brother.[233] Under interrogation, and with no immediate hope of release, Henry had seen fit to disclose most of the plot's details.

Some at court propounded that Stephen of Perche pardon most of the offenders, even if many of the plotters clearly merited death or, at the very least, lengthy imprisonment. Gilbert of Gravina suggested otherwise. He had his own reason for this.

Richard of Molise Accused

Richard of Molise, it may be remembered, had nearly come to blows with Gilbert of Gravina, the queen's cousin, during an argument about the flight of Caïd Peter to Africa. At Richard's urging, Matthew of Aiello successfully managed to have Gilbert sent away from the court on the pretext that he was needed on the peninsula to fend off an impending invasion by Frederick Barbarossa. True, Barbarossa did eventually make his way into Papal territory, but he was forced to withdraw before invading the Kingdom of Sicily. Nevertheless, duplicitous Gilbert, who was envious of Richard's rank as *familiare*, had never forgotten this affront. He enmity was at least explicable.

At a royal audience, Bohemond of Manopello[234] accused Richard of having covertly supported the recent conspiracy. At first, Margaret found this absurd, but if her own brother could not be trusted, then who could she trust? On the other hand, Bohemond was a confederate of her brother.

For his part, Richard of Molise vigorously denied the ludicrous allegation that painted him as a miscreant, challenging to trial by single combat anybody who accused him of such a flagrant betrayal.

Further accusations followed, intended, more than anything, to erode Richard's credibility in the eyes of the queen. Their substance was that he continued, illegally, to hold the County of Mandra, as well as some royal towns around Troia. To this the *familiare* responded that Mandra had been entrusted to him temporarily by Caïd Peter and the Troian towns by Turgisio, that region's chamberlain. Turgisio, who was present, refuted this.

SOVEREIGNTY

An impromptu jury led by the high justiciars, but excluding Matthew of Aiello, the other *familiare* present, then conferred to discuss the charges against Richard. This was not entirely proper but Margaret and Stephen did not object to it. In any case, the queen was the ultimate authority in the matter.

The sanctimonious "judges" decided that Richard held Mandra and the Troian towns legally so long as Caïd Peter guaranteed his possession, but effectively lost this tenure as soon as Peter fled the *Regnum*. Richard protested this casuistry, saying that justice was being corrupted, but Stephen did not wish to contradict a jury led by high justiciars. The travesty of justice that condemned Richard bore all the hallmarks of a vengeful show trial for which the verdict had already been determined.

The accused nobleman was not allowed to exonerate himself. Instead of his accusers being required to prove his guilt, Richard was expected to prove his innocence.[235]

The *familiare* was arrested, and imprisoned in the castle on the rocky mountain overlooking Taormina to the south of Messina.

A number of others were condemned for being directly involved in the conspiracy. Most, like Bartholomew of Parisio, were imprisoned. Walter of Moac demanded trial by combat, and this duel was scheduled.[236]

Henry of Montescaglioso was imprisoned at Reggio in Calabria. Stephen ordered Odo Quarrel to hold him there until he could be taken to Spain. Margaret had decided to send him to the court of her brother, King Sancho, at Pamplona, with a thousand ounces of gold. The plan was for seven galleys under Odo's command to take Henry as far as Arles. From there, the fickle prince could make his way overland to Spain.

In exchange for Gravina, Gilbert requested the affluent County of Loritello. If this discouraged the return of Robert, its exiled holder, so much the better, at least from Gilbert's point of view. Stephen granted this request, which angered the residents of Loritello who had hoped that Robert might one day return to them.

It had been an awful winter. How many more like it could Margaret hope to survive?

Palermo

Margaret's presence in Messina had reminded the people of her power, but this was little more than a bittersweet victory. Now she really did not know who to trust. Like her kindred sovereigns, she was learning that royal authority was tenuous, and dangerous for whoever held it.

The regent found time in early March to grant the Agrò forest to the Most Holy Savior abbey.[237] These lands had belonged to a Greek Orthodox monastery, and the number of such communities was dwindling while those of the Roman Catholics increased. The queen also exempted a monastery from an import tax[238] and ceded the manor of Rahal el Melum Rameth, near Milazzo, to the nunnery of Santa Maria delle Scale[239] of Messina, in the care of Antiochia, its abbess.[240]

Following a visit to inspect Santa Maria delle Scale, where a royal chapel was consecrated, Margaret and her sons left Messina on the twelfth of March. On the way to Palermo, they stopped at a number of coastal towns. The most important was Cefalù, where they were welcomed by the bishop, Boson of Gorron, who very much wanted the bodies of Roger II and William I to be entombed in his cathedral. The royal party arrived at Palermo on the twentieth.

Conspicuously absent from the entourage was Richard of Molise, the *familiare* now imprisoned at Taormina on the other side of the island. Whatever he thought of his fellow *familiare*, Matthew of Aiello, who had spent the winter with the royal party at Messina, had made no effort to defend him. There was a certain logic to this, regardless of the working relationship that had existed between the two men. Quite simply, Matthew now had one less peer with whom to share his power.

We do not know if Margaret had misgivings about Richard's sentence; the evidence against him was flimsy indeed, but she never abjured her contention that he was guilty. She needed an exegesis. More importantly, she needed allies, and if, as Richard claimed, his loyalty to the queen had never faltered, Margaret made a grave error in permitting him to be incarcerated. In choosing not to exercise her authority, she had renounced it. What is more, she alienated a *familiare* who otherwise would have remained one of her most steadfast allies.

Margaret found herself somewhat more isolated than she had already been, even if this reality was not immediately obvious. But she knew that her trial by fire had not yet ended, and she had three more years to serve as regent before William reached the age of majority.

Disloyalty was rampant. The *familiare* Matthew of Aiello, the chamberlain Caïd Richard and Bishop Gentile of Agrigento perceived a changed situation now that Gilbert of Gravina and his large contingent of knights were no longer present to bolster the power of Stephen of Perche, the chancellor. The absence of Richard of Molise, who also commanded some knights, only reinforced their belief that Stephen was underprotected and could now be overthrown.

As usual, there were pretexts for the claim that the chancellor was acting inappropriately. One of the more credible among these was that the Frenchman[241] to whom Stephen had given the Sicilian lands of the late Bonello was mistreating the local people. This allegation bore a grain of truth because only the people classified as serfs, be they Arab or Greek, were obligated to remit the kind of taxes[242] the French baron was collecting.

Deceptively, the complaint painted Matthew, Richard and Gentile as defenders of the populace despite their disdain for the common folk. Unfortunately, in rendering judgment in the matter Stephen relied on the advice of two French counsellors[243] rather than Sicilians knowledgeable in local law.

The traitorous triumvirate wasted no time contemplating an attack on Stephen, conspiring to kill him on Palm Sunday, the Sunday before Easter, which fell at the end of March.[244] Their scheme called for him to be struck down whilst leaving Palermo's cathedral with the royal cortege.[245]

Obviously, the assassination plot required the participation of a certain number of accomplices if it were to be successful. The chief conspirators were adept at stabbing somebody in the back verbally, but the task of doing so literally, with a real sword, was assigned to a professional. In the event, the plan was aborted after several knights involved in it were arrested and divulged some of its details.[246]

For now, Stephen's detractors sought wider support for their cause. One of their tactics presented itself in the reaction of Stephen's counsellors to the French baron's taxation on peasants. Exploiting this, the trio disseminated the rumour that the populace of the entire *Regnum* would soon be subjected to these taxes, which until now were unheard of.

It didn't take long for Stephen to determine the source of these detrimental rumours. He suspected that Matthew of Aiello might be the mastermind of the most recent defamation scheme. Matthew was summoned to court, where he was formally accused of treason. Unable to defend himself against such an accusation, the *familiare*, who was also high notary of the realm, was summarily incarcerated. The chroniclers differ slightly in their assessments of Matthew's character.[247]

The chancellor didn't stop with Matthew of Aiello. Stephen wanted to arrest Caïd Richard, who he felt certain was involved with Aiello in the disinformation campaign that was eroding his prestige.

But here Margaret drew the line, forbidding the arrest of

the palace chamberlain.[248] The most that Stephen achieved was having Richard confined to the palace and prohibited from communicating with his company of knights.

Daily Life

By 1168, Margaret found herself in the midst of ruling and, for the most part, governing a kingdom of more than two million people.[249] What was a typical day like for the most powerful woman in Europe?

She usually woke up early and attended matins in the palace chapel with her sons and a few ladies of the court. Some days this was followed by liturgy (mass) in the chapel or in one of the nearby churches, such as Mary Magdalene, where two of her sons were buried. Then she would have breakfast. Commoners might consume one or, with luck, two meals per day, but royalty sometimes had three.

During the morning, the queen met in audience with the chancellor, the *familiares,* the bishops, the high justiciars or other courtiers. Except for Stephen of Perche and a few trusted advisors, private meetings were rarely granted. She issued decrees and dictated letters.

The children, meanwhile, studied with their tutors. Margaret saw them again at lunch, which was the main repast of the day.

After lunch, the queen might return to the chamber where she met with the court in the morning. Here she could convoke additional audiences or read the letters which had arrived during the day. By now, it was more likely that William, the young monarch, would be present at some of these meetings.

If she were inclined to visit the Genoard park with her children, or take them to one of the city's souks, she would probably do so in the afternoon.

Margaret had very little free time, but she probably spent it reading. It is probable that her vision was still good. She was in her thirties, rather slender and quite fit.

In the evening the family might have a third meal, something less substantial than lunch. On some evenings Margaret and the children attended vespers. There was time for leisure on Sunday.

The queen and her children might occasionally venture beyond the environs of Palermo, to places that were only a day's ride away, but their stay in Messina for four months was exceptional.

Margaret was rarely alone. She was almost always accompanied by ladies-in-waiting, typically damsels in their twenties, and perhaps a nun or two. We do not know the names of these women, but it is possible that there were youngish Norman or Navarrese cousins among them. Palermo's palace was not merely a royal residence; it was the kingdom's administrative center, and at any time at least a hundred people were there. One encountered guards, chamberlains, notaries, scribes, sundry courtiers and visitors, servants, cooks, tailors and the occasional monk. The staff still included a few eunuchs, but during Margaret's regency the maidens of the harem were relegated to such tasks as weaving.

The royal family's living quarters, as we have seen, were in the Pisan tower, the only tower that has survived *in toto* (if much altered) until our times.

We know of no female advisors in the queen's intimate circle, certainly not by name. Indeed, we have only sparse information to suggest who was in that circle except for counsellors such as Stephen of Perche. However, it seems likely that there were a few female intellectuals among Margaret's close friends. Some may have been slightly older. In this connection, it should be borne in mind that Margaret's contemporary, Henry II of England, was only two years her senior; many of Margaret's royal advisors, like his, were forty or fifty years old. These avuncular figures were a priceless asset.

The extent of a queen's isolation from her people depends on the nature of the kingdom itself, and even the woman's personality. Here it must be remembered that Palermo was one of Europe's largest cities, so Margaret need only stroll a few steps from the palace to meet many of the people she ruled.

Agrigento

It wasn't long before Gentile, the Bishop of Agrigento, realized that the plan to discredit Stephen, and perhaps even kill him, had been foiled. What was worse, the other two conspirators in his malevolent trio had been removed from circulation.[250] Gentile, despite his name, was anything but gentle. So profound was his perfidy that even a local manifestation would satisfy it, if only temporarily.

Gentile was one of the prelates who spent more time in the capital than in his own bishropic. Now he found a reason to justify his presence in Agrigento. Accompanied by a few knights, he headed there covertly, traveling along obscure roads.

There was a reason for such secrecy. Bedevilling as certain prelates were, the queen had come to prefer having the more troublesome bishops in Palermo, where she could keep an eye on them.

The Agrigentans themselves rarely lamented Gentile's prolonged absences. Its timeless Greek temples attested to the city's survival over many long centuries. If the most heinous tyrants of antiquity had failed to break Agrigentan will, the local bishop hardly stood a chance of doing so.

Suppression was not always in Gentile's interest. Early in April of 1168, his strategy consisted chiefly of manipulation. Many of the people in the towns around Agrigento were recent converts from Islam.[251] The ardor of these new Catholics led a good number of them to embrace Christianity just as zealously as they had professed the Muslim faith of their ancestors, and they held bishops in high esteem.

Resorting to the usual tropes, Gentile sought to exploit his flock's confidence in him. He impudently announced that Matthew of Aiello had been imprisoned illegally, and that Stephen of Perche planned to usurp royal authority by marrying Margaret.

In his crazed rantings, the bishop underestimated the Arabs' loyalty to the queen, whilst straining credulity. In Agrigento and the surrounding manors he convinced nobody. Open rebellion was the last thing anybody wanted.

Within days, those at court noted Gentile's absence; perhaps they missed his habitual tirades and chronic gossip. Margaret sent to the bailiff of Agrigento a justiciar[252] bearing an order for the bishop to report to the royal court at once, accompanied by the same justiciar.

Back in Palermo, Gentile faced a hearing. There was no dearth of witnesses to offer evidence against him, and their testimony was unassailable. His treachery exposed, he was held in custody, but the punishment of a prelate was more appropriately handled by the Pope. To that end, the queen sent a letter to Pope Alexander soliciting a response to the situation. Meanwhile, Gentile was escorted to the royal fortress at San Marco d'Alunzio, where he was detained pending a Papal reply.

Any hope of a successful conspiracy or rebellion might have ended with Gentile's arrest. It so happened that troubles in northeastern Sicily began to take on a life of their own, threatening the peace of the entire *Regnum*. Most of this can be attributed to one man, Odo Quarrel.[253]

Messina

Just days after sending Bishop Gentile to San Marco, Stephen had to contend with problems created by Odo. It may be recalled that Odo Quarrel was supposed to accompany Henry of Montescaglioso, Margaret's bothersome brother, to France.

The chancellor was annoyed to learn that his assistant was still in Messina long after he was scheduled to depart. Knowing something of Odo's avarice, Stephen hastily dispatched a letter tactlessly ordering him to set sail within three days, telling him to forget exploiting Messina for his own gain.

Odo had embarked on a scheme to exact his own tax from ships leaving Messina, or simply passing through its straits, on the way to the Holy Land. This was tantamount to extortion, and it enraged the Messinians, as well as the merchants. But the abuses didn't end with Odo himself.

Some of his French companions, who were given to getting drunk as they wandered aimlessly through the city's streets, entered a gaming house and began to insult the men gambling there. At first the gamblers, fearing reprisal from the chancellor if they responded to the aggressors, tolerated the unprovoked abuse. Finally, unable to further endure the pejorative words of the foreigners, they beat the men.

When news of this incident reached Odo's ears, he summoned Andrew, the city's governor, and demanded that the gamblers be apprehended immediately and brought to him. Andrew demurred, suggesting that any punishment be delayed until the local populace was more tranquil; he explained that in recent weeks the Messinians had been growing restless as the result of rumours, so it might be imprudent to arrest the gamblers at this moment. Seeking a conciliatory tone, the governor stopped short of excoriating Odo. Vilifying the chancellor's assistant directly would hardly be politic; indeed, it could have dire consequences. For now, comity and appeasement might be more effective than bitter words. Having witnessed, just months earlier, the demise of his predecessor, Richard of Aversa, Andrew thought it possible to catch more flies with honey than with vinegar.

Odo's approach, on the other hand, was to swat any fly that crossed his path. Known for his intolerance and short temper, the haughty mandarin bristled that the supposed influence of peasants did not concern him. The prosecution of these men would serve as a deterrent for others.

Given no choice, Andrew went to the house where the altercation had transpired. The crowd of men gathered there had no intention of being scolded. They began to assault the governor, who quickly mounted his horse and fled amidst a flurry of stones being hurled at him.

The Messinian gamblers and their friends were speakers of Greek. The "Latins" of the city, along with foreign merchants who were there on business, had other grievances, such as Odo's tax on shipping. These men incited the Greeks, saying, among other things, that Queen Margaret had married Stephen of Perche, and that young King William was in danger, if indeed he was not already dead. The governor and his judges were reluctant to enforce order for fear of provoking a general riot.

Within days, news of the unrest engulfing Messina and its purlieus reached Margaret back in Palermo.

Before pandemonium ensued, the queen took the uncommon step of composing a letter to be read publicly at Messina. Issued jointly in her name and that of her son, the king, it sought to assuage the Messinians' fears, exhorting the people to remain loyal to the sovereign and his officers. It explained the reasoning behind the recent decisions against Bishop Gentile, Caïd Richard and Matthew of Aiello, and how Stephen ensured that the three conspirators were not punished too harshly despite the gravity of their treason. Margaret's missive was not intended to prompt panegyrics for the queen or her chancellor; it was only meant to placate the vast swath of society that was getting ready to rebel against royal authority. The final passage reassured the people that Queen Margaret and King William were well and unharmed.

Unfortunately, nobody but the governor and his judges (and Hugh Falcandus) ever learned the contents of the royal letter.

Andrew called the people together at the new cathedral. Here, as the governor procrastinated reading the letter aloud, rumours circulated among the crowd. Existing falsehoods were embellished and new ones were created. By the time Andrew finally began to read the letter, his voice was drowned out, lost in a sea of shouts and screams. The unruly horde had been carried away by a wave of imaginative lies: Stephen of Perche had been crowned king; William was dead, his younger brother besieged at Palermo's seaside castle; Geoffrey, the brother of Stephen of Perche, was coming to Sicily to marry Constance, the young daughter of King Roger II, and rule in her name.

Finally, a self-appointed leader enjoined the people to assassinate Odo Quarrel, suggesting that they then liberate the queen's brother, Henry of Montescaglioso, who, the man said, had always been benevolent to the Messinians. Andrew, whose purview it was to maintain order, implored the mad mob to abandon these ideas, but his words went unheeded.

Wasting not a moment, the people assaulted Odo's house, which was adjacent to the royal palace. This initial attack failed, and Odo managed to escape to the palace, which an angry crowd surrounded once it became known that he was inside.

At the harbor, some of the people armed themselves, commandeered seven galleys, boarded the ships and crossed the strait to Calabria, where the royal chamberlain[254] permitted the Messinians to enter the gates of Reggio. There a local crowd escorted them to the fortress where Henry was imprisoned.

The knights guarding this castle attempted to defend it by tossing stones upon the intruders, who nonetheless persisted in demanding that Henry be freed. The knights refused, declaring that they would hand the prisoner over to the Messinians only if ordered to do so by a competent authority. The rebels accepted this proposal, crossed back to Messina, and returned with James the Innkeeper, the man who the chancellor had sent to outfit the galleys that were to take Henry to France. The knights were expecting a judge, if not the governor himself; at the same time, there was only enough food in the castle to last three days. They reluctantly acceded to the Messinians' demand.

As soon as Henry of Montescaglioso was freed, he crossed over to Sicily, where he was acclaimed by the Messinians.

The revolution had begun.

Chapter 14
PALIMPSEST

"No one provokes me with impunity."

— Mary, Queen of Scots

A few days were to pass before detailed reports of the most recent events at Messina arrived at the court in Palermo during the middle of April 1168.[255] For now, Henry of Montescaglioso had seized control of one of Europe's most important cities, a key to shipping and a gateway to the eastern Mediterranean. Ironically, the Messinians were not supporting Henry out of affinity for him so much as the belief that he was their best hope of supporting the monarchy which they believed had been threatened. The unsubstantiated rumours of the young king's death led the people to embrace his uncle.[256]

Odo's Demise

The people wanted odious Odo Quarrel, dead or alive. For the moment, he was still in the royal palace near the sea. The castellan responsible for protecting the palace was reluctant to turn him over to an angry horde, but he cooperated with Henry, who sent a squad of men with a notary to take an inventory of Odo's possessions, and especially the money he had accumulated from his illegal tax.

At this point Odo was taken into custody. During the night he was removed from the palace, placed on a boat, and transported to the old seaside castle[257] near the harbor, where he was imprisoned. The more astute Messinians suspected that Henry was protecting Odo to ensure that the corrupt cleric, being the assistant and close friend of the chancellor, might intervene on the rebels' behalf with the royal court, whoever was running it. At the very least, as a hostage Odo would make an effective bargaining chip in the negotiations Henry envisaged with Margaret.

The best way to avoid this, the leaders of the avenging mob reasoned, was simply to eliminate Odo, but nobody said anything about killing him.

Instead, the throng demanded that Henry consign Odo to them for corporal punishment. Here they made mention of the grave offenses the treacherous man had perpetrated against the monarch he served, and against the people of Messina. Reluctant as he was to comply with this request, Henry thought it impolitic to defy the popular sentiment of people whose support he may yet need.

Odo had already been divested of his money and precious gems, so no harm was seen in placating public desires.

Therefore, the queen's half-brother permitted the mob to attach the tyrant's feet to a sturdy donkey that then dragged him naked down the streets. Some scraped skin, along with a few superficial bruises inflicted by a mild cudgelling, would ensure that Odo emerged from the experience chastened but essentially unscathed. This scenario, terrible as it is to the modern mind, was not altogether unorthodox in the twelfth century. Following the macabre spectacle, Henry intended to throw the man into prison. The premise in this reprisal was that a generous dose of humiliation might serve Odo well.

Henry was expecting little more than a token gesture that would satiate the public appetite for justice.

But that is not what was delivered. The queen's half-brother had neglected to recognize the fact that he was witnessing the excessive response of an unruly crowd, not a sentence, however harsh, meted out by a justiciar and supervised by guards.

Before long, Odo was stabbed to death. Then his body was chopped into pieces. His head was placed at the end of a lance and paraded along the city streets. It was this savage spectacle that set the stage for what was to come.

Seized by an uncommon furor, the Messinians began running amok, killing any men they could find in the city who hailed from beyond the Alps. In this they were motivated in large measure by a loathing for French knights like those who had arrived with Odo Quarrel and harassed the gamblers a few days earlier. Even here, the splenetic mob's frenzy was misdirected, for there were many German, French and English merchants and pilgrims in Messina who had nothing to do with Odo of Quarrel or the chancellor he had served.

Henry put an abrupt end to this wanton violence by announcing that anybody who committed murder would be tried and summarily punished. Clearly, there was a method to Henry's madness. Indeed, he was not mad at all.

Military Operations

Undaunted, Margaret considered a response to the burgeoning rebellion led by her half-brother. She was told that a number of knights could be mustered hastily from Palermo and some towns to the east. They could be sent along the Tyrrhenian coast toward Messina. Even though the April rains might hamper the knights' advance somewhat, it was fortunate that these coastal roads had been widened and repaired on the chancellor's orders the previous autumn.

The immediate problem was a question of numbers. At the very least, the size of such a force would have to be sufficient to dissuade the Messinians from rebelling further. For this a full-fledged army was required, and that would take time.

Henry's advisors surmised the royal court's reaction, even if they suspected that King William himself might be dead. They had to defend the areas to the west of Messina, and for that they needed Rometta.[258] This fortified city straddling the Peloritan Mountains overlooked the Tyrrhenian coast near Milazzo, where there was a seaside castle. Controlling it was a paramount strategic necessity because any troops arriving by land from Palermo had to pass through this area.

Rometta had no baron; it was a royal town where the castellan guarded a small fortress. Most of the inhabitants were speakers of Greek. A few promises[259] were sufficient to dislodge the castellan, and the Messinians left a small garrison at Rometta's castle. The next operation would be far more onerous.

Its objective was Taormina, where Richard of Molise was imprisoned in a castle atop a rocky mountain overlooking the Ionian Sea far below. The town was famously impregnable, being one of the last strongholds in Sicily to fall to the Normans during the previous century.[260] Bearing this reality in mind, Henry led an army of Messinian knights and archers to Taormina as furtively as he could, along obscure mountain passes.

The element of surprise worked to the attackers' advantage, and the town was subdued with minimal effort. The problem was the fortress; here their efforts were repulsed.

Like Rometta, this was a royal town. Matthew, the castellan, defiantly refused to relinquish his prisoner. He could not be enticed, bribed or intimidated. But perhaps he could be persuaded.

Exasperated, Henry sent the brother of Matthew's wife with entreaties. This man begged the castellan, his brother-in-law, to release the prisoner, saying that he should think of the lives of his sister, nieces and nephews, who were being held hostage in Messina pending Richard's release. Matthew was unmoved, responding that, as a question of honour, he would not capitulate, even if the cost of refusal was his own life or that of his sister.

Matthew's brother-in-law finally took another approach. He persuaded the jailer, with whom he was acquainted, to free Richard while Matthew was asleep. This led to a skirmish and the death of the castellan. With this, Henry's forces took the castle.

Henry of Montescaglioso and Richard of Molise now controlled a strategic chunk of Sicily. Significantly, the northeastern region was the gateway to the peninsular part of the *Regnum*.

The two men had never been very fond of each other, but politics makes strange bedfellows.[261] Margaret's half-brother had always been troublesome, even disloyal. Richard, on the other hand, had been imprisoned following a trial motivated by little more than envy; his loyalty to Margaret had never wavered, and he probably did not deserve the fate that befell him.[262]

Henry and Richard might share doubts about Margaret's wisdom in acquiescing to their imprisonment, but this was overshadowed by their visceral hatred of Gilbert of Gravina and Stephen of Perche.

Back in Palermo, Stephen was alarmed at the fall of Taormina and the release of Richard of Molise, a competent warrior. An immediate response was necessary, but this was not forthcoming with any urgency, for there was an unforeseen impediment at court.

One of the figures at larger European courts, such as Sicily's, was the astrologer, something of a cross between a sorcerer and an astronomer. The most sophisticated among them came from the Muslim lands, and in Palermo astrologers were probably part of the Arabs' *dar al-hikma,* or "house of wisdom," a secular place of learning. The study of astrology found its way into other fields, such as meteorology and agriculture.

One of the era's better known astrologers was Adelard of Bath, who visited Sicily and then introduced the Muslims' knowledge of astronomy and geometry to England, where he served as the tutor of a young Henry II.[263]

Not surprisingly, there were astrologers among William's teachers.[264] Peter of Blois, the chief tutor, did not object to the young king learning about the zodiac, the stars, comets, eclipses and the phases of the moon, and neither did Margaret. The boy was developing a serious interest in astrology, and it was indeed considered a science in the twelfth century, when it was distinguished from astronomy little more than alchemy was differentiated from chemistry. Seen in its best light, astrology was usually thought to complement religion rather than contradict it.

Was Margaret herself very interested in astrology? Probably not. But her son, who was present at ever more meetings, was growing obsessed with it. Therefore, it was not surprising that the young monarch turned to astrologers to determine a good time to attack the rebels in Messina.[265]

Here the queen was left with little choice. Even if she thought the horoscope useless, by mitigating the influence of the court astrologers she would be casting doubts upon their legitimacy. Worse, she would be seen to be contradicting, even chastising, her son before the eyes of his subjects. This may explain why she did not act, but her indolence delayed action when every passing day was crucial. The result was grave inefficiency at a moment when nothing short of a timely response would suffice.

The *Regnum* risked a civil war.

If Stephen of Perche could not immediately attack Henry and Richard, he would attempt to cripple them logistically. Because the rocky hills around Messina yielded little grain, the city's ravenous demand was usually satisfied with wheat from Calabria; that source was not viable this year because the region had suffered a preternaturally meager harvest the previous autumn. Knowing this, the chancellor cut off the supplies from Catania, whose plains produced plenty of grain.

Requiring a large army, the chancellor sought allies on the island to participate in the postponed military attack. The Lombard towns[266] expressed their unequivocal support for the queen. Between knights, footmen and archers, these communities alone could raise an army twenty thousand strong.[267] These loyal subjects encouraged Stephen to act soon, and he assured them that a day had been chosen to march on Messina. He did not mention that the day had been selected by astrologers.

Henry and Richard were more than capable of leading an army. Killing was their stock in trade. By now, they may have known that William and Margaret were alive and well. If so, the fact did not dissuade them. What they really wanted was to topple Stephen of Perche from his lofty perch. Then they would deal with Gilbert of Gravina.

With the widening dissent, Roger of Gerace, one of the barons who had conspired with Bishop Gentile of Agrigento but escaped notice, saw an opportunity to further his interests. To that end, he rode to Cefalù to solicit the support of Boson, its bishop, who controlled the royal city on the Tyrrhenian coast and was known to be one of Stephen's critics. Although Boson was, in principle, amenable to supporting the Messinians, there was little he could offer them materially, for the chancellor had already stationed a garrison of knights in the mountaintop citadel that overlooked the cathedral and town.

From this vantage point, it was possible for sentinels to guard the coast for many miles; on a clear day one could see the volcanic Aeolian Islands to the northeast.

This made it obvious to the insurgents that the mobilization of troops to be used against them was proceeding, however sluggishly. Rapid as the rebels' advance had been thus far, its success was by no means assured. Fortunately for Henry and Richard, some allies of like mind were working toward the same objective on another front.

Crown Immunity

Like Richard of Molise, the *familiare* Matthew of Aiello had been imprisoned following a trial on the basis of sketchy evidence. Were both arrests no more than a ploy by Stephen of Perche to eliminate the two men most likely to challenge his authority? This we shall never know.[268]

What emerges from the scant facts known to us is the distinct possibility that, as chancellor, Stephen of Perche was occasionally overzealous, even unwise, inclined to paint several men with the same scornful brush. Whilst Margaret's capricious half-brother merited discipline for his treason, the *familiares* had never shown themselves to be overtly disloyal, nor had they ever confessed to their purported guilt. Had Stephen succumbed to hubris? Some thought so.

The rebels' hatred was never targeted directly at Margaret except through surreptitious rumours. Perhaps they viewed the queen as a victim of Stephen's thirst for power. Of course, Henry, Richard and Matthew wanted to slake some ambitions of their own; they sought control. Apart from that, however, there was no common thread running through the motivations of Stephen's detractors. The men shared no philosophy or political view significant enough for the chroniclers to record. They were, quite simply, European Christian men of their time. That they resented the presence of somebody they viewed as a usurper of their perceived birthrights reflected little more than nastiness nurtured in the depths of the mind.

"The queen can do no wrong." Crown immunity is a modern legal concept rooted in medieval practice. It was one of the fundamental principles underpinning the lengthy reign of England's Queen Victoria, and the even longer reign of Britain's next queen regnant, Elizabeth II. Another legal doctrine that survives in England is appointment, dismissal or even incarceration "at the queen's pleasure." In the Kingdom of Sicily this principle was enshrined in the Assizes of Ariano, which confirmed royal authority as the ultimate law of the realm. This idea had existed long before the twelfth century; no medieval monarch of Europe ruled without it, and there is nothing to suggest that Margaret ever abused her reginal rights.

Margaret and the young king were unimpugnable, indeed untouchable. They were not simply "above the law." They themselves were the final arbiters of the law. Anybody brazen enough to openly defame the monarch or regent risked permanent incarceration, even death.

The rebels knew this. It was a sacrosanct fact of life, and it meant that any maneuvering against the chancellor would have to result in a "surgical strike" against him, and against him only, were it to bear fruit. This was not just a question of law. A handful of knights and barons could not hope to control a city the size of Palermo if things turned violent. The loyalty of the people was, first and foremost, to the sovereign; Bonello's revolt had shown the bedlam that could break out when the populace rebelled against the rebels.

As a purely military operation could be haphazard, the rebels resorted to trickery within the palace walls, where Matthew of Aiello was being held prisoner.

Matthew's incarceration was something more akin to "house arrest" than conventional captivity. His imprisonment in the royal palace did not confine him to a jail; indeed, the palace dungeon no longer served that purpose. Since the deposed *familiare* was not isolated, he communicated with people in the palace. In this way, he learnt of the revolts in northeastern Sicily and the recent transfer of some men in Stephen's elite corps of bodyguards to Cefalù and other strategic towns.

It so happened that the royal castellan, Ansaldo, a close ally of Stephen of Perche, was absent from his post, confined by illness to a high floor in another tower of the palace. This gave Matthew an opportunity to convince the man's colleague, Constantine, to enlist the majority of the palace personnel to assassinate the chancellor on an appointed day.[269] The plan was for them to attack Stephen and the two close associates, Roger of Avellino and John of Lavardin, who arrived with him most mornings at a certain gate.[270]

The threshold of the palace, at least in theory, was a kind of Rubicon; within its walls no visitors, not even knights, were allowed to carry swords and daggers.[271]

As there were, in total, some four hundred men between servants and guards, this diabolical strategy stood a good chance of success.[272]

Opportunism was rife in Palermo, where it took very little for some greedy ruffians in the Kasr district near the palace and cathedral to agree among themselves to attack whichever faction seemed more likely to be overpowered once the expected fighting began. Ideally, from their warped point of view, this would be Stephen, whose death would permit the criminals to pillage the wealth of gold they thought was kept in his house.

Umpteenth Plot

Stephen suspected that something was afoot; there usually was. Ansaldo confirmed that there was a plot against the chancellor, and that a large number seemed to be involved thus far. Stephen's life was in danger. The castellan went on to counsel his friend to go to a fortified town of the hinterland that he could use as a base. From such a place, he could summon the troops he needed from the Lombard[273] towns and any other localities where the fealty of the populace had not yet been compromised.

Ansaldo suggested that Stephen depart the capital immediately, paying no heed to the date established by the astrologers to march on the enemy. In this way, he could assemble a force without delay. Then the young king could join him.

Was Margaret's presence presumed? Probably.

Ansaldo's plan was essentially sound, but Stephen of Perche did not follow through on it. Instead, he took the advice of some of his French knights, and particularly that of Robert of Meulan.[274] These men advised him against leaving the king in Palermo, believing the capital to be safe. The fundamental flaw in this counsel was that these men-at-arms, being foreigners, had no idea of the degree to which the Palermitans were capable of conspiring. Many secrets lurked in the shadows cast by the palace walls.

The day finally dawned for the attack planned on Stephen. That morning found a few of the murderous servants waiting just inside the gate the chancellor usually entered. Upon arriving, Stephen was expected to step through with two or three trusted associates, leaving his company of armed knights outside the wall.

But this morning he did not arrive.

Somehow, Odo, the master equerry, the man responsible for the horses stabled within the palace's curtain wall, had found out about the plan. Early in the morning he went to Stephen's house to alert him.

Having been warned of the plot, the chancellor dismissed

the knights waiting outside his house to escort him to the palace. Several of his friends remained with him.

As soon as he learnt of this, Constantine, the traitorous assistant of the palace castellan, ignited a rebellion by sending a large number of servants into the city with orders to incite the populace against the chancellor. Claiming that Stephen was about to abscond from Palermo by sea with chests of gold belonging to the king, the servants goaded the citizens into taking up arms and encircling Stephen's house.

Nearby, Hervé "the Florid," who was resented not for his loyalty to Stephen but because he was a braggart, and Roger of Avellino were trotting their horses outside the palace. A large mob attacked the two. Hervé was struck off his horse and stabbed to death with swords. Roger rode into the flat area south of the city gate at the edge of the Genoard.[275] Here the crowd was about to assault him with lances when King William, who had heard the noise, suddenly appeared at a window and ordered the people to desist, threatening them with punishment if Roger was harmed.

The events unfolded with an uncommon fury as a frail decorum devolved into chaos. Partaking in the rebellion were the chancellor's most vociferous critics, whose steady stream of gossipy propaganda spurred hundreds of ordinary Palermitans to join them just as the rabid Messinians had acted against Odo Quarrel. The stark difference was that Odo's sins were real, whilst most of those attributed to Stephen had been crafted by fabulists animated by vested interests to remove him from power, by force if necessary. The chancellor's denouement, the rebels hoped, would be fast and fierce.

From a tower window, Margaret could see the violence enveloping the Kasr district. Fearing the worst should the insurrection sweeping the city go unchecked, she ordered Roger of Avellino to be taken to the seaside castle in the Kala, where he could be protected and assist in its defense.

Meanwhile, the crowd at Stephen's house was growing larger by the minute. Among these people were the royal longbow archers who, Falcandus tells us, were never the last to arrive at riots when there was any chance for lucre to be had.[276]

Stephen had left the protection of his residence to Simon of Poitiers. This man-at-arms placed knights and foot men around the perimeter of the house's wall, but the crowd's sudden onslaught threatened to overwhelm them.

Seeing that the situation was critical, the chancellor moved quickly to escape with a few trusted friends[277] into the bell tower of the church adjacent to his house, along with several other French knights. Amongst them was Robert of Meulan, who just a few days earlier had advised Stephen to remain in Palermo because a revolt in the city seemed unlikely. Overconfident Robert might live to eat his presumptuous words, but first he had to survive the present peril. It was turning into a long day.

To better see what was happening, Margaret ascended the steps along a narrow passage to the roof of the Pisan Tower. Much of her view of the streets below was blocked by the low buildings.[278] But she could see the bell tower where Stephen and his companions had taken refuge, and the scene didn't look good.

William was with his mother. The young king was learning firsthand the form a rebellion could take in a large city. It was a sober lesson in the reality of ruling a kingdom.

Accompanied by a brave company of knights, Roger of Tiron, the high constable, made his way to the bell tower and assailed the most aggressive attackers.[279] But he and his men were overwhelmed by the onslaught of the armed mob and forced to retreat.

Meanwhile, the mob attacked Stephen's house even more truculently than before. The knights besieged within its walls fought back just as ferociously.

With the collapse of public order, Matthew of Aiello and Caïd Richard were able to leave the palace unopposed. The pair ordered the servant musicians to go sound horns and drums outside the chancellor's house. Summoning the people to battle in this way was a royal prerogative, so another segment of the populace, consisting of Muslims as well as Christians, assuming that the signal had been given on the queen's orders, arrived to reinforce the assault.

Margaret and William could see that the violence was concentrated in the area around Stephen's house and the church next to it. The palace, though by now largely abandoned by the guards, was not under attack. What the queen and her son were witnessing was unchecked street fighting on an unprecedented scale. Numbering fewer than a hundred, the loyal knights did their best to defend the chancellor and themselves against thousands.

The fighting at the house was intense, but in the end the edifice was overrun by rioters who gained entrance to it through a passage from the church next door. This led to the knights at the house being taken prisoner by rebels led by Constantine, the disloyal castellan who had instigated the disorder in the first place.

With the chancellor's house finally taken, the crowd could focus its efforts on the bell tower, where Stephen and his company continued to defend themselves. Having reached an impasse, the rioters began to consider ways to overcome the resistance, perhaps by building a siege engine to attack the tower, or simply by piling wood and igniting a fire whose heat would force the structure's porous bricks to crumble.

Margaret was now desperate. She wanted the people to desist. Something had to be done, and right now.

Not without grave misgivings, the queen proposed that she and William leave the palace to go speak to the people. Matthew of Aiello forestalled this, explaining that all the arrows and stones flying about made an unannounced public appearance too risky.[280] His words were not devoid of reason, for safety was indeed a factor to consider; Margaret remembered how an earlier revolt had claimed the life of one of her sons. Nonetheless, Matthew's words conveniently camouflaged the fact that the young king's presence would almost certainly convince the Palermitans to cease the hostilities, which were initiated earlier in the day on the pretext of a royal order.

Margaret did not yet know how the revolt had begun, but she had her own suspicions about who instigated it, and she saw the violent results.

By the end of the afternoon, the conspirators were beginning to succumb to some fears of their own. A problem appeared just as the sun began to disappear behind the rugged mountains to the south of the city. The crowd was likely to disperse at dusk, with no guarantee that even a few of the fickle Palermitans would remain to prevent the chancellor and his knights escaping in the darkness. Short of imprisoning Margaret and her sons, it would be impossible to prevent the young king from emerging to address his subjects the next day; indeed, the people might even demand it, just as they did during Bonello's revolt years earlier.

All along, the rebels' objective had been to eliminate Stephen of Perche, yet they had failed to overpower him. In seeking to checkmate their nemesis, they had achieved nothing more than a sour stalemate. It was time to negotiate. This was done in the king's name, if not with his willing consent.

In the haggard twilight, the voice of reason emerged from the smouldering embers.

If he agreed to leave, Stephen would be guaranteed safe conduct out of the realm. He and the men who had come with him from France would be supplied armed galleys to take them to whatever land they wished, and the Sicilian barons with him in the tower could retain their estates in the *Regnum*. Stephen's mercenary knights were given the choice of continuing their service to the king or accepting passage to a place of their choosing. These terms were accepted. The deposed chancellor and a small company would sail to Jerusalem[281] via Constantinople.

Caïd Richard, Matthew of Aiello, Richard Palmer, John of Malta and Romuald of Salerno jointly gave their word that the conditions of the agreement would be respected. The next morning, after bidding his cousin a sad farewell, Stephen renounced his status as Palermo's archbishop-elect and boarded his galley, setting sail on a westward course around Sicily. The only encumbrance proved to be a problem with his galley that forced him to purchase another vessel at Licata. Before long he was in the Holy Land.

Queen's Counsel

Stephen's departure left Margaret melancholy, but she had little time to dwell on her sorrow. She needed solid advice. Unfortunately, it was not forthcoming from any quarter except, perhaps, the feckless astrologers or a handful of sycophants. Having placed so much faith in one man, the queen had alienated some who otherwise might have been more willing to take up her cause. Peter of Blois, the royal tutor, was a worthy confidant, but he had left shortly after his friend Stephen.

A few days after Stephen of Perche departed, Henry of Montescaglioso arrived in Palermo's harbor with a score of armed galleys. Accompanying him were Bishop Gentile of Agrigento, who he had freed from San Marco d'Alunzio, and his ally Richard of Molise.

Margaret was anything but gratified to see these three again. Most of all, she abhorred seeing her half-brother.

The queen was coerced into appointing a number of *familiares*. The list included the notary Matthew of Aiello, the archdeacon (and royal tutor) Walter, Caïd Richard, Bishop Gentile of Agrigento, Richard Palmer, Bishop John of Malta, Archbishop Romuald of Salerno, Roger of Gerace, Richard of Molise and, worst of all, Henry of Montescaglioso. The only consolation in having ten headaches instead of two or three was that they might fight enough among themselves to permit Margaret to serve as an effective referee. The doctrine of *divide et impera* would serve her well.

Collectively, these *familiares* represented the most important elements of the ruling class, namely the baronage, the bureaucrats and the clergy. In principle, this might provide political stability.

A certain faction of historians has taken to referring to this expanded group of *familiares* as a "council of regency," a characterization predicated on the belief that the queen's authority suddenly evaporated under the torrid Sicilian sun. There is a morsel of truth in this. However, it was rare for more than four or five of these men to be present at court at the same time.[282] Margaret was still the nexus of power in the Kingdom of Sicily.

A complementary theory, little explored until now, is that the effect of the "council," whatever its initial intent, was to give a voice to the baronage. Here, arguably, we see the first seeds of representative government, which eventually took root at the end of the next century with Sicily's first parliament.[283] Although it cannot be compared to England's *Magna Carta*, which was a formal charter of baronial rights, the "council" certainly gave the nobles a greater influence at court than they otherwise could have expected.[284]

In the other great Norman realm, King Henry's Assize of Clarendon introduced certain rights that, in a perfect world, could redress perceived injustice of the kind claimed by Sicily's rebellious baronial element. Trial by jury, novel disseisin and other elements of what came to form the foundation of common law[285] might well have been instituted in Sicily. This may have obviated the very premise of some complaints because it is quite likely, based on what little we know, that Matthew of Aiello and Richard of Molise would not have been found guilty had their cases been heard by a competent jury.

Continuously forced to respond to immediate challenges to her authority, Margaret had little time to address fundamental legal questions. Even if she did, some subjects might well have questioned her prerogative, as regent, to bring about substantial changes in her son's name. At all events, if it became known that certain principles of a hypothetical Sicilian common law were indeed inspired by notions derived from the Maliki School, as a few modern juridical scholars[286] have suggested, the more bigoted Christians would have resented the statutes for their Islamic origin. By the time Margaret became regent, there weren't even many erudite scholars left at court to advocate for new laws.

Apart from the crisis that saw the expulsion of Stephen of Perche, grave as it was, there was very little to stimulate the queen to effect sweeping additions to the existing law. Unlike the English king, whose actions were motivated in part by a jurisdictional "turf war" with the Catholic Church, Margaret's relationship with the Papacy was consolidated by such things as the apostolic legateship. For now, the Assizes of Ariano[287] would have to suffice, and Margaret would have to endure an expanded cadre of *familiares*.

The first act of the newly-appointed *familiares* was to expel Gilbert of Gravina (and Loritello) from the *Regnum*. Sensing that she had no choice, Margaret agreed to this, however reluctantly.[288]

She drew the line at their request to attaint or exile Hugh of Catanzaro, a kinsman of Stephen of Perche.[289]

Falcandus tells us that the *familiares* relented for two reasons. On the one hand, Hugh was violent and unpredictable, and therefore capable of waging an insurgency against them; on the other, the *familiares* wished to mitigate the queen's anger.[290]

Apart from Margaret's feelings and Hugh's belligerent temperament, the *familiares* had good reason to fear the Count of Catanzaro. Unlike Stephen's other companions, who had few ties to the Kingdom of Sicily, Hugh had a link to it that was worth fighting for. The large chunk of Calabria he controlled was held by right of his wife, the heiress Clementia, who once flirted with Matthew Bonello. Hugh had enough resources, and enough support from the Calabrian baronage loyal to his wife's family, to raise a formidable army of his own.

After the first few chaotic months, the power of the *familiares* was more like a placid pond than a raging river. But even a docile lake can be dangerous for those unable to swim. Fortunately, Margaret knew how to survive in perilous waters, and she refused to let herself drown in her own tears.

As individuals, some of the *familiares* wielded considerable influence at court. Matthew of Aiello ensured that John, his brother, was consecrated Bishop of Catania as planned. This took place in July.[291]

The queen restored to Richard of Molise the prosperous lands he had held until his imprisonment.

Henry of Montescaglioso was finally granted his wish for more territory when he was invested with the Principate, a large county that included territories around such cities as Salerno and Avellino. The queen reasoned that this concession, ludicrously generous as it was, would keep her half-brother far away from the royal court. Margaret's only modicum of satisfaction in this gesture came the moment Henry made submission by kneeling before her and William to swear fealty to the monarch.

The *familiare* Walter, archdeacon of Cefalù, had no hope of being consecrated bishop of that diocese so long as Bishop Boson[292] was alive, and he was hardly content to serve exclusively as rector of the palace chapel. Almost as soon as Stephen had left the *Regnum,* overbearing Walter began seeking supporters who might endorse his appointment as Archbishop of Palermo. He reassumed the role of royal tutor held until recently by Peter of Blois, soon emerging as the most important *familiare*.

By the autumn, exiled Robert of Loritello learnt of recent events. For months, he had been sending Margaret letters requesting that she lift his exile. Reasoning that he might reclaim his old manor now that Gilbert of Gravina was no longer in the *Regnum,* he began sending insistent letters to the regent asking for it back. Margaret had to think about this.

She was busy dispatching correspondence of her own, to such people as Thomas Becket, who had sent letters to the queen[293] and to her chancellor[294] thanking them for providing hospitality to his nephews.

Not surprisingly, Richard Palmer corresponded with his countryman. Ostensibly acting on behalf of the King of France but perhaps at Margaret's urging, the Archbishop of Canterbury asked Richard to intervene to recall Stephen of Perche to Sicily.[295] Richard, of course, wished to keep Stephen as far away as he could.

By the end of 1168, a certain calm had been restored to the kingdom. Margaret's authority had diminished slightly, but hers was still the most powerful voice in the *Regnum*.

Chapter 15
LEADERSHIP

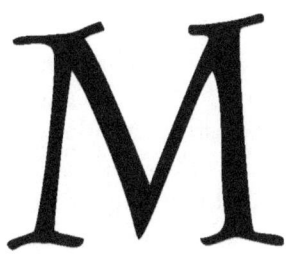

"Throw me to the wolves and tomorrow I'll return leading the pack."

— Anonymous

One of the differences between a she-wolf and her male counterpart is that the female is more inclined to defend her pups. In Margaret we find that rarity of rarities, the alpha female, ready and willing to lead the pack. By early 1169, it was clear that this would be a solitary duty. The queen regent found herself without familial peers to assist her.

Of course, she was capable of taking decisions on her own. She decided to permit Robert of Loritello, her son's distant cousin, to return from exile; this might bring him into her camp. Other problems were more complex.

In the wake of the resignation and departure of Stephen of Perche, the chancellorship was not filled and the archbishopric of Palermo was vacant. The queen's failure to make these appointments might elicit subtle dissent in certain quarters. No matter.

Hoping, however wistfully, that her cousin might someday return and reassume his former post, Margaret saw no immediate need to appoint another chancellor.[296] Not being eager to see the concentration of power in one courtier, the *familiares* voiced no objection to this lacuna.

As the Archbishop of Palermo was, *ex officio,* the Primate of Sicily, a position that brought with it its own privileged place in the kingdom's power structure, the queen, at least for the moment, saw no urgency in advancing any names for it. For now, reticence was a trait that might serve her well.

The taciturn regent would have her way eventually. It would be best for her political detractors not to view her silence to imply consent.

Walter

As the royal tutor, Walter, who was also the rector, or dean, of the palace chapel, spent more time at court than any other *familiare*. He even had a tiny office in the palace. Although he never became chancellor, Walter was, effectively if unofficially, the chief *familiare,* and we find his signature as the first witness in many royal decrees.

Like Stephen, Walter had been sent to Sicily by Margaret's kinsman Rotrou of Rouen. However, having arrived earlier than, and separately from, Stephen and the hated French knights, Walter never came to be closely associated with them in the public mind. Spared the bitter animus directed at them, he was not expelled with the others.

If Walter was related to Margaret or Stephen, it was only through a very distant, tenuous kinship.[297] He may not have been a close friend of Stephen, but neither was he an enemy. In any case, he never defended him with much vigor, and in the end he added his voice to the opposition.

With Stephen of Perche and Peter of Blois gone, Walter

LEADERSHIP

was the best advisor Margaret could expect to find, even if he would never be a trusted confidant. The queen bore the indelible memory of how years earlier, during the revolt that claimed the life of her son, Walter was one of the opportunists who exploited the public sentiment of the moment to advocate the abdication of her husband.

Tireless were his efforts to garner enough support to justify being elected the capital's archbishop. Before long, he renounced his position in the diocese of Cefalù to be appointed archdeacon of Agrigento, a more important see.[298] This suggests a certain amity with Gentile Tuscus, Agrigento's bishop.

Falcandus claims that Walter attempted to gain the appointment as Archbishop of Palermo by paying a violent mob to frighten the local clergy into supporting him. The queen hoped Pope Alexander III would refuse to ratify this election on the grounds that Stephen, having renounced his archiepiscopal status under duress, was still archbishop-elect.

The chronicler contends that Margaret sent Peter of Gaeta, subdeacon of the Papal Curia, seven hundred gold ounces to give the Pope to encourage Rome's support.[299] This account, if truthful, implies that the regent's actions were tantamount to bribery. In this she was not alone, for the baronage, which endorsed Walter, made its own entreaties to the Pontiff, along with a bribe even more substantial than Margaret's.

After contemplating the situation, the Pope decided to confirm the election of Walter who, by February, had already begun to behave as if he were archbishop, witnessing charters with that title and celebrating liturgy in the cathedral.[300]

Pope Alexander kept the gold Margaret had sent him but, seeking to spare her feelings, he delayed sending Walter's charter of appointment to Palermo. Margaret was not happy about losing so much gold in a nugatory effort, but by now she had more urgent matters to address.

Natural Disaster

Early in the morning of the fourth of February a violent earthquake shook eastern Sicily and southern Calabria. Its epicenter was near the city of Catania, which it all but levelled.[301] Some fifteen thousand Catanians perished. Most of the people in Lentini were killed. There was damage from Messina down to Syracuse. Castles crumbled at Modica and other towns, and from Taormina the snow-capped summit of Mount Etna was observed to sink somewhat.[302]

Lending the catastrophe an apocalyptic air was its occurrence during the vigil of the feast of Saint Agatha, Catania's heavenly patroness. The city's cathedral was dedicated to her, and its collapse[303] crushed Bishop John of Aiello, the brother of Matthew the *familiare*, along with forty-five monks inside for matins.

Margaret and her sons made their way to Catania to comfort the people as best they could. Here William spoke publicly in his first official address to his subjects: "Let each of you pray to the God he worships. He who has faith in his God will feel peace in his heart." Such words reflected William's kind disposition to all the Abrahamic faithful he ruled.[304]

Nothing could portend such a catastrophe, let alone explain it. To the medieval mind, a disaster of this magnitude could be nothing less than an act of a wrathful God. Some thought it foretold even worse cataclysms to come. In a letter to Richard Palmer, Peter of Blois expressed the opinion that the earthquake was God's vengeance.[305] According to Falcandus, there were people who believed that Stephen of Perche, said to be at the court of Constantinople, might return, flanked by Robert of Loritello and a faction of the baronage, to take control of the court.

This speculation ended when news arrived that Stephen had died in Jerusalem, where he was buried with full honours in the Templars' chapter house.[306]

With this, Margaret realized there was no purpose to be served in crying over spilt milk. She would have to face her destiny alone.

Generations

Three years earlier, when the Emperor of Constantinople proposed betrothing his daughter to Margaret's son, the queen's reaction was tepid. But that was then. The young king was now fifteen; he would reach the age of majority in two years.

Recent events had shown that he was becoming a decisive young man, intelligent and confident. The time had come to begin the search for an appropriate wife for him.

The Byzantine proposal, interesting as it was, did not appeal to the queen. Her affinity for Norman society prompted her to look toward the northwest. She was not the only one in her family to entertain such a notion.

Alfonso VIII of Castile, the son of her beloved sister Blanca, was making overtures to Henry II of England to marry one of the English king's daughters. Alfonso was the same age as William, but his life thus far had taken a far more cumbersome course.

Margaret's brother-in-law, Sancho III of Castile, died in 1158, just two years after Blanca, leaving young Alfonso as an orphan in the care of what became a succession of Castilian noblemen. Warring factions fought over custody of the young king. It saddened Margaret to learn that her brother, the King of Navarre, exploited this tragedy to seize some border territories that belonged to Alfonso, who was his late sister's son. This included La Rioja, where Margaret and Blanca were born.

As much as Margaret wanted to help her nephew in Castile during the hardships facing him, there was little she could do.

She had hoped that her half-brother, Henry of Montescaglioso, a knight errant by nature, would have returned to Spain with his men, perhaps to end up fighting at young Alfonso's side, but that was not to be.

Out of necessity, Alfonso had come of age and was now ruling a kingdom with the support of some loyal barons who did their best to look after him, advise him and defend his interests. Quarrels among the Castilian baronage and a chronic conflict with Sancho, the King of Navarre, made this a fruitless task. Thoughts of her nephew's destiny tormented Margaret.

Thinking about her son's future, the regent learned that Matilda, one of the daughters of Henry II and Eleanor of Aquitaine, had recently wed the Duke of Saxony. There were two princesses left, and Eleanor, the elder, was not yet eight years old. Despite the girls' tender years, however, it could not hurt to make a discreet inquiry. Margaret wasn't seeking promises, only possibilities.

Golden Rule

For the moment, she had to rule the *Regnum*. This entailed establishing policy when necessary, but more often confirming feudal grants, founding monasteries and, of course, protecting the rights of all the subjects. She had little time to think about those who had left. The eunuch and onetime *familiare* Caïd Peter, for example, was now an admiral in the service of Abu Yaqub Yusuf, the Almohad emir. It will be remembered that once he left Sicily Peter reassumed his original name, Ahmed; to this he had since added the surname *es-Sikeli*, "the Sicilian."

In February, the queen permitted Matthew of Aiello to establish a tax-exempt monastery on his property in Palermo. The salutation of this charter, which is typical of those issued during the regency, refers to "William, benevolent King of

Sicily, Duke of Apulia and Prince of Capua, with Lady Margaret his Queen Mother, resplendent in their great and glorious royal generosity."[307]

Several such charters survive. Another example, dated May 1169, confirms the rights to an abbey in northeastern Sicily formerly granted by John of Aiello, Matthew's brother, the late Bishop of Catania. This monastery, which seems to have been uninhabited by this time, once housed Byzantine monks.[308]

These charters reveal something of the form the court had assumed. Caïd Richard was the master chamberlain, assisted by Caïd Martin, the royal chamberlain. The *familiare* Matthew of Aiello was high notary. Richard of Molise was also present.

Stephen's death removed the last theoretical impediment to Walter's formal appointment as Archbishop of Palermo, and Pope Alexander formalized it by decree in June.[309] Margaret then had to endure attending the petulant prelate's consecration in Palermo's cathedral in late September.[310]

Walter convinced her to appoint his brother, Bartholomew, as a *familiare*, but the archbishop's avarice did not stop there. He also prevailed upon the queen to concede to him the feudal rights of the mills of the manor of *Bur-Ruqqad,* or Brucato, as well as other lands.[311]

Margaret had her own way of reminding pompous Walter that the Kingdom of Sicily wasn't his personal theocracy. This involved adding a layer of power to the court hierarchy. She appointed Matthew of Aiello, the *familiare* and high notary, her vice chancellor. This was a slightly ironic title as there was no high chancellor for him to serve under. Nevertheless, it sent the clear signal that the *Regnum* was a monarchy, not a dictatorship, and that Margaret was still in charge.[312]

By Christmas, Henry II had expressed his consent to the marriage of his youngest daughter, Joanna, to King William. This was not a formal, binding decision, and Joanna was just four years old, so the wedding was still about a decade away, but the English monarch's agreement was a hopeful sign. Without delay, the queen sent ambassadors to discuss the matter with the Pope.

The beginning of 1170 was a good time to think about the year just ended. There was peace and stability in the kingdom, whilst the treasury, the diwan, was as rich as ever. Margaret found Walter and his ilk overbearing, if not downright obnoxious, but she managed to achieve a tolerable coexistence with them. More important than her needs was the necessity of rebuilding Catania and the other localities destroyed during the previous year.

To the north of the kingdom's border, Pope Alexander III spent a good part of his pontificate exiled from the city of Rome, which was a hotbed of unrest rooted in the ambitions of Frederick Barbarossa and the occasional anti-pope. The Pontiff resided instead at Benevento, Gaeta and Anagni. Gifts like the gold he received from Margaret and the Sicilian barons the previous year made this exile bearable.

In January, the Pontiff received as Margaret's ambassadors Robert of Loritello and Richard Palmer, whose brief it was to seek approval for the idea of the marriage of William to Joanna, the youngest daughter of King Henry of England. These emissaries were more reliable than others the queen might have sent; Robert was distant kin to her son and Richard was English by birth.

At England's royal court, like Sicily's, life proceeded unhindered despite political complexities. King Henry's dispute with Thomas Becket, who Pope Alexander supported, had yet to be resolved.

The Sicilians were anything but oblivious to what was transpiring in England, and the matter was doubtless discussed, if only perfunctorily, by the two Sicilian ambassadors and the Pope. It did not impede the negotiations, but Becket himself was displeased, personally offended by what he viewed as disloyalty on the part of the two emissaries, with whom he was familiar, and perhaps even Margaret. In a letter to the Bishop of Ostia he wrote that, "Even the King of Sicily, in whose dominions you live, has been promised the daughter of the King of England if he will join in effecting our ruin."[313]

That criticism was misplaced and simply erroneous. Margaret was merely seeking to secure a marriage for her son. Like many, she hoped for a resolution to a conflict that had already dragged on for years. Thomas Becket further asserted that Richard Palmer was offered the bishopric of Lincoln, as if this were comparable to the importance (and climate) of Syracuse, if he supported King Henry politically and financially.[314] There seems to be no basis for Becket to have believed such a thing; most of the money he mentions would certainly have to come from the treasury of the *Regnum,* and that would require Margaret's approval.

Margaret supported Becket[315] whilst Matthew of Aiello, who was now her vice chancellor, was inclined to endorse King Henry's views. Yet the Kingdom of Sicily took no official position in the dispute, and during the summer of 1170 the Archbishop of Canterbury and the King of England seemed to reach a compromise.

As the months passed, the queen continued the business of running a kingdom. As always, the greater number of decrees she issued in her son's name dealt with feudal and ecclesiastical rights. Typical of these is a charter of October, in which she granted a hermit monk of the Byzantine tradition a small manor and the rights to a mill.[316]

Margaret's improvised strategy of "divide and conquer" was beginning to achieve its desired result. Archbishop Walter viewed Matthew of Aiello as a rival, and their rapport was sometimes difficult. Over time, however, the two men developed a reasonably efficient working relationship.[317]

By the Christmas season of 1170, it seemed as if the marriage agreements of William II to Joanna of England and that of his cousin Alfonso VIII of Castile to her elder sister, Eleanor, would soon be confirmed.

The English monarch hoped to benefit from these unions. Princess Eleanor's marriage to Alfonso would provide Henry more security along the southern border of Aquitaine and other regions he ruled by right of his wife. Joanna's marriage to William would more closely link England, Normandy and Henry's various French lands to the affluent Kingdom of Sicily.

No account was taken of love. Henry's daughters would be expected to embrace the husbands chosen for them, just like Margaret herself had done many years earlier.

For his part, Alfonso wanted support from King Henry, whose lands extended to the Pyrenees, to offset the territorial ambitions of his avaricious uncle, Sancho of Navarre. By surrounding Navarre in this way, the young King of Castile hoped to restrict Sancho's expansion into Castilian territories beyond La Rioja.

Margaret's motives were more nuanced. She had no lofty political or economic objectives in arranging her son's marriage to Henry's daughter, but closer ties with Henry and his dominions on the continent would not be unwelcome.

These incipient wedding plans were torn asunder by an event that occurred in the last days of December.

Thomas Becket had been murdered in Canterbury by four of Henry's knights. In the aftermath of this tragedy, the English sovereign risked becoming a pariah.

Chapter 16
THOMAS BECKET

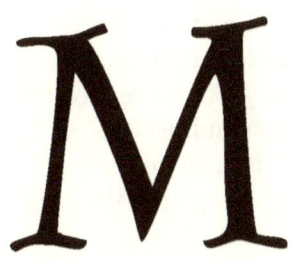

"You can kill a man, but not an idea."

— Benazir Bhutto

He was one of the most influential prelates of his century. In death, if not in life, he came to be admired, and then venerated, across Catholic Europe. His letter[318] to Queen Margaret is the only snippet of her correspondence that survives, but the eloquent epistles of Thomas Becket fill many volumes, painting a punctilious portrait of his personal character and his theological views. No discourse on the concepts of national sovereignty, ecclesiastical authority or the separation of church and state is truly complete without a consideration of the unholy feud between Henry II, King of England, and his onetime friend, Thomas Becket, Archbishop of Canterbury.[319]

Roots

Thomas Becket was born in London on the twenty-first of December, the feast of Saint Thomas the Apostle, probably in 1119, to Gilbert Becket and his wife, Matilda, both of Norman ancestry. Thomas had at least three sisters, namely Mary, Agnes and Rose, but no brothers who survived to adulthood. Gilbert was a prosperous merchant who eventually became a property holder and sometime sheriff.

A wealthy friend of Gilbert Becket was Richard of Aigle, a kinsman of Margaret of Navarre through her mother. Young Thomas went hunting and hawking with this baron, who he came to regard almost as an uncle.

The boy's education began at Merton Priory and continued in London, perhaps at the school of Saint Paul's Cathedral.[320] Being residents of Cheapside, his parents had a connection with this church.

Around the age of twenty, Thomas studied for a year in Paris. By the time he returned, his mother had died and his father's business was suffering. To avoid penury, Thomas made use of his writing skills by earning a living as a clerk, first for a kinsman who was a justiciar, and then for Theobald of Bec, Archbishop of Canterbury. Thomas did not declare a calling to the priesthood, but before long Theobald was sending him on missions to the Papal court. Following these experiences, which must have made an impression on the young man, the archbishop sponsored his education in canon law in Bologna and Auxerre.

Such an education was not unlike that of Stephen of Perche and Peter of Blois. In this social class we find the promising sons of wealthy families destined for scholarly pursuits rather than service as knights, notaries or merchants. These intellectuals were the kind of young men likely to become the advisors of kings and cardinals.

Not only did his sojourn across the channel provide Thomas an exceptional education, it had the benefit of removing him from the strife resulting from the royal succession crisis that has come to be known as the "Anarchy." This civil war between baronial factions supporting one or the other descendant of William the Conqueror to rule England was detrimental to the entire kingdom.

Yet the scholar had to return to his homeland sooner or later, and Theobald, his sponsor, found him a succession of posts in ecclesiastical service. In 1154, the year the "Anarchy" ended with Henry II, at the age of twenty-two, being crowned King of England, Theobald made Thomas the Archdeacon of Canterbury.

Chancellor

However devout he may have been, Thomas still was in no hurry to be ordained a priest, but through his exemplary service to Theobald he became known as a learned and pragmatic man, more thinker than scrivener. In 1155, Theobald recommended him to become the chancellor of King Henry II.

This post involved collecting monies owed the crown, whether from barons or bishops. Thomas performed his duties efficiently, bringing order to the royal accounts. He and the king become good friends, passing much time together hunting and conversing. Thomas was Henry's closest confidant. Being thirteen years the king's senior, he may even have been something of a mentor to him.

Close as they were, the two men had very obviously different mentalities. Henry's lifestyle was austere; he enjoyed simple pleasures. Even his attire was simple, virtually indistinguishable from what any rustic baron wore whilst hunting. A pragmatist, he deplored ceremony for its own sake. Thomas cultivated a slightly more elegant image that reflected his taste for luxury.

The story is told of how Henry sent Thomas ahead of him to Paris in 1158 to negotiate the marriage of the young heir apparent to the daughter of King Louis VII of France. Henry suggested that the chancellor make an effort to impress the French.

Taking this recommendation to heart, yet relishing the task, Thomas brought with him every kind of fur and silk garment, along with lush carpets and exquisite furnishings, in eight large carts and on the backs of a dozen mules. Over two hundred foot men led the endless train of courtiers, esquires, heralds, archers, falconers and servants who preceded Thomas and his elite company of knights and prelates. The king himself arrived later, dressed unpretentiously, with just a few knights in tow.[321]

But Henry's ideals transcended his ascetic approach to life. The monarch believed that justice should be available to all his subjects, and that some semblance of equality could prevail under the law. True, there were barons and there were serfs, and a feudal order that kept every man in his place (with little thought given to women), but the long civil war he witnessed as a boy convinced the king that just laws could bring about a fundamentally just society.

Thomas Becket agreed with these principles. Amongst their prominent proponents were Richard of Luci, the chief justiciar (England's highest judge), and Ranulf of Glanville, the erudite scholar who succeeded him.[322]

With Henry's introduction of civil (secular) tribunals, a law emerged that was "common" throughout England. Decisions might establish precedent, ensuring consistency in the prosecution of the same crime in different parts of the realm.

Henry's common law[323] did not completely supplant existing principles. His grandfather, Henry I, had proclaimed a very rudimentary legal code, the Charter of Liberties.[324] Nonetheless, the new laws forever changed the face of England's juridical landscape.

Archbishop

The legal system instituted by Henry II, with its itinerant judges, was effective so long as the bishops did not encroach on its jurisdiction by claiming immunity for the clergy, which was about one-sixth of the population. The king wanted his legal system to function on its own, independently of Papal influence. He reasoned that ecclesiastical support was necessary if his reforms were ever to be accepted without resistance.

In 1161, an opportunity presented itself with the death of Theobald, Archbishop of Canterbury.[325] Henry's simple solution was to ensure that somebody who shared his own views assumed this important post as Primate of England.[326]

To Henry, the obvious choice, or at least the most expedient one, was Thomas Becket, whose perspectives about royal authority and the law were not unlike his own.

The next year, Thomas was ordained to the priesthood and elected archbishop. Following his consecration, he seems to have realized that it would be difficult to serve two masters, so he resigned from the office of chancellor. (Here is a parallel of sorts to the situation of Stephen of Perche a few years later.)

In accepting the pallium, did Thomas Becket undergo a conversion that altered the form of his religious faith and his sense of the king's importance? Most historians believe so, but we can never know what subjective considerations motivated him.

Only rarely did Becket seek to ingratiate himself with antagonists, and now his dogmatism revealed itself. Whereas, as chancellor, his knowledge of canon law never impeded his support of the new system of justice, as archbishop he became its critic.

Although Becket's greatest criticisms seemed to focus on just a few laws, much more was at stake. The archbishop thought that conceding one or two points would lead to the collapse of the authority of the Catholic Church altogether.

Was the conflict between Thomas Becket and King Henry rooted in nothing more complicated than a clash of personalities? Such a thesis would be a gross oversimplification, but greater accommodation may well have been reached if both the archbishop and the monarch were less adamant in the totality of their views. Differences in character certainly aggravated matters. Henry was known for his violent temper, Thomas for his stubbornness. It was an explosive combination.

In January 1164, the Constitutions of Clarendon were enacted. Their preamble mentions the earlier laws of Henry's grandfather, "which should be observed and enforced in the realm."[327] Yet these new statutes were very clearly intended to curb the power of the ecclesiastical courts and Papal authority. Becket was saddened to see among the names of the signatories supporting the Constitutions that of his old friend, Richard of Aigle.

Disputes between laymen and clerics were to be decided by the civil courts, in some cases by a jury of "twelve lawful men." The Constitutions forbade the excommunication of English subjects, and even prohibited clergy from leaving the kingdom without prior royal consent.

A few church powers were retained in some form. For example, clerics accused of crimes could be tried in ecclesiastical courts, but with an officer of the civil (secular) court present; if convicted, the cleric would be remanded to the civil court for punishment. Because the judges of the ecclesiastical court could not order a punishment that would spill blood, a priest found guilty of murder might be defrocked but penalized no further, whereas a civil court would more likely order mutilation or even death.

The Constitutions found consent with the other prelates but enraged Thomas Becket, who viewed the laws as an affront to the apostolic authority of the Roman Church, and therefore an offense to God Himself. In this he was "more Catholic than the Pope" who, oddly enough, advocated less obstinate positions in some of these matters. This did not reflect Pope Alexander's sympathy for Henry's views, but rather his fear that strong opposition might drive the King of England to support the anti-pope, a threat being used by Emperor Frederick Barbarossa in an effort to manipulate the Papacy.

Thomas eventually voiced assent to the Constitutions but never confirmed his approval with a seal or signature. If Henry had even the faintest shadow of a doubt about Becket's opposition to the reforms, it vanished as the months passed.

The defiant Archbishop of Canterbury knew that repercussions would follow, but in this the king was creative. Taking what he thought to be the path of least resistance, Henry accused Thomas of malfeasance committed during his tenure as chancellor. He summoned him to appear at a great council at Northampton Castle in October to answer these charges. When convicted, Thomas stormed out of the trial and fled to France, where he received sanctuary from King Louis VII.

Exile

In 1166, with Thomas in exile, Henry enacted the Assize of Clarendon.[328] Very little of this dealt with ecclesiastical authority. Instead, it transferred much power from the barons to the royal judges. Trial by jury was instituted based on an evidentiary model, replacing such methods as compurgation, an accused person being released if a certain number of his friends swore that they believed him, and trial by single combat, a knight duelling an opponent to decide his case.[329]

Henry took reprisal against the prelate's family, which he exiled, and (as we have seen) eventually two of Becket's nephews were granted hospitality by Queen Margaret in Sicily.

By 1167, Pope Alexander III was actively intervening in the dispute through the diplomacy of one emissary after another. Whilst he agreed with Thomas in theory, the Pontiff saw no point in allowing the controversy to drag on for years.

A meeting between the king and the archbishop east of Paris early in 1169 resolved nothing, ending with both parting in exasperation.[330]

Henry was just as obdurate as Becket. He arranged for his young son, Prince Henry, to be crowned *rex filius* by the Archbishop of York, whose see contested Canterbury for primacy in England.[331] This was meant to humiliate the exiled Becket, as everybody knew that the privilege of coronation belonged to Canterbury alone. The coronation took place in June 1170.

Becket's reaction was to excommunicate the Archbishop of York, along with the bishops of London and Salisbury who assisted him in crowning Henry the Young King.[332]

Convinced that the senior Henry had gone too far, Pope Alexander confirmed Becket's excommunications of the bishops and others. Fearing that an interdict on England might be the next misfortune to befall his reign, the king met with Thomas in France in late July. The exile formally ended and the two tacitly agreed to ignore, for now, the myriad jurisdictional complications arising from the Constitutions of Clarendon.

Thomas Becket returned to England in early December. In Normandy, Henry was distressed to learn that his erstwhile friend refused to lift the excommunication of the Archbishop of York. Worse yet, the archbishop excommunicated other subjects in what seemed like an attempt to test Henry's resolve, if not his laws.

Saint

Seeing Henry's displeasure, four of his knights went to Canterbury to confront the archbishop. There, in the cathedral, they struck down Thomas Becket with their swords at the hour of vespers on the evening of Tuesday, December twenty-ninth.

Henry repudiated this heinous act, disavowing any responsibility for it. The assassins, though publicly condemned, went unpunished except for banishment from the court and excommunication.

Saint Thomas of Canterbury was canonized in February 1173. Remorseful King Henry II did public penance at the martyr's tomb in Canterbury Cathedral in July of the following year. This involved being flogged by monks.

This permitted the king's reputation to be rehabilitated in the eyes of the Pope and other sovereigns. Although some of the laws contested by Thomas Becket were suspended for a time, the greater number survived. In England, trial by jury supplanted trial by ordeal and principles of common law endured. Henry faced squabbles not with churchmen but with his own wife and sons.

Thomas Becket's story was widely recounted; in Sicily it was described by Romuald of Salerno.[333] The next decade saw a great number of churches founded in the saint's name across western Europe. The Sicilians dedicated the mother church of Marsala to Thomas Becket, and the earliest public holy image of him is a mosaic icon in Monreale Abbey. A small church was erected in his honour in Palermo near the place where his nephews lived.[334]

In England, meanwhile, pilgrims like those famously described by Chaucer flocked to Canterbury.

rit oportunum: pmoueatis. Thomas
cant archs: margarete regine sicule:

Serenissime dñe & in xpo kme Im.
margarete illustri regine sicu
loy Thomas diuina dispensa
tione cant ecclie ministr' humilis. sa
lutē, & sic temporalit' regnare in sici
lia: ut cum anglis etnalit' exultet in
gl'a. Licet faciem u'ram nō noue
rim, gl'am tñ non possum ignorare;
q'm & genosi sanguinis illustrat cla
ritas: & multarū magnarūq; u'tu
tum decorat titulus. & fame celebri
tas numosis p'conus reddit insignē.
S; inter cetas uirtutes q's cum aliis au
ditorib; g'tantr amplectim': libalitatm
u're debem' & qua nunc possum' de

Letter of Thomas Becket to Margaret (see page 359)

Chapter 17
TRANSITION

"The most difficult thing is the decision to act. The rest is merely tenacity."

— Amelia Earhart

Nothing in the first days of 1171 marked the year as beginning very differently from any other.[335] Queen Margaret passed the Christmas season with her sons, as always. There were no serious conflicts within the *Regnum,* and no foreign threats. The seasonal snow on the mountains beyond Palermo was a reassurance that some things never change. The queen was at the pinnacle of her power.

Reginal Duties

The news of the murder of Thomas Becket was startling not only for the death itself, but for the brutality with which the archbishop was said to have been killed. Ultimately, a king was held responsible for the actions of his knights, especially when a few of them acted together and claimed to be exercising his will. There was no telling how long it would take for the King of England to emerge from this quagmire, but the fingers being pointed at him as the presumed culprit did not bode well for his reputation abroad.

Margaret was not one of the people pointing fingers. Much as she may have admired Thomas Becket, her experience dealing with prelates in her own realm had taught her something about the complexities that arose when the royal and ecclesiastical spheres overlapped. If she could not commiserate fully with Henry, it was because the specific jurisdictional issues in England differed from those confronting her in Sicily. It was not her place to judge him.

Henry's problem with the Catholic Church would have to be resolved with alacrity, for he now risked excommunication for himself and interdict for his kingdom. The betrothals of his daughters to the sons of the two Jiménez sisters were probably the last things on his mind. Yet, like many other matters, they were predicated on a solid rapport with the Papacy.

There was still time to find William a suitable bride. Indeed, another offer soon arrived from the Emperor of Constantinople. This reiterated his proposal of several years earlier. His daughter was still available, although no longer his universal heiress as a son had been born since he last tendered Margaret a proposal that William wed Maria. This time, Margaret decided to accept the offer.[336]

As the most influential *familiares,* Matthew of Aiello and Walter the Archbishop of Palermo worked together well enough for a later chronicler to describe them as "two firm pillars" supporting the Kingdom of Sicily.[337] That portrayal may well have reflected popular sentiment.

Now, at the age of thirty-six, Margaret could begin to think about retiring from the most important public role of her life. Her elder son, the heir, was nearing seventeen, the age of majority. Margaret would always be his mother, for a queen is always a queen, and one did not speak of retiring to "private life" in the manner of a president or prime minister leaving a term of office, but her formal duties would no longer make her the center of attention.

This passage was not simply a question of a few sun spots, gray hairs or facial lines. The last few years had been full of enough unwieldy courtiers and hard choices to make anybody feel the effects of time.

But Margaret had survived these challenges. She could even decide to confront others. She was, by the standards of her era, middle-aged and might live another thirty years.

She was devout, perhaps even more so than most monarchs of her time, all of whom, like her, ruled by the grace of God, in whom she placed her faith.

For the moment, her time was consumed by such tasks as rendering "extraordinary" decisions in matters referred to her. Most cases involving bishops were addressed by the queen rather than by a civil authority such as the justiciars. In March, Margaret restored to Gentile, Bishop of Agrigento, a mill of which, according to a surviving charter, the prelate had somehow been defrauded.[338] Other decrees defended the rights of Muslims and Jews.

Cities like Jerusalem, Tudela and Palermo might accommodate all of their religious factions in something approaching harmony, but that was not true everywhere. In May, the Christians of Blois, a city on the Loire, massacred some forty Jews on the contrived pretext of the murder of a Christian child.

By 1171, the composition of the population of the realm Margaret ruled in her son's name could be identified by religion in a general way. The Jews were the only religious minority of note in the peninsular part of the Kingdom of Sicily. On the island of Sicily, perhaps one in four subjects were Muslim, and no more than one in ten were Jewish.

God and Country

The world around her was undergoing one of those subtle shifts that alters the form, if not the spirit, of religion every now and then.

To the south of Sicily, a Sunni family succeeded a Shia dynasty. The death of the last Fatimid caliph brought changes to the African lands running along the Mediterranean all the way to the Red Sea. Cairo, the family's capital, had been founded not long after the Fatimids made their way to Egypt from Tunisia.[339] In September 1171 Saladin, a Kurd, established what was to become a new ruling house. His Ayyubids, who had a natural religious affinity for the Sunni Abbasids of Baghdad, were intent on asserting their power around Jerusalem. Islam spanned three continents, influencing regions from Spain to what is now Pakistan.

The Christianity of some regions on the fringe of Europe was being brought into line with Rome's customs and rites. After a band of English knights had occupied part of Ireland, King Henry, not wishing to see them establish a rival kingdom on the island, reminded them that he was their lord. He and a large invasion force would land in Ireland in October. Pope Alexander approved the conquest of Eire so long as Henry encouraged its people to embrace the same liturgy and traditions as the Catholic Church in England, setting aside certain distinctively Celtic practices. The same Pontiff made an effort to more firmly integrate the people of Finland into Rome's fold.

In Sicily, as we have seen, the Christians were becoming ever more Latin. Margaret was eyeing some abandoned Greek monasteries on the eastern side of the island with a view to establishing Roman Catholic houses for the religious orders, especially for nuns.

Building churches was becoming something of a competition, a kind of medieval one-upmanship, in Norman Sicily.

Great churches were the super-tall skyscrapers of their day. Maio of Bari built San Cataldo to challenge the Martorana of George of Antioch next door; Matthew of Aiello built Saint Mary of the Latins in the Saqaliba district and later endowed the Magione in the Khalesa quarter, while Walter wanted to leave his mark on Palermo with a new cathedral. Each power player had his own "pet project."

As queen, Margaret had the resources to beat the boys at their own game. That's how she would spend her retirement.

Acumen

Was Margaret a competent leader, perhaps even an exceptional one? The quality of leadership depends greatly on context, and especially the challenges one faces, as much as personal ability. Difficult as Margaret's regency was, it would have been far more arduous, indeed potentially catastrophic, if it involved anything like repelling a large military invasion such as the one attempted, and aborted, by Frederick Barbarossa. The challenges from prelates in Sicily were nothing like the ideological war of words between Henry II and Thomas Becket, and as Margaret's regency was ending Henry stood on the threshold of an internecine squabble that would degenerate into armed conflict against his own sons.

It could be argued that the scheming, conspiring efforts to undermine the queen's authority were more difficult to respond to, and defeat, than a transparent military or juridical attack. There can be no doubt that some of the verbal barbs launched in Margaret's direction were, by their very nature, misogynistic, intended to exploit a woman's perceived vulnerabilities in an age that saw very few females in positions of leadership.

Viewed from such a perspective, Margaret's regency cannot be regarded as anything less than a success. Not every decision she made was unflawed, but perfection is not the measure of great leadership. Triumph in the face of adversity is what makes good leaders great.

Constance, the posthumous daughter of King Roger II, was about the same age as young William. As a girl reached the age of majority two or three years before a boy, she was already a woman, and actually William's aunt. Constance and her mother spent little time at court, so far as we know, preferring the tranquility of San Marco d'Alunzio. Yet the daughter of Sicily's first king saw in Margaret the rare example of a woman who could, and did, lead a kingdom. It was an inspiration that would serve Constance well, and over the next few years the two women would come to know each other better.[340]

And what of the populace? Did the people view their queen regent as a leader they could support?

What scant indications exist tell us that they did. Looking at the minorities, Islam flourished despite many conversions to Catholicism, and the Jews were protected.

The few major revolts were not upheavals motivated by widespread injustice but, rather, rebellions instigated by aristocrats. The ringleaders of the revolt that led to the exile of Stephen of Perche negotiated with the chancellor precisely because they feared that by nightfall the Palermitans they had incited to riot would abandon the effort and return to their humble hearths.

A unique occasion occurred in the middle of 1171 when one of Margaret's most famous countrymen visited Sicily. It was to be the last noteworthy event of her regency.

Chapter 18
BENJAMIN OF TUDELA

"He who has courage and faith will never perish in misery."

— Anne Frank

Benjamin of Tudela arrived in Sicily during the summer of 1171. Would that he had borne with him recent news from Navarre, but Benjamin had been travelling around the eastern Mediterranean for years before reaching Sicily along his return route to Spain.[341]

Teacher, Merchant, Traveler

Benjamin ben Jonah was born in the prosperous, multicultural town of Tudela around 1130. It will be remembered that this town came into the possession of Margaret's mother as a gift from Rotrou of Perche. Tudela was the most important center of learning in Navarre. During the twelfth century, Jews and Muslims made up at least half its population.

Benjamin was chiefly a rabbi and merchant, but his travel diary is the best record of its era for its descriptions of the

Jewish populations of southern Europe and western Asia. It is also something of an ethnography, and a census of Jews. His expedition may have begun as a pilgrimage; it ended up being an adventure.

Whilst there is some ambiguity about the precise dates that he passed through each place he describes, some in great detail, we know that he set out upon his journey from Zaragoza, in Aragon, in 1165. He followed the Ebro River to Tarragona before heading toward Barcelona and Girona. He then followed the French coast to Marseilles, where he boarded a galley that took him to Italy.

Here he stopped at Genoa, Lucca, Pisa and Rome before crossing the peninsula to Apulia, from whence he set sail for Greece. He visited Salonika and then Constantinople.

From there, he followed the coast of Asia Minor southward. A highlight of his trip was the Kingdom of Jerusalem. Benjamin eventually made his way to Mosul and then opulent Baghdad, the largest city known. Next he ventured into Persia, and thenceforth into the desert of Arabia. It is thought that, embarking at Basra, he sailed around the peninsula and up the Red Sea to Egypt.

Whether by land or by sea, Benjamin and his companions arrived at Damietta and Cairo, taking time for an excursion to visit Alexandria.

They then sailed from Damietta to Messina. This nautical voyage took almost three weeks.

Benjamin's Sicily

Writing in Hebrew, Benjamin describes Messina and the orchards around it, mentioning that there were around two hundred Jews in the city. From there, it took him two days to arrive at Palermo, where some fifteen hundred Jews lived. He notes that there was still a large Muslim population in the capital.

Like bin Jubayr[342] some years later, Benjamin of Tudela paints the picture of a splendid city full of gardens fed by rivers and springs. The royal palace and the mosaics of its chapel are mentioned.

Benjamin stayed at the royal court and among the city's Jews for a week or two. Margaret enjoyed a chance to reminisce about Navarre with a native. His diary suggests that Benjamin visited Trapani, as he mentions the coral harvested there, but this is uncertain.

He saw Palermo's magnificent synagogue, described by a fifteenth-century visitor, Obadiah ben Abraham of Bertinoro, as a squarish structure boasting a splendid courtyard enclosed by a colonnade. (Today the synagogue site is marked by a church, San Nicolò da Tolentino, whilst the mikveh is preserved under the Jesuit cloister of Casa Professa.)

Brief though his visit to Sicily was, Benjamin's account offers us information of the kind not readily found in other sources. It is invaluable for its insight by an outsider who saw good reason to note things unlikely to be pondered by a native who viewed them as commonplace. That, of course, is the great advantage of travelogues.

Benjamin of Tudela visited over three hundred localities, including such places as Saint Catherine's Monastery in the Sinai and various ancient archeological sites. Although he did not visit the African coast beyond Egypt, he covered the European and Asian parts of the Mediterranean world. In many of these areas, all three Abrahamic faiths flourished.

By 1173 he was back in Spain. He seems to have died there in that year.

William's Majority

Late in 1171, William reached the age of majority. He began to rule without the need for a regent.

There may have been a public celebration to mark the rite of passage. If so, the details of this birthday feast are unknown to us. As William was already a crowned monarch, there was no need for another coronation.

Majority meant that William no longer had any need for tutors. Henceforth, Walter the archbishop would be an advisor.

Margaret graciously accepted matronhood. She stepped down without stepping back. Her motherly instincts would never abandon her. Yet, as protective as she may have felt of her sons, the elder one, the king, was now a man. She would stand behind him but never beside him.[343]

William was the show, the man upon the stage. Margaret would work with him, only now her efforts would be behind the scenes. Together they would achieve great things, but exclusively in William's name, for the queen regent had become the queen mother.

Chapter 19
MONREALE

"You should know that our passion for building is more fervid than ever. It is a diabolical thing. It consumes money. The more you build, the more you want to build. It is an affliction, like being addicted to alcohol."

— Catherine the Great of Russia

Following the monarch's first Christmas as a sovereign ruling his own kingdom, the initial months of the majority of King William II in 1172 were occupied by plans for him to meet Maria, the daughter of the Emperor of Constantinople, in Apulia during the coming spring.

Margaret urged her son to exercise his full authority gradually, one step at a time, eschewing reactions that might lead to open disputes with men whose egos were notoriously fragile. An effort was made at appeasement.

Amongst the few royal charters that survive from these years is one that permits Walter, the Archbishop of Palermo and chief *familiare*, to try adulterers in his archdiocese.[344] Adultery is an example of something that was a crime in both ecclesiastical law and in the civil law enshrined in the Assizes of Ariano.[345] Too few cases are known in Palermo for us to ascertain exactly how this archiepiscopal authority was applied in practice, but Walter's jurisdiction included Roman Catholics, not Muslims, Jews or Greek Christians.

Another royal gesture, however, involved a project that Walter found slightly unsettling, even unnerving, and it would trumpet Margaret's triumph.

God's Builder

One of the peaks overlooking the Genoard park to the immediate south of Palermo has come to be called *Mount Caputo*. Except perhaps for a tiny Arab village, the mountain seems to have been uninhabited until 1172.[346] Favored for its hunting, it afforded the visitor a commanding view of the city. The site was known for its springs.

Margaret loved such places so much that she was already undertaking the construction of an abbey near Maniace in the Nebrodian Mountains on the site of a dilapidated Greek monastery.[347] It didn't take much to convince William to pursue a similar project near the capital, where he and his mother could oversee the details.

With royal involvement, the place was renamed, appropriately enough, *Mons Regalis,* "Royal Mountain." It is now called *Monreale*. Mother and son planned to erect Sicily's most beautiful church on this spot, along with the island's largest monastery and a walled town.[348] A castle would be built on the rocky summit overlooking the church.

The planning of such a project could not be kept secret for very long. Walter, the Archbishop of Palermo, was chagrined to hear about it.[349] He wanted funding for his own enterprise, an expansion of Palermo's cathedral.

Historians generally agree that, whatever moved William to

begin his venture at Monreale, one of the reasons was to make a public gesture of his independence from his former tutor, Walter, Primate of Sicily. In a time when tangible symbols were the most salient, Monreale was a royal reproach, a sign that Walter's power was on the wane.

Writing long afterward, the chronicler Richard of San Germano believed that the construction of the abbey church at Monreale was suggested to the king by Matthew of Aiello. He tells us that Matthew despised Walter, and vice versa, yet the two *familiares* behaved amicably toward each other in public. He goes on to report that Monreale reflected a certain diminution of Walter's effective power.[350] Not surprisingly, the chronicler overlooks Margaret's influence and, for that matter, William's role.[351]

Yet Peter of Blois, the king's former tutor, seems to have surmised William's intention to distance himself from Walter upon reaching the age of majority, if not earlier. This the young monarch did by interrupting his formal studies as soon as he could.

Peter later exploited this fact to compare William II of Sicily unfavorably to a much older Henry II of England: "Although your king has studied well, ours is far more learned. In fact, I have had the chance to assess the practical education of both monarchs. As you know, the King of Sicily was my pupil for a year, having already studied with you to acquire a knowledge of general studies and literature. He was able to benefit from my special efforts to motivate him, but as soon as I departed from the kingdom he fell into the habit of reading frivolous books and enjoying royal pleasures."[352]

There may be some truth in this. Few sovereigns were as erudite as Henry of England. However, Peter may have overlooked, or chosen not to see, William's quest for independence.

Although the King of Sicily and his guests could stay at the castle above Monreale, there would also be a comfortable palace on the north side of the church's apse (what remains of this edifice is now the city hall). From the highest floor of the palace, the royal family could see Palermo, just a short ride away, yet enjoy the privilege of being, quite literally, above the fray whose petty intrigues infested the court in the city far below. Margaret appreciated this, and so did William, who had been raised amidst a succession of troublesome plots.

From the outset, Monreale Abbey, officially "New Saint Mary's," was intended to be part of a vast monastic complex of the Benedictines, far larger than Saint John of the Hermits near the royal palace in Palermo. The monks of Cava, near Salerno, were happy to oblige the king by sending some of their number to Monreale.

By longstanding tradition, major Benedictine abbeys like Cassino and Cava were autonomous, answering, through their order's hierarchy, to the Pope himself. Local diocesan bishops had little say in monastic administration. Pope Alexander granted Monreale's Benedictines a similar privilege.[353] This meant that they were outside Walter's jurisdiction. All he could do was watch as the new church took shape.

King William endowed the monastery with extensive lands and towns populated largely by Arabs: Corleone, Jato, Partinico, Battallario, Calatrasi.[354] The Arabs' villages bore names like *Rahal Algalid* and *Menzil Zarsun*. This was a vast, fertile territory bordering the Archdiocese of Palermo. No wonder Walter was distressed.

In aggregating these estates for the Benedictines and removing Monreale from Palermo's ecclesiastical authority, was the hand of Margaret at work, snatching power from Walter's grasp just as he had tried to wrest it from hers? The possibility cannot be ruled out. If not vindictive, the queen was certainly shrewd. It was a trait acquired through her experience with jackals.

With Papal and royal approval, the abbot of Monreale gradually obtained authority over numerous monastic estates in Sicily, such as those Margaret founded around Maniace, and some in regions as far afield as Apulia.

The construction of the town, the hilltop castle, the royal palace and the walls encircling the abbey seems to have been initiated in 1172, but two years were to pass before work began on the church and monastery following Papal approval for the project.

The greater part of the church's Romanesque superstructure was completed by 1180. Although a Gothic cathedral of comparable size might take decades to build, a church like Monreale's could be completed in less time so long as the work went uninterrupted and there were enough men assigned to the project.

It would be another few years before the mosaics in the church and the columns in the cloister were completed.

Building such a monument required a monumental effort. What follows is a very concise overview (maps follow the text of this chapter).

The Church

Whether one refers to it as a basilica, *duomo* or cathedral, the church around which Monreale was built is impressive. The layout is a classic cross plan with a transept. The two massive towers were meant to serve as fortifications. The floor area measures slightly over four thousand square meters (more than forty thousand square feet), the nave being just over a hundred meters (at three hundred thirty feet) in length.

The nave is positioned generally, but not precisely, on an east-west axis *ad orientem,* with the apse toward the east. This tradition dates from the early centuries of the Church in Greece and elsewhere in Europe. In former times, the celebrant faced the altar and apse during liturgy; this is still true in the Orthodox Church, and it was the case in the Catholic Church until the twentieth century, when altars were positioned so that the priest faced the congregants.

There was initially a Byzantine templon, essentially a low iconostasis (icon screen), separating the sanctuary from the nave.

Inside the church is a wide central aisle between two narrower ones, for a total nave width of forty meters. Eighteen columns support the arches. These pillars were not built for the church; they were taken from a temple in Rome, and many of their capitals bear the likeness of Roma, one of that city's deities.[355] Most of the columns are made of syenite, an igneous rock very similar to granite but bereft of more than rare traces of quartz. It takes its name from Syene (Aswan) on the Nile, where the Romans quarried it.

The church's wooden roof replaces the one destroyed by fire in 1811. The original ceiling had muqarnas "stalactites" similar to those of the chapel in the palace in Palermo.

An interesting detail is the occasional use of *strata* of timber between some of the large stones of which the thick walls are constructed; this serves as a soft buffer to absorb seismic shock that creates fissures during earthquakes.

Among the distinctively Arab features are the geometric motifs of the exterior of the three apses, typical of Fatimid designs.

The Mosaics

What most strikes the visitor are the walls covered with mosaics set upon an endless field of gold tesserae. At six thousand three hundred and forty square meters (nearly seventy thousand square feet), thus eclipsing the wall area of the mosaics of Saint Mark's in Venice by around thirty percent, this is the largest medieval display of its kind in Italy. It was inspired by the mosaics of the Palatine Chapel in Palermo.

Many figures are icons, while others are Biblical scenes. The Old Testament is depicted on the walls of the central aisle. The mosaics of the lateral aisles and those above the sanctuary depict the New Testament. Many are accompanied by inscriptions in Latin or Greek.

All the saints but one are venerated in the Orthodox Church. The lone exception is Thomas Becket, depicted in the central apse; this is the earliest public image of Saint Thomas of Canterbury.

Overlooking the royal thrones in the presbytery, one mosaic shows King William II offering the church to the Virgin Mary, while another shows the same king being crowned by Christ, recalling the mosaic in the Martorana Church depicting Roger II receiving the crown from Jesus. The two lions *passant guardant* facing each other in the triangular mosaic immediately above the royal throne on the north wall resemble the heraldic beasts in the royal coat of arms of England (displayed by English kings beginning with Richard Lionheart) and the lions flanking the royal throne dais in the Palatine Chapel in Palermo's Norman Palace, repeated in a motif of the exterior of the apse of that city's cathedral.

Dominating everything is the imposing icon of Christ Pantocrator, "Ruler of All," looking down from high in the central apse above the main altar. At thirteen meters wide and seven meters high, this is thought to be the largest medieval image of the Pantocrator to survive. Indeed, the extent of Monreale's mosaics dwarfs that of any similar display that survives from the Middle Ages in what was once the Byzantine world. Beneath the Pantocrator is the Theotokos, the Mother of God; below this is a window of fine Fatimid design.

Begun in 1180, the mosaic work took about a decade to complete.

The Cloister

If Monreale's mosaics leave an impression, so does its large cloister. The colonnade is formed of two hundred twenty-eight pillars, most in pairs.

The Fatimid fountain in one corner is very similar to the one in Palazzo Falson in Mdina, Malta. The water spouts from the faces of men and lions carved in relief into a sphere set upon a column of zigzag motifs. When the water spurts out, the fountain's ensemble gives the appearance of a palm tree, representing life. The fountain was probably intended to be placed in the center of the cloister in representation of the spring of eternal life in the garden of Paradise of all three Abrahamic faiths.

Most of the cloister and its decoration are essentially Provençal in style, and it is from that region that its chief sculptors were recruited. Some of the same artisans carved similar capitals at Maniace and elsewhere.

Into the columns' capitals are carved all kinds of Biblical, mythological and natural scenes and personages. There are archers, lions, mermen, boars, and Norman knights bearing long shields devoid of heraldic devices.[356] The Arab warriors are depicted holding round shields. Also present are owls with monks' heads representing vigilance. There are grapes representing autumn and even the depiction of blowing leaves. One scene shows lions devouring men and stags. The double-tailed mermaid sitting among the evangelists and their symbols is Melusina, whose legend was popular in northern Europe. Along the eastern colonnade is a capital showing William II offering the cathedral to the Blessed Virgin Mary and Baby Jesus.

The columns themselves vary in design superficially. Some bear sculpted motifs while others are decorated in patterns with mosaic tiles. The alternating pairing of smooth and decorated columns was meant to create a subliminal sense of endless movement linked to the infinity of God or Allah.

Bordering the cloister is a refectory and dormitory. Beyond these is a large courtyard, the *belvedere,* from which the entire Gulf of Palermo is visible.

The Royal Tombs

Queen Margaret and two of her sons, Roger and Henry, whose remains were transferred from Mary Magdalene in Palermo, rest in the north semitransept. In the opposite (south) semitransept are the two Williams.[357]

Margaret's original sarcophagus was porphyry, which preserved her body remarkably well until 1811, when lightning struck the cathedral's wooden roof, setting off a fire. Fed by the resinous Nebrodian fir (a timber harvested in Sicily) of which the ceiling was constructed, the flames severely damaged her tomb and those of her sons Roger and Henry. The queen's remains were subsequently placed into a sarcophagus constructed in 1846 modelled on the original one but made of marble. An epitaph in mosaic (described in a later chapter) appears in the wall above the tomb.

A curious detail is the altar near Margaret's tomb dedicated to King Louis IX of France, who died crusading in Tunisia. A reliquary preserves his heart and viscera, placed here during a solemn ceremony in 1270 by his brother, who was then King of Sicily.[358]

Bronze Doors

Two impressive sets of bronze double doors bearing panels depicting Biblical scenes grace the church. Forged in 1186, the doors beneath the main portico at the end of the nave are by Bonanno "Pisano" of Pisa. The pair of Byzantine design under the north portico is the work of Barisano of Trani. Similar bronze doors designed by both sculptors are conserved in churches elsewhere in Italy.

What one finds at Monreale transcends any single work of art. Here Margaret and her son fashioned part of the Kingdom of Sicily into a piece of the Kingdom of Heaven.

+HIC REGINA IACES REGALIB
EDITA CVNIS: MARGARITA TIBI
NOMEN·QVOD MORIBVS VNIS:
REGIA PROGENIES PER REGES
DVCTA PROPAGO: VXOR REGIS
ERAS: ET NOBILITATIS IMAGO:
SI TAC ERM QVIBVS IPSA NE
PLES PRECONIA MVNDV: REGE
W. SATIS E PEPERISSE SECVNDV
+VND ETIES CENTV·DECIES V IIETTI
BVS ANNIS: POST hOMINEM XPM
MIGRAS NECIS ERVTA DAMPNIS:
LVX EA QVA POPVLIS DANT PETRI
FESTA CATENE: hIS TE DE NEDVE
TVLIT AD LOCA LVCIS AMEN E

Margaret's mosaic epitaph and marble sarcophagus

Mosaic icon of Thomas Becket at Monreale

Arab fountain in the cloister of Monreale Abbey

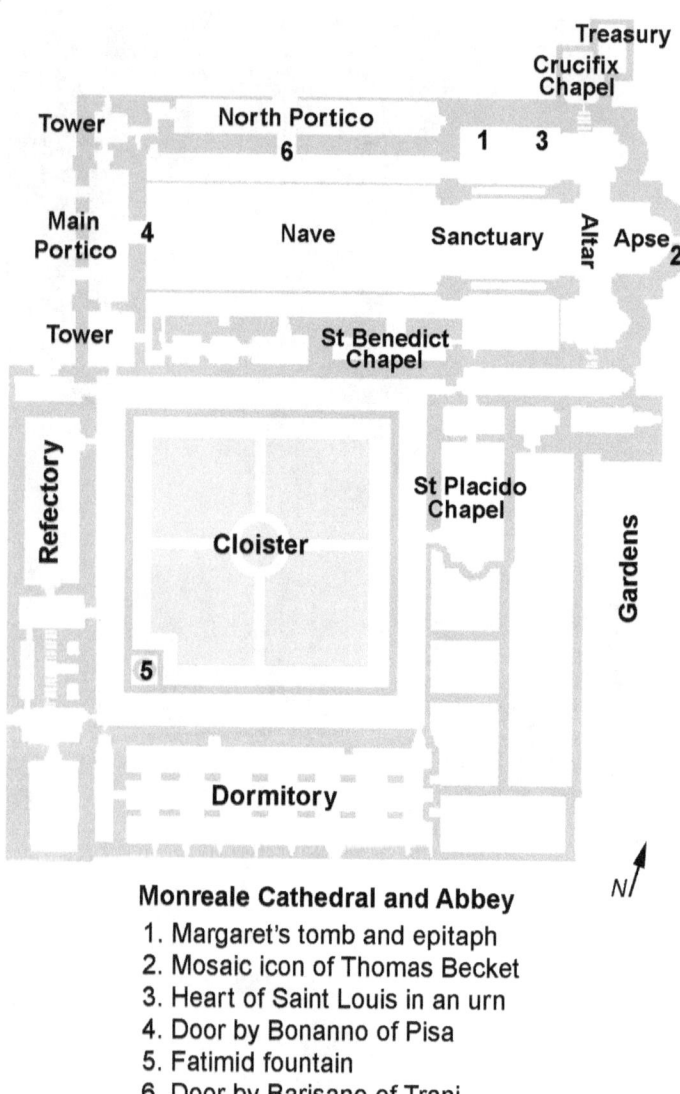

Monreale Cathedral and Abbey
1. Margaret's tomb and epitaph
2. Mosaic icon of Thomas Becket
3. Heart of Saint Louis in an urn
4. Door by Bonanno of Pisa
5. Fatimid fountain
6. Door by Barisano of Trani

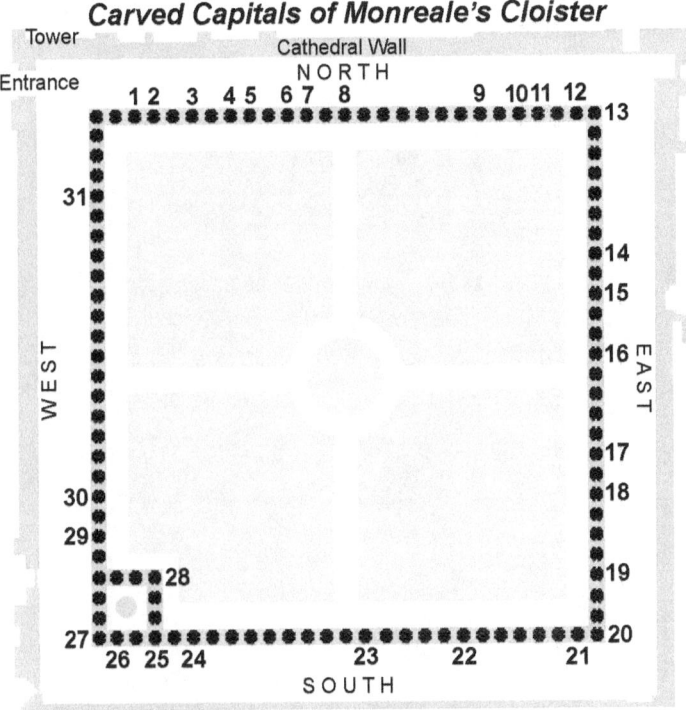

Carved Capitals of Monreale's Cloister

1. Arab archer and swordsman
2. Lions and other beasts
3. Merman (triton) and knights
4. Parable of Lazarus
5. Knights and Saracens
6. Windswept leaves
7. Men killing beasts
8. Life of John the Baptist
9. Story of Samson
10. Norman knights
11. Massacre of the Innocents
12. Evangelists and mermaids
13. Magi, Annunciation, etc.
14. Men supporting capitals
15. Vigilant owls, harpies
16. Men, beasts, lizards
17. Joseph of Old Testament
18. Abraham sacrifices Isaac
19. Resurrection of Jesus
20. Willam and Margaret (?)
21. Lions devour men and stags
22. Acrobats
23. Eagles supporting capital
24. Arab killing sheep or goat
25. Mounted Norman knights
26. Harvesting of grapes
27. Apostles, Flight into Egypt
28. Wine barrels, seasons
29. Prophets and angels
30. William II offers cathedral to Virgin
31. Lion slaughters pig as Norman knight and Saracen warrior watch

MARGARET, QUEEN OF SICILY

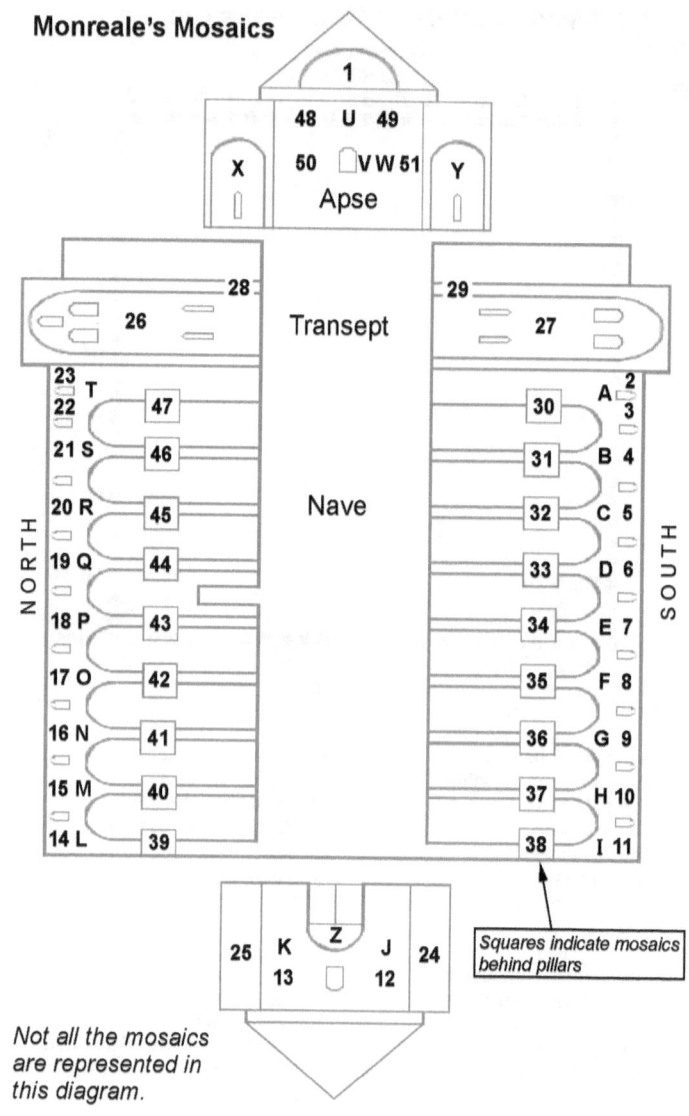

Key to Numeration of Principal Mosaics in Monreale Cathedral

1. Christ Pantocrator (ruler of all)
2. God creates Heaven and Earth
3. God divides light from dark
4. God divides waters
5. God separates lands from seas
6. Creation of sun, moon, stars
7. Creation of birds and fish
8. Creation of Adam and animals
9. God rests
10. Adam placed in Garden of Eden
11. Adam dwells in Eden alone
12. God creates Eve
13. Eve presented to Adam
14. Eve tempted by serpent
15. Forbidden fruit consumed
16. God confronts Adam and Eve
17. Expulsion from Eden
18. Adam and Eve toiling
19. Sacrifice of Cain and Abel
20. Cain kills Abel
21. God confronts Cain
22. Lamech kills Cain
23. Noah commanded to build ark
24. Miracle of loaves and fishes
25. Healing of crooked woman
26. Events from life of Jesus
27. Miracles of Jesus
28. William crowned by Christ
29. William dedicates church to Mary
30. Possessed woman healed
31. Healing of leper
32. Healing of lame man
33. Peter rescued from water
34. Raising of widow's son
35. Healing of woman's hemorrhage
36. Raising of Jairus' daughter
37. Peter's mother-in-law healed
38. Loaves and fishes (also 24)
39. Crooked woman healed (also 25)
40. Man suffering edema healed
41. Healing of ten lepers
42. Healing of two blind men
43. Money changers expelled
44. Jesus saves adulteress
45. Paralyzed man healed
46. Healing of lame and blind
47. Magdalene washes Jesus' feet
A. Noah constructs ark
B. Animals board Noah's ark
C. Dove arrives
D. Animals exit ark
E. Rainbow signifies God's covenant
F. Drunken Noah in vineyard
G. Tower of Babel constructed
H. Abraham meets angels at Sodom
I. Abraham's hospitality
J. Lot protects angels
K. Lot flees destruction of Sodom
L. God commands sacrifice of Isaac
M. Angel stops sacrifice of Isaac
N. Rebecca offers water to servant
O. Rebecca journeys to meet Isaac
P. Isaac with sons Esau and Jacob
Q. Isaac blesses Jacob
R. Jacob flees Esau
S. Jacob dreams of ladder
T. Jacob wrestles with angel
U. Theotokos and Jesus enthroned
V. Saint Sylvester
W. Saint Thomas Becket
X. Saint Paul enthroned
Y. Saint Peter enthroned
Z. Theotokos and Infant Jesus

48. John, Philip, Bartholomew, Luke, James, Peter, Archangel Michael
49. Angel Gabriel, Paul, Andrew, Mark, Thomas, Simon, Matthew
50. Martin, Agatha, Anthony, Blaise, Stephen, Peter of Alexandria, Clement
51. Lawrence, Hilarion, Benedict, Mary Magdalene, Nicholas

The nave

Chapter 20
QUEEN MOTHER

"To deny fate is arrogance. To declare that we are the sole shapers of our existence is madness."

— Oriana Fallaci

Margaret was no longer regent. Inevitably, the day arrived for William, who was now an adult, to act independently of her. In the early days of May in 1172, the king and his young brother, Henry, who was then twelve, left with a large entourage for Taranto, where they were to meet Maria of Constantinople, to whom William was betrothed the previous year.[359] This was the first time that Margaret's sons left their mother's presence for more than a day or two, and it was to prove a fateful occasion.

Whatever maternal misgivings she had, Margaret knew this to be a necessary step. Apart from its obvious purpose, the excursion into the mainland would give the people of the *Regnum* a chance to see their young king ruling on his own. This could not help but reinforce his authority in the eyes of the nobility and the clergy.

Lost Princess

It had been agreed with Manuel Comnenus of Constantinople that his daughter would arrive with several galleys and a number of emissaries, knights, ladies-in-waiting and servants. A legation of Sicilian ambassadors had visited the Byzantine court to ensure that Maria, who was nearly two years older than William, was sufficiently healthy, intelligent and attractive to become Sicily's queen consort.

With the birth of her half-brother, Alexius, Maria was no longer Manuel's universal heir to the Byzantine throne, but she was just as eligible as any other princess to become William's bride, for her father's empire was an important ally. Unstated was another aspect of the union that was not to be overlooked.

In the event of the childhood death of her brother, who was not yet three, Maria would again become Manuel's heiress, an eventuality that might well open the door for William to claim the Byzantine Empire by marital right. This possibility did not escape Manuel or, for that matter, any other monarch whose interests touched Mediterranean shores, especially Frederick Barbarossa.

William waited at Taranto for about ten days. Presuming a timely departure from Constantinople, there was no immediate explanation for a delay in Maria's arrival. The seas were calm this time of year. The route of her flotilla would take Maria through the Aegean, following the Greek coasts into the Ionian to Corfu and then to Apulia.

Not wishing to spend too much time idly waiting, William left a company of prelates and nobles at Taranto to receive Maria while he and his brother went to pray at the sanctuary of Saint Michael on Mount Gargano, a site very important to the Hauteville dynasty.[360] They then went to Barletta for a few days.

As the days passed, it became obvious that Maria was not going to arrive. An armed flotilla sailing through friendly coastal waters did not risk an attack by pirates, and there were no storms, so the royal court could only conclude that Manuel Comnenus had reneged on his word. If that matter were not grave enough, the event itself left William greatly dismayed. The young man had expected to meet the woman who would be his wife. Instead, he departed Apulia without so much as an explanation for her failure to appear.

Receiving word of the incident, Margaret was equally frustrated. More than once, Manuel of Constantinople had proposed the union of his daughter to her son, finally committing to it formally, only to abandon the idea now. Not only was this annoying, it was highly offensive to royal dignity. It was enough to anger any mother.

The lack of an explanation, or indeed any communication, from the Byzantine court only added insult to injury.

Lost Prince

From Apulia, William and his company headed to the western side of the peninsula. Before long, he was passing through Benevento, a Papal enclave within the Kingdom of Sicily. At this point, young Henry began to complain of illness.

The king thought it best to send his brother to Salerno. Not only did that city have a good medical school and exceptional physicians, it was a convenient port from which to embark for Sicily.

Matthew of Aiello and Archbishop Walter remained with William. Despite their concern for Henry, both *familiares* wanted to be as near to the king as possible.

From Salerno, young Henry returned by sea to Palermo accompanied by a small retinue. During the sea voyage, his physical condition did not improve.

In Sicily, the illness only worsened. Henry died in the middle of June.

Having visited Capua, William soon headed to Salerno, where the royal galleys were waiting to take him to Sicily. He embarked without further delay and set sail for his capital.

Upon reaching Palermo, William learned of his brother's death. He did not take it well.

The people of Palermo attended yet another royal funeral. Margaret was beside herself with grief. The long arm of death had snatched three of her sons from this earth.

But the political repercussions of Henry's premature passing transcended even a mother's anguish. Henry's death brought with it dynastic ramifications that could change the course of history.

The young prince had been first in line to the throne. Now there were no legitimate male heirs in sight.

Constance, the posthumous daughter of Roger II, became heiress to the throne. It will be remembered that she was around William's age, even though she was his aunt. The idea that she might become queen in her own right was antithetical to the principle of Salic Law that excluded females from the line of succession; male primogeniture was the norm.

If Constance were to marry, her husband might rule in her name *jure uxoris,* by marital right. Until now, Constance's mother, Beatrice of Rethel (the widow of Roger II), had made no effort to find the girl a husband, and neither had Margaret. Constance was living in a convent, having expressed the intention of taking vows and becoming a nun. Married life did not seem to interest her.

Finding William a wife to produce heirs was more important than ever.

A proposal came from the Holy Roman Empire when ambassadors representing Frederick Barbarossa offered the hand of his daughter, Beatrice Hohenstaufen.

This German offer was not accepted, but neither was it immediately refused. The issue was complex.

Margaret and William both knew that Pope Alexander and Frederick Barbarossa had yet to negotiate a peace with each other. Jeopardizing Sicily's rapport with the Papacy was not a good idea, especially now that Papal support was being sought for the ambitious project at Monreale.

After careful contemplation, William refused to wed Frederick Barbarossa's daughter. The rebuke, accompanied as it was by William's refusal to negotiate a new treaty with the Holy Roman Emperor until the Papal dispute was resolved, enraged Barbarossa.

Other monarchs were more willing to cultivate good relationships with the Papacy, if only out of necessity. In England, Henry II reached what seemed like an accommodation with Pope Alexander III in the wake of the Thomas Becket assassination.[361] Could this serve to resuscitate the abandoned betrothal of Henry's daughter to Margaret's son? Margaret hoped so.

Matronage

Between mourning for her lost son and fretting over the future of her last living child, Margaret had a great deal on her mind. If she confronted depression, she did not succumb to it.

The canonization of Thomas Becket in February 1173 only served to remind her of the earlier tragedy that ended in her friend's martyrdom, and her dashed desire for William to wed young Joanna of England.

Faced with uprisings in France supported by his own sons, King Henry could be forgiven for ignoring the subject of the betrothal of his daughter to the King of Sicily.

Letters from the English king advised fellow monarchs of developments in his realm. One such letter arrived at Palermo. Margaret encouraged William to respond amicably.[362] She gave little thought to Henry's insolent sons. It was his daughter, Joanna, who interested her; the queen was beginning to think it possible to salvage the plan for the young princess to marry William.

At some point in 1173, Margaret ventured into northeastern Sicily. She visited Beatrice of Rethel and Constance before trekking into the Nebrodian Mountains to inspect the monastery being built at Maniace.

None of these royal dames ever traveled with anything less than a company of knights, esquires, grooms, ladies-in-waiting, servants, and perhaps a friar and scrivener. At the bare minimum, that meant no fewer than twenty people.

We know rather little of the sense of sisterhood that existed among Margaret, Beatrice and young Constance, but there was now a dearth of legitimate Hauteville males. Despite the ambitions of the *familiares* who governed the *Regnum* from one day to the next, dynastic power rested firmly in the hands of William and Margaret.

Margaret enjoyed a unique status as queen mother. Several charters relating to the monasteries she founded in the Nebrodian Mountains cite her authority exclusively.[363] We find, for example, the phrase *dominae Margaritae gloriosae reginae matri,* without William being mentioned explicitly.[364] Within a few years, Maniace became a vast network of holdings outside the ecclesiastical jurisdiction of the Archbishop of Messina, ceded to the authority of the abbot of Monreale.[365]

Nothing like a "mini-kingdom" was ruled by Margaret in northeastern Sicily once her son reached the age of majority. However, using the royal castle at San Marco d'Alunzio as her base, she exercised her authority with a certain degree of autonomy.

Politics as Usual

One of the people that Margaret, as regent, had permitted to return from exile was Tancred of Lecce, the illegitimate grandson of Roger II who had participated in the Bonello revolt. During the middle of 1173, William decided to entrust the wayward prince with commanding a fleet to support a Fatimid uprising against Saladin's ambitious Ayyubid government, which had designs on the Holy Land.

The plan, a response to a request by Almaric, the King of Jerusalem, was for the Sicilian fleet to land at Alexandria. Tancred's forces were to be supported by the Fatimid insurgents and, more importantly, an army sent by Almaric from Palestine. The attack was to take place in July of the following year. This meant that William had to invest in the construction of almost three hundred galleys at the shipyards of Messina and Brindisi.

If all went according to plan, William would assert his authority in the eastern Mediterranean. At home, he was doing so through the construction of Monreale's church and monastery.

News reached the Sicilian court that William's cousin (Margaret's nephew), Alfonso VIII of Castile, intended to resume his own plan to marry Eleanor, the daughter of Henry II, in view of the English monarch's formal reconciliation with the Papacy. This, understandably, prompted Margaret to think that William could indeed marry Eleanor's little sister, if only the details could be worked out.

With two major projects under way, marriage was probably not foremost in William's mind.

During the regency, Margaret was fortunate to be able to avoid war. Frederick Barbarossa's attempt to invade the *Regnum* had ended as a fiasco, and there were no military threats from other quarters. The queen supported Pope Alexander financially in Papal efforts against the Holy Roman Emperor in Italy, but that was a far cry from direct military involvement. William's effort in Egypt was different. Would it be successful?

In July of 1174, the Sicilian fleet commanded by Tancred arrived at Alexandria to support the friendly Fatimids in their struggle against the adversarial Ayyubids. Here two unexpected problems presented themselves, and Tancred might have elected to abort the principal assault had he known about either one. In Egypt, Saladin had recently captured and killed the leaders of the Fatimid insurgency; in Palestine, Almaric had unexpectedly died, so no army arrived from Jerusalem. This left the Sicilians alone. Formidable as the landing force was, it was beaten back, suffering heavy losses. In the end, Tancred had to content himself with some raids along the African coast, and Saladin's acquisition of territory continued unabated.[366]

If any political benefit could be gleaned from the unsuccessful Egyptian expedition, it was that young King William had shown the world, Christian and Muslim alike, his capacity to prosecute military campaigns and his willingness to defend his allies. Tactical failure did not, in itself, diminish these virtues so laudable in a king. The Egyptian debacle does not seem to have spawned angst in William's mind.

Whilst William was flexing his muscles in Muslim territory, Henry II of England was having his flesh whipped by the monks of Canterbury as penance for his persecution of his onetime friend, Thomas Becket.

We know not what Margaret thought about these developments. She could not have had great regrets about her son, as king, asserting himself to the world, but her campaign to build monasteries interested her more than William's campaign against a Muslim dynasty. She had considered Becket her friend, yet she harbored no antipathy toward her brother sovereign and contemporary, Henry II.

Henry's act of penance was the last step in his spiritual rehabilitation. It paved the way for the Sicilian king to again solicit the English king for his daughter's hand in marriage. For the moment, however, Henry still had to contend with the rebellion of his sons.[367]

In December 1174, Pope Alexander III confirmed to Monreale's Benedictine monastery the status and privileges of an autonomous "major abbey" despite the fact that its construction was far from complete.[368] This (as mentioned earlier) placed it outside the ecclesiastical jurisdiction of Walter of Palermo and any other archbishop. It permitted the abbot to wear a mitre[369] and exercise authority similar to that of a bishop.

Years before their completion, the monastery and church at Monreale had already managed to kill two birds with one stone, enhancing royal prestige while attenuating Walter's power.

By 1175, King William II of Sicily had launched a military campaign and secured jurisdictional independence for a major monastery he had founded. Actions spoke louder than words. There could be no doubt about his authority, and no question of his maturity.

Margaret need not agree with her son's every decision, but she no longer had to worry about his capacity to think for himself.

Nonetheless, although statecraft was outside her responsibility, a certain diplomatic detail found her in perfect accord with her son, and here the she-wolf revealed her nature.

In September 1175, William signed a treaty with the Venetians to protect shipping and trade.[370] Interestingly, it explicitly mentioned galleys in the service of the Byzantine Empire being beyond the protection of the King of Sicily, effectively placing such vessels in the same category as pirate ships.[371] Clearly, the humiliation visited upon him by Maria's failure to arrive at Taranto three years earlier was still fresh in William's mind.

Whilst Margaret may not have met the Venetian ambassadors who came to Palermo to sign the treaty, William probably discussed it with her. Like her son, the queen mother was still deeply offended by the poor behavior of the Emperor of Constantinople.

Mother and son were founding or revitalizing monasteries all over the *Regnum,* and especially in Sicily. Monreale and Maniace, of course, were their favourites. William went so far as to make the abbot of Monreale the justiciar for all of the monastery's lands.

Although he found time to forgive the English king's behaviour and approve the Sicilian sovereign's foundation of a major Benedictine monastery, Pope Alexander III, who was still living outside Rome, had his hands full. The longstanding Papal dispute with Frederick Barbarossa continued, with the Holy Roman Emperor supporting an antipope, Callixtus (John of Struma). Yet, despite the many demands on his time, Alexander was well aware that the youngish King of Sicily still needed a queen consort.

The Pope had never abrogated or renounced his approval of the proposed marriage between William Hauteville and Joanna Plantagenet.[372] He knew about the two emperors, Manuel and Frederick, advancing their daughters as candidates to become, through marriage, Queen of Sicily.[373] He knew of the death of Henry, Margaret's younger son.

Alexander was grateful for Margaret's support, but his concern about the royal succession was more firmly rooted in his own interests than in hers. The endless conflict with Barbarossa had revealed the vulnerability of the Papal dominion in central Italy to the hegemony of the monarchs whose realms bordered its northern and southern frontiers.

The Supreme Pontiff might wield the power of excommunication and interdict, but such weapons had their practical limits, especially when a monarch like Barbarossa could choose the pope or antipope he preferred. Useful as an army of angels was in the spiritual realm, defending territory against an earthly invader boasting great material resources was a predicament best avoided.

The security of his alliance with the powerful *Regnum Siciliae* to the south of the Papal lands depended on its dynastic continuity from one generation to the next, something that could be ensured only by the birth of legitimate sons.

Late in 1175, the Pope of Rome decided to remind the King of England about the agreement made with Queen Margaret before Thomas Becket's murder. Henry II, for his part, needed solid alliances as much as Alexander III needed safe borders. It was time to form a union.

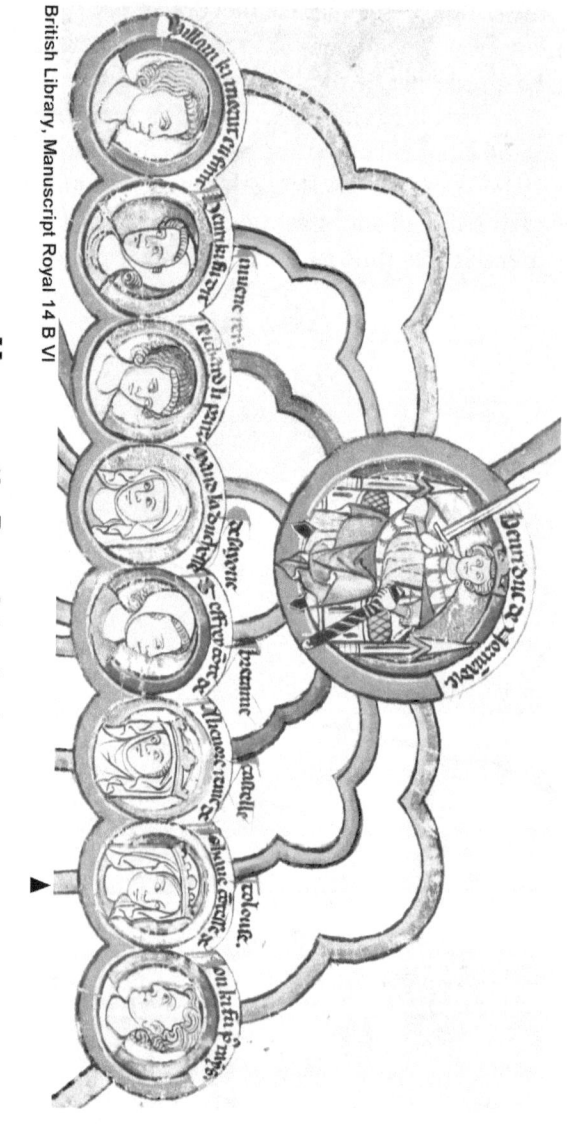

British Library, Manuscript Royal 14 B VI

Margaret's Daughter-in-Law

Joanna of England (second from right) and her siblings as the children of King Henry II of England in a fourteenth century manuscript illumination

Chapter 21
MOTHER-IN-LAW

"Your work is the rent you pay for the room you occupy on earth."

— The Queen Mother, née Elizabeth Bowes-Lyon

In 1176 Margaret found herself working to establish several convents for Benedictine nuns. One of these was established at San Marco d'Alunzio, where the Hautevilles' familial castle was located on a rocky mountain. This nunnery answered to the authority of the abbot of Maniace who, in turn, fell under the jurisdiction of the abbot of Monreale. Founding convents was not Margaret's only effort.

The queen mother was also working to build a family for her son. To that end, she sent ambassadors to England to revive plans for the betrothal of William to Joanna.[374]

Joanna of England

Joanna had been raised, for the most part, in France with her mother, Eleanor of Aquitaine, the estranged wife of Henry II. Queen Eleanor had taken her sons' side in their war against her husband. Although this was not the royal couple's only marital squabble, it led to Henry imprisoning his own wife in England; in 1176 Eleanor was living under "house arrest" in Winchester.

Margaret may have sympathized with the suffering of her sister queen, but she could not let Eleanor's plight interfere with plans to finalize the dynastic marriage proposed years earlier.[375] The two queens lived in very different realities. One of the differences was that Eleanor had four living sons, whereas Margaret had only one, and William needed a bride.

We know far more about the details of the betrothal of Joanna of England to William of Sicily than we do about the great majority of royal unions negotiated in Europe during the twelfth century.[376] So complete are the surviving records of it that the event, as it has become known to us, is the very archetype of its era.

Firstly, Margaret turned to a trusted prelate, Rotrou of Rouen, the kinsman who had sent Stephen of Perche to her court years earlier. Rotrou offered to go to England to meet with Henry. Accompanying him were two bishops, Elias of Troia and Arnolf of Capaccio, along with a faithful nobleman and justiciar, Florio of Camerota. With a company of knights and servants, these four ambassadors reached England early in April 1176.

There was never really any doubt that Henry would consent to this marriage; he had already agreed to its conditions a few years earlier. In the meantime, he had also approved the betrothal of another daughter to Margaret's nephew, the King of Castile.

Nonetheless, the King of England followed the formality of meeting in council with the prelates and high nobles of his court to grant his royal assent before sending William's ambassadors to meet Joanna at Winchester, where she was living with Queen Eleanor.

Considering Joanna's tender years, this was a precocious betrothal even by the standards of the twelfth century; the girl was six months shy of her eleventh birthday.

At Winchester, the ambassadors were presented to Queen Eleanor, who permitted them to meet the young princess. Her beauty and poise were obvious enough. The men were curious about the girl's health and intelligence.

Communication was no obstacle, as Joanna spoke Norman French. The men asked her a few questions. Having heard something about the fiery temperaments of her mother and father, they were at least a little interested in Joanna's personality.

Eleanor and her daughter probably had a few questions about William, especially if, perchance, the Queen of England had heard the rumour that the King of Sicily kept a harem. Then again, Eleanor had long ago resigned herself to her own husband's extramarital affairs; it was a part of life she might, albeit very delicately, explain to her daughter.

The ambassadors overwhelmingly approved of Joanna.

Brooking no delay, they made their way back to London to discuss the betrothal details with the king. There they explained that, as Queen of Sicily, Joanna would receive a large dower that included, among other lucrative manors, the wealthy county of Mount Sant'Angelo.[377]

Rotrou of Rouen was present, along with Cardinal Hugh Pierleoni, the Pope's permanent ambassador to the English court. Henry's next step was to send his own ambassadors to Palermo to convey his personal greetings to William, his future son-in-law.

Meanwhile, the Sicilian ambassadors, Elias, Arnolf and Florio, remained in England as Henry's guests whilst Joanna prepared for her voyage. They would accompany her to Sicily. The princess and her ladies-in-waiting would be ready to depart in four months.

Henry visited his daughter during the middle of August to wish her well, and to remind her of the importance of the role she was about to assume.

The Journey to Sicily

In October, Henry received a letter[378] from William thanking him and setting forth some details of Joanna's journey. The day of the departure eventually arrived. Joanna embraced her mother, Eleanor, knowing she might never see her again.[379] Her retinue then set out for Sicily with a large company of prelates and nobles. With them Henry sent his future son-in-law gifts of fine horses, clothes, gold and silver, and precious vases.[380]

The royal party included Archbishop Richard of Canterbury and Bishop Geoffrey of Ely, along with Bishop Giles of Evreux and Hugh of Beauchamp.

Among the travelers was Hamelin of Warenne, King Henry's half-brother. Not all of these clerics, courtiers and kinsmen would accompany Joanna all the way to Sicily. Some would go only as far as Saint-Gilles, on the French coast, where a flotilla of Sicilian galleys would meet Joanna. Elias of Troia, Arnolf of Capaccio and Florio of Camerota, being William's ambassadors, were to travel with the company to Palermo.

Joanna, of course, was the youngest of the travelers, and one of the few women. On the leg of the journey over land, the large royal party, with its many wagons, traveled much more slowly than a pair of couriers or a company of knights would have ridden over the same distance.

Having crossed the English Channel, the company was met in Normandy by Joanna's eldest brother, Henry the Young King, who accompanied them to Poitiers. From there, her brother Richard escorted the company southward through Aquitaine.

In late November, Joanna and her suite arrived at Saint-

Gilles, where twenty-odd Sicilian galleys were waiting for them. She had just celebrated her eleventh birthday.

Unfortunately, the two galleys bearing precious gifts that William had sent his father-in-law were lost at sea. This was reported by Bishop John of Norwich, one of Henry's returning ambassadors, who described a terrible voyage from Messina to Saint-Gilles.

Leading the Sicilian flotilla were Alfano, Archbishop of Capua, Richard Palmer, Bishop of Syracuse, and Robert, Count of Caserta. Most of the royal retinue embarked, but Richard of Canterbury and Geoffrey of Ely returned to England to report to Henry that the first part of the journey was successful.

The galleys set out along the Italian coast, occasionally stopping along the way. The waters of the Tyrrhenian, the same sea that had claimed the galleys carrying gifts for King Henry, were choppy this time of year. Joanna was unaccustomed to sea travel. She suffered a bout of sea sickness that necessitated stops along the coast more frequent that what had been planned.

Joanna and her suite finally reached the waters of the Kingdom of Sicily. They disembarked at Naples to celebrate Christmas and give Joanna a few days' rest. At this point it was decided to travel over land, stopping at Salerno and Calabria. This took longer than an itinerary by sea, but it was less injurious to Joanna's physical condition. It also offered the advantage of affording her a glimpse of the peninsular part of the *Regnum*. Naples was gradually increasing in population and importance, while Salerno, with its splendid cathedral and palace, was one of the kingdom's most important cities.

Royal Wedding

When Joanna reached Palermo in early February 1177, William was waiting for her at one of the city's eastern gates. It was nearly nightfall when Bishop Giles of Evreux presented her to the King of Sicily. Joanna mounted a palfrey and rode with William through a city lit by lamps and torches. Exultant crowds hailed the couple and their endless entourage.

Accompanied by her ladies-in-waiting and servants, the bride-to-be was received by Queen Margaret at the Zisa palace[381] on the other side of the Genoard.

On Sunday, the thirteenth, Joanna was wed to William in the chapel of the royal palace beneath the benevolent gaze of the Pantocrator. Here she was crowned and anointed Queen of Sicily.

On this occasion, according to Romuald of Salerno, William was crowned for the second time, *in cappella sua desponsavit, et se et eam gloriose coronari fecit, et solemnes de illa nuptias celebravit*. The nuptials and twin coronations were performed by Archbishop Walter, who could finally enjoy the satisfaction and prestige of having crowned a king.

With Joanna's coronation, Margaret officially became queen mother.

Back in England, Henry and Eleanor received a report of the magnificent event. The only disappointment was the loss of the two galleys transporting gifts for Henry and, perhaps, for Eleanor.

The dynastic marriage formed an esoteric link between the mothers of the spouses. We Italians call it *consuocera*. The word describes the relationship between two mothers whose children have wed each other. The marriage between William and Joanna made the two queens, Margaret and Eleanor, *consuocere*.

It was hard to say whether the new alliance of England with Sicily would yield any advantages beyond trade, but that was quite enough. Besides, there was no telling when Henry might need an ally in the Mediterranean.

Three Queens

The Kingdom of Sicily now had three queens. There was Beatrice of Rethel, the "queen dowager," the widow of Roger

II. There was Margaret, the queen mother. Then there was young Joanna, the newly-crowned queen consort, who was not yet even a teenager. As heiress, Constance, the daughter of Beatrice living in a convent, was a potential queen.

There was no telling when Queen Joanna might bear children. For the moment, she was little more than a child herself.

One of the gifts she brought for her mother-in-law was sent from Bishop Reginald of Bath. This was a gold reliquary, formed into a pendant, bearing relics of martyred Thomas Becket.[382] It bears the only contemporary image of Margaret known to us.

Significantly, it reflects the widespread extent of the veneration of Saint Thomas of Canterbury that existed in 1177. Joanna could be counted among those who accorded the saint a special reverence.

Margaret's transformation into a mother-in-law was as painless as such a change could be. Perhaps she came to think of Joanna as the daughter she never had.

Although Walter, the Archbishop of Palermo, performed the wedding and Joanna's coronation, the fact that both rites were celebrated in the royal chapel, and not in his cathedral, may be a significant detail.[383] Here we confront medieval perceptions of importance and prestige; Walter wanted to erect a new cathedral in Palermo, yet years were to pass before his wish came true.[384] For now, resources were being invested elsewhere; work continued on Monreale's church and cloister.

In July, Romuald of Salerno represented William at the negotiations that culminated in the Treaty of Venice.[385] This brought peace between the Papacy and the Holy Roman Empire. Abandoning his support of an antipope, Frederick Barbarossa recognized Alexander III as Pope whilst regularizing his relations with Papal allies like the northern Italian communes and Sicily.[386]

South of the Alps, the chief effect of this heretofore elusive treaty was a rare era of peace over the next few years. For the Kingdom of Sicily, it meant domestic security throughout William's reign.

This was Sicily's golden age.

Yet the *Regnum,* like other European kingdoms, had its shortcomings. Manorialism was a fact of life, and Monreale's abbot, being the feudal lord of a chunk of the Sicilian hinterland analogous to a vast barony, was beginning to act the part of a zealous baron. When several Muslims, not wishing to accept their status as his serfs, left the territory only to be repatriated, the perfervid prelate made the men swear on the Koran never to leave again, for they were tied to the land.[387]

Margaret was bound to her sense of duty. Even so, with William finally married, she could look forward to a more quiet life.

Chapter 22
PATRONESS

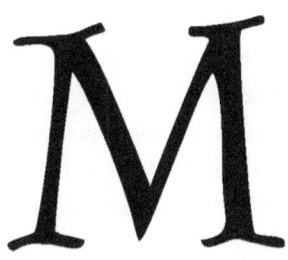

"The end crowneth all the work."

— Elizabeth I of England

By early 1178, a number of Margaret's projects were nearing completion. An impressive church, dedicated to the Holy Spirit, was being erected outside Palermo's city walls near the Oreto River.[388] It was given to the Cistercians[389] but assigned to the episcopal jurisdiction of Archbishop Walter, perhaps as something of a consolation to him for the lack of a new cathedral in Palermo. Indeed, Walter was showing himself to be uncharacteristically cooperative in order that he might obtain royal support for the grand church he envisaged; he even conceded some additional rights to Monreale's abbot.[390]

Mission

In addition to recent foundations, the crown supported a number of existing monasteries. Amongst the Benedictine abbeys outside local episcopal jurisdiction was one in Calabria where the poet William of Blois[391] had once been the abbot.[392] Unlike his brother, the royal tutor Peter of Blois, he had decided to remain in the kingdom for some time following the departure of Stephen of Perche. At his brother's urging, William finally returned to his native France.

By 1178, Maniace boasted a thriving religious community. Besides Maniace, Margaret patronized the abbey of Saint Philip of Fragalà, near Frazzanò. Like Maniace, it was built on the site of a Greek monastery. Here the queen was following in the footsteps of an earlier regent, Adelaide del Vasto, the widow of Count Roger I of Sicily.[393]

As her duties in the capital were ever fewer, Margaret visited Maniace sometimes, and also spent time with the nuns of the new convent at San Marco d'Alunzio near the Hauteville castle.[394] Constance probably lived at this nunnery for a time; indeed, Margaret may have founded it for her.[395]

Sometimes Beatrice of Rethel and Constance escorted Margaret back to Palermo, remaining in the capital for a month or so. Margaret's long absences were made possible by her son's complete independence and the fact that court intrigues were rarer and rarer.

In reality, the court was wherever the king was. William occasionally had to travel around the *Regnum,* accompanied at times by Matthew of Aiello.[396] By now, the king probably had other trusted advisors, nearer his own age, whose names are unknown to posterity. Then there were the older advisors he consulted often: Romuald of Salerno, Tancred of Lecce, the abbot Theobald of Monreale, the justiciar Florio of Camerota.

Margaret's confidants were her own ladies-in-waiting, certain trusted abbesses and the queen dowager Beatrice.

In Palermo, Joanna had several ladies-in-waiting who had come with her from England. The youngest was probably around twenty-two.

It was unrealistic to expect Joanna to begin bearing children very soon, but she knew that she was expected to give birth to as many as possible, preferably male.

Because of the young age of the new queen consort, certain reginal duties were still assumed by Margaret, usually accompanied by Joanna. Much of this involved little more than the act of being visible.

Appearances were almost everything. The simple fact that the two queens, accompanied by a small retinue of ladies-in-waiting and knights, strolled through Palermo's souk on a busy morning was sufficient to reassure the people that their monarchy was healthy, wealthy and prosperous.[397] The presence of the royal family at public religious ceremonies reinforced this.

The Palermitans do not seem to have been quite as obsequious to royalty as, by way of comparison, the Londoners, but they understood that only a strong king could defend their interests. This feeling was most keenly felt among the Muslims, who still comprised some thirty-five percent of the city's population, and the Jews.

As the former regent, Margaret enjoyed a special prestige. To the typical subject, who drew little distinction between the legal status of one queen and another, she was simply, as always, *la regina*.

Even in the twelfth century, the populace was more likely to actively support a king who seemed to have a harmonious rapport with the common folk. Margaret needed no confirmation of this principle beyond her own experience in Sicily, and it was something that, by way of example, she taught her daughter-in-law.

It was important for a queen to be aloof without appearing to be too remote.

Here the strategy of Margaret, who had been regent, differed from what Joanna had seen in her own mother, Eleanor, who was still in confinement at Winchester. The Kingdom of Sicily was a different world.

Royal Wisdom

The tenure of Romuald Guarna of Salerno in Sicily was nearing its end. He left Palermo for Salerno, of which he had long been the absentee archbishop, in March 1178.

In May, several ambassadors of Frederick Barbarossa, their journey delayed somewhat, arrived at Palermo. They confirmed the peace negotiated in Venice, swearing a further treaty with the Kingdom of Sicily for the next fifteen years. Margaret, some *familiares* and nobles were present for this momentous event.

Romuald of Salerno recounts a peculiar incident that occurred following the meeting. According to established practice, Frederick's ambassadors were escorted from Sicily northward through the *Regnum* on their return by a company of knights led by a military commander.[398] This journey proceeded through the mountains without incident until the party reached the wooded environs of Lagonegro at the northern boundary of Calabria. There they were attacked by a large crowd of peasants.

The ambassadors sought refuge in a house which the peasants attacked by hurling stones. The crowd of thieves managed to seize the trunk borne by one of the ambassadors, stealing a silver cup and the royal charter William was sending to Frederick; their interest in the charter was its gold seal.

As soon as the company reached Salerno, they reported the incident. Romuald thus heard about it, and notified the king. Enraged at the news, William immediately sent justiciars to the scene of the crime with an armed force bearing explicit orders to find, try and hang the perpetrators. The robbers were found at Barletta, Troia, Salerno, Capua and San Germano, and duly hanged publicly to send a message that law and order would prevail in the kingdom.

William then issued another charter bearing a gold seal and

sent it to Frederick.

Another violent incident occurred around the same time at Faiano, near Salerno, when Matthew, a Benedictine abbot, was hacked to pieces with swords and lances; some claimed this murder was instigated by monks who hated the unpopular abbot. Led by Florio of Camerota, William's justiciars investigated the crime, learning that, indeed, the peasants who did the killing were acting on the orders of some local monks. Speedy justice in this case made it clear that clerics were not exempt from royal authority.[399]

In August, John of Struma, the antipope Callixtus, deprived of support from the Holy Roman Emperor, who now recognized Alexander III as Pope, renounced his claim to the pontificate. He knelt before Alexander, who forgave him.

This is the last event described in the chronicle of Romuald, who by now resided in Salerno, his archbishopric. For historians, this leaves a dearth of detailed information from chroniclers present at court after 1178.[400]

Amongst the many architectural projects being undertaken was construction of a palace similar in style to the Zisa. Situated on the opposite side of the Genoard, near the Kemonia River not far from the road leading to Monreale, the Cuba, being surrounded by a lake, was equally impressive. Like the Zisa, the Cuba, which takes its name from the Arabic *qubba*, "cupola," is still standing.[401] Boccaccio mentioned it in his *Decameron*, where it is a setting in the sixth story of the fifth day, involving John of Procida.

By 1179, with the *Regnum*, the central Mediterranean and northern Italy pacified, it was possible for Margaret and her family to contemplate a future devoid of obvious hardship.

New Saint Agatha's Gate in the Norman-era city wall bordering the old souk district in central Palermo

Chapter 23
QUIETUS

"In my end is my beginning."

— Mary, Queen of Scots

Margaret learned that, in Spain, her brother, Sancho VI of Navarre, had reached a peace with her nephew, Alfonso VIII of Castile, ending a long feud. This dispute was arbitrated by Henry II of England, whose daughter, Eleanor, was now married to Alfonso. By 1179, Eleanor, who was a few years older than Joanna, had given birth to a daughter, Berengaria, and established a shrine to Thomas Becket in Toledo's cathedral.[402] The martyred Archbishop of Canterbury was being commemorated across western Europe.

Matriarch

Margaret's plan to commemorate Saint Thomas in Monreale was wholeheartedly embraced by Joanna. More immediately, though, what the queen mother most hoped for was that Joanna, who was fifteen, would become pregnant soon. For now, Constance, the posthumous daughter of Roger II and aunt of William II, was still heiress presumptive.[403]

Manuel Comnenus of Constantinople died in 1180, leaving his heirs to fight over the Byzantine succession. Margaret would not want that kind of thing to happen in Sicily. The best way to ensure against such a catastrophe was for William to have a few sons.

It is possible that during 1181 Joanna gave birth to a child, rumoured to have been named Bohemond and to have died in infancy. However, only one chronicler reports the event, and he was not in Sicily. Robert of Torigni, a Norman, was the abbot of Mont Saint-Michel and godfather to Eleanor, the daughter of Henry II. Significant as his chronicles are, Robert's statement about Bohemond is probably inaccurate.[404]

So far as we know, Margaret never became a grandmother. Indeed, it is highly possible that her son, the king, could not produce heirs.[405]

In a report corroborated by Arab sources, Robert of Torigni also tells us that the same year, 1181, saw the arrival in Palermo of an embassy from Tunisia that confirmed a decade-long treaty with the Kingdom of Sicily. The impetus for this trade accord was an event that occurred two years earlier, when a Sicilian fleet encountered a floundering ship taking the daughter of the Almohad caliph to her wedding to a Muslim emir and returned the girl to her grateful father.[406]

Muslim marriages, like Christian and Jewish unions, were, as ever, arranged by parental consent, yet the complications of conjugal life were universal, especially where important families were concerned. By now, Margaret may have begun to suspect a fertility problem in her son's marriage. In the twelfth century, of course, it was often impossible to know what, precisely, that impediment was. It was instinctive to find fault with the wife rather than the husband, but the physicians of the *Regnum,* which boasted one of Europe's finest medical schools at Salerno, knew better than to blame the woman whenever there was a lack of children. Nevertheless, another year or two would have to pass before Margaret's suspicions reached the point of credibility.[407]

Was William thinking about sons?

Monumental Effort

Now, in 1181, Monreale's splendid church was clearly visible from Palermo. It was an impressive sight that envious Archbishop Walter could not ignore.

At Margaret's urging, or at least with her support, King William began to contemplate the avaricious prelate's request for a new cathedral in Palermo. It was normal to draft the details of such a project a year or two before construction was scheduled to begin. In this case, the availability of a work force was a determining factor; these hundreds, even thousands, of men would not be free until the structural work on Monreale was complete.

The dimensions of the new cathedral would compensate for whatever it lacked in beauty. As the church of the Primate of Sicily, it would be larger than any other cathedral in the *Regnum*. Its nave was intentionally longer than that of Monreale's *duomo*. This kind of rivalry in church architecture had long become commonplace, and in later times it even infected the New World.[408]

The squarish nave of Palermo's earlier basilica, which had been altered by such details as muqarnas when it was converted to a mosque, was perpendicular to that of the new cathedral; a few parts of this original structure would be preserved.

The cathedral Walter inherited was already somewhat larger than what William and Margaret were building at Monreale. Writing in the tenth century, the visitor Mohammed ibn

Hawqal, who knew magnificent mosques in his native Baghdad, described what was then the Great Friday Mosque of Palermo as being large enough to accommodate seven thousand worshippers. It had at least seven large mihrabs, one of which can still be seen near the stairs leading down to the crypt.

Except for the addition of a Catalan Gothic portico and an unsightly cupola, the exterior has been modified rather little over the centuries. Unfortunately, most of the interior, which is now covered in stucco, reveals very little of the original Romanesque design, which featured Norman, Fatimid and Byzantine details.

After Monreale, Cefalù boasts the most impressive Sicilian cathedral of the Norman age to be found in Sicily; it was inspired by the Romanesque churches of Normandy. Nor are certain Norman churches on the mainland, such as those at Bari and Gerace, to be overlooked.

Margaret and William had a personal concern about the construction of Walter's cathedral. Attached to Palermo's original basilica was the chapel dedicated to Mary Magdalene that housed the royal tombs. Plans called for these to be transferred to another church of the same name to be hastily built at a site nearby.[409]

Passages

Pope Alexander III, who had long been Margaret's ally, died in August 1181. His most lasting achievement was the reformative Third Lateran Council, largely a dilatory attempt to curtail corruption and make the Papacy more efficient. Many occupants of the See of Peter were wicked misanthropes. Pope Alexander, a true man of God, was the exception. His successor was Ubaldo Allucingoli, an octogenarian cardinal who took the name Lucius III. Perhaps not surprisingly in view of his age, Lucius was a bit of a reactionary; his pontificate was destined to last just four years.

Except for sending a fleet to the island of Majorca[410] as part of a half-hearted Christian effort to oust the Muslims, William's military exploits during this period were few. Most of his time was occupied with domestic affairs. Elsewhere, however, events transpired that had a subtle ripple effect on the Kingdom of Sicily.

In April 1182, the Greek populace of Constantinople erupted against the many Italian merchants in the city.[411] Few of the victims were Sicilian; most were Genoan or Pisan. Thousands of Roman Catholics were attacked and killed indiscriminately. Not even the Papal ambassador was spared. This prompted William and other European monarchs west of the Adriatic to contemplate an invasion of the Byzantine territories.

That was not Margaret's concern. Although she resented the way the late Manuel Comnenus had treated her and her son, the queen mother's only effort involving the Byzantines was to convert their abandoned monasteries in northeastern Sicily into Latin abbeys and to perpetuate their artistic traditions at Monreale. Mosaics were beginning to cover the walls of Monreale's *duomo*.

Margaret continued her routine inspections of Monreale, occasionally visiting the monasteries under her patronage in the Nebrodian Mountains.

At the town of Patti was the tomb of Adelaide, the third wife of Roger I of Sicily and mother of Roger II. The two women had much in common. Like Margaret, Adelaide had been the patroness of monasteries in this mountainous region, and she was the regent of Sicily following her husband's death.[412] Margaret had to think of tombs other than Adelaide's.

As construction was beginning on Archbishop Walter's new cathedral, the queen mother oversaw the transfer of the royal tombs in the Mary Magdalene chapel of Palermo's existing basilica to the small church nearer the royal palace. She intended for her husband and sons to be transferred to Monreale eventually.

Margaret still wanted a grandson and she still did not have one.

By January 1183, William was making one of his periodic tours of the peninsular part of the *Regnum,* visiting Capua, Salerno and the Benedictine abbey at Cassino, among other localities.[413] As the senior members of the royal family, and with the vice chancellor and the *familiare* Archbishop Walter attending the king during his travels, the two queens, Margaret and Joanna, were left in charge at Palermo as the *de facto* "governors" of Sicily in William's absence.[414]

Meanwhile, the new Pontiff, Lucius, erected Monreale into a metropolitan archdiocese.[415]

William was back in the capital by April, when he issued a charter relegating to serfdom a great number of Sicily's rural Muslims.[416]

Margaret, who was now forty-eight, spent the next few months at Palermo and in the new royal palace at Monreale. The summer was as warm as ever.[417]

On Sunday, the thirty-first of July, she attended liturgy. It would be her last time, for that night she went to sleep, never to awaken.[418] We do not know what claimed her life, only that it ended.

A few days later, her funeral at Monreale[419] was attended by thousands who hiked up the mountain to commemorate their queen. The chief celebrant was Abbot William, recently consecrated as Archbishop of Monreale.

Here, in the cathedral she loved, lies one of Sicily's most beloved women.

Her epitaph[420] is eloquent in its simplicity: "Here in regal dignity lies Queen Margaret, distinguished by her noble spirit, the consort of a king, the mother of princes, the regent for

King William II the son she bore. Commended to Heaven on the Feast of Saint Peter in Chains, in the year one thousand one hundred and eighty-three. Amen."

Legacy

As queen consort, Margaret was her husband's unwavering advisor. As queen regent, she stood against the encroachments of the baronage and defended the rights of the common people. As queen mother, she championed the efforts of her son and built great churches.

What we do in this life shapes the impressions we leave to posterity, for better or worse. The interpretation of somebody's life forms the blueprint for what historians sometimes call "legacy." Until her husband's death, Margaret Jiménez had only a vague idea of what her legacy might be. One day she was the king's wife, the next day she was running a kingdom.

Struggle is the child of adversity. The greater the struggle, the greater the achievement gained by overcoming it. The most daunting challenges are the ones we don't see coming, those we are not prepared to confront. We can dislike them but we cannot disown them, for they are our inalienable birthright. They make us who we are, and we would be the lesser without them. Less strong, less wise, less individual, perhaps less dignified. Those who rise to overcome unexpected challenges earn our esteem.

Margaret was raised to be a wife and mother, not the leader of a polyglot nation of millions. A consort, not a regent. Certainly not a she-wolf in sheep's clothing. In an age when might made right, she was taught to wield words, not swords.

Leadership and statecraft were not part of her education in Pamplona. Regency was a gritty task nothing like the queenship little girls dreamt of. Margaret had no time for an existential crisis.

So rarely did a European queen become regent that the duty bore only the faintest outlines of a job description. Yet there was nothing ersatz about Margaret's five-year regency.

The women in Margaret's elite sorority were too few, and separated by too many miles and mountains, for there to be anything more than a tenuous sisterhood among them. One of these women, Maude, the mother of Henry II of England, died in Rouen sixteen months into Margaret's regency, and despite knowing a few of the same people the two queens never met.

Except for the occasional letter, the general lack of communication between such women meant that there was little mentoring between those of one generation and the next. Constance, the posthumous daughter of King Roger, was fortunate to find in Margaret the living example of a queen who actually governed a kingdom; in her turn she became, like Margaret and Maude, the most powerful woman in Europe for several years.

"You cannot find peace by avoiding life," observed Virginia Woolf. Margaret confronted life without hesitation. Her mentors were her own instincts. Mistakes would be made. She would learn from them. Experience was her teacher.

The record tells us that, in her pellucid intent to keep peace in the kingdom, the queen jailed one or two men who may have been innocent of their alleged crimes. Such incidents were exceptional. As regent, Margaret was rarely as ambivalent or capricious as many rulers of her century.

The seeds, even the saplings, of enlightened reform can be discerned in some of Margaret's policies during the chancellorship of Stephen of Perche. The queen's attempts to curtail corruption in officialdom bore the accoutrements, if not the substance, of democracy. Although such reforms proved little more than an evanescent excursion into a world that could have been, they were significant for their time. There is no evidence to suggest that Margaret's husband, had he lived and reigned longer, would have made a comparable effort to eliminate the corruption of the court notaries or high officials like Robert of Calatabiano in Palermo and Richard of Aversa in Messina.

Thrust into her place in the world by the unsteady hand of fate, Margaret shaped a corner of Europe into her own niche by reacting with courage to every challenge thrown before her. Her essential strategy was simple survival, yet she was more than a survivor.

Margaret was expected to maintain the *status quo* in a prosperous land threatened from within and without. At the very least, she was a temporary "caretaker" ruler required to pass unto her son a nation as whole and hale as the kingdom founded by her father-in-law. We should resist the temptation to characterize her very simply as a "power player," for she resorted to the crude use of raw, royal power only when she had no choice.

Her wisdom was exceptional. She was just, but rarely vindictive. Endowed with the royal power of life and death, she ruled benignly yet firmly, seeking to avoid meting out capital punishment even when the outright elimination of her adversaries would have solved her immediate problems. She respected the rule of law, and she was fortunate to have an efficacious legal code, the Assizes of Ariano, as her guide.

For the most part, she was pragmatic, a realist. There is not so much as a hint that Margaret's ego thrived on flattery or the superficial. She did not suffer fools gladly.

With the possible exception of the eunuchs, sycophants at her court were few. No trace of gratuitous vanity was ever attributed to her. There is no evidence to suggest that Margaret consciously applied Aristotle's modes of persuasion (pathos, ethos, logos) to win people over to her way of thinking through the use of rhetoric, but her strength of character prevailed over the efforts of some notoriously ferocious foes. Part of her strategy was the smile that Falcandus found so incriminating.

The Sicilians loved her. If we knew little more about Queen Margaret, that would be enough to suggest her innate rectitude. Her charisma, so far as we know, did not transcend the mystique accorded most medieval queens.

She marched in step with her time. Norman Sicily was very much part of the "Renaissance of the Twelfth Century," with its scholasticism, vernacular literature, and majestic architecture.

Would that we could, very literally, transport ourselves back in time to interview the steel butterfly that was Margaret of Navarre. A delicate flower crowning a stem as steadfast as the trunk of an oak. A graceful woman whose claws could draw blood.

Would we be impressed more by her fondness for frankness, or by her simple pragmatism? Might Margaret the woman revise the impressions expressed in these pages of Margaret the queen?

May history be kind to the daughter, wife and mother of kings who transcended docility to lead a nation.

Let us tread lightly on the legacy of great queens, who bequeath us a precious patrimony.

EPILOGUE

"God and posterity will show me more favour."

— Lady Jane Grey

The memory of their Spanish queen did not soon fade from the Sicilians' memory, but their attention turned to focus on the king's wife. Virtually nothing is known about Joanna's time as queen consort, except that she bore no children. In the spring of 1184, she went with William to Calabria to comfort its population following a destructive earthquake powerful enough to force the collapse of Cosenza's cathedral.

The traveler bin Jubayr arrived in Sicily too belatedly to meet Margaret, but he left us a perceptive description of what he found.[421]

A year after Margaret's death, William arranged the marriage of his aunt, Constance, to Henry, a son of Frederick Barbarossa. This may have reinforced Sicily's bonds with Germany, but any child of Constance would be a Hohenstaufen, not a Hauteville. The queen dowager Beatrice of Rethel, Constance's mother, died a few months after the betrothal.

In 1185, while Constance was making her way northward to marry[422] Henry Hohenstaufen, William launched an invasion of the Greek lands to the east of the *Regnum,* something he had been considering ever since the Byzantine massacre of the Latins at Constantinople a few years earlier. Leading this incursion was Tancred of Lecce and an able admiral named Margaritus of Brindisi. The Sicilian advance toward Constantinople was stopped by Emperor Isaac Angelus Comnenus, with whom the King of Sicily made peace four years later.

When Saladin captured Jerusalem late in 1187, the only military opposition to arrive from Europe was the Sicilian fleet led by admiral Margaritus. The next year, Margaritus relieved the Knights Hospitaller, who were besieged by Saladin at their large fortress, Krak des Chevaliers.

With other Christian kings, William was already contemplating a Third Crusade to take back the Holy City.

When King William II of Sicily died in November 1189, his aunt Constance was his designated heir.[423] The Sicilians, not wishing to see the *Regnum* fall into the hands of the Holy Roman Emperor, crowned illegitimate Tancred of Lecce their king. Initially, there was nothing Constance could do about this.

Henry II of England died in the same year, succeeded as king by his son Richard Lionheart.

In 1190, Constance's father-in-law, Frederick Barbarossa, met his end while riding across a river in what is now Turkey. His son, Constance's husband Henry VI, was crowned Holy Roman Emperor in Rome the following year.

Queen Joanna, Margaret's daughter-in-law, survived William and in 1191 she went on the Third Crusade with her brother, Richard Lionheart, who tried to marry her off to Saladin's brother as a peace offering. Returning to Europe, she wed Raymond VI of Toulouse as his third wife. (Joanna died following childbirth in 1199.)

Thinking to overthrow Tancred, Constance and her husband invaded the *Regnum*. This incursion ended with Constance being captured. She was rescued in 1192.

With Tancred's untimely death in 1194, Constance again claimed the Kingdom of Sicily as its lawful queen regnant. This time she was successful. By her husband, Henry VI, she bore a son, Frederick II. This ushered in Sicily's Swabian era. Frederick was Holy Roman Emperor, King of the Germans, King of Sicily, and eventually King of Jerusalem. Following in the intellectual tradition of his grandfather, Roger II, erudite Frederick led Sicily into a second golden age.

Margaret's brother, Sancho VI "the Wise" of Navarre, died at Pamplona in 1194. His daughter, named Berengaria (like the daughter of Alfonso VIII of Castile), had wed Richard Lionheart in 1191, thus becoming Queen of England and daughter-in-law of Eleanor of Aquitaine. Berengaria's marriage to Richard was childless.

Margaret's nephew, Alfonso VIII of Castile, is celebrated for his part in Spain's *Reconquista*. He defeated an Almohad force at the Battle of the Navas de Tolosa in 1212, but died two years later.

Looking back across many generations, we can see that the people who touched Margaret's life were the most colourful figures of their era. The patina of the passing centuries has not lessened their legacy, nor has it tarnished hers.

The story of Margaret Jiménez of Navarre is the story of every woman who rises to face the unknown and defeats it. Her story is our story.

The royal throne dais in the Palatine Chapel

CHRONOLOGY

M

"The stream of time, irresistible, ever moving, carries off and bears away all things that come to birth, plunging them into utter darkness, both deeds of no account and deeds which are mighty and worthy of commemoration."

— Anna Comnena

This succinct timeline is intended merely as a general framework to lend context to the history and events recounted in the preceding pages. It is not meant to present in detail those events that occurred during Margaret's lifetime, or to substitute the narrative text in this monograph.

998-1019 - Rule of Jafar al-Kalbi in Sicily. Construction of Favara palace in Palermo is attributed to this emir.

1000 - Norse civilization in northwestern France (Normandy) assimilates with local culture. Approximate period of Norse landings in Newfoundland.

1002 - Defeat of Al Mansur ibn Abi Aamir (Almanzor) leaves most of Navarre and Catalonia in Christian hands.

1004 - Fatimids establish large library and *dar al-hikma* (house of wisdom) in Egypt.

1008 - Fatimids re-establish diplomatic relations with China.

1016 - Norman knights first participate in battles in Italy. First Turkish raids in Armenia.

1018 - Bulgarian lands conquered by Byzantines, who also defeat Italians (Lombards) at Battle of Cannae, in Apulia, where many Norman knights are felled.

1019-1037 - Rule of Ahmed al-Akhal in Sicily.

1035 - County of Aragon becomes a kingdom.

1037-1040 - Rule of Sicily by Abdallah Abu Hafs, usurper.

1038-1042 - Byzantine forces of George Maniakes briefly occupy parts of eastern Sicily; army includes Greeks, Normans, Lombards, and Norse Varangian Guard under Harald Hardrada.

1040 - Hasan as-Samsam begins his rule in Sicily; deposed in 1044.

1042 - Normans establish Melfi as their Italian capital

1044 - Sicily divided into four qadits. Rivalry among emirs worsens.

1045 - Zirids of Tunisia rebel against Fatimids to unite with Abbasids of Baghdad. Cathedral of Gerace (Calabria) consecrated.

1052 - García Sánchez III of Navarre establishes Church of Santa María la Real at Nájera.

1053 - Following death of Hasan as-Samsam and extinction of Kalbid dynasty, three important emirs divide control of Sicily: Ibn al Hawas at Kasr' Janni (Enna), Ibn at Timnah at Syracuse and Catania, Abdullah ibn Hawqal at Trapani and Mazara. Normans defeat Lombards at Battle of Civitate.

CHRONOLOGY

1054 - Great Schism between eastern and western Christianity. Sicilian Christians initially remain "eastern" (Orthodox). Supernova observed by astronomers in Asia; becomes Crab Nebula.

1055 - Seljuk Turks occupy Baghdad.

1056 - Agnes of Aquitaine regent of Holy Roman Empire until 1061.

1057 - Tunisia invaded by Banu Hilal of Arabia, with Zirid lands reduced in size.

1060 - Unsuccessful Norman attack in coastal northeastern Sicily.

1061 - Battle of Messina. City and parts of Nebrodian and Peloritan region occupied; permanent Norman presence in Sicily.

1065 - Kingdom of Castile founded. Seljuk Turks invade Georgia.

1065-1067 - War of the Three Sanchos among three Jiménez cousins ruling Castile, Navarre and Aragon.

1066 - Battle of Hastings leads to complete Norman conquest of Saxon England. Battle of Messina forms partial pattern of this invasion of an island from a continent. (Some Norman knights fight at both battles.)

1071 - Normans attack Palermo; Norman invaders are led by Robert de Hauteville, Arab defenders by Ayub ibn Temim. Byzantines lose Battle of Manzikert to Seljuk Turks.

1072 - Battle of Palermo ends in January with Norman occupation under Roger and Robert of Hauteville. Greek Orthodox Bishop Nicodemus removed from authority over Christian community.

1074 - Seljuk Turks seize Jerusalem from Byzantine control.

1075 - Investiture Controversy begins as conflict between Papacy and Holy Roman Emperors.

1077 - Excommunicated Henry IV, Holy Roman Emperor, does penance at Canossa.

1078 - Arab poet ibn Hamdis leaves Sicily.

1079 - Frankish settlement begins along Way of Saint James in northeastern Spain.

1081 - Suppression of revolt led by self-appointed "emir" Bin al Wardi (Bernavert) at Catania; another of his revolts is quashed at Syracuse in 1085.

1083 - Roger I appoints Latin (rather than Orthodox) Bishop of Palermo and Gallican Rite is introduced in new churches.

1084 - Bruno founds Carthusian Order in Germany.

1085 - Alfonso VI of Castile seizes Toledo from Moors.

1087 - Ibn Hammud, Emir of Kasr'Janni (Enna), last major Arab stronghold in Sicily, surrenders to Normans; Noto falls in 1091.

1091 - Byzantine Greeks defeat Pechenegs at Battle of Levounion.

1094 - El Cid conquers Valencia.

1095 - Roger II, future King of Sicily, is born. Pope Urban II preaches First Crusade.

1096 - First Crusade begins; some Norman knights participate under Bohemond of Hauteville (later Prince of Antioch), brother of Roger I.

1097 - Odo of Bayeux, Earl of Kent, younger brother of William the Conqueror, dies in Palermo *en route* to the Crusade while visiting Roger I.

1098 - Roger I, as Great Count of Sicily, becomes Papal apostolic legate, with right of approval over bishops. Cistercian Order founded in France.

1099 - Crusaders conquer Jerusalem. Death of El Cid in Spain.

1100 - Crusaders control Palestine in the wake of the First Crusade and crown Baldwin first King of Jerusalem. García Ramírez (father of Margaret) born in Spain to Ramiro Sánchez, Lord of Monzón, and Cristina, daughter of the Cid.

CHRONOLOGY

1101 - Roger I, Great Count of Sicily, dies, succeeded by Simon, his eldest living, legitimate son, who is still a minor. Roger's consort, Adelaide del Vasto of Savona, is regent.

1104 - Alfonso I "the Battler," a cousin of García Ramírez, becomes King of Aragon and Navarre.

1105 - Roger II succeeds his elder brother Simon (1093-1105) as ruler of Sicily under Adelaide's regency.

1108 - Bohemond of Antioch becomes vassal of Byzantine Emperor.

1109 - Bertrand of Toulouse occupies Tripoli (Lebanon).

1112 - Roger is knighted (this ceremony marks his age of majority and sovereign authority following "regency" under his mother).

1113 - Order of Saint John (Knights Hospitaller) based in Palestine chartered by Pope Paschal II. Establish commanderies in Sicily and later (in 1530) receive Malta from Charles V, King of Sicily and Holy Roman Emperor.

1116 - García Ramírez succeeds his father, Ramiro Sánchez.

1119 - In Spain, Alfonso the Battler takes control of Tudela from Moors. Knights Templar founded in Palestine.

1120 - Council of Nablus establishes legal code for Kingdom of Jerusalem.

1121 - Betrothal of young Margaret of Aigle to García Ramírez. Presumed year of birth of William I of Sicily.

1122 - Concordat of Worms between Papacy and Holy Roman Empire.

1123 - First Lateran Council, opened by Pope Alexius II, forbids Roman Catholic clerics wives or concubines; until now Catholic priests were permitted to marry before ordination. Rotrou III "the Great" of Perche takes possession of Tudela.

1125 - Christian army defeats Seljuk Turks at Battle of Azaz.

1126 - In Spain, Almoravids take control of Monzón and its environs.

1128 - Portugal declares independence from León, which recognizes its monarch, Alfonso Henriques, in 1143.

1130 - Roger crowned first King of Sicily (known henceforth as "Roger II"). On his orders Saint John of the Hermits, an Orthodox monastery in Palermo, is ordered rebuilt as Benedictine abbey, completed in 1148. Palatine Chapel rebuilt to present form during this period. García Ramírez occupies Monzón in the name of Alfonso the Battler.

1131 - Cathedral of Cefalù erected.

1132 - Birth of Sancho VI "the Wise" of Navarre, brother of Margaret.

1134 - Birth of Blanca (who wed Sancho III of Castile), sister of Margaret, at La Guardia in La Rioja. García Ramírez elected king by Navarrese nobles and bishops.

1135 - Birth of Margaret Jiménez of Navarre, future Queen Regent of Sicily, at La Guardia in La Rioja. García Ramírez crowned King of Pamplona. Beginning of "Anarchy," a civil war over royal succession, in England.

1136 - Construction of Saint-Denis near Paris; Gothic movement begins.

1138 - Death of Anacletus II ends Papal schism (which began in 1130); Innocent II universally recognized as Pope. Major earthquake around Aleppo.

1139 - Second Lateran Council, convened by Pope Innocent II, makes celibacy mandatory for Roman Catholic priests, reiterating a canon established in 1123 but not widely enforced. Innocent recognizes Roger II as King of Sicily.

1140 - Roger II promulgates Assizes of Ariano, introduces ducat.

1141 - Death of Margaret of Aigle, mother of Blanca and Margaret Jiménez.

1143 - Martorana Church (Palermo) built in Norman-Arab style for Greek Orthodox community by George of Antioch. Nilos Doxopatrios, Orthodox cleric, authors a theological treatise supporting the Eastern Church.

CHRONOLOGY

1145-1148 - Second Crusade; participation by Sicilian knights is limited.

1146 - Legal principles expressed in Assizes of Ariano are in force by this time.

1147 - Almohads displace Almoravids in northwestern Africa and southern Spain.

1148 - Betrothal of Margaret of Navarre to William I of Sicily.

1149 - Margaret of Navarre weds future William I of Sicily.

1150 - Death of King García Ramírez, father of Margaret; accession of Sancho VI of Navarre.

1151 - Blanca Jiménez weds Sancho III of Castile. William I of Sicily crowned *rex filius*.

1152 - Birth of Roger, first son of Margaret and William.

1153 - Birth of Robert, second son of Margaret and William. End of "Anarchy" in England. First Treaty of Constance between Papacy and Holy Roman Empire to prevent Byzantine conquests in Italy.

1154 - *Book of Roger* completed by court geographer Abdullah al Idrisi. Roger II dies and reign of King William I begins. Birth of Constance, Roger's posthumous daughter. Accession of Henry II in England.

1155 - Birth of William II, third son of Margaret and William I. Birth of Alfonso VIII of Castile, son of Blanca (Margaret's sister). Frederick I "Barbarossa" Hohenstaufen crowned Holy Roman Emperor.

1156 - Death of Blanca, Margaret's sister. Treaty of Benevento between Papacy and Kingdom of Sicily.

1158 - Birth of Henry, fourth son of Margaret and William. Thomas le Brun (Thomas Brown), treasurer at William's court, returns to England to reform exchequer of Henry II, thus influencing European accounting principles.

1159 - Death of Robert, secondborn son of Margaret and William. Arrival in Sicily of Gilbert of Gravina, Margaret's cousin.

1160 - Mahdia, last Norman stronghold in North Africa, is lost.

1161 - Matthew Bonello leads revolt of Norman barons, resulting in death of Roger, firstborn son of Margaret and William. Rhum Sultanate makes peace with Byzantine Empire.

1165 - Design and construction of Zisa palace begin.

1166 - Death of William I; reign of young King William II begins under Margaret's regency. Arrival in Sicily of Rodrigo (Henry), Margaret's half-brother.

1167 - Margaret appoints her cousin, Stephen of Perche, chancellor.

1168 - At Messina, Margaret oversees trials of Rodrigo (Henry) and others. Stephen of Perche deposed and expelled.

1169 - Major earthquake in Catania and southeastern Sicily. Walter becomes Archbishop of Palermo.

1170 - Thomas Becket murdered in Canterbury Cathedral.

1171 - Margaret's regency ends when William II reaches age of majority. Benjamin of Tudela visits Sicily. Saladin deposes Fatimids, establishes Ayyubid rule.

1172 - Death of Henry, Margaret's fourthborn son. Planning and construction begin on Monreale Abbey.

1173 - Thomas Becket canonized.

1174 - Sicilian fleet led by Tancred of Lecce attacks Alexandria.

1175 - William II signs treaty with Venetians. Henry II of England signs treaty with Irish.

1176 - Betrothal of William II to Joanna of England. Byzantines lose much of Anatolia to Seljuk Turks.

1177 - Wedding of William II and Joanna of England. Treaty of Venice between Pope and Holy Roman Emperor.

CHRONOLOGY

1178 - Sicilian treaty with Holy Roman Empire. Romuald Guarna of Salerno leaves Sicily.

1179 - Third Lateran Council convened by Pope Alexander III.

1181 - Sicilian treaty with Tunisia. Pope Alexander III dies.

1182 - Massacre of the Latins in Constantinople.

1183 - Death of Margaret, Queen of Sicily. Monreale becomes archdiocese.

1184 - Major earthquake in Calabria. Bin Jubayr visits Sicily. Construction of Palermo's new cathedral.

1185 - William II invades Byzantine lands.

1186 - Constance, daughter of Roger II, weds Henry VI, future Holy Roman Emperor.

1187 - Saladin captures Jerusalem. William II sends fleet to Palestine.

1189 - Death of William II. Succeeded as King of Sicily by Tancred of Lecce. Richard I "Lionheart" crowned King of England.

1190 - Richard Lionheart, brother of Queen Joanna of Sicily, occupies Messina with Philip II of France for several months *en route* to Third Crusade. Death of Frederick I "Barbarossa," Holy Roman Emperor; succeeded by Henry VI.

1191 - Henry VI and Constance defeated in attempted invasion of *Regnum*, with Constance captured. Construction of Magione church (Palermo) by Matthew of Aiello.

1192 - Constance is rescued. Isabella I crowned Queen of Jerusalem.

1193 - Death of Saladin.

1194 - Death of King Tancred. Holy Roman Emperor Henry VI arrives in Palermo and rules by right of his wife, Constance, Queen Regnant of Sicily, who gives birth to Frederick II. Death of Margaret's brother, Sancho VI of Navarre.

1195 - Constance crowned Queen of Sicily.

1196 - Joanna, widow of William II, weds Raymond VI of Toulouse.

1197 - Death of Henry VI, Holy Roman Emperor, husband of Constance. Basilica of Saint Nicholas (begun in 1089) consecrated in Bari.

1198 - Death of Constance; she is succeeded by her son, Frederick II. Teutonic Order founded under Hohenstaufen patronage.

1199 - Death of Joanna at Rouen.

GENEALOGICAL TABLES

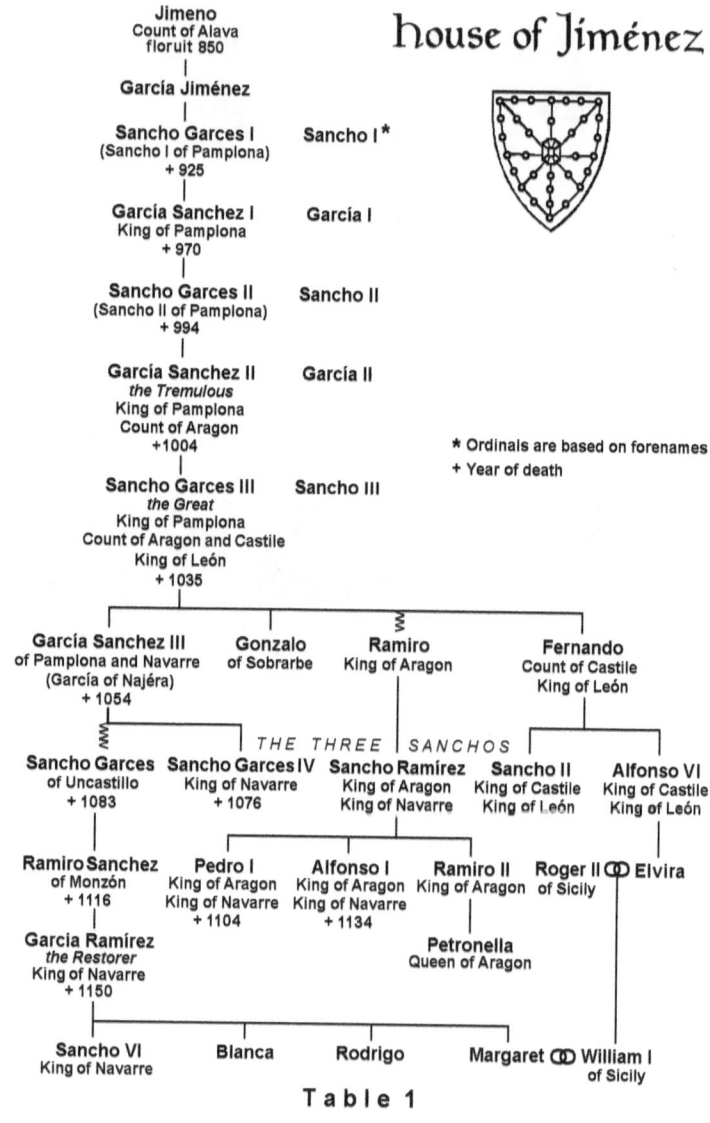

Table 1

GENEALOGICAL TABLES

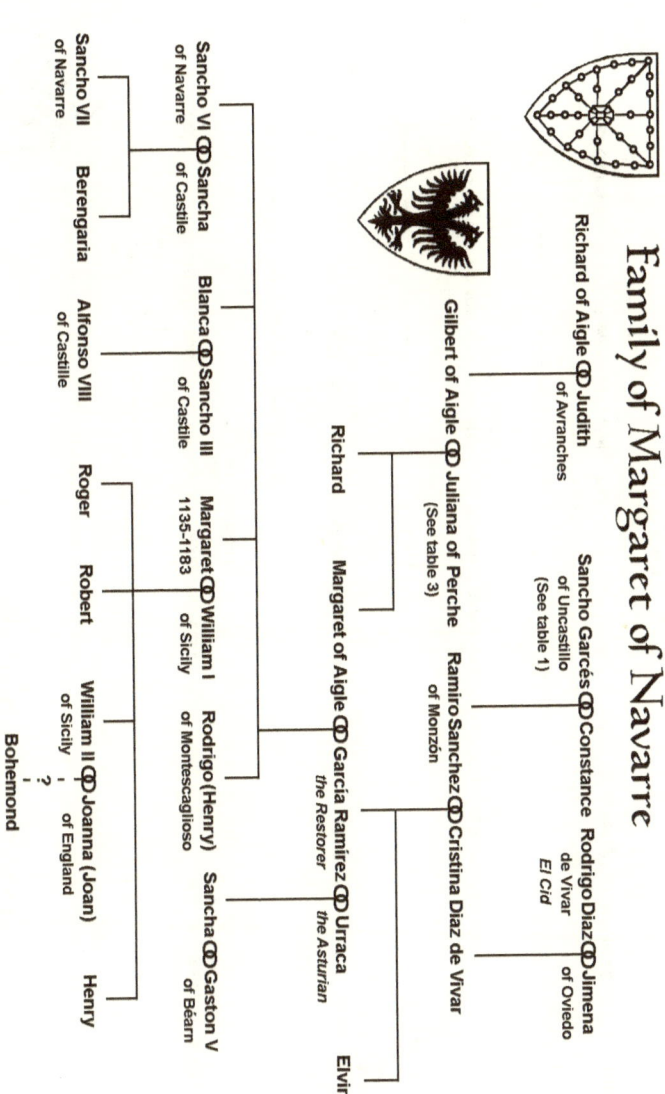

Table 2

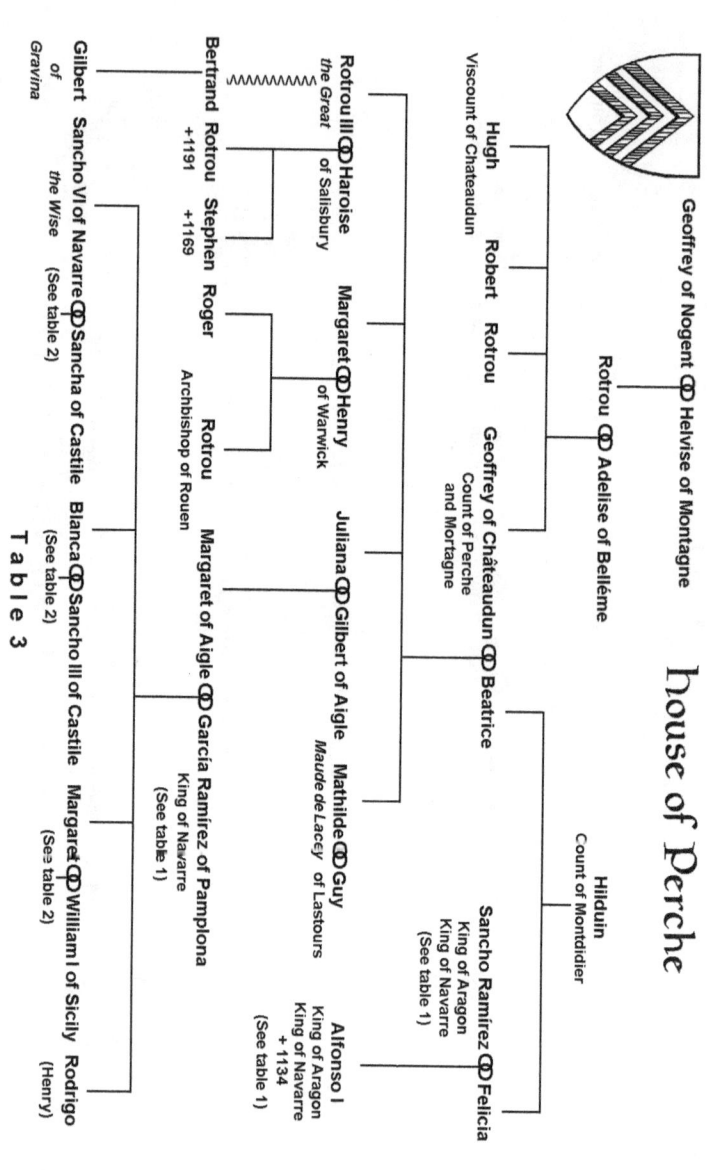

Table 3

GENEALOGICAL TABLES

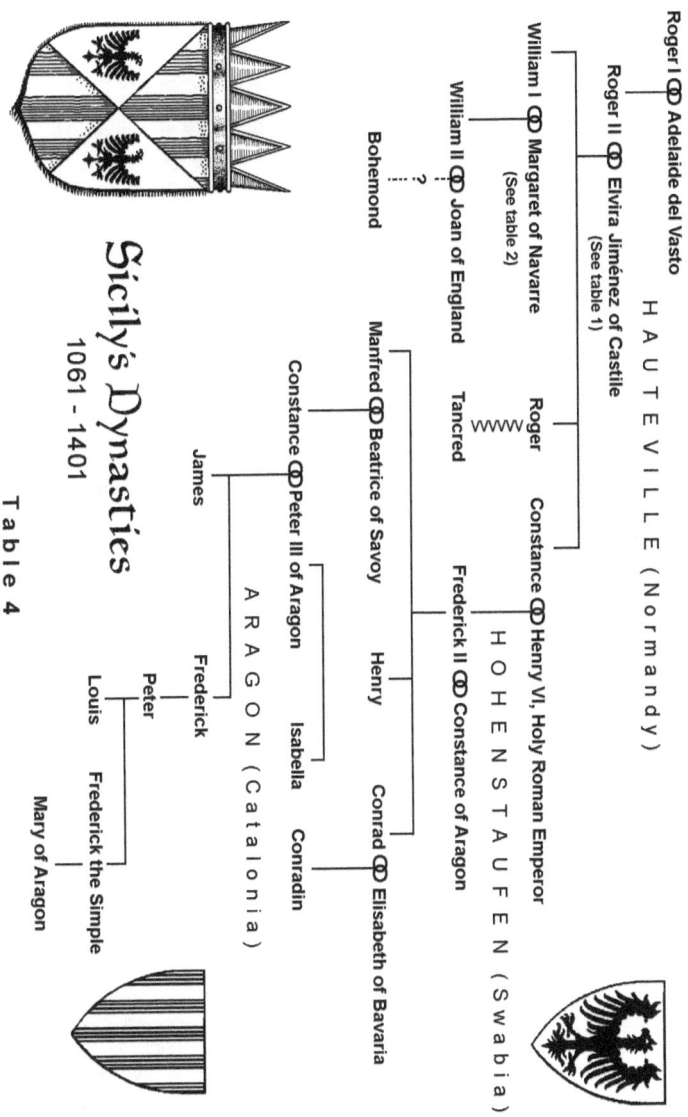

Sicily's Dynasties
1061 - 1401

Table 4

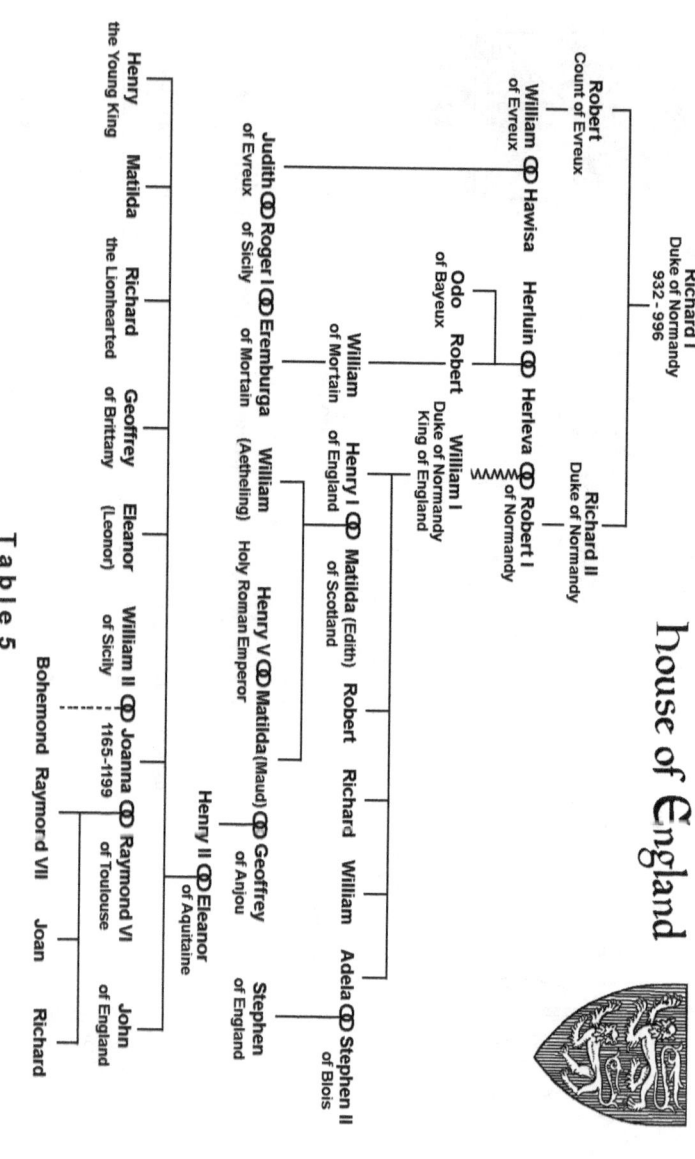

Table 5

Appendix 1
BIN JUBAYR

Some of the most important descriptions of Norman Sicily come to us from Arab and Muslim sources. These are especially important in their objectivity because, unlike visitors from northern, Christian Europe, those from prosperous Muslim regions brought to their observations a somewhat more sophisticated point of reference. They weren't easily impressed by the more superficial aspects of a wealthy kingdom. Idrisi is the best known of the Arab geographers to have visited Sicily (indeed he lived here on the island), but another is equally distinguished. He visited Sicily after Margaret's death.

Abu Hussain Mohammed bin Ahmad bin Jubayr (or Jubair) al-Kenani was born around 1145 in Valencia, then a thriving region of "Moorish" Spain, and by 1182 he was high secretary for the Emir of Granada. The following year Jubayr left for a Hajj (pilgrimage) to Mecca. His travels took him across the Mediterranean, reaching Alexandria in the spring of 1183. On his way back to Spain, in early December 1184, he reached Sicily, where he was shipwrecked at Messina but given hospitality by an Arabic-speaking monarch, William II. His Sicilian travels took him westward by ship, with stops at Cefalù, Termini, Solunto and finally Palermo. Following a week in the capital, he departed by land for Trapani, passing Alcamo along the way.

Among many other features, he describes several castles which no longer exist. He refers to a military fleet under construction; these were probably galleys for William's invasion of Greece in 1185.

In Palermo he found a city of gardens and streets in a metropolis that combined "the benefits of wealth and splendor," comparing it to Cordoba. He mentioned its limestone buildings, springs and rivers.

He remarked that the Christian women dressed with much the same modesty as their Muslim sisters, and wore scarves or veils; his description leads us to infer that many of them spoke Arabic.

He also described the Martorana Church, and specifically its bell tower (perhaps higher then than now). He observed that the city of Messina was predominantly Greek Orthodox, with a dwindling Muslim community. Some of his comments are cryptic. He mentions a tax on Muslims, without making clear whether this tax was also levied upon Christians and Jews.

Jubayr recorded the story of the words of King William II to his subjects following the horrific earthquake of 1169: "Let each of you pray to the God he worships; he who has faith in his God will feel peace in his heart."

It is clear from his writings that Jubayr was devout in his Sunni faith, perhaps even something of a dogmatist. But the winds of religious intolerance were gathering force, and perhaps that is what he inferred from what he saw in Sicily, where he might have hoped to see more Muslims.

Jubayr's record is useful in establishing the continuity of the Palermitan cultural atmosphere over the centuries. It is, in effect, a link in a chain. Mohammed ibn Hawqal, a merchant from Baghdad with a penchant for geography, described an Arab-Byzantine Sicily in the time long before Idrisi and Jubayr, and a capital just as prosperous as in the time of Jubayr.

Jubayr also visited Jerusalem and other places, and wrote about these. He died in Alexandria in 1217.

Appendix 2
CHRONICLERS AND VISITORS

Many original sources were consulted in the writing of this book, forming its essential foundation. Apart from architectural features (Margaret's funerary epitaph), these were written records such as chronicles, charters and letters. The chief chroniclers whose work was consulted, Hugh Falcandus and Romuald of Salerno, are considered in the following appendices. Here we'll succinctly describe the contributions of other chroniclers, commentators and visitors associated with Sicily, Navarre, Normandy and England in Margaret's time.

Many chroniclers were monks. A few were travelers, typically intellectual traders. If "Falcandus" was a court official, he was the rare "exception that proves the rule." Anna Comnena, a Byzantine princess and the first woman to write a history, was even more exceptional. Most traders, minstrels and heralds were seasoned travelers, monks somewhat less so, although religious orders like the Benedictines had monasteries across Europe, forming what was a *de facto* ecclesiastical and intellectual network.

To this list could be added a number of Spanish, French and English chroniclers who made passing references to the Jiménez or Hautevilles, perhaps in connection with their own dynasties, such as England's Plantagenets. Here the chronicles of William of Puylaurens and Robert of Torigni come to mind. In the eastern Mediterranean we find Nicetas Akominatos Choniates and William of Tyre.

Charters, decrees and various manuscripts, such as those consulted in researching the life and times of Queen Margaret, tell us only a small part of the story. The chroniclers were the journalists of the Middle Ages, offering us details and perspectives we could not likely find elsewhere. Our knowledge of past events would be much the lesser without them.

The identities of many chroniclers are unknown. We do not know who wrote the *Gesta Roderici,* the chronicle of the deeds of El Cid.

Historians distinguish between *annals,* which are essentially "diaries" that record a sequence or chronology of events as they occur, and *chronicles,* "narratives" which typically lend more detail and insight to the events they recount. In many cases, however, the difference between the annal and the chronicle is rather subtle. By definition, both are contemporaneous to the events they describe, and one imagines their writers recording notes before composing "finished" entries in an annal or narratives in a chronicle.

Writing in 1867, William Stubbs drew the distinction in these terms:

"The difference between chronicles and annals was not, as it has been sometimes stated, that the former belong to universal, the latter to national or particular history, but that the former have a continuity of subject and style, whilst the latter contain the mere jottings down of unconnected events. The annals are the ore, the chronicles are the purified metal out of which the historian elaborates his perfect jewel."[424]

He went on to define the chronicle by paraphrasing Gervase of Tilbury, saying that, "a contemporary chronicle is a record of acts and events which the actors and eyewitnesses thought worthy to be remembered."

CHRONICLERS AND VISITORS

For our purposes, such definitions will suffice. The accounts by Benjamin of Tudela and bin Jubayr are, strictly speaking, a different literary form, namely travel diaries or "travelogues." Idrisi's geography is rather similar in format to these travelers' writings. Thomas Fazello's work is a "secondary" history drawn from various sources of information.

Alexander of Telese. Completed around 1136, the *Ystoria Rogerii Regis* was reportedly commissioned by a sister of King Roger II. Alexander was a monk in the Calabrian town of Telese, where he is thought to have lived until around 1143.

Amatus of Monte Cassino. This important chronicler was a Benedictine monk, author of the eloquent *L'Ystoire de li Normant,* which was written soon after 1080 and survives as a (later) French translation.

Ali ibn al-Athir. Born in 1160, al-Athir directed his attention to the eastern Mediterranean but makes occasional reference to other regions, and to events such as the Crusades. He died in Mosul in 1233.

Benedict of Peterborough. A highly informative chronicle dealing with the reigns of Henry II and Richard I of England was attributed to this abbot until the twentieth century. Scholars are now in general agreement that it was, in fact, the work of Roger of Howden (see below).[425] The chronicle of "Benedict" provides information about the betrothal of Joanna, Henry's daughter, to William II of Sicily, such as her voyage through France with her brothers Henry and Richard.

Benjamin of Tudela. Born around 1130 in the same region as Queen Margaret, Rabbi Benjamin's travels offer us much information about the Mediterranean world, and not just that of the Jews, during the twelfth century. He is described in his own chapter.

Hugh Falcandus. Irascible Hugh Falcandus (whoever he was) is described in a dedicated appendix.

Falco of Benevento. Born around 1070, this chronicler wrote the *Chronicon Beneventanum* and other works. Of Lombard ancestry, he was antipathetic toward the Normans. Falco died during the reign of Roger II.

Gerhoh of Reichersberg. This cleric shed light on the Normans' rapport with the Papacy. He died in 1169. A compilation of his more important works was published in 1897 in the *Monumenta Germaniae Historica* series.

Godfrey Malaterra. The *De Rebus Gestis Rogerii Calabriae et Siciliae Comitis et Roberti Guiscardi Ducis Fratris Eius*, written by this Benedictine monk, is an important contribution. Malaterra died before 1130.

Romuald Guarna of Salerno. The author of the informative *Chronicon sive Annales* is described in his own appendix.

Mohammed ibn Hawqal. In his *Kitab al-masalik wa l-mamalik*, this merchant from Baghdad with a penchant for geography described an Arab-Byzantine Sicily in the year 972 (361 AH), long before Idrisi and Jubayr, when Palermo was already a prosperous capital. He spent much time in Asia and Africa. He died shortly after 978.

Herbert of Bosham. Having studied in Paris, this cleric is best known today as Thomas Becket's friend and biographer. He authored the *Life of Saint Thomas*, which notes the saint's complex relationship with Reginald of Bath, who presented the gold reliquary to Queen Margaret. Some historians believe that Herbert died in Calabria. William Fitzstephen, Herbert's contemporary, wrote a complementary biography of Becket.

Abu Abd Allah Abdullah Mohammed ibn Mohammed ibn Ash Sharif al Idrisi (or Edrisi). Present in Sicily by 1145, Idrisi became the court geographer. Descended through a long line of distinguished and aristocratic personages from the Prophet Mohammed, Idrisi seems to have spent his youth in Sabtah, now Ceuta (in Morocco), where he is thought to have been born, but his family had commercial interests in Sicily. His *Book of Roger* is a key record of Sicilian geography in the twelfth century.

Abu Hussain Mohammed bin Ahmad bin Jubayr (or Jubair) al-Kenani. This visitor who arrived in Sicily following the death of Margaret was described in the previous appendix.

Orderic Vitalis. This English-born Benedictine monk spent much of his adult life in Normandy, where he wrote his monumental *Historia Ecclesiastica*, a chronicle that covers the history of those regions until Orderic's death around 1142. The *Historia* makes mention of the adventures of crusading Rotrou of Perche in northeastern Spain as early as 1114, and recounts something of the exploits of García Ramírez in the years immediately before Margaret's birth.

Peter of Blois. This Breton cleric educated in Bologna arrived in Sicily in September 1166 with his brother, William. He became tutor of the young king and one of Margaret's advisors. He left shortly after Stephen of Perche departed, ending up at Canterbury and then Bath, although he was back in Sicily with Richard Lionheart in 1189. A number of Peter's letters survive. He lived until around 1211. Peter's brother, William, was the abbot of a monastery in Calabria (see note 392).

Peter of Eboli. This later chronicler served at the court of Constance, daughter of Roger II. His *Liber ad Honorem Augusti* is a good source for the early years of the Hohenstaufen reign, but also such figures as Archbishop Walter of Palermo and Matthew of Aiello. He died after 1220.

Ralph of Diceto. Made archdeacon of Middlesex in 1152, this French-educated chronicler lived most of his life in England, where he became dean of Saint Paul's. His *Ymagines Historiarum*, with its focus on the years from 1180 to 1202, mentions William II and his consort Joanna.

Richard of San Germano. Born around 1165, this cleric was a notary at the Benedictine monastery at Cassino. His *Chronica Regni Siciliae* covers the history of the *Regnum* from the death of William II in 1189 until 1243. Richard died in 1244.

Roger of Howden (Hoveden). Roger was a confidant of Henry II of England and probably a monk, although rather little is known about him. His description of the conflict with Thomas Becket is highly informative. He accompanied Richard Lionheart on crusade and is thought to have died in 1201. His *Annals* were published in English in 1853. An excerpt from these (describing the dower of Joanna of England) appears in this book. The chronicle long attributed to Benedict of Peterborough (see above) is now recognized by most scholars as Roger's work.

William of Apulia. Completed around 1098, his *Gesta Roberti Wiscardi* is a chief contemporary source of information for the Normans' conquest of southern Italy. William's work suggests he was a layman and possibly a Lombard. He probably died before 1120.

tentatū. liberatus est igitur rex à coniuratis, neq; tamen prius quàm pacto conueniret, nihil se à turba grauius & atrocius regis causa perpessuros: illico enim rege reddito, in oppidū Cacabū transfugerunt salui & incolumes. Multa gessit hic rex in Italia, maxime quidem in Calabria, & Apulia: lōgéque, & late bellis seditiosis agitatus est. Sed vbi sedata tandē omnia vidit, nullis iam hostibus reliquis in Siciliam reuersūs, palatio sese abdidit, voluptuoso ocio & quieti vacaturus, interim dum regnum ab externis tumultibus respiraret. Deniq ue fato proximus conuocatis curiæ magnatibus & archiepiscopis Salernitano & Rhegino, vltima voluntate Gulielmum maiorem natu filium regni successorem instituit. Henricum vero Capuæ principem, & Reginam Margaretam Hispanani natione, Regis Nauarrorum, vt colligo, filiam, regni & regis pueri gubernatricem, dum puer ætate regno suffecturus sadoleceret. Quibus ad eum modum rebus dispositis, dysenteria morboque diuturno dissolutus interiit. Mortuus autem in palatio sepultus est, donec proceribus euocatis qui, quæ ad nouum regem coronandum necessaria erant procurarent, more lugubri, conclamato funere, totius ciuitatis luctu maximo, de loco sepulchri in id sacellūquod Siciliæ regū Mausolea continet, translatus est. quáquam templum esse Panhormi ingés alii scribunt historici à Gual-

Mors Gulielmi.

Mausolea regum Siciliæ.

First mention of Margaret in the printed edition of the chronicle of Hugh Falcandus (see page 32).

Appendix 3
HUGH FALCANDUS

The chief source for the life and times of Margaret in Sicily until 1169 is a chronicle written by a man known to posterity, at least since the middle of the sixteenth century, as "Hugh Falcandus."

This encompasses Margaret's regency from the death of her husband, William I, in 1166, almost to the age of majority of her son, William II, in 1171. In reading the chronicle of Falcandus, one should bear in mind that he does not recount events in precise chronological order. Nevertheless, his narrative is somewhat more detailed than that of Romuald of Salerno.

The oldest surviving manuscript known to us is *Codex Vaticanus Latinus 10690*, dating from circa 1230. Retained by the Vatican Apostolic Library since 1903, it was previously held by the Benedictines of the San Nicolò l'Arena monastery in Catania and is divided into several sections but not actual chapters. As we shall see, this was not the only manuscript to survive into modern times, and it was not the basis for the post-incunable *editio princeps* published in Paris.

Whoever Falcandus was, it is clear that he had close, if not privileged, access to the royal court in Palermo. The tone of his writing is often cynical, even sardonic, and historians have long questioned his objectivity, as well we should. Yet his chronicle has been seriously studied for centuries, and one of the surviving codices bears annotations attributed to Petrarch and Boccaccio.

Evelyn Jamison, perhaps the greatest medievalist of her time to focus on Norman Sicily, cogently argued in her *Admiral Eugenius of Sicily: His Life and Work and Authorship of the Epistola ad Petrum and the Historia Hugonis Falcandi Siculi* (1957), that Falcandus was quite possibly Eugenius of Palermo, who died in 1202.

Born into a family of able Greek administrators, Eugenius was fluent in both Greek and Latin, and proficient enough in Arabic to render a Latin translation of Ptolemy's classic, *Optics*, around 1154, and it is quite possible that he translated other works as well. Both his father (John) and grandfather (his namesake Eugenius) were also "admirals" in the service of the Hauteville dynasty. The family appears to have been quite wealthy, and still had a connection to the Greek Church in the middle of the twelfth century.[426] The Eugenius under discussion was made a court officer by William II around 1188, before which he had administered the royal *diwan*. He finished his illustrious career in the service of the young Frederick II, having "transitioned" from the Norman court to that of the Swabians.

With equal erudition, Gwenyth Hood advanced another widely-supported theory, specifically that Falcandus was Hugh Foucault (who died in 1197), Prior of Saint-Denis and Argenteuil, whose surname, sometimes *Foucaud,* is readily latinized to something very similar to *Falcandus,* there being no "universal" orthography for Latin surnames derived from Norman French or most other languages. Professor Hood applied a sophisticated philological method to the question. See Hood, Gwenyth, "Falcandus and Fulcaudus Epistola ad Petrum Liber de Regno Sicilie: Literary Form and Author's Identity," *Studi*

Medievali, June 1999, 3rd Series, XL, pages 1-41.

Another candidate advanced for authorship by scholars is a certain Falcus, or Falco, sometime canon of the royal chapel in Palermo. Such speculation proves little more than the lasting allure of the ongoing mystery to modern scholars.

Martin Gervais de Tournay first published the chronicle in Paris in 1550 as *Historia Hvgonis Falcandi Sicvli de Rebus Gestis in Siciliae Regno.*

Tournay's transcription was made from a manuscript, now presumed lost, which was then in the possession of Matthew Longuejoue, Bishop of Soissons, and which may well have been copied from the autograph attributed to Foucault.

The surviving manuscripts, being copies, may vary slightly from the autograph written by the hand of Falcandus, possibly on fragile paper (rather than more durable vellum or parchment) as was typical in Sicily during the twelfth century, and for which Frederick II, with his Constitutions of Melfi, decreed that parchment henceforth be used for important official documents.

To Falcandus is also attributed the concise *Epistola ad Petrum Panormitane Ecclesie Thesaurarium de Calamitate Sicilie* discussed by Jamison and others.

It is generally accepted that the essential details cited by Falcandus are reasonably accurate, and indeed some are readily corroborated by contemporaneous sources. The challenge for the modern scholar lies in discerning what is most likely factual from what probably is not. For the most part, Falcandus is blatant enough in his character assassinations for us to distinguish fact from subjectivity. Indeed, a few of his descriptions of personalities may be quite precise.

The translations which appear in this book are by the author herself. A few editions of Falcandus published after 1550 are mentioned in the Sources.

In the past, historians effected their own translations of the work of Falcandus. John Julius Norwich did so for *The Kingdom in the Sun 1130-1194* (1970). Ferdinand Chalandon (1875-1921) undertook some translations into French for his *Histoire de la Domination Normande en Italie et en Sicile* (1907), where he mentions the enigmatic Sicilian chronicler in the Introduction of the first volume. Henry Gally Knight, in his monograph *The Normans in Sicily* (1838) quotes Falcandus, and his source appears to be the Paris printing of 1550; he also quotes the (inaccurate) aperçu that the surname ascribed to Walter *Offamilias* means "of the Mill" (see note 297).

Though obviously trained as a classicist, Falcandus clearly made use of a certain amount of medieval vernacular to express himself, and (as we have seen in the *Offamilias* example) the modern historian must consider context. Among medievalists, two oft-cited examples are the word *milites* which in the twelfth century meant *knights* rather than *foot soldiers* (one of its classical definitions), and *servi* which were more likely *serfs* than *slaves*. Words such as *baro* and *baronis* (baron) were typically medieval.

Martin Gervais de Tournay published his *Historia* a century after Gutenberg printed the Bible. Thus the first Falcandus book saw print during a period (not long after the *incunabula* era) characterized by an effort to publish medieval manuscripts. Decade by decade, a new wave of learning engulfed Europe as these works were disseminated, the first press in Paris being established around 1470.

Running to nearly two hundred numbered pages, the *Historia* of 1550 features a lengthy preface, the *Praefatio,* and useful marginalia indicating personages, events and other details.

Falcandus disliked Romuald Guarna of Salerno, who he almost certainly knew personally. (See the following appendix.)

Appendix 4
ROMUALD OF SALERNO

Archbishop of the prosperous diocese of Salerno from 1154 until his death in 1181, Romuald Guarna of Salerno was born into the nobility that held estates in parts of southern Italy. His *Chronicon sive Annales* covers part of the middle of the twelfth century, complementing other works such as those of Falcandus. However, it is not quite so detailed as the chronicle of Falcandus in reporting events at court.

The chronicler was the second prominent archbishop of Salerno named *Romuald*, and thus is sometimes known as "Romuald II."

The origins of the Guarna family, sometimes *Varna* or *Avarna*, are debated; by most accounts it was of Norman stock, perhaps even related to the Hautevilles. The Guarna were a family of clerics and jurists. At Salerno's medical school, Romuald studied other subjects as well as medicine. These included law, history and theology. He reputedly knew a young Gilles of Corbeil.

Romuald succeeded William, a Norman, as Archbishop of Salerno, and served Pope Paschal II as a diplomat.

Delegating some of his episcopal duties to underlings, he served as an effective diplomat for King William I and then for William II. Accompanied by Bishop Hugh of Palermo, in

1156 he negotiated the Treaty of Benevento with Pope Adrian IV. Two decades later, he concluded the Treaty of Venice.

He was Archbishop of Palermo from 1161 to 1166. Although he may have resented Maio of Bari and advocated against William I during the Bonello revolt, this does not seem to have attenuated his standing. Indeed, he performed the coronation of William II.

Romuald's self-serving chronicle, but not his ambitious career, ended by 1179, the same year that saw him participating in a church council condemning the Albigensians (Cathars) as heretics.

Archbishop Romuald was one of the *familiares* appointed to assist Queen Margaret in governing the *Regnum*.

His exact date of birth is unknown to us, but when Romuald died in 1181 he may have been seventy. He was succeeded as archbishop by Nicholas of Aiello.

Despite its unabashed *protagonismo,* especially beginning around 1159, Romuald's chronicle is less opinionated than that of his contemporary Hugh Falcandus, or at least less overtly critical of its subject.

Appendix 5
LETTERS

A small body of surviving correspondence offers us insight into the rapport between the Sicilian and English courts during the regency and in the years before the wedding between Margaret's son, William, and Henry's daughter, Joanna.

From Thomas Becket to Queen Margaret

A surviving letter sent to Queen Margaret from Thomas Becket late in 1168 thanks her for granting refuge to two of his nephews, as well as other kin, during the exile of the archbishop (and some members of his family). He makes reference to her request to assist in prompting the return of her cousin, Stephen of Perche, formerly the chancellor. The letter is borne by Thibauld, Prior of Saint-Arnoult de Crepy, who shall elucidate (verbally) more information than Thomas does in the correspondence itself. This translation is from the book by John Allen Giles[427] published in 1846; the Latin original was published by him the previous year.[428]

The Translation:

"To the most serene lady and dearest daughter in Christ,

Margaret, the illustrious Queen of Sicily, Thomas, by divine appointment humble minister of the church of Canterbury, sends health, and thus to reign temporally in Sicily, that she may rejoice forever with the angels in glory!

"Although I have never seen your face, I am not ignorant of your renown, its fame supported by nobility of birth and by greatly numerous virtues. But amongst other perfections which we and others praise, we owe a debt of gratitude to your kindness, which we are now endeavouring to acknowledge, for the generosity with which you gave refuge to our fellow exiles, Christ's poor ones, our own kin who fled to your realm from him who persecutes them. You have consoled them in their distress, which is a great duty of religion. Your wealth has relieved their indigence, and the amplitude of your power protected them in their needs. By such sacrifices God is well pleased, your earthly reputation is enhanced and made known, and every blessing is poured upon you. By these means you have bound ourself also to you in gratitude, and we devote all that we possess and all we are to your service. As the first fruits of our devotion, we have used our good services to present your request to the most Christian king, as you may know by the requests which he had made to our dear friend, the King of Sicily, and by the words of the venerable prior of Crepy, whose literary attainments, single-mindedness and sense of justice make him dear to all good men. He is a man of correct life, sound doctrine, and perfect sanctity in human judgment. We beg of you to hear him with as much reverence as you would listen to the entire Western Church were it assembled at your feet. And I beseech you, not only out of respect for his person, but in high regard for the Church of Cluny, whose necessities he is charged with and which is reputed throughout all the Latin world to have possessed, within its walls, all the glory of virtue and perfection from the time of our first ancestors. In other respects also, I ask you, if it so please you, to place as much confidence in all that he shall tell you as coming from me, as if I myself had said it. Farewell."

The Original:

"Serenissime domine, et in Christo carissimae Margarete, illustri reginae Siculorum, Thomas divina dispensatione Cantuariensis ecclesiae minister humilis, salutem, et sic temporaliter regnare in Sicilia, ut cum angelis aeternaliter exultet in gloria.

"Licet faciem vestram non noverimus, gloriam tamen non possumus ignorare, quam et generosi sanguinis illustrat claritas, et multarum magnarumque virtutum decorat titulus, et famae celebritas numerosis praeconiis reddit insignem. Sed inter caeteras virtutes, quas cum aliis auditoribus gratanter amplectimur, liberalitati vestrae debemus, et qua nunc possumus devotione, gratias referimus ampliores, quae coexules nostros, proscriptos Christi, et consanguineos nostras, fugientes ad partes vestras a facie persecutoris, consolata est in tribulatione sua, quae profecto magna pars verae et Deo gratissimae religionis est, si pro justicia patientibus clementia ferat solatium, si pauperibus opulentia suffragetur, si sanctorum necessitatibus absoluta potestatis communicet amplitudo. Talibus enim hostiis promeretur Deus, exhilarescit et dilatatur gloria temporalis, et omnium bonorum gratiosus conciliatur affectus. His meritis inter alios specialiter tamen promeruistis et nos, qui totum id quod sumus et possumus ad vestrum devovimus obsequium. Cujus devotionis primitias, quas pro tempore potuimus excellentiae vestrae nuper optulimus, preces vestras apud regem Christianissimum promoventes, sicut perpendere potestis ex precibus ejus dilecto nostra illustri regi Siciliae porrectis, et ex verbis venerabilis prioris Crispiniacensis, quem et eruditio litterarum, et vitae sinceritas et integritas famae bonis omnibus amabilem et commendabilem reddunt. Est enim vir probatissime conversationis sanae doctrinae, et quantum ad humanum spectat examen, perfectae pro tempore sanctitatis, quem tanta reverentia a sublimitate vestra desideramus et petimus exaudiri, quanta totam occidentalem ecclesiam, si vestris pedibus assisteret, audiretis. Et hoc quidem tum pro suae personae reverentia, tum pro merito et auctoritate Cluniacensis ecclesiae, cujus procurat necessitates, quae in orbe Latino dinoscitur, a diebus patrum nostrorum in monastica religione perfectionis gloriam quasi propriam possedisse. In caeteris, quae vobis ex parte nostra dixerit, ei, si placet, credatis ut nobis. Valete."

From Thomas Becket to Richard Palmer

The request of the Archbishop of Canterbury to prevail upon his countryman, Richard Palmer, to seek the return of Stephen of Perche coincides with Margaret's wishes. This is another fine translation by John Allen Giles.[429]

"Your humanity makes us, by comparison, guilty of presumption, and the bounty which you have displayed towards our relations makes us doubly debtors to you and yours. In this interchange of kindnesses we are compelled, and not unwillingly, to contract debts with so kind a creditor, trusting that God will discharge all our obligations, for it is He alone that can release those who fear Him. You have entertained our fellow exiles and kin; and without doubt have thereby entertained Him who promises to repay all that shall be lent to the poor in his name. You have gained praise among your countrymen, and glory among posterity, and made us your debtors. God does not permit us to meet. Receive, therefore, the bearer of this letter as my second self, and trust him as you would trust me. He is distinguished for his literary attainments, as well as his moral conduct, and amongst the monks of Cluny he is a model for imitation. He is charged with commissions from his brethren, from his most Christian majesty, and from me. By receiving him with respect, you will receive us also, that pious king and me, whose agent he is. There is one thing remaining, which I will whisper into your ear, and which I hope you will grant me: To do your utmost with the king and queen to procure the recall of that noble-minded man, Stephen of Perche, Archbishop-elect of Palermo, both for reasons which at present shall be nameless, and because by doing so, you will confer a lasting favour on the French king."

From William II to Henry II

In the spring of 1173, the sons of King Henry of England and most of his baronage in France rose up against him. The tense situation between King Henry and his sons, Henry and Richard, was eventually resolved, if ever tenuously. When the revolt broke out, he sent letters to a number of brother sovereigns, including William II, who had only recently reached the age of majority. We do not know how much Margaret influenced William's response to the King of England. Henry Riley, whose translation of Joanna's wedding charter appears in another appendix, translated this letter from the *Annals of Roger de Hoveden*.

"To Henry, by the grace of God the illustrious King of the English, Duke of Normandy and Aquitaine, and Count of Anjou, William, by the same grace King of Sicily, Duke of Apulia and Prince of Capua, wishes the enjoyment of health, and the desired triumph in victory over his foes.

"On the receipt of your letter, we learned a thing of which indeed we cannot without the greatest astonishment make mention, how that, forgetting the ordinary usages of humanity and violating the law of nature, the son has risen in rebellion against the father, the begotten against the begetter. The bowels have been moved to intestine war, the entrails have had recourse to arms, and, a new miracle taking place, quite unheard of in our times, the flesh has waged war against the blood, and the blood has sought means how to shed itself.

"And, although for the purpose of checking the violence of such extreme madness, the inconvenience of the distance does not allow of our power affording any assistance, still, with all the loving kindness we possibly can, the expression of which, distance of place does not prevent, sincerely embracing your person and honour, we sympathize with your sorrow, and are indignant at your persecution, which we regard as though it were our own.

"However, we do hope and trust in the Lord, by whose judgment the judgments of kings are directed, that He will no longer allow your sons to be tempted beyond what they are able or ought to endure; and that He who became obedient to the Father even unto death, will inspire them with the light of filial obedience, whereby they shall be brought to recollect that they are your flesh and blood, and, leaving the errors of their hostility, shall acknowledge themselves to be your sons, and return to their father, and thereby heal the disruption of nature, and that the former union, being restored, will seal the bonds of natural affection."

Appendix 6
THE PENDANT

The only contemporary image of Margaret known to us, which may indeed be a merely symbolic representation, is a gold reliquary pendant made by skilled goldsmiths in Canterbury, a center of this craft. This was given to her by Bishop Reginald of Bath, whose name appears on it: "Bishop Reginald of Bath consigns this to Queen Margaret of Sicily." Clockwise, beginning from the cross at the middle-top of the border, this Latin inscription on the obverse reads: ISTUD REGINE MARGARETE SICULORUM TRANSMITTIT PRESUL RAINAUDUS BATONIORUM.

Seven tiny relics of Saint Thomas Becket were once preserved under a crystal. These are described in the inscription on the reverse side: DE SANGUINE SANCTI THOME MARTYRIS DE VESTIBUS SUIS SANGUINE SUO TINCTUS DE PELLICIA. DE CILITIO. DE CUCULLA. DE CALCIAMENTO. ET CAMISIA. "Of the blood of Saint Thomas Martyr. Of his vestments stained with his blood: of the cloak, the belt, the hood, the shoe, the shirt."

The majuscule characters are typical of the ecclesiastical engraving and inscriptions of the twelfth century; the lettering rendered in mosaic in the epitaph above Margaret's tomb in Monreale is very similar (see the photograph in this book).

Bishop Reginald "Fitzjocelin" (de Bohun) of Bath, whose ambivalent relationship with Thomas was described by Herbert of Bosham, probably presented this pendant to Margaret on the occasion of her son's marriage, in 1177, to Joanna, the daughter of King Henry II of England.

Becket was murdered in late 1170. He was canonized in 1173. Fashioned between 1174 and 1176, the gift was probably an acknowledgment of Margaret's support for Becket, specifically for giving refuge to his kinsmen in Sicily, and for her support of the Church generally. There is debate as to whether the image depicts Margaret being blessed by Reginald, or by Becket himself, though the latter is the majority view among scholars.

Measuring 5 x 3.1 x .7 centimeters (nearly 2 inches in height), the pendant is exceptional for the mere fact of its preservation. The great majority of English goldsmiths' work of this period was melted down over the centuries. Hallmarks were not used in the twelfth century; the gold purity of the pendant is approximately twenty-two karats, which is slightly less than that of gold coins minted during the same period.

The engraving is quite similar in style to various drawings and illuminations of its era. For comparison, particular reference is sometimes made to those of the unfinished Winchester Bible, and specifically its Ecclesiastes (fol. 268r). Forming the pattern of what were to be painted illuminations, the manuscript's drawings resemble the lines of the pendant's figures.

Margaret is shown bowing slightly for the bishop's blessing. Her gaze seems to be fixed on something she is holding in her hands, perhaps the reliquary itself. Not much can be inferred from this simple representation except that Margaret is depicted as rather slender and statuesque, nearly as tall as the prelate invoking the benediction.

Long and tortuous has been the reliquary's journey from Canterbury to Palermo and then around Italy, finally crossing the Atlantic during the middle years of the twentieth century. It is now part of the collection of the Metropolitan Museum of Art in New York, where it is usually displayed in the Treasury gallery at the Cloisters Museum in Fort Tryon Park in Upper Manhattan, catalogued under accession number 63.160. Part of a significant bequest made in 1963 to the museum by Joseph Pulitzer (1913-1993), who acquired it from the Italian collector and art dealer Piero Tozzi, it was first described at length by Thomas Hoving (op.cit.) in 1965.

Codex Vaticanus Latinus 8782, folio 91 recto

The legal code issued by King Roger II at Ariano in 1140 recognizes "the diversity of our people."

Appendix 7
ASSIZES OF ARIANO

This is the *corpus* of law of the Kingdom of Sicily in force when Margaret lived there. Taking a cue from the Code of Justinian whilst definitively asserting royal authority in specific areas, it established generally uniform jurisprudence, whereas until the first decades of the twelfth century cases were often decided (based on the subject's religion) according to Canon, Maliki or Halakha law, and sometimes by *judicium dei*, "the judgement of God," of which trial by ordeal is the most obvious example.

The *Assizes* were most likely drafted in 1140 (their traditional date) or shortly thereafter, a decade following Roger's coronation and establishment of the *Regnum Siciliae*. Their connection with the town of Ariano is uncertain.

There exist fine published translations of the text into Italian, French and English. Here, for the benefit of jurists and Latinists, and to avoid ambiguity in interpretation, is the original text of both extant manuscripts; these were transcribed decades after Roger's reign.

Codex Vaticanus Latinus 8782 has forty-three statutes (clauses), or "assizes," and a preface. This is probably the more faithful to the original document.[430] A later manuscript, *Codex Casinensis 468,* is abbreviated in form but includes seven additional statutes. Both codices were rediscovered during the nineteenth century.

That the contemporary chronicler Falco of Benevento mentions Roger's controversial introduction, at Ariano, of the ducat but not the new legal code suggests to some scholars that the *Assizes* were issued somewhat later and elsewhere. Moreover, the fact that the *Assizes of Capua* of Frederick II were deemed necessary in 1220 might lead a skeptic to question the application (or dissemination) of the earlier *Assizes of Ariano*. Thus far, a manuscript copy of the *Assizes of Ariano* dated to circa 1140, if it survives, has yet to be discovered.

The following texts incorporate minor stylistic editing, such as full words in place of abbreviations. Numeration of the statutes in the second codex was added by the author.

Codex Vaticanus 8782

Dignum et necessarium est o proceres si quod de nobis et universi regni nostri statu meritis non presumimus; a largitate divina gratia consecuta recepimus; divinis beneficiis quibus valemus obsequis respondeamus, ne tante gratie penitus ingrati simus. Si ergo sua misericordia nobis deus pius prostratis hostibus pacem reddidit, integritatem regni, tranquillitate gratissima, tam in carnalibus quam in spiritualibus, reformavit, reformare cogimur iustitie simul et pietatis itinera, ubi videmus eam et mirabiliter esse distortam. Hoc enim ipsum quod ait, inspiramentum, de munere ipsius largitoris, accepimus, dicente ipso: per me reges regnant et conditores legum decernunt iustitiam. Nichil enim gratius deo esse putamus, quam si id simpliciter offerimus, quod eum esse cognovimus, misericordiam scilicet atque iustitiam. In qua oblatione regni officium quoddam sibi sacerdotii vendicat privilegium.

Unde quidam sapiens legisque peritus iuris interpres, iuris sacerdotes appellat. Iure itaque qui iuris et legum auctoritatem per ipsius gratiam optinemus, eas in meliorem statum partim erigere, partim reformare, debemus et qui misericordiam consecuti sumus in omnibus eas tractare misericordius, interpretari benignius, presertim ubi severitas earum quandam inhumanitatem inducit. Neque hoc ex supercilio quasi iustiores aut moderatores nostris predecessoribus in condendis legibus interpretandisve nostris vigiliis arrogamus, set quia in multis delinquimus et ad delinquendum et ad delinquendum procliviores sumus, parcendum delinquentibus cum moderatia nostris temporibus apta conveniens esse censemus.

Nam et ipsa pietas ita nos instruit dicens: Estote misericordes sicut et pater vester misericors est.

Et rex et propheta: Universe vie domini misericordia et veritas. Et proculdubio tenebimus, quia iudicium sine misericordia erit ei qui iudicium fecerit sine misericordia.

Volumus igitur et iubemus ut sanctiones quas in presenti corpore sive promulgatas a nobis, sive compositas nobis facimus exhiberi, fideliter et alacriter recipiatis.

ASSIZES OF ARIANO

I. De legum interpretatione

Leges a nostra maiestate noviter promulgatas pietatis intuitu asperitatem nimiam mitigantes mollia quodam moderamine exaucuentes; obscura dilucidantes, generaliter ab omnibus precipimus observari, moribus, consuetudinibus, legibus non cassatis pro varietate populorum nostro regno subiectorum, sicut usque nunc apud eos optinuit, nisi forte nostris his sanctionibus adversari quid in eis manifestissime videatur.

II. De privilegio sanctarum ecclesiarum

Noverint ergo omnes nostre potestati subiecti, quoniam in voto nobis semper fuit, et erit, ecclesias dei pro quibus dominus Ihesus sanguinem suum fudit, protegere, defensare, augere modis omnibus, sicut et proienitores nostri consueta liberalitate, id ipsum facere studuerunt, ideoque multa et innumera beneficia a deo consecuti sunt semper in melius. Itque sacrarum ecclesiarum res omnes et possesiones in nostra post deum et sanctos ejus custodia collacatas atque commissas ab omnibus incursibus malignantium, gladio materiali nobis a deo concessas defendimus et inviolatas custodimus; principibus, comitibus, baronibus et omnibus nostris fidelibus commendamus, scituri, quod nostrum decretum quisquis violare voluerit, nostram se sentiat ledere majestatem.

III. Monitio generalis

Monemus principes, comites, barones, maiores atque minores, archiepiscopos, episcopos, abbates, cunctos denique qui subditos habent cives, burgenses, rusticos, sive cuiuscumque professionis homines, eos humane tractare, misericordiam adhibere, maxime cum debitum adiutorium conveniens et moderatum valent ab ipsis quos habent subditos, postulare. Gratum enim deo faciunt, et nobis maximum gaudium, cuius potestati atque regimini divina dispositio, tam prelatos subdidit quam subiectos. Quod si fuerit neglectum, nostram spectabit sollicitudinem male factum in melius reformare.

IV. De rebus regalibus

Scire volumus principes nostros, comites, barones universos archiepiscopos, episcopos, abbates, quicumque de regalibus nostris magnum vel modicum quid tenet, nullo modo, nullo ingenio, possit ad nostra regalia pertinens alienare, vel vendere, vel in totum vel in partem minuere, unde iura rerum regalium minuantur, aut subvertantur sive aliquod etiam dampnum patiantur.

V. De sanctarum reliquiarum venditione

Sanccimus nemini licere martirum, vel quorucumque sanctorum reliquias vendere, vel comparare. Quod si presumptum fuerit, nondum pretio numerato nichil ets consecuturus si venditor emptorem voluerit convenire. Si autem numeratio facta est, emptori repetitionem non esse, fiscum vero vendicare. Nostram spectabit providentiam temeritatem contrahentium cohercere, et ubi decuerit, reliquias cum consilio antistitum collocare.

VI. De confugio ad ecclesiam

Presente lege sanccimus per loca regni nostri omnia deo propitio in perpetuum valitura nullos penitus, cuiuscumque condicionis de sacrosantis expelli ecclesiis, aut protrahi confugas, nec pro his venerabiles episcopos, aut yconomos exigi, que debentur ab eis qui hoc moliri aut facere presumpserit, capitis periculo, aut bonorum omnium ammissione plectendis. Interim confugis victualia non negentur. Sane si servus, aut colonus, aut servus glebe se ipsum subtraxerit domino, vel furatus res ad loca sancta confugerit, cum rebus quas detulit, domino presentetur, ut pro qualitae commissi subeat ultionem, aut intercessione procedente restituatur et gratie. Nemini quippe ius suum est detrahendum.

VII. De privilegiis ecclesiarum non violandis

Si venerabilis ecclesie privilegia cuiscumque fuerint temeritate violata dolove suppressa commissum iuxta dampnositatem ecclesie compensetur. Quod si non sufficiat ad condempnationis mulctam, regis iudicio vel officialium arbitrio committetur. Nichilominus pro qualitate commissi regis providentie, vel officialium arbitrio subiacebit.

VIII. De episcoporum privilegio

Episcopus ad testimonium non flagitetur, nisi forte in causis ecclesiasticis, vel publicis, cum necessitas, aut regis auctoritas postulaverit. Presbiteri non cogantur corporale sacramentum in negotiis exibere; diacones, subdiacones et infra positos altari sacri ministros, ab obsequiis sordidis alienos esse precipimus; presbiteros tantum non etiam ceteros omnibus angariis personalibus prohibemus.

IX. De illicitis conventiculis

Conventiculam illicitam extra ecclesiam in privatis edibus celebrari vetamus, proscriptionis domus periculo imminente, si dominus eius in eam clericos novam vel tumultuosam conventiculam celebrantes, susceperit non ignarus.

X. De ascripticiis volentibus clericari

Ascripticios sine voluntate et assensu eorum quorum iuri subditi sunt, et potestati, nullus episcoporum ordinare presumat, neque de aliensa parrochia, per litteras commendatorias secundum canonum instituta, vel ab episcopo, vel a proprio capitulo. Hii quorum ascripticii sunt, si quod premium pro data licentia consecrandi suscepisse convicti fuerint, huiusce ascriptii perdant qui dedit pecuniam ab ordine cadat, fisco vero cum omnibus rebus suis vendicetur. Solent sancto voto atque proposito sanctis occasionibus pravitas se ingerere, et dei servitium atque ecclesie ministerium perturbare. Ne ergo sinistrum aliquod aliquando possit nostris institutionibus obviare, si forte in rure vel in vico ecclesia assignatos habuerit sacerdotes quibus decedentibus sint alii (subrograndi et) domini ruris vel vici super ascripticiis, episcopo fieri subgorationem negaverint, presertim cum ex ipsis ascripticiis persona ydonea ab episcopo expectatur, dignum nostre clementie videtur, atque iustissium ad iustam petitionem ecclesie ascripticiorum dominum iure cogendum; filii vero decedentis presbiteri ad asripticiorum condicionem reddatur omni occasione remota.

XI. De raptum virginum

Si quis rapere sacratas deo virgines aut nondum velatas causa iungendi matrimonium presumpserit, capitali pena feriatur, vel alia pena quam regia censura decreverit.

XII. (sic)

Iudeus paganus servum christianum nec vendere, nec comparare audeat, nec ex aliquo titulo possidere seu pignori detinere. Quod si presumpserit, omnes res eius infiscentur, et curie servus fiat. Quem si forte ausu vel nefario vel suasu circumcidi vel fidem abnegare fecerit, capitali supplicio puniatur.

XIII. De apostatantibus

Apostantes a fide catholica penitus execramus, ultionibus insequimur, bonis omnibus spoliamus, a professione vel voto naufragantes legibus coartamus, successiones tollimus, omne ius legitimum abdicamus.

XIV. De ioculatoribus

Mimi et qui ludibrio corporis sui questum faciunt, publico habitu earum virginum, que deo dicate sunt, vel veste monachica non utantur, nec clericali; si fecerint verberibus publice afficiantur.

XV. De pupillis et orphanis

Pupillis et orphanis pietatis intuitu, multa privilegia priscis legibus confirmata pro qualitate temporum quibus absolverint in ultimo delegamus nostri iudicibus ubi iactura tollerabilis non est, favorabiliter commendamus. Mulieribus nichilominus ubi non modice lese sunt, propter fragiliorem sexum, legum equitatem sectantes tam per nos, quam per officiales nostros ex pietatis visceribus subveniendum decrevimus, sicut decet et oportet.

XVI. De indigne anelantibus ad sacerdotum

Nemo sacerdotum dignitatem pretio petere audeat, contumeliam pro premio reportaturus et penam, mox ut fuerit propria petitione detectus. Ille enim honore se privat, qui inpudenti fronte, velud importunus expostulat.

XVII. De sacrilegiis

Disputari de regis iudicio, consiliis, institutionibus, factis non oportet. Est enim par sacrilegio disputare de eius iudiciis, institutionibus, factis atque consiliis et an is dignus sit quem rex elegerit, aut decernit. Multe leges sacrilegos severissime punierunt, set pena moderanda est arbitrio iudicantis, nisi forte manufacta templa dei fracta sunt violenter, aut dona et vasa sacra, noctu sublata sunt, hoc enim casu capitale est.

XVIII. De crimine maiestatis

Quisquis cum milite uno vel cum pluribus, seu privato scelestem inierit factionem aut factionis dederit, vel susceperit sacramentum, de nece etiam virorum illustrium, qui consiliis et consistorio nostro intersunt, cogitaverint et tractaverint, eadem severitate voluntatem sceleris qua effectum puniri iura voluerunt, ipse quidem ut pote reus majestatis gladio feriatur, bonis eius omnibus fisco addictis; filii vero eius nullum unquam beneficium sive a nostro beneficio seu iure consensum optineant. Sit ei mors solacium et vita supplicium. Quod si qiusquam de factiosis mox sine mora factum detexerit, veniam et gratiam mox sequatur. Crimen majestatis post mortem rei etiam incipit et tractatur; rei ù memoria condempnatur, adeo ut quicquid contraxerit, fecerit, statuerit, a die criminis nullam habeat firmitatem; set omne quod habuit, fisci iuribus vendicetur. Hoc crimine qui parentem purgaverit, eius successionem meretur. Hoc crimine tenentur omnes, quorum consilio fugiunt obsides, armantur cives, seditiones moventur, concitantur tumultus, magistratus necantur, exercitus deseritur, ad hostem fugitur, sociis proditur, dolo malo cuneus discinditur, bellis ceditur, ars desolatam relinquitur, sociis auxilium denegatur, cetaraque hujusmodi sicut regii consilii explorator, summissor et publicator, et qui susceperit hospitio hostes regni, et ductum prbeuerit non ignarus.

XIX. De nova militia

Divine iustitie consentientes probanda probamus contrarium refutamus. Sicut, enim, nullatenus exasperandi sunt boni, ita beneficiis non sunt fovendi mali. Sanccimus, itaque tale proponentes edictum, ut si quicumque novam militiam arripuerit, contra regni nostri beatitudinem, atque pacem, sive integritatem, militie nomine et professione, penitus decidat, nisi forte a militari genere per successionem duxerit prosapiam. Idemque statuimus de sortientibus qualiscumque professinis ordinem, ut puta si vel auctoritatem iudicii optinuit, sive notariorum officium, ceterisque similibus.

XX. De falso

Qui litteras regias aut mutat aut quas ipse scripsit notho sigillo subsignat, capitaliter puniatur.

XXI. De cutendibus monetam

Adulterinam monetam cudentibus, vel scienter eam accipientibus, penam capitis irrogamus, et eorum substantiam publicamus; consentientes etiam hac pena ferimus. Qui nummos aureos vel argenteos raserint tinxerint, vel quocumque modo imminuerint, tam personas eorum, quam bona omnia publicamus.

Ubi questio falso inciderit, diligens inquisitio mox sequatur, argumentis, testibus, collatione scripturarum, et aliis vestigiis veritatis. Non solum accusator probationibus honeretur, set inter utramque personam iudex sit medius, ut omnibus que competunt exquisitis, demum sententiam ferat. Capitali post probationem supplicio secuturo si id exigat magnitudo supplicii, vel alia pena pro qualitate delicti.

XXII. De falso instrumento

Qui falso instrumento nesius utitur, falsi crimine non punitur. Qui falsitatem testibus astruxerit, falsi pena cohercetur.

XXIII. De abolitione testamenti

Amator testamentorum, publicorum instrumentorum, celator, delator, perversor, eadem pena tenetur. Si quis patris testamentum deleverit, ut quasi ab intestato succedat, patris hereditate privatur.

XXIV. De officialibus publicis

Qualitas persone gravat et relevat penam falsi. Officiales reipublice, vel iudicis qui tempore amministrationis pecunias publicas subtraxerint, obnoxii crimini peculatus, capite puniantur, nisi regia pietas indulserit.

XXV. De bonis publicis

Qui sua negligentia bona publica deperire, vel minui permiserit, in persona propria et rebus suis, constituetur obnoxius, et hoc prospectu pietatis rege. Qui sciens furantibus assensum prebuerit, eadem lege tenetur.

XXVI. De coniugiis legitime celebrandis

Quoniam ad curam et sollecitudinem regni pertinet leges condere, populum gubernare, mores instruere, pravas consuetudines extirpare, dignum et equum visum est nostre clementie, quandam pravam consuetudinem, que quasi clades et lues huc usque per diuturna tempora, partem nostri populi perrependo pervasit edicti nostri mucrone decidere, ne liceat vitiosas pullulas de cetero propagare. Absurdum quippe moribus repugnans sacrorum canonum institutis, christianis auribus inauditum est, matrimonium velle contrahere, legitimam sobolem procreare, indivisibile vite consortium alligare, nec dei favorem et gratiam nuptis nuptiarum in stabulis querere, et tantum in Christo et ecclesia ut dicit apostulus sacramentum confirmandum per sacerdotum ministerium creare. Sancimus itaque lege presenti deo propitio perpetuo valitura, volentibus omnibus legitimum contrahere matrimonium necessitatem imponi, quatinus post sponsalia nuptias celebraturi sollempniter quisque pro suo modulo seu commodo, limen petant ecclesie sacerdotum benedictionem post scrutinium consecutum anulum ponat, pretii postulationique sacerdotali subdantur, si volunt futuris heredibus successionem relinquere.

Alioquin noverint ammodo molientes contra nostrum regale preceptum, neque ex testamento, neque ab intestato se habituros heredes legitimos, ex illecito per nostram sanctionem matrimonio procreatos. Mulieres etiam dotes, et aliis nubentibus legitime debitas non habere. Rigorem cuius sanctionis, omnibus illis remittimus, qui promulgationis eius tempore, iam matrimonium contraxerunt.

Viduas vero volentibus ducere, huius necessitatis vinculum relaxamus.

XXVII. De adulteris

Generali lege presente sancimus pietatis intuitu, cui viscera tota debemus, quotiens a nostra provisione et ordinatione iura regentibus accusatio adulterii aut stupri fuerit presentata, oculo non caligante personam despicere, condiciones notare, etates et consilium animi investigare, si deliberatione vel consultatione, vel lubrico etatis proruperint, ad facimus, vel prolapse sint. Utrum earum fortuna tenuis sit an torosa, petulantia stimulate fuerint, an dolore maxime materiali. Ut, his omnibus perquisitis, probatis vel manifestis, non de rigore iuris, set de lance equitatis, super commissis excessibus, lenior vel asperior sententia feratur. Sic, enim, perfecta iustitia divine iustitie respondebit. Nam nec nos poterit illa divina sententia: in qua mensura mensi fueritis remetietur vobis.

Legum igitur asperitate lenita, non ut olim gladio agendum, set rerum ad eam pertinentium confiscatio inducetur, si filios legitimos ex eo matrimonio violato, vel alio non habuerit. Periniquum est successione quippe fraudari, qui nati sint eo tempore quo thori lex legaliter servabatur. Aut viro traenda est, nullatenus ad vite periculum servituro, set ultionem thori violati, nasi truncatione, quod sevius et atrocius inducitur persecuturo. Ultra enim, neque viro, neque parentibus sevire licebit. Quod si vie eius noluerit in eam dare vindictam, nos huiusmodi maleficium non sinemus inultum, precipimus publice flagellandum.

Qui coram se spectante, vel arbitrio, permittit cum ganeis suam coniugem lascivire, non facile poterit vero iudicio accusare. Viam quippe mechandi aperit, qui cum possit prohibere consentit.

Quamvis uxorem suspectam quis habeat, eum lenocinii non dapnamus. Quis enim alieni thori iure inquiet quietem. Quod si patenter deprehendimus quempiam habere uxorem questuosam, dignam nostris temporibus mox sequimur pene vindictam, eum quoque pena infamie condempnamus. Femine penitus, et adulterii et stupri severitate iudiciaria prestentur immunes, quas vilitas vite dignas legum observatione non credit.

XXVIII. De eodem

Que passim venalem formam exhibuit, et vulgo prostitutam se prebuit, huius criminis accusationem ammovit. Violentiam tamen ei ingeri prohibemus, et inter boni testimonii feminas, ei habitationem vetamus. Adulter, adultera simul accusari non possunt, alter singulariter est accusandus, et rei exitus expectandus. Nam si adulter defendi poterit, mulier est secura, nulli ulterius responsura. Si vero fuerit condempnatus, tunc demum mulier accusatur.

Lex delectum non facit, quis primum conveniri debeat. Set si uterque presens est, vir conveniendus est primum.

Repudium in accusatione est semper permittendum; neque violentia seu detentio est adhibenda.

XXIX. De lenocinio

Lenas sollicitantes alienam scilicet castitatem genus criminis pessimum, tamquam ipsas adulteras puniendas presente lege sanccimus. Matres virgines filias venalicias proponentes, et maritalia federa fugientes, ut lenas ipsas persequimur, scilicet ut nasus ejus abscidatur. Castitatem enim suorum viscerum vendere inhumanum est et crudele. Quod si filia se ipsam tamen prostituerit, mater vero solummodo consentit, iudicum arbitrio relinquatur.

XXX. De violatione thori

Si providentia rege celsitudinis nullo modo patitur inter regni nostri militem baronum nostrorum quemlibet alterius castrum invadere, predas committere, cum armis insurgere, vel inique fraudari, quin pro commisso bonorum omnium iactura ipsum afficiat, quanto amplius dampnandum censemus si compatris et vicini thorum violare presumpserit. Intolerabile prorsus de iure videtur. Sanccimus itaque si de tali facto nobis aliquando fuerit proclamatum, manifestum fuerit, vel probatum, bonorum omnium mulctatione plectendum. Si maritus uxorem in ipso actu adulterii deprehenderit, tam uxorem, quam adulterum occidere licebit, nulla tamen mora protracta.

XXXI. De adulterio

Lex maritum lenocinii pena cohercet, qui uxorem in adulterio deprehensam, retinuerit, adulterumque dimiserit, nisi forte sine sua culpa ille diffugit.

XXXII. De desistendibus ab accusatione

Qui post crimen adulterii intentatum uxorem receperit, destitisse videtur ab accusatione ideoque suscitare qustionem ultra non poterit.

XXXIII. De iniuriis privatis personis illatis

Quod iuri et rationi est consentaneum satis iure cunctis est gratum, et quod a ratione equitatis dicrepat, universis ingratitudinem representat. Nulli igitur mirum si quod in homine deus carius et dignius posuerit, cum negligitur atque despicitur, et inprobo iudicio vilipenditur, sapiens et honestatis amicus rationabiliter indignatur. Quid enim absurdius quam equa lance pensari ubi iumenti cauda decerpitur, et ubi honestissimi viri barba depilatur.

Pro suggestione ergo populi nostro regno subiecti atque supplicatione legum suarum ineptitudinem cognoscentis hanc legem et edictum proponimus. Ut cuicumque de popularibus excusato, tamen et deliberatione barba fuerit depilata, reus talis commissi pena huiusmodi feriatur solidis aureis scilicet regiis sex; si vero in rixa factum fuerit, sine deliberatione et studio, de eisdem solidis III.

XXXIV. De iniuriis personis illatis curialibus

Observent diligentissime iudices, ut in actione iuriariarum, curialium dignitatem personarum considerent, et iuxta personarum qualitatem sententiam ferant, eorum scilicet quibus fiunt, et eorum qui faciunt, et quando ubi temeritas presumitur, et iuxta qualitatem personarum sententiam ferant; ipsis autem facta iniuria, non ad ipsos dumtaxat, set etiam ad regie dignitatis spectat offensam.

XXXV. De mederi volentibus

Quisquis ammodo mederi voluerit, officialibus et vicibus nostri se presentet, eorum discutiendus iudicio. Quod si sua temeritate presumpserit, carcere constringatur, bonis ejus omnibus publicatis. Hoc autem prospectum est, ne quilibet nostro regno subiecti periclitentur imperitia medicantum.

XXXVI. De plagiariis

Qui sciens liberum hominem vendiderit hac pena legitima teneatur, ut ex bonis suis venditus redimatur; ipse vero maleficus curie nostre servus sit, bonorum suorum residuo publicato. Quod si non poterit redimi, pro servo tradatur parentibus venditi, bonis eius curie addictis. Quocumque autem venditus redeat, maleficus curie servus fiat, fillis etiam post hunc casum nascentibus subiectis curie perpetue servituti.

XXXVII. De siccariis

Qui aggressorem vel latronem in dubio vite discrimine constitutis occiderit, nullam ob id factam calumpniam metuere debet.

XXXVIII. De infantibus et furiosis

Infans sine malignitate animi et furiosus si hominem occiderit, non tenetur. Quia alterum innocentia consilii, alterum fati infelicitas excusat.

XXXIX. De fure

Nocturnum furem qui occiderit, impune ferat si aliter comprehendi non potuerit, dum modo clamore id fiat.

XL. De incendiariis

Qui dolose domum incenderit capitis pena plectatur, velud incendiarius. In maleficiis voluntas spectatur non exitus; nichil enim interest occidat quis an mortis causam prebeat.

XLI. De precipitatoribus

Qui de alto se ipsum precipitat, et hominem occiderit, et ramum incautus prohiciens, non proclamaverit, seu lapidem ad aliud iecit, hominemque occidit, huic pene non succumbit.

XLII. De poculo

Mala et noxia medicamenta, ad alienandos animos, seu venena quis dederit, vendiderit, habuerit, capitali sententia feriatur. Poculum amatorium, vel aliquem cibum noxium, quisquis instruxerit, etiam si neminem leserit, impunis non erit.

XLIII. Si iudex litem suam fecerit.

Iudex si accepta pecunia reum quem criminis et mortis fecerit, capitis periculo subiacebit. Si iudex fraudulenter atque dolose sententiam contra leges protulerit, auctoritate iudiciaria inrecuperabiliter cadat, notetur infamia, rebus eius omnibus publicatis. Quod si ignorantia a iuris sententia oberraverit, ferens iudicium pro simplicitate animi manifesta, regie misericordie et providentie subiacebit.

Codex Casinensis 468

Leges a nostra maiestate noviter promulgatas, generaliter ab omnibus precipimus observari, moribus, consuetudine, et legibus non cassatis, nisi forte nostris his sanctionibus adversari quid in eis manifeste videatur.

1. De privilegiis ecclesiarum

Primo itaque iura sanctarum ecclesiarum, res omnes et possesiones earum in nostra post deum et sanctos ejus custodia collacatas ab omnibus incursibus malignantium, gladio materiali a deo nobis concesso defendimus et inviolatas custodimus; quisquis hoc nostrum decretum violare voluerit, nostram senserit ledere maiestatem.

2. Ut domini subiectos humane tractent

Monemus, princeps, comites, et barones, omnesque dominos, subiectos humane tractare, misericordiam adhibere, maxime cum debitum adiutorium et moderatum et conveniens volent ab ipsis, quos habent subiectos, postulare.

3. Ut regalia non minuantur

Quicumque de regalibus nostris magnum vel modicum quid tenet, nullo modo, nullo ingenio possit ad nostra regalia pertinens donare, vendere, vel alienare, vel in totum vel in partem minuere.

4. De sacrosanctis ecclesiis, et episcopis, et clericis

Sancimus nemini licere sanctorum reliquias vendere vel comparare. Sancimus sub capitis periculo nullos penitus cuiuscumque condicionis de sacrosanctis ecclesiis expelli aut protrahi confugas; nec pro his venerabiles episcopos vel iconomos exigi que debentur ab eis; nec ipsis confugis interim victualia negentur. Servus vero, colonus, seu gleba servus, subtrahens se domino, vel furatus res ad loca sacra confugiens, cum rebus quas detulit domino presentetur.

Privilegia ecclesiarum inconcussa serventur. Episcopus ad testimonium non flagitetur, nisi forte in causis ecclesiasticis vel publicis, et cum summa necessitas, aut regis auctoritas postulaverit. Diaconos et subdiaconos et infra positos altari sacri ministros, ab obsequiis sordidis, alienos esse precipimus. Presbiteros vero tantum non etiam ceteros ab angariis personalibus prohibemus.

5. De illicitis conventiculis

Conventiculam illicita extra ecclesiam in privatis edibus celebrari vetamus.

6. Ne servi vel ascripticii clericentur

Ascripticios sine voluntate eorum quorum iuri subditi sunt, nullus episcoporum ordinare presumat. Iudeus, paganus, servum christianum, nec compare audeat nec ex aliquo titulo possidere.

7. De ioculatoribus

Mimi et mime, et qui ludibrio corporis sui questum faciunt, publico habitu veste monachica, vel clericali non utantur; quod si fecerit, verberibus publice afficiantur.

8. De raptu

Si quis rapere sacratas virgines, aut nondum velatas causa iungendi matrimonium presumpserit, capitali pena feriatur.

9. De apostatis

Apostatas insequimur ultionibus, bonis omnibus spoliamus. A professione vero naufragantes seu voto legibus coartamus, succesiones tollimus, omne ius legitimum abdicamus.

10. De pupillis et orphanis

Leges que pro pupillis et orphanis faciunt relevamus. Mulieribus lesis ex pietatis visceribus propter fragiliorem sexum subveniendum decrevimus sicut decet, et quatenus oportet.

11. De sacrilegis consiliis

Disputari de regis iudiciis, consiliis, institutionibus et factis non oportet; talis disputatio par sacrilegio computatur. Multe leges sacrilegos severissime punierunt, set pena moderata est arbitrio iudicantis, nisi forte manu facta templum dei fractum est violenter, aut dona et vasa sacra noctu sublata sunt, hoc enim casu capitale est.

12. De crimine maiestatis

Quisquis cum milite uno aut pluribus seu privato villano scelestam inhierit factionem aut factionis dederit vel susceperit sacramentum, de nece etiam virorum illustrium, qui consiliis et consistorio nostro intersunt, cogitaverint et tractaverint, eadem enim severitate voluntatem sceleris qua effectum puniri iura voluerint, ipse quidem ut pote reus majestatis gladio feriatur, bonis eius fisco addictis. Filii vero eius nullum unquam beneficium sive a nostro beneficio seu iure confertum optineant;sit ei mors solacium et vita supplicium. Quod si quisquam de factiosis mox sine mora factam detexerit, et premio a nobis et honore donabitur.

Is vero qui usus fuerit factione, si vero tamen incognita adhuc patefecerit et conciliorum archana absolutione tantum ac venia dignus habebitur; sic tamen, si suis assertionibus veri fides fuerit opitulata, laudem maximam et premium a nostra clementia consequetur; alioquin capitali pena plectetur.

Crimen maiestatis post mortem rei etiam incipit et tractatur, et rei memoria condempnatur adeo ut quicquid contraxerit, fecerit, statuerit, a die criminis nullam habeat firmitatem; hoc crimine qui parentem purgaverit, eius successionem meretur.

Hoc crimine tenentur omnes quorum consilio fugiunt obsides, armantur cives, seditiones moventur, concitantur tumultus, magistratus necantur, exercitus deseritur, ad hostem fugitur, dolo modo cuneus scinditur,socius proditur, bellis ceditur, arx desolatur vel relinquitur, sociis auxilium denegatur, cetaraque huiusmodi, ut regii consilii explorator, sive missorum publicator et qui susceperit hostes regni hospitio, vel ductum prebuerit non ignarus.

13. De jnjuriis curialium

Observent iudices diligentissime, ut in actionem injuriarium curialium personarum dignitatem et qualitem eorum quibus illate sunt, et eorum qui faciunt, et quando, et ubi, huiusmodi temeritates presumuntur, et sic ferant sententiam; quia non ad ipsos dumtaxat, sed ad regie dignitatis spectat offensam.

14. De crimine falsi

Qui litteras regias aut mutat, aut quas ipse scripsit notho sigillo subsignat capitaliter puniatur. Qui falso instrumento utitur nescius, falsi crimine non punitur.

Adulterinam monetam cudendibus vel scienter eam succipientibus, et utentibus, penam capitis irrogamus, et eorum substantiam publicamus; consentientes etiam, hac pena ferimus.

Qui nummos aureos vel argenteos raserit, tinxerit, vel aliquo modo minuerit, tam personas eorum, quam bona omnia publicamus.

Qui falsitatem testibus astruxerit falsi pena coherceantur.

Motor testamentorum publicorum, instrumentorum celator, deletor, perversor, eadem pena tenetur.

Si quis patris testamentum aboleverit, ut quasi ab intestato succedat, patris hereditate privetur.

Qualitas persone gravat et relevat penam falsi.

15. De coniugiis

Sancimus lege presenti, volentibus omnibus legitimum contrahere matrimonium necessitatem imponi, quatenus post sponsalia celebraturi nuptias sollempniter quisque pro modulo suo seu quomodolibet limen petat ecclesie, sacerdotum benedictionem post scrutinium consecuturum anulum ponat, preci postulationique sacerdotali subdantur, si voluerint futuris heredibus successiones relinquere. Alioquin amodo molientes contra regale nostrum edictum, neque ex testamento neque ab intestato, habituros se legitimos filios heredes ex illicito matrimonio per nostram sanctionem noverint procreatos; mulieres etiam aliis nubentes legitimas dotes debitas non habere. Viduas vero volentibus ducere hoc necessitatis vinculum relaxamus.

16. De crimine adulterii

Generali lege sancimus quotiens nostra provisione et ordinatione iura regentibus accusatio adulterii vel strupi fuerit presentata, oculo non caligante personas despicere, condiciones notare, etates et consilium animi investigare, si deliberatione, consultatione, vel lubrico etatis proruperint ad facinus vel prolapse sint, an dolore maxime maritali; ut, his omnibus perquisitis, probatis vel manifestis, non de rigore iuris set de lance equitatis super commissis excessibus levior vel asperior sententia proferatur. Sic enim profecto iustitia nostra divine iustitie respondet.

Legum igitur asperitate lenita, non ut olim gladio agendum, set rerum ad eam pertinentium confiscatio inducetur, si filios legitimos ex eo matrimonio violato vel alio non habuerit. Iniquum enim est eos successione privari, qui nati sunt eo tempore quo thori lex legaliter servabatur. Aut viro tradenda est nullatenus ad vite periculum servituro, set ultionem thori violati nasi truncatione quod sevius et atrocius inducitur persecutor; ultro enim nec viro nec parentibus sevire licebit. Quod si vir eius noluerit in eam dare vindictam, nos maleficium huiusmodi non sinemus inultum; precipimus igitur publice flagellandum.

Qui coram se spectante, vel arbitrio permittit cum ganeis coniugem suam lascivire non facile nostro iudicio poterit accusare. Viam quippe peccandi mechandi aperit, qui cum possit pohibere consentit.

Quamvis uxorem suspectam quis habeat, quamvis famosam, si tamen fidem habet, eum lenocinii non dampnamus; quis enim iure thori alieni inquietet quietem. Quod si patenter deprehendimus quempiam habere incestuosam uxorem, dignam mox sequemur pene vindictam; eum quoque pena infamie condempnamus.

Femine penitus et adulterii et stupri prestentur immunes iudiciaria severitate, quas vilitas vite dignas legum observatione non credidi, sicut ministre caupone.

17. De meretricibus

Que passim formam venalem exhibuit, et vulgo prostitutam se prebuit, huius criminis accusationem amovit; violentiam tamen ei ingeri prohibemus, et inter boni testimonii feminas habitare vetamus.

18. De accusatione adulterii

Adulter et adultera simul accusari non possunt, alter singulariter est accusandus, et rei exitus expectandus; nam si adulter defendi poterit, mulier est secura, nulli ulterius responsura. Si vero fuerit condempnatus, tunc demum mulier accusatur.

De crimine adulteri pacisci non licet, et par delictum accusatoris prevaricatoris et refugientis veritatis inquisitionem. Qui autem pretium pro comperto stupro accepit, pena legis Julie de adulteriis tenetur. Crimen adulterii maritum retenta in matrimonio uxore, inferre non posse nemini dubium est.

Lex delectum non facit, quis primum debeat conveniri, set, si uterque est presens, vir convenendus est primum. Repudium in hac accusatione pretermittendum, neque violentia seu detentio adhibenda.

19. De officialibus rei publice

Officiales rei publice vel iudices qui in tempore amministrationis pecunias publicas subtraxerint, obnoxii crimine peculatus, capite puniuntur, nisi regia pietas indulserit.

Qui sua negligentia bona publica deperire vel minui permiserit, et in persona propria et in rebus suis constituetur obnoxius; et hoc prospectu regie pietatis.

20. De furtis

Qui sciens, furanti sinum prebuit, eadem pena tenetur.

21. De crimine lenocinii

Lenas sollicitantes alienam castitatem genus criminis pessimum tamquam ipsas adulteras puniendas, presenti lege sancimus.

Matres virgines filias venalicias proponentes et maritalia federa fugientes, ut lenas ipsas persequimur, scilicet ut nasus earum abscidantur; castitatem enim et virginitatem suorum viscerum vendere inhumanum est et crudele; quod si filia se ipsam tamen prostituit, mater vero tantum consentit, iudicis arbitrio relinquetur.

Crimen lenocinii contrahunt, qui deprehensam in adulterio uxorem in matrimonio tenuerit, non qui suspectam adulteram habuerunt.

22. De eodem

Si providentia rege celsitudinis nullo modo patitur inter regni nostri limitem baronum nostrorum quemlibet alterius castrum invadere, predas committere, cum armis insurgere, vel inique fraudari, quin pro commisso bonorum omnium ipsum iactura afficiat; quanto amplius dampnandum censemus, si compatris vel vicini thorum violare presumpserit quis intolerabile prorsus de iure videtur. Sancimus itaque si de tali facto nobis aliquando fuerit proclamatum, et manifestum fuerit vel probatum, bonorum omnium mulctatione plectendum.

23. De vindicta adulterantium

Si maritus uxorem in ipso actu adulterii deprehenderit, tam adulterum quam uxorem occidere licebit, nulla tamen mora protracta. Lex maritum lenocinii pena cohercet, qui uxorem in adulterio deprehensam retinuit, adulterumque dimisit; nisi forte sine sua culpa ille diffugerit.

24. De desistentibus ab accusatione

Qui post crimen adulterii intemptatum uxorem receperit, destitisse videtur, ideoque suscitare questionem ultra non poterit.

25. De plagiariis

Qui sciens liberum hominem vendiderit, hac pena legitima teneatur, ut ex bonis suis venditus redimatur; ipse vero maleficus curie servus sit, bonorum suorum residuo publicato; quod si ex rebus ipsius redimi non poterit, pro servo tradatur parentibus venditi, bonis eius curie addictis; quocumque autem casu venditus redeat, maleficus curie servus fiat, filiis etiam post hunc casum nascentibus subiecti sint curie perpetua servitute.

26. De sicariis secundum legem corneliam

Qui aggressorem vel latronem, in dubio vite discrimine constitutis occiderit, nullam, ob id factum, calumpniam metuere debet. Qui aggressorem ad se venientem ferro repulerit, non homicida set defensor salutis est.

Nocturnum furem qui occiderit, impune feret, si aliter comprehendi nequiverit, si modo cum clamore id fiat.

Infans sine malignitate animi et furiosus si hominem occiderit, non tenetur; quia alterum innocentia consili alterum facti infelicitas excusat

Nichil interest occidat quis, an mortis causam prebeat.

In maleficiis voluntas spectatur non exitus.

Qui de alto se ipsum precipitat et hominem occidit, qui ramum incautus deiciens non proclamavit, seu lapidem aut aliud deiecit hominemque occidit, huic pene succumbit.

27. De incendiis

Qui dolose domum incenderit, capitis pena plectetur velut incendiarius.

28. De noxiis medicaminibus

Poculum amatorium vel aliquem cibum noxium quisquis instruxerit, etiam si neminem leserit, impunis non erit.

29. De eisdem

Mala et noxia medicamenta ad alienandos animos, seu venena qui dederit, vendiderit, habuerit, capitali sententia feriatur.

30. De iudice depravato

Si iudex accepta pecunia reum quemlibet criminis et mortis fecerit, capitis periculo subiacebit.

Si iudex fraudulenter atque dolose sententiam contra leges protulerit, auctoritate iudiciaria inrecuperabiliter cadat, notetur infamia, rebus eius omnibus publicatis. Quod si iuris ignorantia a iuris sententia aberraverit, ferens iudicium pro simplicitate manifestum regie misericordie subiacebit.

In maleficiis voluntas spectatur non exitus.

31. De arripientibus novam militiam

Quicumque novam militiam arripuit contra regni nostri beatitudinem et pacem sine integritate militie nomine et professione penitus cadat, nisi forte a militari genere per successionem duxerit prosapiam.

32. De tironibus

Nullus tiro ga aut veteranus aut censibus obnoxius ad militia accedat.

33. De iniuriis privatorum

Cuicumque de popularibus ex consulto tamen et deliberatione barba fuerit depilata, reus soldorum aureorum VI regalium pena condempnetur; si vero in rixa factum fuerit, sine deliberatione, solidorum III.
Vel iumenti cauda decerpitur.

34. De fugacibus

Si quis temerario ausu presumpserit bona in quiete et tranquillitate regni habita, cum pro ipso laborare expedit, labores fugiendo obmittere, omnia bona sua dominus eius habeat, et illius persona curie assignetur.

35. De seditionariis

Si quis in exercitu seditiones, iurgia seu aliud fecerit, uti exercitus noster turbetur, persona eius cum omnibus suis bonis mercedi curie subiacebit.

Si quis ficte vel fraudulenter ad magnum exercitum non venerit, seu, postquam venerit, ab exercitu sine licentia curie recesserit, capitalem subibit sententiam, vel in manibus curie tradetur, ut ipse et eius heredes culusti fiant.

36. De mordisonibus

Comperit nostra serenitas infra regni nobis a deo concessi fines quorundam immanitate clandestina incendia, tam in urbanis quam rusticis prediis, perpetrari, arbores quoque et vites furtim cedere. Proinde hac edictali pragmatica sanctione in perpetuum valitura deo propitio sancimus, ut si quis amodo de hujusmodi reatu fuerit appellatus, si suspectione careat et eius conversatio per bonorum testimonia illibata consistat, pro tenore veterum legum, aut cuiuscumque loci consuetudine se expurget. Si vero tanti reatus non levis suspitio de eo fuerit, vel preterite vite sue probrosus cursus extiterit, opinionemque eius apud bonos et graves dehonestaverit, de calumpnia prius actore iurante, non ut actenus set ceteris super hoc legibus sopitis et moribus, igniti ferri subeat iudicium. Predicti denique criminis confessus aut convictus, dampno prius lese partis de eius facultatibus resarcito, vite sue periculum, vel membrorum suorum privatione pro bene placito maiestatis nostre incurret.

37. Que sit potestas justitiarii

Sancimus ut latrocinia, fracture domorum, insultus viarum, vis mulieribus illata, duella, homicidia, leges parabiles, calumpnie criminum, incendia, forisfacte omnes, de quibus quilibet de corpore et rebus suis mercedi curie debeat subiacere, a iustitiariis iudicentur, clamoribus supradictorum baiulis depositis, cetera vero a baiulis poterunt definiri.

38. De intestatis

Nuper ad nostri culminis pervenit audientiam quod cum aliquis burgensium vel aliorum hominum civitatum intestatus decedit, sive filii ex eo existant sive non, res eius ad opus curie nostre capiebantur, quod admodum maiestati displicuit et grave tulimus.

Nos itaque, ex solita nostre benignitatis gratia, hanc pravam consuetudinem penitus resecare volentes, precipimus, ut, si quis burgensium vel aliorum, qui in ipsa civitate devenerit, intestatus decesserit, si ex eo filius vel filia exierit, ipse sui patris heres existat, et tertia pars omnium rerum eius pro ipsius anima erogetur.

Si vero nulli filii ex eo existant, tunc proximiores eius tam ex linea ascendentium et descendentium quam ex latere venientium, qui de iure ei succedere debent, heredes existant, si de feudo vel de servitio non fuerit, tertia tamen parte rerum suarum pro defuncti anima distributa.

Si autem filius vel filia ex eo nullus exierit, vel alius tam ex linea ascendentium quam et descendentium, vel ex latere venientium, qui de iure ei succedere debeat, tunc etiam tertia parte omnium rerum suarum ut dictum est integre pro defuncti anima prestita, residuum ad opus curie nostre capiatur.

Si vero cum herede seu sine herede testatus decesserit, ultima eius voluntas in integrum observetur.

39. De excessu prelatorum et dominorum

De prelatis autem ecclesiarum sic a regia munificentia statutum est, ut in his tantum ab hominibus suis adiutorum exigant, vidilicet, pro consecratione sua, cum ad concilium a domino papa vocantur, pro servitio exercitus nostri, si quando in exercitu servierint, vel si vocati fuerint a rege vel missi, pro corredo nostro si quando in terris eorum nos hospitari vel corredum ab eis recipere contigerit. Et in his tantum casibus a prelatis omnibus, comitibus, baronibus et militibus moderate secundum facultates hominum suorum audiutoria exigant et accipiant.

40. Rescriptum pro cleris

De eo autem quod male interpretatum est videlicet quod de nostre maiestatis constitutione villani non audeant ad ordinem clericatus accedere, sine voluntate et assensu dominorum suorum, ita statutum est, quod si aliquis villanus est et servire debet personaliter intuitu persone, ut sunt ascripticii et servi glebe, et alii huiusmodi, qui non respectu tenimentorum vel alius beneficii servire debent, set intuitu personarum, que persone eorum sunt obligate servitis isti quidem, sine assensu et voluntate dominorum suorum ad ordinem clericatus accedere nequerunt. Illi vero, qui non intuitu personarum set respectu testimentorum vel aliquorum beneficiorum que tenent servire debent dominis suis, si voluerint ad ordinem clericatus accedere, liceat eis etiam sine voluntate dominorum suorum, prius tamen renuntiatis his que tenent a dominis suis.

Appendix 8
CHRONICON EXCERPTS

These are the author's translations of the sections most directly relevant to Queen Margaret, especially those which mention her by name. Part of the *Chronicon* of Romuald of Salerno, which is not as lengthy or detailed as the chronicle of Falcandus, has been published in English translation.[431] The chronicle of Falcandus ends in 1169, but that of Romuald details events until late 1178. All of the following translations are original; the passages beginning with Thomas Becket are the first translations from the *Chronicon* ever published in English, while the others were effected without reference to existing (published) translations. For ready identification, the initial sentence of each section is also presented in the original Latin of the manuscripts, which, like the *editio princeps,* lack chapters. Details such as dates are indicated within [brackets]. The texts appear in the order in which Romuald presents them.

Construction of the Zisa Palace

Eo tempore Rex Guilielmus palatium quoddam altum satis et miro artificio laboratum prope Panormum aedificari fecit, quod Zisam appellavit, et ipsum pulchris pomiferis et amoenis viridariis circumdedit, et diversis aquarum conductibus et piscariis satis delectabile reddidit.

At that time [1165] King William ordered to be erected near Palermo a rather high palace, built with admirable technical competence, which he called the Zisa, surrounded by fruit trees and splendid gardens, rendering it pleasurable with numerous fountains and lakelets.

Margaret becomes Queen Consort at William's Accession

Defuncto autem Rege Rogerio, Guilielmus filius ejus, qui cum patre duobus annis et mensibus decem regnaverat, illi in regni administratione successit.

With the death of King Roger [February 1154], his son, William, who had reigned alongside his father for two years and ten months, succeeded to the throne. Following the death of his father, and in the presence of the realm's great nobles, William was solemnly crowned on Easter, which was very near [4 April]. Among those in attendance was Robert of Bassonville, Count of Conversano and matrilineal cousin of the King.

Margaret's Marriage to William, Son of Roger II

Rex autem Guilielmus, adhuc vivente patre cum esset princeps capuanorum, Margaritam filiam Garsie Regis Navarre duxit uxorem, de qua plures liberos hubuit: Rogerium quem ducem apulie constituit, Robertum quem capuanorum principem ordinauit, Willelmum et Henricum.

When his father was still alive, William, whilst Prince of Capua, wed Margaret, daughter of García, King of Navarre [in 1149], who bore him several sons, namely: Roger, who he created Duke of Apulia, Robert, who he invested as Prince of Capua, and William and Henry.

Frederick I [Barbarossa] was very annoyed to learn of the pact between the King of Sicily and Pope Adrian IV, as well as the Papal recognition of the investiture (sic) of young William with the Kingdom of Sicily [crowned as *rex filius* in 1151] and the Duchy of Apulia.

Margaret Named Regent

Rex autem Guilielmus circa Quadragesimam fluxu ventris et molestia coepit affligi.

During the beginning of Lent [March 1166], William was struck by a bout of dysentery. For a time the condition subsided, but by the middle of Lent it worsened, and the King believed himself at the gate of death. He repented and confessed himself, freed some prisoners, forgave a redemption tax he had imposed in Apulia, and made his last testament. In this will he named his elder surviving son, William, as his heir, and confirmed the younger, Henry, as Prince of Capua, as he had already designated.

The King left much money to be spent [for the poor and to glorify God] for the salvation of his soul, and decreed Queen Margaret, his wife, to be keeper and governor of all the realm and of his sons.[432] Finally, he appointed as royal counsellors [familiares] Richard, Bishop-Elect of Syracuse, and Matthew, his High Notary, both being wise, prudent men who were proven experts in law and known to his wife and sons.

Death of William I

Sed quum praedicta passio ingravesceret, rex Guilielmus Romualdum salernitanum archiepiscopum, qui in arte erat medicinae valde peritus, ad se vocari praecepit.

As the illness became grave, King William called to his presence Romuald, Archbishop of Salerno, who was learned in the art of medicine. Arriving around Easter [24 April], the prelate was received with honour and he prescribed a number of remedies. However, trusting in the authority of his own counsel, the monarch used only the cures he thought most beneficial. And so, the Saturday following Easter, the fever rose and the dysentery worsened.

The King died, aged forty-six, during the afternoon of the seventh day (sic) of May, of the fourteenth indiction, around the ninth hour of daylight [3 PM], having reigned alongside his father and then alone for fifteen years and ten months.[433] He was entombed in the chapel of Saint Peter [the Palatine Chapel] in the royal palace.[434]

He was tall, robust and attractive, proud, desirous of prestige, victorious in naval and land battles. He was despised in his realm, where he was feared more than loved. He was greedy in obtaining money for himself and not very generous in spending it on others.[435]

In bestowing honour and wealth he edified those loyal to him. He prosecuted traitors, condemning some to penury and others to exile.

Frequently did he attend liturgy, and he showed great respect for the clergy. He had the Palatine Chapel decorated with marvelous images in mosaic, enhanced by precious stones, its walls covered in various types of marble. He had it appointed in gold and silver, with lush tapestries. The chapel was served by numerous clerics, endowed by as many ecclesiastical benefices. The monarch ensured every reverence toward God in the divine office celebrated there.

Accession of William II

Quo defuncto, Guilielmus, filius ejus maior, natus annos duodecim, illi in regno successit.

The deceased sovereign was succeeded by William, his eldest son, who was aged twelve years. On the Queen's command, and on the advice of the archbishops, barons and people, he was proclaimed King two days following his father's death.

Indeed, on that day of his coronation, he arrived at the Church of Saint Mary [the cathedral] in Palermo escorted in pomp by a royal cortege that bestowed great glory upon him. He was anointed and crowned by Romuald, Archbishop of Salerno, in the presence of numerous archbishops, bishops and barons. In great honour, and to the joy of the people, he processed to the palace with the crown on his head.

Margaret's First Acts as Regent

Regina vero, utpote mulier sapiens et discreta, manifeste cognoscens animos populi sui, propter molestias quas a rege Guilielmo passi fuerant, plurimum esse turbatos, illos ad amorem et fidelitatem filii sui beneficiis credidit provocandos.

The Queen, being a wise and prudent woman, and knowing well the spirit of the populace, which was very disturbed for the mistreatment the subjects had endured under the late William I, undertook through many concessions to instill their love and fealty toward her son. Acting on sage counsel, she opened the jails and released many prisoners, restoring their lands and forgiving their debts.

She allowed counts and barons who had left the realm to return, restoring to them the estates that had been confiscated. By royal grace, she very generously granted many lands to churches, counts, barons and knights.

Through these and many other acts the fealty and spirit of affinity of the people for her son increased greatly, to the point that those who were already loyal became even more ardently loyal and those who were devoted became further devoted to him.

In those times Qaïd Peter, a eunuch who was master chamberlain of the palace, fled with some others to the court of the King of Morocco, taking with him much money.

Manuel [Comnenus], Emperor of Constantinople, learning of the death of King William I, sent ambassadors to his young successor in Sicily to convey the message that he wished to establish, of his own volition, peace with him, William II. He proposed to William the betrothal of his only daughter, universal heiress to his [Byzantine] Empire, along with the right of succession.[436]

The Queen Regent and the King convoked a council to consider this proposal, sending and receiving many ambassadors. They renewed the traditional peace, but the negotiation of the betrothal remained open for the numerous details that had to be stipulated.

For the many concessions made to their subjects, King William and his mother soon earned their esteem, governing the Kingdom in peace and tranquility.

Henry, Margaret's natural [illegitimate] brother, arrived at the court in Sicily. The King granted him the County of Montescaglioso and betrothed to him a daughter of King Roger.

In those same days [in 1166] Stephen, son of the Count of Perche, also arrived in Sicily. This cleric was kin to Queen Margaret, who named him Grand Chancellor and then arranged for him to be consecrated Archbishop of Palermo.

Before long, Stephen was governing the entire realm as he saw fit, having become very familiar with the King and the Queen Regent.[437]

Murder of Thomas Becket Reported

Illis autem diebus Thomas Cantuariensis archiepiscopus, vir religiosus ed Deum metuens, dum pro libertate ed ecclesiarum justitiis Henrico regi angliae viriliter repugnaret, de Anglia exire compulsus ad regem

Lodovicum venit in Franciam, qui eum ob suae religionis reverentiam satis officiose recepit, et per aliquos annos in terra sua honeste detinuit, et quae erant illi necessaria, liberalitate regia ministravit.

In those times, Thomas, Archbishop of Canterbury, a devout and god-fearing man, strove to preserve the rights and freedoms of the Church which King Henry II of England tried to usurp. This forced Thomas into exile in France at the court of King Louis VII, who accorded the cleric every courtesy and for some years granted him hospitality in his realm, providing him with every necessity.

Finally, at the request of Pope Alexander III and King Louis, Thomas, Archbishop of Canterbury, made peace with the King of England, who permitted him to return to his church.[438] Over time, King Henry, acting on the counsel of malicious men, began to provoke the clergy and deprive the Church of her rights.

Coming to learn of this, Archbishop Thomas, defying all fear and never deviating from the path of justice, defended the Church's freedom through words and deeds as a good shepherd protects his flock.

Since the discord increased day by day, with words and actions annoying the monarch ever more, some English knights decided to act in a manner that would please their sovereign. To that end, Hugh de Morville, William de Tracy, Reginald FitzUrse, Richard le Breton and Robert de Broc (sic)[439] ignored the reverence due the priesthood and the fear to be shown in the face of God. On the day following the Feast of the Innocents [29 December 1170], they killed Thomas by striking his head with a sword while he prayed before the altar of the cathedral. They immediately fled, pursued by nobody, keeping their remorse to themselves.

The bells of the city and the abbey rang out to announce news of the evil act. Monks, priests and laity entered the cathedral to find, unspeakably, the body of their pastor who had been cruelly killed next to the altar. Tearfully, between heartfelt groans and sighs, they buried him in honour in his own church during a Pontifical [solemn] liturgy to the sound of hymns.

The just and merciful Lord, who looks upon his own not only in the future but the present, permitted Archbishop Thomas to be venerated as a martyr, as much for the pain he suffered as for the cause he defended. His murder, for having upheld truth, made Thomas famous and celebrated in all the world through many supernatural manifestations and recent miraculous events.

When the Pope [Alexander III] heard of the certainty and veracity of those miracles, the decision was announced to his fellow prelates of the canonization of Thomas as a martyr, his name to be inscribed in the catalogue of martyrs. It was ordered that his martyrdom be celebrated every year on the anniversary of his death.

The King of England heard that public opinion was against him, implying that he had prior knowledge of the crime perpetrated against the Archbishop, and these voices persecuted he who was not to blame. Confident in the purity of his innocence, Henry sent some of his bishops and clerics to Anagni to see Pope Alexander.

Before the Pope and his cardinals, Henry's emissaries publicly swore on the Holy Gospels that their King was innocent of having spilled the blood of that just man, and that he had no part in the crime that was committed. His knights, who did not fear assaulting the Archbishop, had given thought to their deed, recognizing their crime and their dishonesty. They now submitted themselves humbly at the Pope's feet, publicly proclaiming their guilt and their sacrilege, imploring that he permit them to make penance for the crime they had committed.

The Pontiff condemned the guilty knights in the strongest terms for their evil, affirming that the judgement of God would be visited upon them if they did not atone for their sin with a suitable penance.

He ordered them to go on pilgrimage to Jerusalem, barefoot and clad in cilices [hairshirts], visiting the holy places in pain and piety. He ordered them to go thenceforth to Black Mountain, which is near the city of Antioch.[440] There, only by fasting, meditating, praying and grieving for the rest of their lives, ever asking for divine mercy, might they repent of so vile a crime.

Maria Comnenus Fails to Arrive

Eo tempore quum Emmanuel imperator Constantinopolitanus frequentibus nuntiis delegatis filiam suam Zura Mariam Guilielmo regi Siciliae in uxorem tradere promisisset, tandem ex conventione ultriusque partis factum est, quod imperator, praesentibus legatis ejusdem regis, in anima sua jurare fecit, et juramentum suum magnatum suorum jurejurando firmari, quod in termino et loco ab utraque parte praefixo filiam suam regi pro uxore transmitteret.

At that time [1171] Manuel, Emperor of Constantinople, in the frequent messages borne by his ambassadors, had promised the betrothal of his daughter, Maria, to King William of Sicily. At the end of these negotiations, both parties were agreed that the Emperor, in the presence of William's representatives [as witnesses], would swear on his very soul to send his daughter to the King to a place that was mutually agreed upon.

The terms of the betrothal were confirmed by an oath sworn collectively by the Imperial nobles. In the same manner, the King and those near him [the Queen and court] swore to welcome the daughter of the Emperor.

Having done so, William, being a just and god-fearing man, and seeking to honour his oath, went to Taranto with his younger brother Henry, Prince of Capua, and waited there for a time for the arrival of Maria, who was to be accompanied by Manuel's emissaries.

Then the devout prince went to the shrine of Saint Michael on Mount Gargano to pray before going to Barletta, where he stayed for several days.

But the Emperor, abandoning his oath and his promise, failed to send his daughter to meet the King of Sicily at the time and place agreed upon.

Death of Prince Henry of Capua

Quo rex cognito per terram beneventanam transiens, Henricum capuanorum princepem fratrem suum, quia infirmus erat.

Knowing this [that Maria Comnenus had not arrived at Taranto], William, while passing through the Benevento region, sent his brother, Henry, who had fallen ill, ahead to Salerno. Meanwhile, William visited Capua and then made his way to Salerno.

Henry boarded a galley for Palermo. There the illness worsened, and he died in the middle of June in the year of Our Lord 1172, of the fifth indiction, aged thirteen. He was interred with honour next to the tomb of Roger II, his grandfather, in the Church of Saint Mary in Palermo.[441]

Having remained in Salerno for a few days, William boarded a galley with Walter, the venerable Archbishop of Palermo, and Matthew [of Aiello] the Vice Chancellor, and returned to Palermo, where, according to proper usage, he immediately learned of the death of his brother. At first William suffered terribly, both mentally and physically, but he eventually accepted the wise counsel of those loyal to him, finding consolation for his pain through his faith in the Lord.

Proposed Betrothal of Beatrice Hohenstaufen

Interea praedictus cancellarius ex mandato imperatoris nunctios ad Guilielmum Siciliae regem transmisit, suadens et postulans, ut ipse, imperatoris filia in uxorem accepta, cum eo pacem perpetuam faceret et ipsi se amicabiliter couniret.

The chancellor of the Holy Roman Emperor [Frederick I "Barbarossa"], acting on his lord's orders, sent ambassadors to William, King of Sicily, asking him, and prevailing upon him, to stipulate a perpetual peace. To seal this accord, the Emperor asked William to accept his daughter [Beatrice] as his bride.

But King William, being a devoutly religious, Christian ruler, knew that this marriage would not please Pope Alexander III. Indeed, it would have brought with it great damage to the Church of Rome.

Out of reverence for God and respect for Pope Alexander, he chose not to accept a union with the daughter of the Emperor, nor the peace accord presented. For his part, Frederick was greatly offended at this rebuke and did not forget it. His daughter died shortly afterward.[442]

Joanna "Plantagenet" of England

Interea rex Guilielmus consilio Papae Alexandri, Heliam Trojanum electum et Arnulfum caputaquensem episcopum et Florium de Camerota regium justitiarium ad regem Henricum in Angliam misit, ut ei Joannam minorem filiam suam in uxorem daret.

In those times [1176] King William II, acting on the advice of Pope Alexander III, sent to King Henry II in England as his emissaries Elias, Bishop Elect of Troia, Arnolf, Bishop of Capaccio, and Florio of Camerota, royal justiciar, to ask for the hand of Joanna, his young daughter.

Henry, accepting the counsel of Pope Alexander and his princes, happily consented to the request of the [Sicilian] sovereign. He sent his daughter as far as the port of Saint-Gilles in the company of the royal emissaries and some of his own nobles.[443]

Knowing this, King William sent Alfano, Archbishop of Capua, Richard, Bishop of Syracuse, and Robert, Count of Caserta with twenty-five galleys to meet Joanna there. From Saint-Gilles, the three prelates escorted Joanna aboard a galley and set out for Naples. Unaccustomed to sea travel, the girl suffered a bout of sea sickness.

They stopped at Naples to celebrate Christmas. Then they travelled by land via Salerno and Calabria to Sicily. At Palermo, Joanna was met by King William and his great nobles, and received with the great honour due her.

Then King William summoned the most distinguished noblemen of Sicily, and a great multitude of the populace, for his solemn nuptials with the daughter of the King of England in the Palatine Chapel, where the betrothed were married and crowned in the Year of Our Lord 1177 in the month of February of the tenth indiction [on Sunday the thirteenth].

Appendix 9
JOANNA'S BETROTHAL

In addition to the notes by Romuald of Salerno, we have descriptions of Joanna's betrothal and marriage written by several English chroniclers. Beyond providing the details of how Margaret and her advisors found a bride for William II, these texts, more generally, offer insight into royal betrothals of the twelfth century, including Margaret's, with special reference to the Kingdom of Sicily.

From the Chronicle of "Benedict of Peterborough"

Here the description of Joanna's betrothal from the chronicle of "Benedict of Peterborough" (written by Roger of Howden) is presented in English, with the rubrics (headings) from the surviving manuscripts, and especially the Cotton Manuscript, thus *De adventu nunciorum regis Siciliae* for the first section and *Carta regis Willelmi regis Siciliae de dote uxoris suae* for the last one.

Arrival of the Ambassadors of the King of Sicily

Meanwhile [April 1176], there landed in England the bishop elect [Elias] of Troia and the bishop [Arnolf] of Capaccio, with count Florio of Camerota, ambassadors of King William of Sicily. Accompanying them was archbishop Rotrou of Rouen, kinsman of the King of Sicily.

They went to meet King Henry at London, petitioning the monarch to betroth his daughter, Joanna, to their sovereign, William. Before responding to this request, Henry convoked in London his bishop [Gilbert Foliot] and other high prelates and knowledgeable counsellors of the realm. Accepting his counsellors' advice, he sent William's ambassadors to Winchester to see if the girl might be acceptable.

The King of England Betroths his Daughter to King William of Sicily

The ambassadors of the King of Sicily, mentioned earlier, went to see the girl, and they very much approved of her. To conclude the agreement, they then went to see her father, and the Papal legate, cardinal Hugh Pierleoni, and the archbishop of Rouen.

With this, King Henry commanded John, bishop of Norwich, Paris, archdeacon of Rochester, Baldwin Bulot and Richard of Camville to travel on his behalf to the court of William, King of Sicily, with Elias of Troia bearing the message that he [Henry] granted to him the hand of his daughter in marriage.

At the same time, the other ambassadors [Arnolf and Florio] remained in England as King Henry's guests until Joanna's departure.

Peace Between the Archbishops at Winchester

On 15 August, the feast of the Assumption of Mary, King Henry arrived at Winchester, where he held a council. Here a reconciliation was reached between Richard, archbishop of Canterbury, and Roger, archbishop of York. The monarch also visited his daughter, Joanna, before her departure for Sicily.

The council ended with concord achieved among the prelates. Archbishop Richard of Canterbury and bishop Geoffrey of Ely readied themselves to accompany the daughter of King Henry to Saint-Gilles, where a galley sent by King William, to whom she was betrothed, would meet them.

With King Henry and King William having exchanged ambassadors, Joanna prepared for her voyage.

King Henry sent Joanna off unhurriedly, with the dignity befitting her, to meet Henry the Younger, her brother, in Normandy. The King of England made gifts to the King of Sicily of horses, clothes, gold and silver, and precious vases.

There Henry the Younger came to meet his sister, conducting her with the greatest honour to the County of Poitiers of his brother, Richard. Thenceforth, Richard escorted Joanna through the lands he held [Aquitaine]. Then the girl traveled to Saint-Gilles with Richard of Canterbury, Geoffrey of Ely, Giles of Evreux, Hugh of Beauchamp, and Hamelin of Warenne, her father's half-brother.

In December [1176] Richard of Canterbury and Geoffrey of Ely, who had conducted King Henry's daughter to Saint-Gilles, returned to their episcopal sees in England.

Likewise John of Norwich, who had been dispatched to the court of King William of Sicily, returned to England. However, upon arriving with Paris of Rochester, he reported to Henry that during his voyage from Messina to Saint-Gilles he had encountered a storm, and two fine galleys carrying various, precious gifts from William had sunk.

Henry Receives Joanna's Dower Charter

The royal ambassadors consigned to King Henry [1177] the charter of the marriage settlement of his daughter, Joanna, who was given in matrimony to King William of Sicily. Here is what it said. [See the following section.]

From Roger's Annals

This is Henry Riley's eloquent, Victorian translation of the account of the wedding and the text of the marriage charter (and dower inventory) from the *Annals of Roger de Hoveden* (volume 1, pages 413-417) published in London in 1853. (One might note the Anglice "Howden" preferred by Doris Stenton, Frank Barlow and other scholars in more recent times.) Roger's *Annals* are complementary to Romuald's succinct description, translated in the previous appendix. The chronicle of "Benedict of Peterborough" (see above) was most likely written by Roger of Howden, and the text of the dower document was compared to what is reported there (on folios 100-101 of the manuscript); minor corrections in orthography have been made to such details as the names of people and places.

In the year 1176 there came to England, from William, King of Sicily, [Elias] the bishop of Troia, the archbishop elect of Capaccio, and count Florio, as envoys to Henry, King of England, the father, and asked of him his daughter Joanna in marriage for William, King of Sicily, their lord.

A council upon the matter being accordingly held in London, the King, the father, with the consent of all the bishops, earls, and barons of the Kingdom, gave his daughter to the King of Sicily. And with this assent, the King [of England] first sent to the King of Sicily the bishop of Troia, John, bishop of Norwich, Paris, archdeacon of Rochester, Baldwin Bulot, and Richard de Camville, and in the meantime prepared for his daughter, Joanna, the things necessary for her equipment and journey. After these were all completed in a becoming manner, the King sent his daughter, Joanna, to be wed to William, the King of Sicily.

When she had arrived at Palermo, in Sicily, together with Giles, bishop of Evreux, and the other envoys of our lord, the

King, the whole city welcomed them, and lamps, so many and so large, were lighted up, that the city almost seemed to be on fire, and the rays of the stars could in no way bear comparison with the brilliancy of such a light: for it was by night that they entered the city of Palermo. The said daughter of the King of England was then escorted, mounted on one of the King's horses, and resplendent with regal garments, to a certain palace, that there she might in becoming state await the day of her marriage and coronation.

After the expiration of a few days from this time, the before-named daughter of the King of England was married to William, King of Sicily, and solemnly crowned at Palermo, in the royal chapel there, in the presence of Giles, bishop of Evreux, and the envoys of the King of England, who had been sent for that purpose. She was married and crowned on the Lord's day before the beginning of Septuagesima, being the ides of February; and was with due honour endowed with the county of Mount Saint Angelo, the city of Siponto, the city of Vesta, and many other castles and places. Whereupon, the King of Sicily executed in her favour his charter, as follows:

> The Charter of William, King of Sicily,
> which he executed in favour of Joanna,
> daughter of Henry, King of England,
> as to her dower

"In the name of the Father, and of the Son, and of the Holy Ghost, Amen. Amid the other blessings of peace, the nuptial tie binds and fastens most strongly the unison and the concord of human affairs; a rite, both venerable from the weightiness of its obligations, remarkable in the circumstances of its institution, and sanctioned by universal usage, from the beginning of the world and of time; of which the virtues and the comeliness, inasmuch as it has derived its origin from Divine institution, have neither contracted blemish from sin, nor have been sensible of any diminution by desuetude, through the lengthened ages of past time.

"Moreover, to this venerable and mysterious institution this honour is added, that the consent of the man and of the woman to enter matrimony typifies the sacramental bond of Christ and His Church. Being therefore led by the nature of this great and mysterious institution, and by veneration for the same, we, William, by the favour of the Divine grace King of Sicily, Duke of Apulia and Prince of Capua, do unite unto ourselves by the laws of matrimony and the bond of wedlock, with the Divine sanction and under happy auspices, the maiden Joanna, of royal blood, and the most illustrious daughter of Henry, the mighty King of the English; to the end, that her fidelity and chaste affection may produce the blessings of the married state, and that by her a royal offspring may, by the gift of God, hereafter succeed us in the Kingdom, which, both by reason of its endowment with all virtues, and of its title by birth, by the Divine grace, both may and ought to be raised to the Throne of this Realm.

"But, inasmuch as it is befitting our exalted position that so noble and illustrious an alliance should be honored with a becoming dower, by this present writing we do give, and as a dower, do grant to the before-named queen, our most dearly beloved wife, the county of Mount Saint Angelo, the city of Siponto, and the city of Vesta, with all the rightful manors and appurtenances thereof. We do also grant for her service, out of the manors of count Godfrey, Alesina, Peschiza, Bicum, Caprile, Barano, and Filizi, and all other places which the said count is known to possess as of the honour of the said county of Mount Saint Angelo. In like manner, we do also grant for her service, Candelari, Saint Clair, Castel Pagano, Bersenza, and Cagnano.

"We do also grant, that there shall be as of the honour of the said dower, the monastery of Saint Mary de Pulsano, and the monastery of Saint John de Lama, with all the manors which those monasteries hold of the honour of the aforesaid county of Saint Angelo — upon condition that the Queen, our aforesaid wife, shall always recognize all the rights of our heirs, who by our ordinance shall succeed us in the Kingdom, and shall do unto our said heirs, fully and unreservedly, all services for the aforesaid manors, according as the tenure in fee thereof shall require, and shall always observe her fealty to them.

"Wherefore, in remembrance of the said gift and grant, and for the inviolable establishment thereof, we have commanded this present charter to be written by the hand of Alexander, our notary, and, the golden bulla, our seal, being impressed thereon, to be confirmed with our said seal, and graced therewith.

"Unto which, by our command, the personages of our household and others have subscribed their names in manner following:

Walter, archbishop of Palermo.
Alfanus, archbishop of Capua.
Richard, bishop of Syracuse.
Bartholomew, bishop of Agrigento.
Reginald, archbishop of Bari.
Nicholas, first archbishop of Messina.
Ruffus, archbishop of Cosenza.
Theobald, bishop and abbot of New Saint Mary.
Robert, bishop of Catania.
Guy, bishop of Cefalù.
Elias, bishop elect of Troia.
Justus, bishop of Mazzara.
Robert, bishop of Tricarico.
Peter, bishop of Caiazzo.

John, bishop of Potenza.
Robert de Bizino.
Robert Malcovenanz
Alexander Gupille
Matthew, royal vice-chancellor
Robert, count of Caserta.
Amphusus, count of Scrulac.
Jocelyn, count of Loret.
Hugh, count of Catanzaro.
Richard, count of Fundano, admiral.
Walter of Moac, admiral of the King's ship Fortunatus.
Aldewin of Candida, seneschal of our lord the King.
Berardus Gentili, constable of the palace of Messina.
Richard, keeper of the records in the royal palace.
Bamalis de Montefort, chief justiciar.
Persicus, chief justiciar of the royal court.
Frederick, justiciar of the royal court.

Given at the flourishing city of Palermo by the hands of Walter, the venerable Archbishop of Palermo, Matthew, vice-chancellor of the King, and Richard, the venerable bishop of Syracuse, members of the household of our lord the King, in the year from the incarnation of our Lord one thousand one hundred and seventy-seven, in the month of February, being the tenth year of the indiction; and in the eleventh year of the happy reign of our lord William, by the grace of God, the mighty and most glorious King of Sicily, Duke of Apulia, and Prince of Capua. Amen."

Sealed with the seal of William, King of Sicily. Here follows in the original, the form of the bulla or seal, which contains around the margin the words *Dextera Domini fecit virtutem. Dextera Domini exaltavit me. Dextera Domini fecit virtutem.* "The right hand of the Lord hath created my might. The right hand of the Lord hath exalted me. The right hand of the Lord hath created my might." In the central portion is a cross surmounted by the words *Divina favente dementia Willielmus rex Siciliae et ducatus Apuliae et principatus Capuae.* "By the favour of the Divine mercy, William, King of Sicily, Duke of Apulia, Prince of Capua." The cross is supported by the following words. *Hoc signum sibi praeferri a vexillifero facit cum ad bellum aliquod procedit.* "This sign he causes to be borne before him by his standard-bearer when he goes forth to battle." [This is identical to the seal affixed to a charter issued in 1169; see the following appendix.]

From the Ymagines Historiarum of Ralph of Diceto

The account by Ralph of Diceto is essentially similar to those of Roger of Howden and adds only a few details, among these the route of John of Norwich, chief ambassador of the King of England, to Palermo via Auvergne, Valence, Embrun, Genoa, Gaeta and Messina. A passage recounts the terrible sea voyage of John of Norwich, his stay in Sicily and his return to England. The entry for Joanna's marriage mentions her arrival at Saint-Gilles and her wedding, performed by archbishop Walter, in February. Ralph of Diceto includes a letter from William to Henry dated 23 August 1176 at Palermo.

William's Letter to Henry

"To Henry, by the grace of God most noble King of England, your friend William, by the grace of God King of Sicily, Duke of Apulia and Prince of Capua, sends greetings.

"We have received your ambassadors in honour, and we thank you for so kindly receiving the three nobles sent to your court asking for your consent in granting us the hand of your daughter in matrimony. Likewise, your ambassadors have expressed to me your consent. As my ambassadors are authorized to act on my behalf, I did not swear a prior oath to this undertaking, but by this letter I hereby confirm their promises to you.

"As the ambassadors have explained, we shall send a fleet of galleys to Saint-Gilles to meet your embassy, from there securely transporting your daughter to our court, and I hope that the nuptials can be celebrated as soon as possible."

Appendix 10
MARGARET'S DECREES

Until her son, William II, reached the age of majority in late 1171, most of the decrees issued in his name made mention of Margaret as regent. What follow are translated extracts from four of the very few royal charters from the regency that have survived into modern times. An effort was made to render these in a style slightly more succinct and clear than the verbose Latin. The essential format of the royal decrees varied very little during Margaret's regency.[444]

Issued in February 1169, the first decree grants Matthew of Aiello the right to establish a convent for nuns on his property on high ground in Palermo's Saqaliba district (corrupted into *Carrabule* in the Latin text). Completed two years later, this was the Benedictine convent that came to be known as "Saint Mary of the Latins," and later "Saint Mary of the Chancellor," erected along what is now Via del Celso between Vicolo Ragusi and the aptly-named Vicolo del Gran Cancelliere (a school now stands on the site). This charter was sealed with the prestigious gold seal reserved for use with the most important royal documents, typically those addressing questions of policy, diplomacy or the general populace; the other charters extracted here bore the more common lead seal.

Issued in May of the same year, the second decree confirms

a privilege granted by John of Aiello, Bishop of Catania, for the Monastery of the Holy Savior of Mount Calanna. Located near Alcara li Fusi (although Mount Calanna itself lies along the slopes of Mount Etna), this was founded earlier as a Greek Orthodox monastery before the arrival of the Normans, and a Sicilian saint, Nicholas Politi, was interred there in 1167. The charter of May 1169 reflects the "latinization" of Sicily's Greek Orthodox monasteries, and the principal abbey at Calanna came to be known as Saint Mary "del Rogato." (Some icon frescos were discovered there recently and restored in 2014.) Consecrated bishop in July 1168, John of Aiello, a brother of Matthew, died in Catania during the earthquake that devastated that city in February 1169.

Both of these royal charters reflect, in some measure, the influence of Aiello and Perche at court; there is no doubt that most decrees of this kind issued during this key period have been lost to time.

We also find Margaret's name alongside her son's in the royal charter of 1170, and one issued early in 1171, where Walter, as witness, is simply "archbishop of Palermo," with Matthew of Aiello referred to as "royal vice-chancellor." William reached the age of majority in 1171; his precise date of birth (see note 88) is not known.

Not surprisingly, Margaret and William are both mentioned in a charter of March 1168 (first indiction) issued by Stephen of Perche, as royal chancellor, conceding the manor of Rahal el Melum Rameth, near Milazzo, to the monastery of Santa Maria delle Scale of Messina, in the care of Antiochia, the abbess.

Most of the letters sent to King William drafted in this era mention his mother. For example, a petition made by the canons of Cefalù in 1169 to entomb Roger II and William I in their cathedral (according to prior royal intent) addresses William II and *clementissima Margarita regina matre,* "most benevolent Margaret the queen mother."

A charter issued during William's majority by the archbishop of Messina in March 1174, relative to the monastery of Maniace founded by Margaret, refers to her in the usual wording as *dominae Margaritae gloriosae reginae matri.*

Nor was this practice anomalous. In a decree of October 1193, the name of Sibylla of Acerra, the queen consort of King Tancred, appears in the decree of her young son, William III, which grants permission for Godfrey Martorana and his wife, Eloise, to establish a nunnery at the church which came to bear Martorana's name. (Tancred's death is usually dated to 20 February 1194 but the date on this charter appears to be correct.)

The bilingual charter of 27 November 1171 (see manuscript H in Sources and note 343), issued toward the end of the minority of William II and therefore the end of Margaret's regency, is presented in the original Latin. The Greek section (the lower portion of the manuscript) is partly damaged where the parchment was folded; lacking a royal seal, the document, which merely confirms rights granted by Roger II and extends these to the monastic refoundation at Maniace, is a contemporary copy (rather than a forgery) of an original charter, and its intent is reiterated by other royal charters of this period. The manuscript is shown in this book. (For the Greek text, see Cusa's *Diplomi Greci ed Arabi* in Sources.)

A fact which lends concordance to Riley's note regarding the royal seal described in the previous appendix is that an identical seal, bearing precisely the same motto, was affixed to the charter of February 1169.

Another observation concerns the status of Walter, Archbishop-Elect of Palermo, referred to (according to the case) as *regis familiarium Gualterii* in the first charter and *regis familiarii Gualterii* in the second one, identifying him literally as a royal *familiare.*

Finally, the listing of the various witnesses at the end of each major charter is useful in establishing the general concordance and accuracy of the chronicles of Falcandus and Romuald, as well as others further afield, such as those of Roger of Howden.

Other royal charters of Margaret's era are mentioned in this book's Sources.

February 1169, of the Second Indiction

+ In the Name of Our eternal Lord and Savior Jesus Christ, Amen. William, benevolent King of Sicily, Duke of Apulia and Prince of Capua, with Lady Margaret his Queen Mother, resplendent in their great and glorious royal generosity, in their ample charity and mercy grant the following:

We respond to the petition of Matthew, high notary and trusted friend, in recognition of his much appreciated service to the late King William [I], of pious memory, by granting him permission to erect on his property, where his house stands, in the Saqaliba district of the city of Palermo, a monastery, free of taxation.

The present, perpetual privilege establishes and confirms his right to dedicate the said monastery to the Virgin Mary, Mother of God, with every human perquisite appertaining to this foundation, that nobody shall ever violate or infringe on the right of Matthew of Aiello, high notary, and his heirs their patronage of the monastery in this place.

We affix our golden seal to the present, perpetual, inviolable privilege, inscribed by Robert, our notary, under the date stated above.

Given at the happy city of Palermo by the hand of the glorious King William in the presence of Walter trusty archbishop-elect of Palermo, Richard [Palmer] venerable bishop-elect of Syracuse, Gentile [Tuscus] bishop of Agrigento, Richard [of Mandra] count of Molise, Caïd Richard the royal master chamberlain, Caïd Martin royal chamberlain, in the year of the Lord 1169 during the month of February of the second indiction, during the third year of the reign of William, by the grace of God King of Sicily, Duke of Apulia and Prince of Capua.

May 1169, of the Second Indiction

+ In the Name of Our eternal Lord and Savior Jesus Christ, Amen. William, benevolent King of Sicily, Duke of Apulia and Prince of Capua, with Lady Margaret his Queen Mother, resplendent in their great and glorious royal generosity, in their ample charity and mercy grant the following:

At the request of God's servant Stephen, a kind and benevolent soul, and in our desiring to bequeath him his wish, we confirm to his jurisdiction, in perpetuity, the Monastery of the Holy Savior at Mount Calanna earlier conceded to him by a privilege of the late John, venerable archbishop of Catania.

We affix our leaden seal to the present, perpetual, inviolable privilege, inscribed by Robert, our notary, under the date stated above.

Given at the happy city of Palermo by the hand of the glorious King William in the presence of Walter trusty archbishop-elect of Palermo, Gentile [Tuscus] bishop of Agrigento, Matthew [of Aiello] our high notary, Richard [of Mandra] count of Molise, Caïd Richard the royal master chamberlain, Caïd Martin royal chamberlain, in the year of the Lord 1169 during the month of May of the second indiction, during the third year of the reign of William, by the grace of God King of Sicily, Duke of Apulia and Prince of Capua.

October 1170, of the Fourth Indiction

+ In the Name of Our eternal Lord and Savior Jesus Christ, Amen. William, benevolent King of Sicily, Duke of

Apulia and Prince of Capua, with Lady Margaret his Queen Mother, resplendent in their great and glorious royal generosity, in their ample charity and mercy grant the following:

To the venerable Stephen, a hermit monk of the monastery of Mount Gibello, in the district of Paternò where that mountain is located, are granted the rights to the Talarico mill. Also granted to Stephen is the manor of Rahat Senec near Lentini. To this decree our notary John attaches a leaden seal.

Given at the happy city of Palermo by the hand of the glorious King William in the presence of Walter trusty archbishop of Palermo, Matthew our vice chancellor, Gentile [Tuscus] our trusty bishop of Agrigento, in the year of the Lord 1170 during the month of October of the fourth indiction, during the fifth year of the reign of William, by the grace of God King of Sicily, Duke of Apulia and Prince of Capua. Amen.

March 1171, of the Fourth Indiction

+ In the Name of Our eternal Lord and Savior Jesus Christ, Amen. William, benevolent King of Sicily, Duke of Apulia and Prince of Capua, with Lady Margaret his Queen Mother, resplendent in their great and glorious royal generosity, in their ample charity and mercy grant the following:

To the trusty Gentile, bishop of Agrigento, is confirmed the Trululim mill, of which the prelate had been defrauded. To this decree our notary Zacharias attaches a leaden seal.

Given at the happy city of Palermo by the hand of the glorious King William in the presence of Walter trusty archbishop of Palermo and Matthew our vice chancellor, in the year of the Lord 1171 during the month of March of the fourth indiction, during the fifth year of the reign of William, by the grace of God King of Sicily, Duke of Apulia and Prince of Capua. Amen.

November 1171, of the Fifth Indiction

+ Margarita, dei gratia regina domini regis. Veniet at nos abbas sancti philippi de sancto marco quemdam de fratribus ecclesie at nos panormum transmisit cum sigillo quod ipsa ecclesia habet statum a comite rogerio qui eam condidit continens homines eiusdem ecclesie liberos esse ab omni in angaria atque servicio. Significavit autem nobis quod baiuli sancti marcii et maniachii et eorum comunitas hominibus et casalibus eius molestiis inferunt. Recipientes autem sigillum vidimus confirmatum a glorioso rege rogerio beate memorie, quapropter concessimus et confirmavimus quicquid in ipso continebatur. Precepimus igitur firmiter tibi ut baiulis maniachii et sancti marci et comuni populo precipias ut deinceps nec hominibus nec casalibus ecclesie predicte ullam inferant molestiam, et ab angaria et a lignaminibus mascali et ab muraliis et ab omni adiutorio ipsos quietos dimittant nec de forfaturis nec de decima ovium se intromittant, ut amodo super hoc nullam proclamationem audiamus, et postquam legeris cartulam des eam abbati prefate ecclesie sancti philippi pro futeris bailis. Datum panormi XXVII die mensis novembris indictionis quinte.

In this charter issued in March 1168 (the date was later altered) in William's name, Margaret's name is also indicated as she was regent.

NOTES

"The cult of the footnote, involving, at its apogee, a page crammed with encyclopaedic detail in small type to a solitary line of text, is no doubt a proof of diligence, but it may also be a tedious form of exhibitionism."

— Sir Harold Acton

Here the author wishes to perpetuate the moribund cult of the endnote.

1. Fazello, Thomas, op. cit. (in Sources), page 463. Here in Italy, where women were granted the right to vote only in 1946 (with the defeated nation's provisional government acting on the orders of the Allied occupiers), it is unsurprising that few detailed biographies were published about historical women until recently. All but ignored were the women who governed Sicily during the twelfth century, namely Adelaide del Vasto (consort of Roger I), Margaret of Navarre, and Constance Hauteville (daughter of Roger II). The dearth of Italian biographies of these women and their male contemporaries (Roger II, William II, et al.) was due chiefly to the unificationist propaganda dominant in the Kingdom of Italy, which strove to focus on national figures rather than "regional" ones such as the medieval rulers of Sicily. (See Alio, op.cit.) In Britain, by comparison, a plethora of works are dedicated to Eleanor of Aquitaine.

2. Formally King of *Pamplona*. His son was to become known, decades later, as *King of Navarre*. Navarre, like Sicily, was initially a county.

3. Margaret's precise date of birth is unknown. The year was ascertained based on such factors as her father's movements and the birthdate of her sister. Additionally, two factors argue for early 1135. Firstly, near-contemporary sources concur that Blanca, Margaret's slightly older sister, was born after 1133. Secondly, sources generally concur that García Ramírez and his wife were wed around 1130. (Through a typographical error in a previous book, the author reported Margaret's year of birth as 1138 when 1133 was intended; at all events, subsequent research in Spain confirmed that 1135 is correct.) William I, who Margaret married, was born around 1121.

4. See Chaytor, op.cit., page 285, for a chronological table listing the various counts of Aragon, Barcelona and Sobrarbe. The author agrees with Chaytor's observation that, "The chronology and order of counts and kings earlier than 950 is extremely uncertain."

5. Consistent with standard Spanish usage, these surnames are simple patronyms, rather than toponyms, so *García Ximenez* literally means "García, son of Ximeno," and *Sancho Garces* literally means "Sancho, son of García." This creates obvious genealogical confusion beyond the identification of just one patrilineal generation. In this book's first genealogical chart, as per general practice, the ordinals are based on given names (forenames), not patronyms. A similar convention gives us the same format for feminine names, according to which the subject of this book would be called *Margarita Garcés*.

6. This book's first genealogical table shows the relationships of the Jiménez rulers of Navarre, Aragon and Castile, and the first map indicates the regions mentioned in this chapter.

7. The Basque language, Euskara, is not Romance, nor perhaps even truly Indo-European. It is believed that the Basques as a people represent a quasi-isolated "pocket" of the civilization that existed long before the Phoenicians landed on the Iberian coasts. Their roots were, in effect, a vestige of the Neolithic era. In recent years, the identification of specific genetic haplogroups and sub-clades among the Basques has supported this theory. However, by the twelfth century the society of the Basques, with its churches and mosques, was generally similar to the cultures around it, in what are now Spain and France.

8. Alas, there is no extant, contemporary record of an *Alberta* among the daughters of William the Conqueror. That hers was a very unusual name in northern Spain during the eleventh century lends credibility to the thesis that she was raised abroad, possibly in Normandy, but there is nothing that attests to William being her father.

9. For *El Cantar de Mio Cid,* see Menéndez Pidal, op.cit. A good modern biography of the Cid is Fletcher, op. cit. Over time, the Cid became the national hero of Spain, his name standing out from the morass of Spanish kings and knights of his century; his exploits were gilded to become something like a folk legend.

10. The knightly dubbing ceremony itself was still quite simple, devoid of the formality introduced later. Many esquires were elevated to knighthood by barons, enfeoffed knights and other feudal lords rather than kings. During this period the status of enfeoffed knighthood in northern Spain was not significantly different from the institution as it existed in France, Italy and England. In Spain, the manorial (feudal) system flourished in territories held by Christians. Nothing precisely identical to this knightly tradition existed among the Muslim population. However, the *furusiyya* code of the Moorish horsemen was vaguely similar to chivalry, and on a few occasions the Cid himself enjoyed the support of brave Muslim horsemen who were knights in everything but name.

11. The expression "blue blood" is thought to have originated in northern Spain (although we know not when), where, as stated earlier, *sangre azul* described the bluish veins visible beneath the skin of those having fair complexions, and perhaps claiming roots in the Visigothic baronage, in contrast to the comparatively swarthy complexions of most of the Moors. The phrase *sangre azul* may well be apocryphal, but the racist concept behind it is not.

NOTES

12. Much information about the life of Alfonso I is drawn from *Chronica Adefonsi Imperatoris* (see the Sources).

13. Our information about Rotrou III "the Great" of Perche comes from various sources, perhaps most reliably the *Historia Ecclesiastica* of Orderic Vitalis. The edition consulted was *The Ecclesiastical History of England and Normandy*, volumes 3 and 4, translated by Thomas Forester (see the Sources). See also the *Chanson d'Antioche* and Thompson, Kathleen, *Power and Border Leadership*, in the Sources.

14. Several chronicles and *chansons* recount the colorful adventures of Bohemond of Antioch. The most famous is Anna Comnena's highly-detailed *Alexiad*, generally regarded as the first European history written by a woman; another is the *Chanson d'Antioche*. (See editions of both in the Sources.)

15. The text of the surviving copy of the marriage contract of 1121 may not be identical to that of the original. See manuscript N in the Sources. In modern usage, the term *dowry* usually refers to property given in the bride's name by her natal family (typically her father but in this case her uncle) to the man to whom the woman is betrothed, whereas *dower* denotes property given the bride by her husband at the time of marriage. The marriage contract was a form of promise, or troth, hence *betrothal*.

16. We find Rotrou of Perche witnessing royal charters of Alfonso I right up until the monarch's death in 1134. However, it is sometimes unclear whether he was a royal lieutenant (Lord *in* Tudela) or a feudal vassal (Lord *of* Tudela). See, for example, the charter of October 1133, document number 270, in *Colección Diplomática de Alfonso I de Aragón y Pamplona* (listed in the Sources). A good analysis of Rotrou's movements during this period is set forth in Nelson, Lynn, op. cit. In 1166, Queen Margaret of Sicily, the daughter of García Ramírez and Margaret of Aigle, referred to her mother's dowry (Tudela) being bequeathed by Rotrou of Perche (see note 179).

17. The Siege of Astorga in 1112. See also note 24.

18. For a few observations, see Thompson, Kathleen, "The Lords of Laigle," in the Sources.

19. Bolea and Huesca were in Aragon.

20. Sancho's birth is usually reported as 21 April 1132. He was probably born at La Guardia.

21. García Ramírez was probably at Monzón when Blanca was born at La Guardia.

22. It seems most likely that Alfonso was indeed wounded but died from a related complication such as an infection. He was almost sixty years old.

23. Here the chief chronicle source is the *Chronica Adefonsi Imperatoris*.

24. For the chief surviving reference to this unorthodox royal testament mentioning all three orders, see the decree of October 1131 in Gran Cartulario de la Catedral de Pamplona; *El Libro Redondo,* folios 59-60. For a transcription see *Colección Diplomática de la Catedral de Pamplona* (in Sources), page 167-169.

25. Although he was probably Aragonese by birth (he may have been from Jaca near Huesca), Sancho de Rosas (or Larrosa), the Bishop of Pamplona who crowned García Ramírez the following year, supported Navarrese sovereignty. Angered by opportunistic Ramiro's ready abandonment of holy orders, Bishop Sancho was willing to fund García Ramírez's military campaign against him. Sancho had been bishop since 1122, and the independence of Navarre, like the cathedral consecrated in 1127, could have only enhanced his prestige. In effect, Sancho became the uncontested, if unofficial, "primate" of Navarre; by way of comparison, Tudela's cathedral was erected on the site of that city's great mosque in 1168, leading to the foundation of a diocese. See Fernandez Perez, op.cit., pages 205-225; also Huesca, op.cit.

26. Urraca, aptly nicknamed "the Reckless," had separated from Alfonso I of Aragon in 1110. Their marriage was annulled in 1112 and Alfonso never remarried. Urraca then wed Raymond of Burgundy, by whom she bore a son, Alfonso VII of Castile (and León). It was chiefly on the tenuous basis of his mother having been the first wife of Alfonso I of Aragon that Alfonso VII of Castile claimed the Aragonese crown. Alfonso VII was born in 1105, when his mother was still married to the King of Aragon; the subsequent annulment made Urraca's affair with Raymond moot and her son (born outside wedlock) was legitimized.

27. Agnes, daughter of the crusader William IX, Duke of Aquitaine, was the widow of Aimery V of Thouars, by whom she had three sons. Although the betrothal was negotiated without delay, Agnes' marriage to Ramiro was not actually celebrated (in Jaca Cathedral) until November 1135. Her proven ability to produce an heir was obviously important to the Aragonese, and indeed she gave birth to a daughter, Petronilla, in the summer of 1136. Interestingly, Ramiro's marriage to Agnes was one of the events that prompted the Second Lateran Council (in 1139) to make the marriages of priests canonically null and void; until that time such unions were legitimate but not sanctioned (legal).

28. See note 3 for the calculation of Margaret's birth date.

29. Pamplona's Romanesque cathedral, like many in western Europe, was later rebuilt in the Gothic style, although the Romanesque façade survived until 1783, when it was replaced by an unsightly Neoclassical one. See also note 25.

30. Like the cathedral, the castle has been much altered over time. Sancho, Margaret's brother, built a fortified palace on the site during the second half of the twelfth century. Little of it remains except the crypt (see the photograph) and a few walls. It now houses an archive. A much larger castle, of which no superstructure remains, was erected early in the fourteenth century outside the old town in what is now Plaza del Castillo.

NOTES

31. Conserved in Gran Cartulario de la Catedral de Pamplona; *El Libro Redondo*, folio 61 recto. For a transcription see *Colección Diplomática de la Catedral de Pamplona* (in Sources), page 173.

32. A document of King Alfonso I of Aragon dated July 1133 and witnessed by Rotrou still identified Tudela with Margaret's uncle. See *Colección Diplomática de Alfonso I de Aragón y Pamplona* (in Sources), document number 265.

33. Conserved in Gran Cartulario de la Catedral de Pamplona; *El Libro Redondo*, folios 72-73. For a transcription see *Colección Diplomática de la Catedral de Pamplona* (in Sources), pages 191-192.

34. In the original, *quem ut eorum plerique qui cum ipso venerant asserebant,* "as was asserted by a number of those who arrived with him."

35. *Hunc ergo regina cum antea Rodericus dicereturm idque siculi nomen abhorrentes velut ignotum et barbarum irriderent, Henricum, appellari praecepit.* Falcandus must have known of the Cid even if many Sicilians did not; he may not have known that *Roderic* was the name of the first Visigothic King of Hispania in 710.

36. As we shall see, Rodrigo eventually sought his fortunes beyond the shores of his native Spain, although there is no evidence of his elder half-brother, Sancho, exiling him. It is remarkable that García Ramírez seems not to have sought to arrange a dynastic marriage for Rodrigo as he did for Sancho, Blanca and Margaret, nor did he grant him any important position or wealthy lands in Navarre.

37. Margaret's death at around thirty-two years of age is thought to have resulted from natural causes. That would not be extremely unusual, but neither would poisoning. If she was as promiscuous as some seemed to believe, and unlikely to change her ways, her death might prove expedient.

38. The *Camino de Santiago,* the Way of Saint James, which is still walked (or hiked) today, was a pilgrim route to Santiago de Campostela in Galicia. Pamplona was a stop along the route for those coming from France.

39. Some historians have characterized Alfonso VII of Castile and León as the "overlord" of García Ramírez, as if the latter were merely a vassal. That may be an oversimplification. Clearly, however, Alfonso was the more powerful "senior partner" in the alliance. Without Alfonso's support, García Ramírez could not ensure the sovereignty of Navarre, which would be vulnerable to a military attack from the combined forces of Aragon and Catalonia (the County of Barcelona) to the east.

40. Urraca survived García Ramírez to return to her homeland, where she was regent of Asturias from 1153 until 1165, hence she is known to historians as "Urraca the Asturian."

41. In 1157, Sancho wed Urraca's half-sister Sancha, a legitimate daughter of Alfonso VII of Castile. Here the difference in age was not very great, as Sancha of

Castile was only about six years younger than Sancho. Blanca was destined to marry Sancho III of Castile, a son of Alfonso VII.

42. Conserved in Gran Cartulario de la Catedral de Pamplona; *El Libro Redondo*, folio 70-71 recto. For a transcription see *Colección Diplomática de la Catedral de Pamplona* (in Sources), page 222.

43. As will be seen, this betrothal was not finalized.

44. Odo, who in his brother's absence sometimes served as the *de facto* regent of England, had stopped in Sicily on his way to the First Crusade, an expedition which he had vigorously promoted.

45. Rotrou III of Perche died from an arrow wound he suffered at the Siege of Rouen in 1144. His son, Stephen, was about the same age as Blanca and Margaret, if not slightly younger.

46. The other legitimate sons of King Roger II to reach the age of majority who predeceased William were Tancred in 1138, Alfonso (Anfuso) in 1144, and Roger in May 1148 (not 1149 as sometimes reported).

47. See genealogical table number 1.

48. See Appendix 9.

49. Referring to the plight of Roger I when besieged at Troina during an unusually cold winter, the chronicler Godfrey Malaterra states that, *Graeci vero et Sarraceni, quibus omnis patria favens pro libito patebat, plurima replebantur abundantia.* "Instead, the Greeks and Saracens received provisions from the entire region and were supplied abundantly."

50. For a general history of the Jews of medieval Sicily, see Simonsohn, Shlomo, op.cit.

51. See Agius, Dionisius, op.cit.

52. For one of the more objective, unbiased histories of this development, which Catholics and Orthodox debate to this day, see Runciman, Steven, *The Eastern Schism* (listed in Sources).

53. For the linguistic implications, see Metcalfe, Alexander, op.cit.

54. Doxopatrios was a distinguished theologian, onetime deacon of Saint Sophia in Constantinople. Composed in Greek at King Roger's court by 1143, his treatise is titled *Orders and Ranks of the Patriarchal Thrones*.

55. This information was provided by the British Library, which kindly permitted the author to view the psalter.

NOTES

56. Jensen, Frede, op.cit., and Mallette, Karla, op.cit.

57. For a translation and the original text, see Mendola, Louis, *Sicily's Rebellion against King Charles* (listed in Sources).

58. The *Dialogue* of Ciullo of Alcamo, the lengthiest poem in Middle Sicilian to survive from the thirteenth century, is reproduced and translated in Mendola, op. cit. supra.

59. The *Kitab al-Tabikh,* literally "Book of Dishes," was written in 1226 by Muhammad al Baghdadi. The only known manuscript is conserved in Istanbul. For a modern English translation, see Perry, Charles, op.cit.

60. For a good description of the *diwan,* see Johns, Jeremy, *Arabic Administration in Norman Sicily* (listed in Sources).

61. The rare tarì was gold, the larger ducat was silver, and the follaris, or follis, was copper. The karruba was a copper coin smaller than the follaris. The gold dinar sometimes seen in Sicily was larger than a tarì. (The design of a coin, particularly its reverse, might vary from one mint to another; coins were struck at Palermo, Messina, Bari, Salerno, Capua and Amalfi.) Among the common folk, many day-to-day transactions were concluded through barter.

62. For more about the Arab archers of the Kingdom of Sicily, see Mendola, Louis, *Frederick, Conrad and Manfred of Hohenstaufen, Kings of Sicily 1210-1258: The Chronicle of Nicholas of Jamsilla* (2016).

63. Segments of several *kanats* survive, not only in the former Genoard but beneath the city of Palermo, where one supplied the mikveh beneath what is now a Jesuit cloister (see the map in this volume) with water from the Kemonia River, which had been diverted underground.

64. The Assizes were based on the Code of Justinian. See Appendix 7 for the original texts and a succinct introduction. For a legal analysis see Pennington, Kenneth, op.cit.

65. This statute was reiterated by Frederick II, King Roger's grandson, with the Constitutions of Melfi in 1231. By the end of the Middle Ages, it had fallen into disuse, and only rarely was anybody in Sicily charged with rape after 1500. In dilatory legislation formulated in 1930, the united Italy defined rape as a crime, but only as "an offense against public decency" akin to pornography, which rarely resulted in prison sentences. Finally, in 1996 (sic), Italy made rape a felony crime as a form of violent assault. It remains a very underreported crime, and the statute itself is not very effective; see Van Cleave, Rachel, op.cit.

66. The issuance of the ducat was mentioned by the chronicler Falco of Benevento. See Appendix 7.

67. When Margaret arrived, most of Sicily's Muslims were Shiites, but the Maliki School of jurisprudence was rooted in Sunni legal principles brought to the island in the ninth century by the conquering Aghlabids, who were Sunnis. Some principles believed to emanate from the Maliki School are the right not to testify to incriminate oneself, proscription of the use of hearsay as evidence in trials, the accused's right to trial by jury, the weight of a contract as right to possession or transfer of property (rather than actual physical possession as sole proof of title), and the importance of judges' decisions in establishing legal precedent. Among the English institutions thought to have been influenced by Islamic law are the Inns of Court and perpetual endowment. As early as 1955, Henry Cattan noted the striking similarity between the perpetual endowment of a trust and the Muslim principle of *waqf*. In contract law we find such similarities as *force majeure* and recission. Another example is that a contract (as for the sale of goods) becomes effective immediately upon acceptance of an offer. This is expressed in Ranulf of Glanville's definition of a valid contract based on agreement and consideration. Some of the earliest efforts in this direction can be seen in the Assize of Clarendon decreed by Henry II in 1166. For more about this, see Makdisi, John, op.cit.

68. The view traces the street now called *Corso Calatafimi*, which follows the route of the path that once traversed the Genoard. Now it is difficult to imagine how this appeared without the unsightly modern buildings.

69. This is the so-called *Sala di Ruggero*, which can still be visited today. Although some of its mosaics already existed in Roger's reign, most are thought to have been completed after 1160.

70. The newer chapel was consecrated in 1140 and completed in 1143. Made of the timber of the Nebrodian fir of Sicily's Nebrodian and Madonian mountains, the wooden ceiling was constructed and painted independently of the chapel and then lowered into position. It seems that most of the mosaics on the walls of the nave were added later, probably during the first years of William's reign, and they would inspire the mosaics of Monreale.

71. Falcandus wrote of William that, compared to the esteem in which Roger held his other sons, "only reluctantly did the father consider him worthy of being a prince," *quem vix pater eodem dignum principatu censuerat*.

72. William's precise date of birth is unknown. The estimate of 1120/1121 is based on the chronicle of Romuald of Salerno (see Appendix 8) and other factors (see note 88).

73. Roger II fathered several sons outside marriage. Prominent among them was Simon, who he made Prince of Taranto in 1144. It would develop that William did not like his illegitimate half-brother, and the antipathy was abundantly reciprocated.

74. Strictly speaking, both Beatrice and Margaret were queen consorts. There is no juridical term for Margaret's position (upon the marriage of Roger and Beatrice)

that is generally accepted by medievalists, but following Roger's death his widow was, arguably, "queen dowager."

75. Estimates of Palermo's population during the Norman era vary widely. There was no formal census, but such statistics as the number of churches and mosques suggest something more than a hundred thousand, and possibly twice that. It was probably the largest city in what is now Italy, and one of the largest in Europe, but smaller than Baghdad.

76. The loyalty of these men to King Roger was beyond cavil. As we shall see, however, they were somewhat less enthusiastic about his son.

77. It is believed that one of Roger's daughters was married to Robert of Loritello, a Hauteville cousin, who we shall soon meet. Another, Adelaide, wed Margaret's half-brother.

78. A miscarriage would not have been recorded unless it resulted in the mother's death. Margaret gave birth to four sons between 1152 and 1158. Statistically, there is an eighty-seven percent probability that a family of four children will be "mixed-gender," consisting of both sons and daughters.

79. Roger seems to have been ill, or at least weakened, for a month or two prior to his death. His ill-health may have been brought on by exhaustion (according to Falcandus), but it ended in a terrible fever (Romuald). A stroke or heart attack cannot be ruled out.

80. The canons of Cefalù reiterated the request for sepulture there in a letter to Margaret and her son in 1169. See Appendix 10.

81. From the very beginning of his chronicle, Falcandus is especially critical of William's character. Romuald is less biased but for many events less detailed.

82. It is presumed that Beatrice still lived at court, at least until her daughter was a few years old.

83. Elected on 4 December 1154 as Pope Adrian IV, Nicholas Breakspear was the only Englishman to occupy the See of Saint Peter. Ambitious Frederick I Hohenstaufen, who later historians called "Barbarossa" for his red beard, was crowned Holy Roman Emperor in Rome by Pope Adrian in June 1155; he had already been King of the Germans (King of the Romans) for three years.

84. It will be remembered that Maio had been chancellor during the very last years of the reign of Roger II. The title *amiratus amiratorum,* the Arabic *amir al umara* (emir of emirs), may be the origin of the modern *admiral,* but that was not its connotation at the court of William I. The chancellor answered to the *amiratus.*

85. Robert's mother, Judith, was King Roger's sister. Robert of Bassonville of Loritello had held the County of Conversano until this was confiscated by Roger.

Loritello, which William gave him, is now Rotello, in the Molise region. See the excerpt from Romuald in Appendix 8.

86. For the size of Robert's army we look to Falcandus. The estimate seems accurate.

87. Falcandus claimed that King Roger had declared in a will that Robert should take William's place if the king's son proved incompetent. However, there is no evidence to support this. Such a will does not survive; as we have seen, Roger himself crowned William *rex filius*.

88. An approximate dating of William's birth (to late in 1154 or early 1155) would be based on the time during 1171 when his mother's name ceases to appear alongside his in royal charters. An earlier date (the middle of 1153) would be based on his being twelve years old at his father's death (as reported by Romuald) and thirty-six (as reported on the epitaph of his tomb) when he died late in 1189. The age of majority for a king to succeed a regency if his successor (his father) was deceased was usually the seventeenth birthday, but this varied.

89. Neither William nor Adrian could have known that in later times the Treaty of Benevento would come to be viewed by historians as something of a turning point in Papal policy because it represented an approach as politically pragmatic as it was theological. Some jurists have posited that in 1156 the Papacy began to manage its affairs as a true state rather than a theocracy.

90. Today the title *Primate of Sicily* is largely symbolic. However, it should be noted that the only other primate in Italy is the Pope. Other traditional titles of this kind held by Italian archbishops are the *Patriarch of Venice* and *Archimandrite of Messina*, both of Byzantine origin. The Archbishop of Palermo is usually made a cardinal. For comparison, the Archbishop of Canterbury is the *Primate of All England* (see note 326).

91. Romuald of Salerno describes this at some length. It need not concern us here except insofar as Barbarossa did not completely abandon his designs on southern Italy.

92. Whether Idrisi was born in Ceuta (in Morocco) is unclear, though his family had mercantile ties to Sicily. It has been suggested that, following his *Book of Roger*, he composed an important geographical work for William I but, if so, it does not survive. He died in Ceuta in 1165.

93. It was quite similar to other feudal rolls of its era. The name *Catalogus Baronum* was attributed to the registry in later times. The typical entry gives the name of a baron (or enfeoffed knight), the name of his manor and the number of knights he was required to provide the king.

94. This was not the Church of Mary Magdalene standing today within what is now a military complex, but a chapel (erected next to the cathedral in 1130) thought

NOTES

to have been destroyed in 1187 to enlarge the cathedral. The royal tombs were moved to the new Mary Magdalene and then to Monreale.

95. King Roger's occupation of Mahdia in the summer of 1148 effectively displaced the Zirid dynasty. The Almohads took the city early in 1160; their caliphate supplanted other rulers in the region, including the Almoravids in Morocco and Spain. To undertake his recent naval campaigns in Apulia and Greece, William (perhaps acting on Maio's advice) had subtracted galleys from ports like Mahdia, thus diminishing Sicilian sea power along the African coast and thereby facilitating Almohad power there. One of Roger's titles was *Rex Africae,* King of Africa.

96. Maio of Bari encouraged the latinization of Sicily's Christians. Soon after George of Antioch built the Martorana for Palermo's Orthodox, Maio erected San Cataldo next to it for the Catholics.

97. Clementia of Catanzaro; despite holding lands in Calabria she spent much time in Palermo.

98. Falcandus quotes a speech which is partly a diatribe against Maio of Bari and partly a plea for Matthew Bonello to marry Clementia (see note 97) and join the rebels in overthrowing Maio.

99. Romuald of Salerno mentions Bohemond of Monopoli, Roger of Acerenza, Philip of Sangro and Roger of Tricarico. Falcandus mentions many more malcontents, including several who had participated in the baronial revolts in Apulia and Campania suppressed by William a few years earlier.

100. These claims come to us from the poison pen of Hugh Falcandus. Matthew of Aiello was a trusted minister who enjoyed a successful career for decades to come.

101. In the original: *Iamque totam fere Siciliam varii super hoc dissonique rumores impleverant, passimque vulgatum erat, admiratum diademata quedam aliaque regis insignia, quae sibi praepararat, multis familiaribus suis ostendisse, nec deerant qui reginam haec ei de palatio dicerent transmisisse. Nam et eius consensu totum hoc fieri eamque Maioni putabant inhonesti contractu foederis obligatam. Plerisque falso videbatur id dici.*

102. Margaret was not the only queen maligned in this way; some of her contemporaries in the reginal sisterhood suffered far worse, videlicet Eleanor of Aquitaine in the works of chroniclers such as Gerald of Wales. See also notes 204 and 205.

103. Crowns were indeed discovered among Maio's possessions following his death, and Falcandus believed this convinced the king of his guilt, but it was later revealed that, in fact, the crowns were gifts being preserved for presentation to William the following year. Maio had commissioned their design and manufacture.

104. Defamatory innuendo about Margaret is absent from the chronicle of Romuald of Salerno.

105. Saint Martin's Day was an important feast in the Middle Ages. In Sicily, it meant that the olives had been harvested and the winter wheat planted. It no longer marks a transition of seasons; Sicily's average mean temperature was slightly lower in the twelfth century than it is now.

106. Falcandus believed (or at least stated) that Hugh was complicit in the plot to kill Maio. This seems unlikely, though the archbishop did not greatly lament Maio's untimely passing.

107. According to Falcandus: *At regina mortem Maionis multo molestius nec adeo patienter audivit, et in Mattheum Bonellum eiusque socios majori quidem impetu indignationis exarsit.*

108. See note 103.

109. Falcandus makes specific reference to Bishop Erveo of Tropea, who actually repaid more gold to the king than he had received from Maio.

110. According to Falcandus: *Itaque reginae ipsius freti consilio, sollicitudinis suae regi causas aperiunt asseruntque non negligendum eius capiti, nisi mature praecautum fuerit, periculum impendere.*

111. Falcandus does not elaborate on the details, but this may have been a loan against some of Bonello's landed estates: *Interim tamen, LX milia tarenorum, tam ab eo quam ab illis qui pro ipso fideiusserant, repeti iubet, quos idem olim, ut patrimonium suum reciperet, curiae spoponderat se daturum. Eorum autem solutionem admiratus, genero parcens, ignorante rege, distulerat.* The debt was grudgingly paid.

112. Adenolf, who was from northern Italy, had served at the palace since 1155.

113. Romuald Guarna of Salerno (the chronicler) became Archbishop of Palermo in 1161 and remained so into the reign of William II.

114. Taranto was much wealthier and far more important than Lecce. The reason Tancred was not deprived of Lecce is because he inherited it not from his father but through his mother, Emma. William seems to have disdained Tancred almost as much as he hated Simon.

115. It is presumed that such a meeting took place in Caccamo Castle, and that is the longstanding historical tradition. Documentation supporting its historicity is lacking.

116. The telling of the events in the following section relies almost entirely on a single account, that of Hugh Falcandus, which seems to be accurate in its essential details.

117. Falcandus and Romuald give very slightly differing (but essentially complementary) accounts of the events in this section. Falcandus' description is the more detailed but the less flattering of King William.

NOTES

118. Sometimes *Henricus Aristippus*, a scholar of Greek who undertook the first Latin translation of the *Phaedo* of Plato and the *Meteorologica* of Aristotle. As an ambassador to Constantinople for two years until 1160, he brought back a copy of Ptolemy's *Almagest* for translation into Latin. William initially trusted him but changed his mind in 1162.

119. Falcandus states that William and Henry were chased down a corridor and caught. In Romuald's account William was confronted by the intruders in a room (which had a window) in the Pisan Tower.

120. From Falcandus: *Nonnulli quoque, per fenestras palatii in plebem quae foris stabat, tarenos habundantissime dispergebant.* The tarì coins were tossed out of a high window of the Pisan Tower, which overlooked a wall (much altered over successive centuries) that faced the city's Halkah district. Compared to the copper follis and silver ducat, the gold tarì was small enough that an adult pelted with a few of these coins would not likely be injured as a result.

121. Although his intent is clear, Falcandus does not refer literally to "concubines" but to "pretty girls." He wrote: *Nec deerant qui puellarum pulchritudinem crederent lucris omnibus praeferendam. Sic homines aetate, moribus genereque diversi, variis nichilominus dissonisque rerum studiis agebantur.*

122. According to Romuald of Salerno: *Sed rex ipse captus est et in carcere positus, regina quoque cum filiis suis in quadam camera honeste est custodita.*

123. From Romuald: *Rex autem huius rei nescius et ignarus et de tam repentino casu attonitus, ad fenestram turris pisane venit, et quosque transevntes cepit ad suum auxilium convocare. Sed cum nullus esset qui succurreret, captum est palatium nemine repugnante, et ex magna parte expoliatum.*

124. The massacre was not entirely arbitrary. The eunuchs, most of whom lived in the palace, had long been viewed as partisan, given to gossip and conniving, and some among their number were known supporters of the late Maio of Bari.

125. From Falcandus: *Eunuchorum vero quotquot inveniri potuerunt nullus evasit. Plures autem eorum in initio rei ad amicorum domos confugerant, quorum plerosque repertos in via, milites occiderunt qui de castello maris exierant, aliique qui iam coeperant per civitatem discurrere.*

126. From Falcandus: *Multi quoque Sarracenorum, qui vel in apothecis suis mercibus vendendis praeerant, vel in duanis fiscales redditus colligebant, vel extra domos suas improvidi vagabantur, ab eisdem sunt militibus interfecti. Postea vero Sarraceni, perturbatione cognita, viribus se quidem ad resistendum impares arbitrati, cum eos praecedenti anno admiratus omnia arma sua curie reddere coegisset, relictis domibus quas plerique eorum in civitate media possidebant, in eam partem quae trans Papiretum est secesserunt, ubi Christianis in eos impetum facientibus, aliquam diu frustra conflictum est. Nam illi ad introitus et angustias viarum nostris tutius resistebant.*

127. Falcandus and Romuald are in agreement that the rebels paraded Roger in the streets of the city.

128. Walter was destined to be consecrated Archbishop of Palermo. For now, he was archdeacon of Cefalù, serving under Boson of Gorron, its bishop, but he spent most of his time at court, eventually becoming dean, or rector, of the Palatine Chapel as well as the royal tutor.

129. However, this was not formalized and the boy was not crowned.

130. According to Romuald, this included (besides himself) Robert of Messina, Richard Palmer of Syracuse and Tustin of Mazzara. It will be remembered that Romuald was Archbishop of Palermo, thus especially influential in the capital.

131. Romuald states that the arrow hit Roger in an eye. That is probably what happened. It is difficult to ascribe much credibility to the theory, advanced by Falcandus (who claims merely to be reporting rumours), that the arrow did not kill Roger but that an angry William brutally kicked the boy out of resentment for his having been proclaimed king by Walter and the people.

132. Roger was entombed with his brother in the Church of Mary Magdalene. This probably was not the surviving church standing within the military complex, but an earlier one (a chapel erected in 1130) later destroyed to enlarge the cathedral. See also note 94.

133. See manuscript T in the Sources.

134. According to Falcandus: *Illi se coniunxerant, praeter Gillebertum Gravinae comitem, qui regis gratiam consanguineae suae reginae precibus impetraverat, et relicta societate comitum, exercitui praeerat in Apulia, Roberti comitis impetum quantum poterat moraturus.*

135. Falcandus tells us that Martin was vindictive toward Christians because his brother had been killed by them during the riots.

136. The phrase "baptized sultan" was coined by modern historians and much favored by Michele Amari.

137. Bonello himself probably died in the prison located in the bowels of the palace.

138. Some of these Punic walls, which include an arched portal, can still be seen.

139. From Falcandus: *Illi vero spe frustrati, ad inferiorem ingressum palatii se transtulerunt, sive ut ad regem indeflexo gressu contenderent, sive ut ibidem in scholis regis filios invenirent, quos eorum preceptor Gualterius, Cephaludensis archidiaconus, in campanarium, primis rei motibus praecognitis, asportarat. Acciderat autem gayto Martino post primum januam in introitu sedenti viros quosdam assistere, quorum unus, irruentibus illis, obvium se dedit, et primos ictus excipiens, eorum impetum retardavit spemque sustulit. Interim enim gaytus Martinus, foribus obseratis,*

intra palatium se recepit. Ita, cum nihil eorum quae speraverant effecissent, subita virorum multitudine circumventi, quae cum Odone magistro stabuli repente confluxerant, ad unum omnes interfecti sunt. Cadavera eorum, proiecta canibus, prohibuit curia sepeliri.

140. There were several classes of justiciar. Those described here may have been "circuit judges," called such because they travelled around the *Regnum* to hear cases.

141. Here the chief source is Falcandus: *Cum ergo regnum ab extrinsecis tumultibus aliquando quievisset, rex autem interim otio quietique vacaret, timens ne quaevis occasio voluptuosum otium impediret, familiares suos premonverat ut nihil ei quod mestitiam aut sollicitudinem posset ingerere nunciarent.*

142. A decade earlier, Idrisi counted only 130 towns, villages and other places of note in Sicily. In fact, there were hundreds of named manors, many held by barons or the church.

143. This may be the *Minenio* mentioned by Falcandus.

144. Blanca's son was King Alfonso VIII of Castile (1155-1214), who in 1174 wed Eleanor, one of the daughters of Henry II of England.

145. For Romuald's description see Appendix 8. Falcandus mentions it only in passing and not by name.

146. According to Falcandus: *Ipse quoque palatium construeret, quod commodius ac diligentius compositum, videretur universis patris operibus praeminere.*

147. Alfonso VIII of Castile succeeded his father, Sancho III, who died in 1158.

148. For Romuald's account see Appendix 8. In the chronicles and in charters, the term *familiare*, from the Latin *familiaris*, refers to the two or three highest ministers who governed the kingdom on the king's behalf. (The distinctive noun *familiare*, rather than *counsellor* or *minister*, shall be used in the chapters to come.) The *familiares* are sometimes referred to as *archons* in charters written in Greek; see manuscript H in the Sources.

149. Romuald and Falcandus both use the same phrase, *totius regni* (the entire kingdom), in defining the scope of her authority. Romuald: *Margaritam reginam uxorem suam totius regni et filiorum suorum tutricem et gubernatricem,* "entrusting Queen Margaret his wife with the governing of the entire realm and the care of his sons." Falcandus: *Reginam autem praecepit totius regni curam et administrationem, quae vulgo balium appellatur,* "to the queen was entrusted the care and administration of the whole kingdom as what is commonly known as a governor," thus explaining that this is what in common parlance was then called a *balius* (a "governor"). In the Medieval Latin of Margaret's time a precise cognate for *regent* was not used, and in Italy the term *viceré* (viceroy) came into use later.

150. Falcandus gives the date of death as 15 May. Romuald states 7 May (see note

152). Historians generally seem to favour the date provided by Falcandus, which is what one reads in most books published in English and French during the last two centuries.

151. Falcandus states that the king's death was kept secret for a few days until arrangements could be made for his son's coronation, and that the late monarch's entombment in the palace was meant to be temporary. This differs slightly from Romuald's account (see note 152).

152. Romuald states that young William was proclaimed king and crowned on 9 May, two days following his father's death (see Appendix 8). This seems credible as Romuald himself performed the coronation in Palermo's cathedral; it does not seem that the boy was already crowned *rex filius*. There is an additional discrepancy between Falcandus and Romuald regarding the young king's age (Falcandus states he was at least thirteen), but Romuald, as his tutor, might be presumed to be better informed on this detail. See also notes 150 and 151.

153. Here reference is made specifically to the years of Margaret's regency (1166-1171). By contrast, Eleanor of Aquitaine, the heiress of a wealthy duchy, was Queen Consort of England (and Duchess of Normandy) as the wife of Henry II from 1154 to 1189, but she never wielded economic or military power comparable to that of the Kingdom of Sicily. Margaret's stepmother, Urraca of Castile, was Regent of Asturias (part of the Kingdom of León) until 1165, but no single Spanish kingdom of the twelfth century could compare to the Kingdom of Sicily in terms of sheer wealth and political influence. The contemporary European queen whose effective power most nearly approximated Margaret's was the Empress Maude, or Matilda, daughter of Henry I of England and consort of the (Salian) Holy Roman Emperor Henry V; by the time she died in 1167, Maude had been Imperial regent in northern Italy (for her first husband), led troops into England (for her second husband Geoffrey of Anjou), and served as regent in Normandy (for her son Henry II of England). In this regard, and though the author does not wish to engage in pedantry, it may be noted that none of the three regions (Normandy, England, northern Italy) Maude governed at one time or another was as wealthy or important as the Kingdom of Sicily during this period. Another queen sometimes included in this elite sorority is Melisende of Jerusalem, who died in 1161.

154. Following the death of his son William II, King William I was accorded the unflattering nickname "the Bad," and it was rooted largely in the harsh criticisms recorded by both Romuald and Falcandus.

155. Much of this is inferred from context and a few comments by the two chroniclers present in Palermo. Until Margaret became regent, it would have been seen as inappropriate to attribute too much political importance to her actions (except insofar as Falcandus criticized them), and at all events a certain degree of sexism was normal during this era.

156. See note 153.

157. For the account of Romuald of Salerno see Appendix 8. The similar description by Hugh Falcandus: *Itaque regina, ut plebem ac proceres sibi filioque gratos efficeret, statuit eorum gratiam copia meritorum elicere, et fidem, si fieri posset, immensis saltem beneficiis extorquere ac primum universa recludi iussit ergastula plurimamque multitudinem virorum, tam in Sicilia quam in adiacentibus insulis, liberavit. Inde redemptionis onus importabile, quod totam Apuliam Terramque Laboris ultima iam desperatione concusserat, omnino censuit amovendum, scripsitque magistris camerariis ut a nemine deinceps quicquam nomine redemptionis exigerent.*

158. In his last days, William I had abolished the redemption tax in Apulia (see "Margaret Named Regent" in Appendix 8). Margaret's policy was distinctive because it abrogated such taxes altogether, throughout the kingdom; in addition to Apulia, Falcandus (see note 157) mentions *Terra di Lavoro*, the region of Naples.

159. According to Falcandus: *Regina vero nihilominus eisdem consentiebat consiliis, nec illius ipsi persecutio displicebat, eo quod adhuc vivente marito suo, cum pro quibusdam negotiis suis aliquotiens electo preces porrigeret, ille ut in prosperis semper elatus, contemptorem induebat animum, superbe nunciis mordaciterque respondens, nunquam eius petitiones efficaciter admictebat.*

160. Richard Palmer was bishop-elect of Syracuse but because he was not yet consecrated he spent little time in that city.

161. This account comes to us from Falcandus.

162. Molise is a region north of Apulia. It reverted to the crown when the man who previously held it died without heirs some years earlier. The territories given to Richard of Mandra made his personal feudal power far greater than Gilbert's.

163. Frederick Barbarossa was indeed planning an invasion, but his chief objective was Rome, which he reached the next year. For now, a few disgruntled barons acting as his surrogates were making raids along the border the Kingdom of Sicily shared with the Papal State to the north.

164. Falcandus does not state explicitly that Margaret was privy to Matthew's manoeuvre (although she probably was), but explains that she exploited the occasion, *Hinc oportune regina, quaesitam occasionem eliciens.*

165. Cardinal John of Naples was a Papal diplomat and not, as his name seems to imply, the Archbishop of Naples. He was the ambassador of Pope Alexander III to the Sicilian court and later played a role in the conflict between Thomas Becket and Henry II of England.

166. Richard Palmer was nominated (but not immediately consecrated) shortly after the death of Syracuse's last bishop and by 1166 the post had been vacant for more than a decade.

167. According to Falcandus: *Assentiente regina idque sibi gratum fore modis omnibus attestante.*

168. In good weather the travel time between Rome and Palermo was around sixteen days.

169. From Falcandus: *Regina mutato consilio respondit: Electi praesentiam curie necessariam esse, nec eum ad praesens posse quopiam proficisci, alias iturum, cum temporis oportunitas pateretur.* This is one of the few instances of anything like a precise quote being attributed to Margaret. See also note 179.

170. The exiled Richard of Aquila had held Fondi, a county midway between Naples and Rome; he was now in the Papal State.

171. Divorce was a personal right in the Kingdom of Sicily, formally codified as recently as the Constitutions of Melfi in 1231. (Only in later times did the Catholic Church "outlaw" divorce altogether, supplanting it with such canonical remedies as annulment.) The dissolution of the marriage described here was more in the nature of an annulment than a divorce because it presumed that the union had never met the canonical requirements for matrimony in the first place. It should be noted that in the twelfth century there was rather little distinction between what we now call *divorce* and *annulment*. (Divorce was again legalized in Italy, quite belatedly, in 1970.)

172. According to Falcandus: *De solvendo quoque matrimonio praecepit curiae familiaribus, ut convocatis episcopis aliisque personis ecclesiasticis, et auditis utriusque partis allegationibus, quod inde dictaret aequitas expedirent.*

173. Therefore, a widower could not lawfully wed his late wife's sister (his sister-in-law) or even her first cousin (his cousin-in-law). Affinity should not be confused with consanguinity, which is kinship by blood (to siblings or cousins).

174. In fact, negotiations for the proposed betrothal continued sporadically for the next few years. For the account of Romuald of Salerno see Appendix 8.

175. See note 35.

176. Not that there were large casinos in Messina, but there were small gaming houses. Most of Henry's money was lost rolling dice or playing "tiles," a game somewhat similar to dominoes.

177. See manuscript A in the Sources. For Walter's status see note 182.

178. Rotrou of Rouen was Queen Margaret's first cousin, one generation removed, being the son of Henry of Beaumont, first Earl of Warwick, and Margaret, daughter of Geoffrey of Perche (sister of Rotrou "the Great" of Perche who we met earlier). See genealogical table 3.

179. From Falcandus, who was almost certainly present, the lengthiest known quote of the words of Margaret of Navarre: *"Ecce, completum video quod plenis semper votis expetii. Nec enim aliter quam fratres proprios diligere quidem et honorare debeo filios comitis*

Perticensis per quem, ut verum fatear, pater meus regnum obtinuit. Nam idem comes patri meo terram amplissimam cum nepte sua, matre mea, dotem dedit, quam in Hispania multis periculis ac diuturnis laboribus expugnatam, Sarracenis abstulerat. Nec ergo mirari debetis si filium eius, matris meae consobrinum, loco mihi fratris habendum censeam, et de remotissimis partibus ad me venientem gratanter excipiam, quem quidem volo jubeoque, ut qui me filiumque meum diligere se fatentur, propensius diligant et honorent, ut eorum gratia erga nos ex hoc ipso fidei dilectionisque quantitatem emetiar."

180. See manuscript A in the Sources.

181. According to Falcandus: *Interea regina voluntatem eius diligenter inquirens, cum intellexisset eum nolle diutius in Sicilia commorari, summa ope niti coepit ut hoc eius propositum immutaret, et gloriam ei divitiasque, quas habiturus erat si remaneret, ostentans simulque transmontanorum inopiam ei frequenter obiciens, socios quoque ipsius propositis ingentibus praemiis hortabatur, ut cum eo se promitterent remansuros, intelligens non posse mentem illius aliter ad id quod postulabat inflecti.*

182. Relying on the date indicated in a forged charter, Chalandon (op.cit.) and others report Stephen of Perche being appointed chancellor in late 1166; the earliest surviving (authentic) charters referring to him as chancellor were issued in 1167. Falcandus does not suggest his appointment before spring 1167. A charter issued in March 1167 (manuscript A in the Sources) was witnessed by a *familiare* (Matthew), the treasurer (Martin) and the royal tutor (Walter), but not by Stephen; Walter's presence is explained by his being rector of the palace chapel which is dealt with in the charter.

183. See Appendix 5.

184. In the Kingdom of Sicily, as in other medieval Norman dominions, there were two forms of property. *Royal* (or "demesnial" or "crown") lands belonged to the king, whilst *feudal* ("manorial") estates were held "in fee" by a baron, knight, bishop or abbot. Here we are using Anglice forms of the Italian terms; certain words occasionally used in England to describe monarchical institutions differ from these, even though the systems in use during the twelfth century were essentially similar. As regards baronial estates, an Italian anomaly was the presence of parallel systems, namely the *Frankish* system (inheritance of an estate by a baron's eldest son) favored by the Normans, versus the *Longobard* system (inheritance by all the sons of a baron) which left estates divided into moieties. A manor such as a barony was administered by a baron or enfeoffed knight, whereas a royal town was governed by a bailiff (or governor); barons and bailiffs both answered to the king. In Sicily, feudal estates usually had at least some serfs, while many royal lands did not.

185. Falcandus uses the phrase *eius successores,* literally "his successors" (heirs generically), who might have been nephews; it was not unusual for a bishop to leave a substantial bequest to his kinsmen. Stephen's generosity thus enfeoffed Richard Palmer, making him a lesser manorial lord. It will be remembered that Richard had come to Italy from England, and therefore held no estates of his own in Sicily. However, the village Richard received, albeit wealthy, was not a walled town (for

which the Latin word *castrum* was used) or a locality protected by a castle but what in Italy is still called a *casale,* from the Latin *casalia.* During this period many smallholdings of Sicily's Arabs and Greeks were being consolidated and absorbed into baronies (and their inhabitants forced into serfdom) while others were acquired by Catholic bishops or abbots; the *casale* granted to Richard Palmer may have been a village amidst such farms.

186. This view is shared by Falcandus and Romuald, but it should be remembered that they were writing their accounts in retrospect.

187. A decade later, Pope Alexander III ordered the prelates who had been living in Palermo for more than six years to report to their bishoprics. By then, the power-hungry clerics had already done much to harm the monarchy.

188. Falcandus implies, but does not state, that the clients were parsimonious.

189. It is interesting to note that in Italy today one must be an attorney to become a notary; this is a holdover from the Middle Ages.

190. The author cannot help commenting that in Italy notary fees are still infamously exorbitant, even subjective, and the bureaucracy is sluggish. Not without reason, Italians sometimes describe our nation's officialdom as "medieval."

191. Many charters issued in Sicily were paper rather than parchment or vellum and thus fragile; in 1231 Frederick II outlawed paper for the most important documents. Not all seals were wax or metal (gold or lead); some were drawn in crimson ink.

192. This is essentially a translation of the account of the incident by Hugh Falcandus. It is interesting that in Italy today there is no fixed limit on what notaries can charge their clients for witnessing documents (see note 190).

193. Here Falcandus prefers the term *stratigotus,* but in some documents the word *balius* is used. These were essentially provincial governors and urban administrators (similar to mayors).

194. According to Falcandus: *Cuius rei fama totum regnum brevi pervadens, plebisque gratiam et favorem ei concilians, tanta nomen eius celebritate diffudit, ut omnes assererent velut consolatorem angelum a Deo missum, qui curiae statu in melius immutato, aurea saecula revexisset.*

195. For some notes on the conversions of Muslims to Catholicism in Sicily during this era, see Metcalfe, Alexander, op. cit.

196. Very little evidence survives to suggest that Stephen of Perche conducted anything like a mass pogrom against the "heresy" of these relapsed converts. It appears that the allegations against them were addressed on a case-by-case basis, which is essentially the kind of approach Pope Alexander suggested for worse crimes allegedly committed by Muslims (see note 198).

NOTES

197. It should be remembered that Muslims and Jews were not the only religious minorities; there were also Greek Orthodox Christians in the *Regnum,* especially in Bari, parts of Calabria and Sicily's Nebrodian region.

198. A letter from Pope Alexander III to Stephen of Perche in late 1167 refers to the matter of punishing Muslims who have raped Christian women and boys, *agendum sit de Sarracenis qui mulieres christianas et pueros rapuerint.* See *Italia Pontificia* (in Sources), volume 10, page 232, document number 31.

199. From Falcandus: *Harum regina precum assiduitate permota, cancellarium primo rogat, deinde renitenti praecipit ut neminis adversus Robertum Calataboianensem accusationes admictat.*

200. To quote Falcandus: *Convocatis ergo curiae familiaribus et episcopis aliisque personis ecclesiasticis, Robertus sub multa frequentia plebis introducitur, omissisque furtis, rapinis, iniuriis civium homicidiis et illata constupratae virgini violentia, periurii, incestus, adulterii quaestio ventilatur.*

201. See Appendix 7, also Pennington, Kenneth, op.cit.

202. Among Sicilian historians, any assembly of barons came to be referred to as a "parliament." This misnomer may be rooted in their ascribing a political meaning to the Middle Sicilian *parlamentu,* literally "conversation." The first Sicilian parliament, leading to the barons' election of Frederick of Aragon as King of Sicily, took place in 1295 and 1296. Aside from prefatorial developments like the *Magna Carta* (in 1215), the inception of an effective parliament in England is usually dated to 1258.

203. In the original: *Reginam, cum hispana sit, francum hunc consanguineum appellare, nimis ei familiariter colloqui et velut rapacibus eum oculis intueri, verendum ne sub nomine propinquitatis amor illicitus occultetur.*

204. By the most widely-accepted definition, *slut shaming* is the defamation or stigmatizing of a woman whose behavior is judged (especially by men) to be promiscuous or sexually provocative; the Middle English *slutte* dates from around 1400. Margaret had already been the target of such slander (see notes 101 and 102).

205. See McCracken, Peggy, op.cit. For an examination of the environment in slightly earlier times, see Stafford, Pauline, op.cit.

206. John of Aiello was consecrated Bishop of Catania on 26 July 1168, having been elected in February. See *Italia Pontificia* (in Sources), volume 10, page 291, document 24; also page 292, document 25.

207. Bellisina may be *Beauce* or *Bellême,* both in France.

208. Aside from feudal toponyms, men were sometimes given nicknames for their towns of origin. Salerno was known for its medical school and, as Falcandus informs us, Salernus the physician was a judge in that city.

209. It will be remembered that Romuald was the best-known physician at court.

210. Among whom were Bohemond of Manopello (who Falcandus tells us was intelligent and eloquent), William of Gesualdo and Richard of Balbano.

211. In the words of Falcandus: *Nunc reliquum quidem esse, ut aut inhonestis reginae votis deservire credatur ipsiusque cancellarii libidini seu potius incestui consentire, aut illicitam eorum familiaritatem se nescire fateatur.* At one point Henry of Montescaglioso, who was no great judge of character, suspected (or was led to believe) that Richard of Molise, rather than Stephen of Perche, was having an affair with Margaret.

212. This passage implies that Falcandus himself did not believe the rumour, which (unfortunately) has made its way into what little has ever been written about Margaret's character: *Qui, cum primum mente dubia vacillaret, dehinc ab ipsis rei principibus qui confinxerant ea cumulatius eadem audiens, plenam hiis quae sibi dicta fuerant fidem adhibuit, relictoque cancellario, consiliis eorum adhesit, quod inde suaderent se facturum pollicitus.*

213. The knights were Christians; most of the archers were Muslims. See also note 62.

214. Falcandus presents the conspiracy of Caïd Richard as a fact.

215. What little was left of this edifice in modern times was completely destroyed by the earthquake of 1908.

216. Neither Falcandus nor Romuald give a specific date for the supposed consecration. For Papal approval, see the letters from Pope Alexander III in *Italia Pontificia* (in Sources), volume 10, page 232, documents number 29 and 30. A charter Stephen witnessed at Messina in March 1168 refers to him simply as "bishop-elect" of Palermo, *datum Messane per manus Stephani Panormitane ecclesie electi et Regii Cancellarii,* for which see *I Documenti Inediti dell'Epoca Normanna in Sicilia* by Garufi (in the Sources), pages 101-102, document 44.

217. For a transcription see White, op.cit., pages 266-267, document 26. Note that the date (and the year of young William's reign) is very clear from the text: *Anno dominice incarnationis millesimo centesimo sexagesimo septimo, mense novembris, indictionis prime, regni vero domini Guillelmi dei gratia gloriosissimi et magnificentissimi Regis Siciliae, Ducatus Apuliae, et Principatus Capuae, anno secundo feliciter.*

218. Also known as Robert of Lauro, sometime high justiciar of northern Apulia. He came to Messina with his son, Roger of Tricarico.

219. See manuscript Q in the Sources.

220. See manuscript T in the Sources. However, it is unclear whether the Messinians petitioning Margaret were referring to these same taxes.

221. This was the "mayor" of Messina. Falcandus prefers the term *stratigotus,* rather

than *balius*, in referring to the local administrator of a demesnial territory. See notes 184 and 193.

222. Not to be confused with the "three estates" of the Middle Ages, namely the nobility, the clergy and the peasantry.

223. If only for the fact of high literacy among the Muslims and Jews, the literacy rate of Sicily's population during the twelfth century was higher than that of the population of the newly-united Italy in 1860 (when it is estimated that fewer than two in ten adults were functionally literate).

224. Most of the women known to have studied at Salerno's medical school lived after the twelfth century; an exception was Sichelgaita, the second wife of Robert "Guiscard" of Hauteville, uncle of King Roger II.

225. Here it should be remembered that in the twelfth century the death penalty was the norm in Europe.

226. It is said that Rosalie, the patron saint of Palermo, was a Norman princess or noblewoman who lived in Margaret's time and perhaps established such a nunnery. The supposed historicity of this claim lacks support in contemporary records.

227. See Appendix 1.

228. Falcandus uses the phrase *Graecos et Longobardos,* literally "Greeks and Lombards" but actually the native Messinians, many of whom spoke Greek, and the (non-Norman) barons from the Italian mainland who had settled in eastern Sicily.

229. From Falcandus: *Quod ubi regina cognovit, anxia cepit distrahi sollicitudine multaeque fluctuationis aestibus agitari. Durius enim in fratrem decernere quippiam tantamque praesumptionem animadversione digna punire crudele quidem tyrampnidique proximum videbatur, sed et si fratri parceret, intelligebat cancellario non dubium capitis periculum imminere, neque posse proditores ab eo quod coeperant absterreri; simulque considerabat indignum eum esse, cui fraternus exhiberetur affectus, qui sororis posthabita reverentia, qui tot eius beneficiorum immemor id solum agere decrevisset quod ad eius dedecus et infamiam non ambigeret retorquendum, multisque rebellandi praebens materiam, regni pacem et quietem niteretur modis omnibus impedire. Huic ergo deliberationi justa succedens indignatio, fraternam ab eius animo clementiam exturbavit, placuitque, congregata curia, comitem sollemni judicio conveniri, convictumque vel confessum interim in aliqua munitionum servari, donec eius indicio ceteri possent proditores agnosci.*

230. Most of these knights were from Navarre and the other kingdoms of northeastern Spain.

231. Falcandus refers to these subjects as "Greeks," because (like the Messinians) the majority of Calabrians spoke this language and frequented churches of the Greek Orthodox rite.

232. This was Bartholomew of Lusci, whose lands near Lecce were placed in the

care of Giles, the abbot of Venosa (who probably came from Navarre).

233. Roger Sorello, whose family held estates around Naples.

234. It may be remembered that Bohemond of Manopello (and Tarsia) had accompanied Henry to Palermo and befriended Stephen of Perche. He was the son of another Bohemond (who died after 1156) briefly imprisoned by King William I for allegedly usurping royal lands. See also note 210.

235. The account by Falcandus is, in itself, insufficient as an analysis of the case against Richard of Molise. The accusations seem to reflect little more than the longstanding grievances against him.

236. Little is known of the duel, or if it even took place, but Walter of Moac (Modica) was master constable by 1171 and he was a witness to the dower charter of Joanna of England in 1177 (see Appendix 9).

237. See manuscript R in the Sources.

238. See manuscript G in the Sources.

239. This church, the so-called *Badiazza* located in the San Rizzo region of the Peloritan Mountains overlooking Messina, was formerly known as *Santa Maria della Valle* (Saint Mary of the Valley), being a Greek Orthodox monastery that became Roman Catholic. In Margaret's time it was a center for the covert forgery of charters. Resembling a fortress, the structure suffered damage in the earthquake of 1908 but was restored and is still impressive.

240. See *I Documenti Inediti dell'Epoca Normanna in Sicilia* by Garufi (in the Sources), pages 101-102, document 44, where Stephen of Perche is identified as "bishop-elect of Palermo," not as a consecrated bishop.

241. John of Lavardin, who was enfeoffed with Caccamo and Prizzi.

242. Specifically, these were periodic tithes (which might be paid in kind) and an annual monetary tribute. The point was that in Sicily these taxes were regulated, whereas in the baron's native France they were left more to the discretion of the local feudatory. It is implied, and indeed suggested by the available evidence, that the serfs of Norman Sicily were treated better than those in France and other regions during the same period.

243. Robert of San Giovanni and Roger of Tiron.

244. Palm Sunday fell on 31 March in 1168.

245. This comes to us from Falcandus. Romuald does not mention the plot explicitly but does tell us that Matthew of Aiello and Caïd Richard were accused of treason.

246. These knights were already in jail by the time Matthew of Aiello was accused, shortly thereafter. According to Falcandus: *Inde capti sunt plerique milites, quos de morte ipsius jusiurandum praestitisse constabat.* The imprisoned knights probably knew the identities of the plot's three organizers; this may have been the basis for Stephen of Perche implicating Matthew of Aiello and Caïd Richard.

247. Falcandus states that Matthew of Aiello "exceeded the others in cleverness," *qui ceteris astutia praeminebat* (implying that Matthew was crafty and conniving). Romuald uses the phrase "sage and prudent," *sapiens et discretus* (thereby implying that the *familiare* was intelligent and probably loyal). This is a good example of the chroniclers describing the same person in somewhat contrasting terms; indeed, Romuald adds that Matthew was arrested "for no reason," *sine causa capi fecit*.

248. Falcandus: *Cumque regina nullatenus consentiret ut Richardus gaytus caperetur*. The chronicler then reiterates that Caïd Richard was a chief instigator.

249. Estimates of the population of the Kingdom of Sicily before 1200 are based to a great extent on such factors as taxation, agriculture, military capacity and the number of churches and mosques, as the Normans undertook nothing like a general census and there were many peasants but (compared to most European kingdoms) few serfs to be counted. Palermo, Messina, Bari and Salerno were quite large by contemporary standards. Although there is a dearth of demographic information for this period, it seems unlikely that there were more than three million people living in the *Regnum* in Margaret's lifetime. For comparison, this may have been roughly equal to the combined population of England and Wales during the twelfth century. Italy, with its wealthy northern communes, was rather highly (and densely) populated compared to most parts of Europe.

250. There were, of course, other sympathizers, such as Roger of Gerace, an important baron, and William of Leluce.

251. This part of Sicily had once boasted a large Berber population.

252. Burgundio, of whom little is known.

253. This is the thesis advanced by Falcandus. Romuald, conversely, does not speculate in this regard. Not only is Falcandus the principal source for most of the events that transpired at Messina in 1168, for most of these he is the *only* source.

254. John Calomeno, about whom little is known.

255. Romuald states mid-April (a week after Easter) for the release of Henry of Montescaglioso, but a necrology at Chartres gives 6 April for the death of Odo which, according to Falcandus, occurred a day after Henry arrived in Messina. Andrew, the governor of Messina, probably sent a messenger to Stephen of Perche explaining the situation.

256. This important point overlooked by many historians is crucial to the analysis

of subsequent events. Henry was not acting against the king or regent, but against the chancellor.

257. Like the palace, this edifice was destroyed long ago. What little of it survived into recent centuries was levelled by the earthquake of 1908.

258. Rometta's very name means "fortress," from the Greek *erymata*. It was the site of a decisive battle that prompted the arrival of thousands of troops from Constantinople in 964. This was part of a revolt of the Greeks against the ruling Kalbids; the emir Hassan al Kalbi was killed during the fighting.

259. Romuald does not mention the incident explicitly, and Falcandus refers to "promises," using the Latin cognate *promissis*, rather than monetary bribes.

260. Using the zodiac as a reference, Godfrey Malaterra (see Appendix 2) states that in the summer of 1079 Roger I took control of the town following a six-month siege: *Sextus erat mensis quo fervidus eminet ensis. Piscibus obsedit servente leone recedit.*

261. This oft-quoted saying is rooted in a line from *The Tempest* (Act 2, Scene 2) by William Shakespeare: "Misery acquaints a man with strange bedfellows."

262. See note 235.

263. See Carey, Hilary, op. cit., pages 10, 27-31.

264. William's affinity for astrology was observed by bin Jubayr (see Appendix 1).

265. We cannot know precisely what it was that influenced the astrologers in casting and interpreting William's horoscope. The most noteworthy astronomical event of this period was the annual Lyrids meteor shower; the more spectacular solar eclipse of 9 April 1168 was not visible over Sicily.

266. The term *Lombard* refers in most cases to the various peninsular Italians who settled in Sicily, having arrived with the Normans (see notes 184 and 228). The towns mentioned by Falcandus are Capizzi, Maniace, Nicosia, Randazzo and Vicari, but there were others having large Lombard populations and therefore willing to support the chancellor, namely Sperlinga, San Filadelfo (San Fratello), Aidone and Butera.

267. This estimate comes to us from Falcandus, and it may be based on a larger number of towns than the five he mentioned (see note 266).

268. Falcandus and Romuald differed in their perceptions of Matthew of Aiello. See note 247.

269. The master castellan was Ansaldo; Constantine was his assistant. Little is known of either one.

270. Roger of Avellino was a distant kinsman of the king; the ancestors of John of Lavardin held a manor on the Loire.

271. According to Falcandus, *ubi nemini liceat armis se vel militibus praemunire,* although there would have been exceptions to the rule. The author's analogy to the Rubicon, of course, refers to Julius Caesar crossing that Italian river with an armed legion in 49 BC (BCE) on his way to Rome, making him and his troops outlaws.

272. Falcandus refers to "four hundred" servants, *qui fere quadringenti erant,* a number that probably included the guards present during the day shift.

273. See note 266.

274. Scion of a Norman family, crusading Robert of Meulan was the nephew of Robert of Leicester, sometime justiciar of Henry II of England; like Stephen of Perche, he was related to Rotrou of Rouen.

275. Outside what is now Porta Nuova, into the present Piazza Indipendenza.

276. *Tunc vero sagittarii curiae, qui nunquam in seditionibus ubi lucri spes appareat ultimi consueverunt occurrere.*

277. Falcandus mentions Carbonello and Bohemond of Manopello (see notes 210 and 234), William of San Severino, Alduin Cantuese, Hugh Lupino (now wed to Clementia of Catanzaro, with whom Matthew Bonello had flirted), and Robert of Meulan (who lived until 1203).

278. There was a church and some buildings in what is now Piazza delle Vittorie between the palace and cathedral.

279. Robert of Tiron, who held several manors in Sicily, was a competent knight and trusted advisor of Stephen of Perche. See note 243.

280. According to Falcandus, the source for this information: *Interea cum rex ad matris petitionem e palatio vellet exire ut ab obsidione populum amoveret, Mattheus notarius ceterique conspiratores qui aderant prohibuerunt egredi, dicentes non esse tutum illuc accedere, nam sagittarum ac lapidum circumquaque turbinem agitari.*

281. Stephen of Perche died in Jerusalem the following year.

282. Over the next few years, the *familiares* rarely acted in unison, although we find one or another (or several at a time) witnessing royal decrees throughout the remainder of the regency. They did not all serve at the same time, and some were more influential than others. However, we find several of them witnessing the dower charter of Joanna of England in 1177 (see Appendix 9).

283. See note 202.

284. As the "council of regency" consisting of numerous *familiares* did not survive in that form into William's majority, it did not become an enduring element in royal rule.

285. For English common law under Henry II, see Hudson, Richard, op.cit. For commentary on the Assizes of Ariano, see Pennington, Kenneth, op.cit.

286. See note 67, and Makdisi, John, op.cit.

287. This is not the place for a detailed treatise on English law during the Plantagenet era, but (by way of comparison) it may be observed that in 1168 England did not have a "statutory" legal code quite so complex or complete as the Assizes of Ariano. However, the Charter of Liberties (issued by Henry I in 1100) is regarded by some scholars as an early precursor of the *Magna Carta*.

288. Like Stephen of Perche, Gilbert of Gravina ended up in the Holy Land. This is stated by Falcandus; for concordance see *Annales Casinenses* (in Sources), entry for 1168, page 312.

289. Hugh of Catanzaro (Hugh Lupino) was one of the signatories of the dower charter of Joanna of England. See Appendix 9.

290. *Sed quia nullius consilii audaciae homo erat ut vel occulte paraturus insidias, vel ex praecipiti magnum ausurus aliquid timeretur, maluerunt ei parcere, sperantes eo ipso posse reginae indignationem aliquatenus mitigari.*

291. See note 206.

292. Boson was Bishop of Cefalù until his death in 1172.

293. For a translation see Appendix 5. See also *Epistolae Sancti Thomae Cantuariensis* (in Sources), volume 1, document number 192, pages 392-394.

294. Ibid, document number 193, pages 394-395.

295. Ibid, document number 150, pages 319-320; translation in Appendix 5.

296. See note 295.

297. Walter's supposed surname "of the Mill" is an anachronistic misnomer popularized by modern scholars in England. Reflecting a misinterpretation of such Latin words as *familiaris* and *offamilias*, it led some historians to believe that Walter was English. In general usage, *familiaris* usually referred to a friend (rather than a relative), apart from its specific meaning at the Sicilian court, where it denoted a counsellor or advisor appointed by the sovereign.

298. Walter may also have had another motive in asserting his influence in southern Sicily, as his brother, Bartholomew, became Archbishop of Agrigento in 1171.

NOTES

299. *His accedebat quod Petrus Caietanus romanae curiae subdiaconus certissime promiserat electionem hanc nihil roboris habituram, septingentasque auri uncias opera studioque reginae acceperat romano pontifici deferendas.*

300. The dating is obvious from several charters referring to Walter as "archbishop-elect" regardless of whether he was already confirmed by the Pope. See, for example, the one issued in February 1169 extracted in Appendix 10.

301. The description suggests the earthquake's magnitude at approximately 8.0 on the Richter scale.

302. The greater part of this description comes to us from Falcandus, although a few details were reported by Romuald. See also the letters of Peter of Blois in *Petri Blesensis Opera Omnia* (in Sources), number 46 on pages 138-140 and number 93 on pages 290-291.

303. Much of the apse survived, and it is the only part of the original structure standing today.

304. This is the view of bin Jubayr (see Appendix 1), who visited Sicily late in 1184. Though recorded years after the event, the quote seems to have been widely known and is probably not merely apocryphal.

305. See letter 46 in *Petri Blesensis Opera Omnia* (in Sources), pages 138-140, written following the murder of Thomas Becket.

306. This is corroborated by William of Tyre in his *Historia Rerum in Partibus Transmarinis Gestarum,* "History of Deeds Beyond the Sea." Stephen's death is the last event mentioned by Hugh Falcandus.

307. See the extract and commentary in Appendix 10.

308. Ibid.

309. This was issued at Benevento on 22 June 1169. See *Italia Pontificia* (in Sources), volume 10, pages 232-233, document number 32.

310. Ibid., page 233, document number 33.

311. Manuscript B in the Sources. A photograph of the charter appears in this book.

312. See the charters of October 1170 and March 1171 in Appendix 10; also the signature in the dower charter in Appendix 9.

313. See Giles, *The Life and Letters of Thomas à Becket* (in Sources), volume 2, page 201.

314. Ibid.

315. This is the consensus of scholars based on the available evidence; no explicit statement (such as a letter) in support of Thomas Becket by Margaret survives.

316. See the extract and commentary in Appendix 10.

317. This is the opinion of chroniclers such as Peter of Eboli; Peter was sometimes critical of Matthew of Aiello. Yet both *familiares* became fixtures at court throughout William's reign; Walter lived until 1190, Matthew until 1193.

318. See Appendix 5.

319. This chapter is not intended as a detailed biography. See the Sources for contemporary records, and the books by Duggan and Barber on the lives of (respectively) Thomas Becket and Henry II. Among those who wrote about Becket shortly after his death are John of Salisbury, Herbert of Bosham and Alan of Tewkesbury. Accounts of his death appear in the chronicles of Roger of Howden, Ralph Diceto and (in an extract translated for this volume) Romuald of Salerno.

320. This church, whose construction was begun by William the Conqueror in 1087, was completed in the Gothic style in 1314 (sic). It was destroyed by the Great Fire in 1666, after which the present cathedral was erected.

321. The source of this account is William FitzStephen's biography of Thomas Becket.

322. Ranulf of Glanville later wrote a detailed summary of these laws, the *Tractatus de Legibus et Consuetudinibus Regni Angliae*. See also note 67.

323. There may have been Maliki influences that arrived via Sicily. See note 67.

324. Except for a single statute protecting church property, the emphasis of this simple proclamation of Henry I was the guarantee of baronial rights (see also note 287). Other pre-existing laws were known, if rarely applied during the reign of Henry II. Written around 1115, the *Leges Henrici Primi* (Laws of Henry I) was a legal treatise that sought to compile the entire body of law that existed in England. This was later superseded by Glanville's treatise (see note 322).

325. Theobald advocated the study of canon law and Roman law, and to that end he brought Vacarius of Mantua, a leading scholar, from Bologna to teach it in England. Vacarius founded the law school at Oxford. See Re, Edward, op.cit.

326. The primacy of the Archbishop of Canterbury was challenged by the Archbishop of York in 1118, and in Henry's reign both archiepiscopal sees claimed it. (See also note 90.)

327. See *Select Charters* (in Sources), pages 135-140.

NOTES

328. Ibid., pages 140-146.

329. This was the kind of trial requested by Walter of Moac in Sicily when accused of treason in 1168 (see Chapter 13).

330. Accounts of this encounter come to us from Herbert of Bosham and Alan of Tewkesbury.

331. See note 326.

332. Henry the Young King lived from 1155 to 1183, predeceasing his father.

333. See Appendix 8.

334. Located along what is now Vicolo Lombardo near the cathedral, this church was entirely rebuilt in the eighteenth century as the chapel of a local family and extensively damaged during the bombings of 1943.

335. For methods used to determine the beginning of the year during this period see Poole, op.cit., pages 41-47.

336. See Appendix 8 for Romuald's description of this betrothal.

337. Richard of San Germano, whose chronicle begins in 1189, uses this phrase verbatim, adding that the great men of the realm referred, in the first instance, to these two courtiers: *His duobus, quasi duabus columnis firmissimis, omnes regni magnates obsequendo adhaeserant, cum per eos quicquid a curia regia peterent, facilius impetrarent.* This may be an accurate description for the last years of the reign of King William, though it is only a retroactive (and anachronistic) characterization; being born in peninsular Italy around 1165, Richard did not have a firsthand knowledge about the regency of Queen Margaret, but his words probably reflect prevailing perceptions.

338. See the extract in translation in Appendix 10.

339. The medieval city of Cairo was founded in 969 by Abu al-Hasan Jawhar al-Saqilli ("the Sicilian"). Despite his nickname, it is possible he was not born in Sicily.

340. Constance eventually joined a convent, but we do not know precisely when.

341. For most of the information presented about Benjamin of Tudela in this chapter, see the translation by Adler, Marcus Nathan, op.cit., which is based on three manuscripts. The book by Adolf Asher was also consulted.

342. For bin Jubayr's visit see Appendix 1.

343. The text of a charter issued at Palermo on 27 November 1171 in Greek and Latin begins (in both versions) with Margaret's name and in the latter language

refers to the queen as *Margarita dei gratia regina mater domini regis,* a formula that differs, if only very slightly, from that used in most royal charters issued until this time. (See manuscript H in the Sources and its original Latin text in Appendix 10.) The subtle variation in wording may reflect Margaret's new status in view of her son reaching the age of majority; or it may be nothing more than a stylistic choice by the scrivener writing the text. In either case, we know that by the spring of 1172 William was acting on his own (see Chapter 20).

344. See manuscript C in the Sources.

345. See both codices in Appendix 7.

346. That an Arab village near the site of Monreale Abbey was called *Ba'lat* or *Ba'lara* is open to question. The oft-repeated claim that a Greek Orthodox chapel was already located on the site of Monreale's *duomo* is based on an erroneous interpretation of the phrase *super sanctam Kuriacam,* properly "the place overlooking" an existing church (not literally "on top of" it) in William's charter of August 1176. See *Catalogo Illustrato* (in Sources), page 11, footnote number 1.

347. Interestingly, the foundation date of Maniace (1172) is given in the *Annales Siculi* (see Sources), page 116. See also *Catalogo Illustrato* (in Sources), page 7. For a detailed summary of sources, see White, op.cit., pages 145-148. See also Radici, Benedetto, op.cit.

348. Numerous records attest to the details of the foundation of this monastery and diocese and its subsequent status. See, for example, *Italia Pontificia* (in Sources), volume 10, pages 272-281; also *Catalogo Illustrato* (in Sources), pages 6-32. For a list of additional original sources, see White, op.cit, pages 132-145.

349. The chief source for Walter's reaction is the prologue of the chronicle of Richard of San Germano (partially quoted in note 350). Although this was written some sixteen years after the fact, it does seem to reflect a perception held by many during the first few years of William's majority.

350. From the chronicle of Richard of San Germano: *Quod idem archiepiscopus ad instinctum ipsius cancellarii factum intelligens (nam odio se habebant ad invicem, quamquam se in publico diligere viderentur, et per invidiam detrahentes libenter unus alteri in occulto) hanc suam injuriam et capitis diminutionem patienter portavit ad tempus. Qui tandem processu temporis cum non posset quod factum fuerat per ecclesiam revocare, hoc fieri subdole procuravit.*

351. Regardless of what Richard of San Germano and other chroniclers state, or refrain from mentioning, charters confirm that Margaret sponsored or endowed a number of other monastic churches in Sicily. Her support of the project at Monreale, just a few miles from Palermo (indeed visible from the Pisan tower), is consistent with these other projects, to which she could dedicate more time now that she was no longer regent.

352. The letter was written to Archbishop Walter of Palermo in 1177: *Nam quum*

rex vester bene litteras noverit, rex noster longe litteratior est. Ego enim in litterali facultatus utriusque cognovi. Scitis, quod dominus rex siciliae per annum discipulus meus fuit, et qui a vobis versificatoriae artis primitias habuerat, per industriam et sollicitudinem meam beneficium scientiae plenioris obtinuit. For the entire letter, see number 66 in *Petri Blesensis Opera Omnia* (in Sources), pages 192-197.

353. This privilege was granted in late 1174 and repeatedly confirmed over the next few years; see *Catalogo Illustrato* (in Sources), pages 7-13. Monreale was eventually erected into an archdiocese. Reference is made to it in several subsequent Papal bulls and royal decrees.

354. This area is still part of the Archdiocese of Monreale. For an example of some Arab smallholdings in each fortified locality (Jato, Corleone, Calatrasi, Battallario) see *Catalogo Illustrato* (in Sources), pages 18-20.

355. Located in the forum near the Colosseum, the site of temples dedicated to Roma and Venus is easily identified by the remains of capitals nearly identical to those installed at Monreale.

356. That the escutcheons, which resemble those of the Bayeux Tapestry commemorating the Battle of Hastings (1066), are not embellished with heraldic insignia suggests that armorial heraldry was introduced in the Kingdom of Sicily after 1180. See Mendola, Louis, "English and Italian Legacy of the Norman Knight Figures of Monreale" (in Sources). In connection with this, it should be noted that the Hauteville coat of arms (blazoned "azure a bend checky argent and gules") displayed in mosaic in the church was added after 1200, there being no contemporary record of the dynasty's use of heraldic insignia.

357. Carved from a porphyry column, the sarcophagus of King William I was transferred to Monreale in 1182 and still survives. The sarcophagus of Frederick II in Palermo's cathedral is very similar.

358. King Louis IX was canonized in 1297. With the destruction (by revolutionaries) of his remains at Saint-Denis except for a finger, more of his bodily relics are conserved at Monreale than anyplace else.

359. Most of the details about Maria's planned arrival at Taranto come to us from Romuald of Salerno. See Appendix 8.

360. According to legend, Saint Michael, who was widely venerated by the Normans of Italy, appeared here during the fifth century. It was a popular pilgrimage site, visited by many pilgrims on their way to the Holy Land. The place itself (Mount Sant'Angelo) was a royal possession which came to be the personal demesne of the queen consorts of Sicily.

361. With the Compromise of Avranches (May 1172), Henry II of England promised to go on crusade. He also swore to guarantee Papal legal jurisdiction in his kingdom in certain cases, effectively renouncing some of the rights he had obtained through the legislation that led to the conflict with Thomas Becket. The king was

absolved of any guilt for Becket's death.

362. For the text of William's letter to Henry see Appendix 5.

363. Margaret founded Maniace in her own name; little explored by historians, this fact is well documented. See the charters of Nicholas, Archbishop of Messina, in March 1174 (in *Catalogo Illustrato,* page 7); Theobald, Archbishop of Monreale, in April 1177 (ibid., page 14); Nicholas, Archbishop of Messina, in May 1178 (ibid., pages 15-16).

364. In the charter of 1174 cited in note 363; also manuscript D in Sources, and Appendix 10. For another interesting example see manuscript S in Sources.

365. See *Catalogo Illustrato,* pages 15-16; White, op.cit., pages 146-148.

366. Saladin advanced on several fronts over the next decade; he conquered Jerusalem in 1187. In response to this, Frederick Barbarossa, Richard Lionheart (son of Henry II of England), and Philip Augustus (Philip II of France) launched the Third Crusade in 1189.

367. The "Great Revolt" ended officially in September 1174 with Henry's sons pledging fealty to their father.

368. See manuscript L in the Sources. Also *Catalogo Illustrato,* pages 8-9; *Italia Pontificia,* volume 10, page 275.

369. This was a rare ecclesiastical rank. A mitred abbot was, indeed, accorded a status almost equal to that of a bishop. The first monks took up residence in Monreale in 1176. An indication of the abbot's power is the fact that by 1177 charters were referring to him as a bishop even though he was not yet consecrated as such. Monreale became a metropolitan archdiocese in February 1183.

370. This followed a rather similar agreement with the Genoans, who had extensive interests in the *Regnum.*

371. See Abulafia, David, *The Two Italies* (in Sources), page 143.

372. The name *Plantagenet* became identified with the dynasty of Henry II centuries after his death. It is based on the belief that his father, Geoffrey of Anjou, liked the broom plant, *planta genista.*

373. Beatrice Hohenstaufen, the daughter of Frederick Barbarossa, died in 1174. Maria Comnenus, the daughter of Manuel of Constantinople, wed Rainier of Montferrat in 1180; she died two years later, possibly by poisoning, following her court intrigues against her half-brother, Alexius, who was briefly Emperor of Constantinople.

374. Officially, of course, the ambassadors were sent by King William II of Sicily.

NOTES

375. While it is quite possible that Margaret corresponded with Eleanor, perhaps sending a letter to be consigned to her by the Sicilian ambassadors, there is no firm evidence of this. By 1176, the two queens shared a devotion to Saint Thomas Becket, although Eleanor, fourteen years earlier, had opposed her husband appointing him Archbishop of Canterbury.

376. See Appendix 9 and the last section of Appendix 8.

377. See Appendix 9 for details of the dower summarized the following year. For Mount Sant'Angelo see note 360.

378. This letter appears at the end of Appendix 9.

379. In fact, mother and daughter did meet again, in Sicily in 1191, when Joanna's brother, King Richard "Lionheart," was on the way to the Third Crusade.

380. See the author's translation at "Peace Between the Archbishops at Winchester" in Appendix 9.

381. See Appendix 9 for the account of Roger of Howden, who mentions "a certain palace," an observation similar to Romuald's. The Cuba palace (along what is now Corso Calatafimi) was not yet built, although it may have been under construction.

382. For a detailed description of this unique object see Appendix 6.

383. The first coronation of William II (shortly following his father's death) was celebrated in the cathedral, which was the preferred place for such a rite. As the church of the Primate of Sicily, it would be the most appropriate venue for the wedding of a reigning monarch, and the coronation of his queen consort.

384. The precise extent of Walter's influence after this time is a matter of scholarly debate. It is the author's contention that the archbishop's power diminished somewhat in real terms, even though, as Primate of Sicily and *familiare,* he remained one of the kingdom's most influential figures throughout William's reign. This is elucidated further in the next chapter.

385. Romuald's chronicle provides one of the most important accounts of this diplomatic event.

386. Italy's northern communes, which were under the authority of the Holy Roman Emperor, were vitally important to Frederick Barbarossa. Beyond their strategic significance, they were far wealthier than most of the cities he ruled in what are now Germany and Austria, thus providing a greater tax base. Frederick's alliance with the Kingdom of Sicily eliminated a potential threat from the south, as it was easy (and economical) for the Sicilian sovereign to send an army northward from Salerno and Naples to defend Rome if needs be.

387. Not all peasants were serfs tied to manorial lands; indeed, "traditional" serfdom was never as widely introduced in Sicily as it was in France and England. (See note 184.) Nevertheless, one of the shortcomings of the Normans' introduction of feudalism in Sicily was that it made serfs of many Muslims while incorporating their smallholdings into baronies and manors. This gave rise to periodic revolts at Jato (in the territory of Monreale), a locality that remained largely Muslim into the next century.

388. This church, restored to its original state, stands amidst what is now a large cemetery. It is known as the site of the Vespers uprising in 1282.

389. Founded in France in 1098 as a splinter from the Benedictines, the Cistercians were growing in importance. To some degree, the establishment of a major Cistercian church in Palermo, in the shadow of the rival Benedictines, probably reflected Walter's attempt to assert his own influence in the monastic environment. At all events, as Primate of Sicily Walter was still the senior prelate of the *Regnum* (see note 90); his brother, Bartholomew, was now Archbishop of Agrigento (see note 390).

390. For the charter of March 1177 exchanging the tithes of the churches of Corleone for episcopal jurisdiction over Baida (a village on the southern edge of the Genoard) see *Catalogo Illustrato*, page 13. Since 1171, Walter's brother, Bartholomew, had been Archbishop of Agrigento, for which see, *exempli gratia,* the charter in *Catalogo Illustrato* (in Sources), pages 20-21.

391. Not to be confused with the Bishop of Lincoln who died in 1209 (see also note 392).

392. The talented William of Blois was the abbot of the monastery of Santa Maria della Matina at San Marco Argentano in Calabria (see Conti, Emanuele, op.cit.). He was once considered for the bishopric of Catania, an appointment which went to John of Aiello. This rejection probably saved William's life, for John perished in the earthquake of 1169. Despite what some modern historians have written, there is no contemporary evidence that William of Blois was ever the abbot of Maniace; charters issued in 1177 and 1178 refer to the abbot of that monastery as "Timothy" (see *Catalogo Illustrato,* pages 14-16). The confusion probably results from poor interpretation of a phrase in letters from William's brother (Peter), *abbas matinensis,* "abbot of Matina," as if it were *abbas maniacensis,* "abbot of Maniace."

393. See manuscripts H, I and J in the Sources. Adelaide del Vasto (who died in 1118 and rests at Patti) was the third wife of Roger I and the mother of Roger II. After Roger I died in 1101, leaving two sons, namely Simon (who died in 1105) and the future King Roger II, Adelaide effectively ruled Sicily until 1112.

394. Despite the oft-repeated idea that Margaret "lived at Maniace" after 1177, there is no evidence whatsoever to suggest that she stayed there for more than occasional visits. She probably spent much more time at San Marco d'Alunzio.

NOTES

395. Reports of Constance's place of residence during these years are not consistent or conclusive. However, we know that she lived in Sicily (Richard of San Germano suggests her occasional presence at the royal palace in Palermo), where she was in frequent contact with her mother, Beatrice, and that she had taken up the monastic life.

396. A number of surviving royal charters attest to this. We find, for example, one issued at Messina in June 1177 approving a donation to a monastery by Matthew of Aiello. Over the next few years, however, William's presence in northeastern Sicily seems to have been rare while Margaret's was fairly frequent.

397. This scenario is based chiefly on prosopography; chroniclers would not waste ink on the account of an everyday occurrence of this kind.

398. Romuald's original text uses the generic term *armigero* for an armed man of noble rank: *Qui accepta a rege licentia, reversi sunt, quodam regis armigero eos, ut moris est, usque ad fines regni deducente.*

399. This case was quite similar, though not identical, to the kinds of circumstances that led to the jurisdictional dispute between Henry II and Thomas Becket, but Romuald of Salerno supported King William's decision to punish the murderous monks.

400. As an example of the kind of sources consulted for the years after 1178, a charter of March 1180 given by William II and witnessed by Archbishop Walter, Matthew of Aiello and Richard Palmer indicates Palermo as its place of issuance. See *I Documenti Inediti dell'Epoca Normanna in Sicilia* by Garufi (in the Sources), pages 171-172, document 71.

401. This palace is located along what is now Corso Calatafimi.

402. Some historians favour 1180 as Berengaria's year of birth.

403. By definition, an heir/heiress presumptive is first in the line of succession until displaced through the birth of an heir (such as a son) nearer to the monarch in kinship. A hypothetical son of William II would be the heir apparent.

404. In the chronicler's own words: *Audivimus a quibusdam quod Johanna uxor Guillelmi regis Siciliae, filia Henrici regis Anglorum, peperit ei filium primogenitum, quem vocaverunt Boamundum. Qui cum a baptismate reverteretur, pater investivit eum ducati Apuliae per aureum sceptrum, quod in manu gerebat.* See *The Chronicle of Robert of Torigni* (in Sources), page 303. Several factors argue against the accuracy of this account. Firstly, it is not corroborated elsewhere, not even by an inscription on a tomb (no tomb of a child of William and Joanna exists). Secondly, Robert was far away in Normandy, not in Sicily, so he was not a witness to events in the *Regnum*. Thirdly, a firstborn son would most likely have been named William, Roger, or even Henry (for Joanna's father or William's beloved brother), not Bohemond. Lastly, Joanna bore no other children by William, although she later gave birth to the children of her second husband, a fact that raises questions about William's ability to father children.

405. We do not have it on reliable authority that William fathered children even outside wedlock. Joanna, by contrast, was certainly fertile, giving birth to three children by her second husband, Raymond VI of Toulouse, between 1196 and her death in 1199. (See note 404 above.) Those who survived her were the future Raymond VII and Joanna (Joan).

406. See *The Chronicle of Robert of Torigni* (in Sources), page 285 (folio 229 in the manuscript).

407. The average age of menarche in Europe in Joanna's time was around thirteen. See Amundsen and Diers, op.cit.

408. The most obvious example of such a rivalry involving churches of traditional design is found in Manhattan. The nave of Saint John the Divine, begun in 1892, was intended to dwarf that of Saint Patrick, completed fourteen years earlier. Both cathedrals are of the Gothic Revival style.

409. See notes 94 and 132.

410. For more about Majorca and the complexities of western Mediterranean politics during this period, see Abulafia's study, *A Mediterranean Emporium: The Catalan Kingdom of Majorca* (in Sources).

411. This "Massacre of the Latins" was described by the chronicler Nicetas Choniates, and William of Tyre mentions it.

412. See note 393.

413. William's presence at Capua in January is attested by a charter issued there; see *I Documenti Inediti dell'Epoca Normanna in Sicilia* by Garufi (in the Sources), pages 188-190, document 76. For his visit to Cassino in February, see *Annales Casinenses* (in Sources), entry for 1183, page 313.

414. Archbishop Walter, Matthew of Aiello, and Richard Palmer (by now Archbishop of Messina) all signed the charter issued at Capua referred to at note 413. This was logical, as the royal court was, in effect, wherever the king was.

415. This is attested by several surviving charters dated February 1183. See, in particular, *Italia Pontificia* (in Sources), volume 10, pages 276-278, documents number 6-11; *Catalogo Illustrato* (in Sources), pages 22-24.

416. See *Catalogo Illustrato* (in Sources), pages 25-26.

417. Margaret lived during what paleoclimatologists call the "Medieval Warm Period." The era known as the "Little Ice Age" began after the middle of the thirteenth century.

418. The only contemporary record of Margaret's date and place of death is her

NOTES

epigraph in Monreale Abbey (see note 420). This reports her death as the Feast of Saint Peter in Chains, which is to say the first of August. In the twelfth century the clergy usually identified a day as beginning at nightfall the previous evening.

419. The new cathedral in Palermo was still under construction. Monreale's *duomo* was essentially completed, although work continued on its mosaics for several more years.

420. Margaret's epitaph (shown on this book's back cover and in Chapter 19) was rendered in black on gold: *Hic regina iaces regalibus edita cunis Margarita tibi nomen, quod moribus unis, regia progenies per reges ducta propago, uxor regis eras et nobilitatis imago, si taceam quibus ipsa reples preconia mundum, regem Wilelmum satis est peperisse secundum, undecies centum decies octo tribus annis. Post hominem Christum migras necis eruta dampnis. Lux ea qua populis dant petri festa catene. His te de nebulis tulit ad loca lucis. Amene.*

421. See Appendix 1.

422. The lavish nuptials were celebrated at Milan in January 1186. On this occasion, Constance was crowned Queen of the Germans as Henry's consort.

423. The fact that Constance was William's designated successor (heiress) is confirmed by the chroniclers Richard of San Germano and Roger of Howden, as well as the author of the *Annales Casinenses*.

424. See Stubbs, William, *Gesta Regis Henrici* (in Sources), Preface, page xii.

425. William Stubbs was one of the first scholars to question its authorship. See also Stenton, Doris Mary; op.cit.

426. A manuscript written in Greek confirms the sale of familial property near the Martorana Church in 1146 by the children of the elder Eugenius for a thousand gold tarì. This document was rediscovered at the Palermo Archive of State late in the last century. See manuscript F in the Sources.

427. See *The Life and Letters of Thomas à Becket* (in Sources), letter 24, pages 303-304.

428. See note 293.

429. See *The Life and Letters of Thomas à Becket* (in Sources), letter 25, pages 304-305.

430. See Paratore, Ettore, op.cit.

431. A translation already published covers the chronicle to February 1168 in *The History of the Tyrants of Sicily* (see Sources), by Graham Loud and Thomas Wiedemann, pages 219-243.

432. See note 149.

433. Falcandus reports 15 May. See note 150.

434. It seems that William may have been moved to the chapel of Mary Magdalene in the cathedral. At all events, he now rests in Monreale.

435. Along with the words of Hugh Falcandus, this is the origin of the enduring epithet of William I as "the Bad."

436. This failed betrothal is described in the main text. Maria "Porphyrogenita" Comnenus was born in 1152. Manuel had his own designs on Sicily, and had suffered defeats at the hands of Roger II in the eastern Mediterranean from 1147 until 1149.

437. Like his contemporary Falcandus, Romuald viewed the ascent of Margaret's cousin Stephen spawning resentment in Richard Palmer and Matthew of Aiello, among others.

438. This is obviously a perfunctory telling of Becket's experience, which is described in far greater detail by English chroniclers. Romuald presumably knew that some of Becket's kin had been granted asylum by Margaret.

439. This probably refers to Ranulf de Broc, brother of Robert. Ranulf was present at Thomas Becket's assassination but was not one of the murderers; he had been excommunicated for siding with Henry II and usurping Becket's estates in England while the archbishop was in France.

440. Located outside the city of Antioch on the Orontes River, Black Mountain was the site of several monasteries and many hermit monks. It may be compared to Mount Athos.

441. Saint Mary Magdalene, the royal chapel attached to the old cathedral (see note 94).

442. Beatrice died in 1174 (see note 373) but not, so far as we know, because of heartbreak from her rejection by the King of Sicily.

443. See Appendix 9.

444. See the charter of November 1171 (at the end of the appendix) and note 343. Margaret, being regent, used her son's seal, not her own. For some observations regarding the charters issued by women in another Norman kingdom during this period, see Johns, Susan, op.cit.

SOURCES AND BIBLIOGRAPHY

The most essential information about Queen Margaret's life in Sicily was drawn from just a handful of original (primary) sources, but supplemented by a good number.

Contemporary Works (Primary Narrative Sources)

The chief editions of the original Latin texts of Falcandus and Romuald (both described at greater length in the appendices dedicated to the two chroniclers) consulted were those published by Giuseppe Del Re in *Cronisti e Scrittori Sincroni Napoletani* (Naples 1845). Note that in these editions the chronicles were not divided into chapters. The excellent 1845 printing also contains additional text from the Salerno Codex of the *Chronicon* (covering the years from 1121 to 1154 in the format of an annal), along with the original Latin text of the *Catalogus Baronum*. There have been numerous publications of these chronicles, some with useful commentary.

As mentioned in the appendix on Falcandus, *Historia Hvgonis Falcandi Sicvli de Rebus Gestis in Siciliae Regno* was published as an *editio princeps* by Martin Gervais de Tournay in Paris in 1550. The first Italian translation of Falcandus was published in 1556 by Antonio Filoteo Omodei. Following Del Re's edition was that of Santini (in 1931). Not to be overlooked is Giovanni Battista Siragusa's *La Historia o Liber de Regno Siciliae e la Epistola ad Petrum Panormitanae Ecclesiae Thesaurarium di Ugo Falcando* (1897), with its excellent analysis of the extant codices; this edition, with its text divided into fifty-five chapters, is the one most frequently consulted by scholars (for a review see Omodei, op.cit.). Several fine commentaries and translations have been published in recent years. In Italian we find Vito lo Curto's excellent *Il Libro del Regno di Sicilia* (2007), which includes a Latin transcription, and Umberto Santini's book of the same title (2008). In

English there is an eloquent translation and introduction by Graham Loud and the late Thomas Wiedemann, *The History of the Tyrants of Sicily by 'Hugo Falcandus' 1154-1169* (1998), which also includes part of Romuald's *Chronicon*.

A "modern" edition of Romuald, published in Italy in 2001 as *Romualdo II Guarna: Chronicon,* is useful for its insightful introductions by Giancarlo Andenna, Hubert Houben and Massimo Oldoni. In English, see Graham Loud's *Roger II and the Creation of the Kingdom of Sicily* (2012), where the translation of Romuald ends at the year 1154. An insightful essay is Donald Matthew's "The Chronicle of Romuald of Salerno" in *The Writing of History in the Middle Ages: Essays Presented to Richard William Southern* (Oxford 1981), pages 239-274.

The chief text of Tudela's diary consulted was *The Itinerary of Benjamin of Tudela* (1907), a translation and commentary by Marcus Nathan Adler. *The Itinerary of Rabbi Benjamin of Tudela* (1840) by Adolf Asher was also useful; this includes a Hebrew text.

There are several fine editions of Idrisi's *Book of Roger*. A good recent edition is *Il Libro di Ruggero* (2008), an Italian translation by Umberto Rizzitano. A detailed map of Sicily based on Idrisi's observations accompanies Luigi Santagati's *La Sicilia di al-Idrisi ne Il Libro di Ruggero* (2010). See also *Carte Comparèe de la Sicile* (1859) by Michele Amari. An extract in translation appears in Graham Loud's *Roger II and the Creation of the Kingdom of Sicily.*

Feudal manors, some dating from the Norman period, are indicated in many locality maps drawn between 1820 and 1850, found in the series *Direzione Centrale Statistiche* retained at the Palermo Archive of State.

See also the appendix dedicated to chroniclers and visitors.

Manuscript Sources (Charters)

For concordance, a number of charters were consulted at archives in Italy and Spain. Those most relevant to Margaret and the facts presented in this book include the following. For the benefit of scholars wishing to consult these manuscripts, it should be noted that cataloguing systems change over time, so since 2007 the collection at the Palermo Archive of State formerly known as *Pergamene Varie* (sundry manuscripts) has been known as *Pergamene di Diversa Provenienza*, literally "manuscripts from various sources," and it is presently housed in the more modernized, more secure Catena division rather than the Gancia off Via Alloro at the opposite end of Piazza Marina. The *Fondo Messina* (Messina Collection) of the Fundación Casa Ducal de Medinaceli, formerly housed in Seville, is now conserved at the archive of the Hospital de Tavera (de San Juan Bautista) in Toledo. Other idiosyncrasies confront the researcher; for example, most Spanish charters and chronicles of the twelfth century are dated with reference to the "Spanish era" dating system that begins with the year 38 BC (BCE), probably based on the infelicitous date that a certain Roman tax was imposed in Iberia. A few charters may be consulted online, where some published transcriptions and extracts are made available. For convenience in identification, the letters A-T correspond to references to each manuscript in this volume's endnotes. The texts of several charters are presented in English in Appendix 10.

A) Tabulario Cappella Palatina: Manuscript number 13 (royal concession of ecclesiastical property in Palermo by Margaret and young William, in March 1167, bearing signatures of Matthew of Aiello, Qaid Martin and Walter the rector and future archbishop).

B) Tabulario della Cattedrale di Palermo: Manuscript number 21 (royal concession of the feudal rights of the mills on the manor of Brucato, the Arabic *Bur-Ruqqad*, to Walter, the newly-consecrated Archbishop of Palermo, in September 1169).

C) Tabulario della Cattedrale di Palermo: Manuscript number 22 (William grants Archbishop Walter of Palermo rights to judge adulterers except for claims falling under civil jurisdiction, 15 April 1172).

D) Tabulario di Santa Maria Nova, Monreale (in the Biblioteca Centrale della Regione Siciliana, Palermo): Manuscript number 8, 1 March 1174, (Nicholas, Archbishop of Messina, exempts Abbey of Maniace founded by Margaret from taxation).

E) Tabulario di Santa Maria Nova, Monreale (in the Biblioteca Centrale della Regione Siciliana): Manuscript number 20, March 1177, (Theobald, Bishop of Monreale, establishes rights of Abbey of Maniace).

F) Archivio di Stato di Palermo, Pergamene Varie: Manuscript number 3, November 1146 (recorded in Greek, confirms the sale of familial property near the Martorana by the children of Eugenius for a thousand gold tarì, includes epitaph to George of Antioch, founder of the Martorana, dated 1151).

G) Archivio di Stato di Palermo, Tabulario di Santa Maria Maddalena of Messina: Manuscript number 50 (Margaret and William order nobles to exempt a monastery from taxation based on established policy, in 1168).

H) Archivio di Stato di Palermo, Tabulario dei Monasteri di San Filippo di Fragalà e di Santa Maria di Maniace: Manuscript 17 (TSFF17), 27 November 1171 (unsealed, probably a copy of an original, sealed charter; recorded in Greek and Latin, confirms privileges of Roger II protecting said monasteries, exempting them from the obligation to provide timber and livestock, lodge men-at-arms, and so forth, effectively exempting them from local civic authority).

I) Archivio di Stato di Palermo, Tabulario dei Monasteri di San Filippo di Fragalà e di Santa Maria di Maniace: Manuscripts 1, 2, 3, 4, 5, 6 (decrees issued early in the twelfth century by Adelaide in the name of her son Roger II chartering the monastery and granting it privileges).

J) Archivio di Stato di Palermo, Tabulario dei Monasteri di San Filippo di Fragalà e di Santa Maria di Maniaci: Manuscripts 7, 11, 12 (decrees made into 1112 endowing the monastery on Adelaide's initiative).

K) Tabulario della Cattedrale di Palermo: Manuscript number 29 (Queen Constance's assignment of some serfs, formerly under the feudal jurisdiction of the late Archbishop Walter, to the authority of the notary Rainaldo, dated April 1196).

SOURCES AND BIBLIOGRAPHY

L) Tabulario di Santa Maria Nova, Monreale (in the Biblioteca Centrale della Regione Siciliana): Manuscript number Balsamo 31, 30 December 1174, (Pope Alexander III grants status and privileges of "major abbey" to Monreale's Benedictine monastery).

M) Vatican Apostolic Library: Codice Vaticano Latino 3880, "Liber Privilegiorum Sanctae Montis Regalis Ecclesiae" chartulary (transcriptions of royal and papal charters relative to Monreale Abbey, several during the reign of William II).

N) Archivo de la Catedral de Tudela: Cajón 1, D. Manuscript number 20 (marriage charter between García Ramírez and Margaret l'Aigle in 1121).

O) British Library, London: Harley Manuscript 5786 (trilingual psalter composed in Sicily in Latin, Greek and Arabic during the reign of Roger II).

P) Archivio di Stato di Palermo: Direzione Centrale Statistiche (maps drawn between 1820 and 1850 showing medieval manors).

Q) Fundación Casa Ducal de Medinaceli (Toledo), Fondo Messina: Manuscript number 1118, November 1167 (Caïd Martin, acting on orders of Margaret and William II, issues this directive in Greek and Arabic restoring authority to Nicholas, Archbishop of Messina; only the Greek text mentions Margaret).

R) Fundación Casa Ducal de Medinaceli (Toledo), Fondo Messina: Manuscript number 109, March 1168, 1st indiction (William II and Margaret cede the Agrò Woods to the Holy Savior monastery of Messina).

S) Fundación Casa Ducal de Medinaceli (Toledo), Fondo Messina: Manuscript number 528, November 1176, 10th indiction (Margaret renews a donation effected five years earlier of some flat land near Milazzo to the Cistercian monastery of Santa Maria at Novara).

T) Fundación Casa Ducal de Medinaceli (Toledo), Fondo Messina: Manuscript number 522, May 1161, 9th indiction (William I confirms to the eldest sons of feudal vassals their hereditary rights to succeed their fathers killed in the service of the king, while conceding the citizens of Messina certain tax exemptions).

Primary Sources in Print

For convenience, these are listed according to content or title rather than the name of the editor, translator or commentator. Others are mentioned in the preceding section, "Manuscript Sources," while a few are included under "Secondary Literature." These sources were useful for myriad details; for example, the *Annales Siculi* mention Margaret founding the monastery of Maniace in 1172, a fact confirmed by royal charters.

Alexiad of Anna Comnena. Translated by Sewter, Edgar Robert Ashton (1969).

Annales Casinenses, in *Monumenta Germaniae Historica,* volume 19. Edited by Pertz, Georg Heinrich (1866), pages 303-320.

Annales Ceccanenses, in *Monumenta Germaniae Historica,* volume 19. Edited by Pertz, Georg Heinrich (1866), pages 275-302.

Annales Siculi, in *Rerum Italicarum Scriptores*, volume 5. Edited by Muratori, Lodovico (1774, reprint Bologna 1928).

Book in Honor of Augustus by Pietro da Eboli. Translation and notes. Hood, Gwenyth. (2012).

Catálogo de los Cartularios Reales del Archivo General de Navarra 1007-1384. Idoate, Florencio (1974).

Catalogo Illustrato del Tabulario di Santa Maria Nuova in Monreale. Garufi, Carlo Alberto (1902).

Catalogus Baronum. Jamison, Evelyn (1972). See also Del Re's *Cronisti,* volume 1, below.

La Chanson d'Antioche. Edited by Graindor de Douai (1862).

Chronica Adefonsi Imperatoris. Edited by Sánchez Belda, Luis (1950).

The Chronicle of Ibn al-Athir for the Crusading Period from al-Kamil fi'l-Ta'rikh by Ali ibn al-Athir. *Part 2, 541-589/1146-1193.* Richards, Donald (2007).

SOURCES AND BIBLIOGRAPHY

The Chronicle of Robert of Torigni. Edited by Howlett, Richard (1889).

Codex Diplomaticus Cavensis. Compilation. Morcaldi, Michele, chief editor (1893).

Codice Diplomatico di Sicilia sotto il Governo degli Arabi. Airoldi, Alfonso (1790).

Colección Diplomática de Alfonso I de Aragón y Pamplona 1104-1134. Edited by Lema Pueyo, José (1990).

Colección Diplomática de la Catedral de Pamplona, volume 1 (829-1243). Compilation. Edited by Gaztambide, José Goñi (1997).

Colección Diplomática Medieval de la Rioja 923-1225 (2 volumes). Rodríguez de Lama, Ildefonso (1976).

Corónicas Navarras. Edited by Ubieto Arteta, Antonio (1989).

Crónica Nájerense. Edited by Ubieto Arteta, Antonio (1985).

Crónica Nájerense. Translated by Estévez Sola, Juan (2003).

Crónica Navarro-Aragonesa, in *Crónica de los Estados Peninsulares.* Edited by Ubieto Arteta, Antonio (1955).

Cronisti e Scrittori Sincroni Napoletani, volume 1 ("Normanni"), edited by Del Re, Giuseppe (Naples 1845); pages 5-71 and 559-563 (Romuald); pages 277-391 (Falcandus); pages 405-439 (Peter of Eboli); pages 571-616 (Catalogus Baronum).

Cronisti e Scrittori Sincroni Napoletani, volume 2 ("Svevi"), edited by Del Re, Giuseppe (Naples 1868); pages 5-100 (Richard of San Germano).

The Deeds of Frederick Barbarossa. Translation of the *Gesti Friderici Imperatoris* of Otto of Freising. Mierow, Charles (1953).

I Diplomi della Cattedrale di Messina. Compilation of the Antonino Amico index. Starrabba, Raffaele (1876-1890).

I Diplomi Greci ed Arabi di Sicilia Pubblicati nel Testo Originale, Tradotti ed Illustrati (2 volumes). Cusa, Salvatore (1868).

I Documenti Inediti dell'Epoca Normanna in Sicilia. Compilation. Garufi, Carlo Alberto (1899).

Italia Pontificia, volume 10 ("Calabria Insulae"). Compilation. Kehr, Paul (1975).

The Ecclesiastical History of England and Normandy, volumes 3 and 4. Translaton and notes of the *Historia Ecclesiastica* of Orderic Vitalis. Forester, Thomas (1854-1856).

Epistolae Sancti Thomae Cantuariensis, volume 1. Compilation. Giles, John (1845).

Gesta Regis Henrici Secundi Benedicti Abbatis (formerly attributed to Benedict of Peterborough), in *Rerum Britannicarum Medii Aevi Scriptores,* volume 1. Stubbs, William (1867).

Historia Roderici, o Gesta Roderici Campi Docti, edited by Risco, Manuel (1792).

The Historical Works of Ralph de Diceto, Dean of London (2 volumes). Stubbs, William (1876).

Kitab al-masalik wa l-mamalik. Mohammed ibn Hawqal, in *Bibliotheca Geographorum Arabicorum* (Leiden 1873).

Kitab surat al-ard, al-Khwarizmi. Hans von Mzik (1926).

The Liber Augustalis or Constitutions of Melfi. Translation and notes. Powell, James (1971).

Materials for the History of Thomas Becket, Archbishop of Canterbury (7 volumes). Compilation. Robertson, James (1877).

Petri Blesensis Opera Omnia (volume 1), Letters of Peter of Blois. Giles, John (1847).

Rogerii II Regis Diplomata Latina (Codex Diplomaticus Regni Siciliae), Diplomata Regum et Principum e Gente Normannorum (series 1). Brühl, Carlrichard (1987).

Rollus Rubeus: Privilegia Ecclesie Cephaleditane, a Diversis Regis et Imperatoribus Concessa, Recollecta et in hoc Volumine Scripta. Mirto, Corrado (1972).

Select Charters and Other Illustrations of English Constitutional History (eighth edition). Compilation. Stubbs, William (1905).

Tabularium Regiae et Imperialis Cappellae Collegiatae Divi Petri in Regio Palermitano Palatio. Garofalo, Luigi (1835).

Tabulario di San Filippo di Fragalà e Santa Maria di Maniace. Silvestri, Giuseppe (1887).

The Life and Letters of Thomas à Becket (2 volumes). Documents in translation. Giles, John (1846).

St Thomas of Canterbury: An Account of His Life and Fame from the Contemporary Biographers and other Chroniclers. Hutton, William (1899).

The Travels of Ibn Jubayr. Broadhurst, Ronald (1952, 2008).

Vita Sancti Thomae by Willian Fitzstephen and Herbert of Bosham, in *Materials for the History of Thomas Becket,* volume 3 (see above).

Secondary Literature

A number of books and articles deal with the reigns of the Jiménez dynasts in Spain, and an even greater number consider the reigns of Roger II, William I and William II in Sicily. The years since 1990 have witnessed an extraordinary proliferation of studies concerning the Kingdom of Sicily under the Normans, spawning eclectic opinions and analyses of every kind, some highly reasoned and others less so. Moreover, a number of studies deal with the role of queens in medieval society. In the following list, mention of a specific modern work does not imply the author's agreement with its contents *in toto*. A few translations (into English) of primary sources are also included here. Defying the academic convention of indicating only the initial of each author's forename, full given names are indicated.

Abulafia, David. "The Crown and the Economy under Roger II and his Successors," *Dumbarton Oaks Papers,* number 37 (Washington, DC, 1983), pages 1-14.

Abulafia, David. *A Mediterranean Emporium: The Catalan Kingdom of Majorca* (1994).

Abulafia, David. *The Two Italies: Economic Relations Between the Norman Kingdom of Sicily and the Northern Communes* (1977).

Agius, Dionisius. *Siculo Arabic* (1996).

Ahmad, Aziz. *A History of Islamic Sicily* (1975).

Alio, Jacqueline. *Women of Sicily: Saints, Queens and Rebels* (2014).

Amari, Michele. *Storia dei Musulmani di Sicilia* (1854).

Amundsen, Darrel, and Diers, Carol Jean. "The Age of Menarche in Medieval Europe," *Human Biology,* number 45, volume 3 (Detroit 1973), pages 363-369.

Amico, Vito. *Dizionario Topografico della Sicilia* (1859).

Aziz, Ahmad. *A History of Islamic Sicily* (1975), sic.

Barber, Richard. *Henry Plantagenet* (1964).

Barlow, Frank. "Roger of Howden," *The English Historical Review,* volume 65, number 256 (Oxford, July 1950), pages 352-360.

Bates, David. "The Representation of Queens and Queenship in Anglo-Norman Royal Charters," *Frankland: The Franks and the World of the Early Middle Ages* (2008).

Beckwith, John. *Early Christian and Byzantine Art* (1979).

Bellafiore, Giuseppe. *La Zisa di Palermo* (1994).

Bennett, Judith, and Karras, Ruth (editors). *The Oxford Handbook of Women and Gender in Medieval Europe* (2013).

Bertinoro, Obadja da. *Miscellany of Hebrew Literature* (1872).

Bowie, Colette. "To Have and Have Not: The Dower of Joanna Plantagenet, Queen of Sicily," *Queenship in the Mediterranean: Negotiating the Role of the Queen in the Medieval and Early Modern Eras* (2013), pages 27-50.

Brandileone, Francesco. *Il Diritto Romano nelle Leggi Normanne e Sveve del Regno di Sicilia* (1884).

Bresc, Henri. *Palermo al Tempo dei Normanni* (2012).

Brühl, Carlrichard. *Urkunden und Kanzlei König Rogers II von Sizilien* (1978).

Bucaria, Nicolò. *Sicilia Judaica: Guida alle Antichità Giudaiche della Sicilia* (1996).

Bucaria, Nicolò, and Cassuto, David. "La Sinagoga e i Miqweh di Palermo alla Luce dei Documenti e delle Scoperte Archeologiche," *Archivio Storico Siciliano,* Series 4, Volume 31 (Palermo 2005), pages 171-209.

Cahen, Claude. *Le Régime Féodal de l'Italie Normande* (Paris 1940).

Caravale, Mario. "La Feudalità nella Sicilia Normanna," *Atti del Congresso*

Internazionale di Studi sulla Sicilia Normanna (Palermo 1974), pages 21-50.

Carey, Hilary. *Courting Disaster: Astrology at the English Court and University in the Later Middle Ages* (1992).

Caruso, Stefano. "Echi della Polemica Bizantina Antilatina dell' XI-XII Secoli nel 'De Oeconomia Dei' di Nilo Doxapatres," *Atti del Congresso Internazionale di Studi sulla Sicilia Normanna* (Palermo 1974), pages 403-432.

Caspar, Erich. *Roger II und die Gründung der Normannische-sicilischen Monarchie* (1904).

Chalandon, Ferdinand. *Histoire de la Domination Normande en Italie et en Sicile* (Paris 1907).

Chappuys, Gabriel. *L'Historie du Royaume de Navarre* (1616).

Chaytor, Henry. *A History of Aragon and Catalonia* (1933).

Cilento, Adele and Routt, David. "Foundation of a Monastery in Byzantine Calabria 1053/54" *Medieval Italy: Texts in Translation* (2009), pages 506-507.

Collins, Roger. *The Basques* (1990).

Collura, Paolo. *Le Più Antiche Carte dell'Archivio Capitolare di Agrigento 1092-1282* (1961).

Columba, Gaetano. "Note di Topografia Medievale Palermitana," *Archivio Storico Siciliano* (Palermo 1910), pages 325-350.

Conti, Emanuele. "L'Abbazia della Matina," *Archivio Storico per la Calabria*, volume 35 (Rome 1967), pages 11-30.

Crouch, David. *The Birth of Nobility: Constructing the Aristocracy in England and France 900-1300* (2005).

Crouch, David. *William Marshall: Knighthood, War and Chivalry 1147-1219* (2002).

Cuozzo, Errico. *Catalogus Baronum: Commentario* (1984).

D'Angelo, Edoardo. *Pseudo Ugo Falcando: De Rebus circa Regni Siciliae Curiam Gestis* (2014).

Davies, Norman. *Vanished Kingdoms* (2012).

Delogu, Paolo. *I Normanni in Italia: Cronache della Conquista e del Regno* (1984).

Demus, Otto. *The Mosaics of Norman Sicily* (1950).

Di Giovanni, Vincenzo. "Appendice alla Topografia Antica di Palermo," *Archivio Storico Siciliano* (Palermo 1899), pages 379-396.

Di Giovanni, Vincenzo. "Il Quartiere degli Schiavoni nel Secolo X," *Archivio Storico Siciliano* (Palermo 1887), pages 40-64.

Di Giovanni, Vincenzo. *La Topografia Antica di Palermo dal Secolo X al XV* (1890).

Domínguez Fernandez, Enrique, and Larrambebere Zabal, Miguel. *García Ramírez el Restaurador 1134-1150* (1986).

Drell, Joanna. "Cultural Syncretism and Ethnic Identity: The Norman 'Conquest' of Southern Italy and Sicily," *Al-Masaq: Journal of the Medieval Mediterranean*, volume 25, issue 3 (London 1999), pages 187-202.

Duggan, Anne J. *Thomas Becket* (2004).

Earenfight, Theresa. *Queenship in Medieval Europe* (2013).

Enzensberger, Horst. "Il Documento Regio come Strumento del Potere," *Potere, Società e Popolo nell'Età dei Due Guglielmi* (Bari 1981), pages 104-138.

Enzensberger, Horst. "Chanceries, Charters and Administration in Norman Sicily," *The Society of Norman Italy* (Leiden 2002), pages 117-150.

Epifanio, Vincenzo. "Ruggero II e Filippo di Al Mahdiah," *Archivio Storico Siciliano* (Palermo 1905), pages 471-501.

Fazello, Thomas. *De Rebus Siculus* (1558-1560).

Fernandez Perez, Gregorio. *Historia de la Iglesia y Obispos de Pamplona* (1820).

Fletcher, Richard. *The Quest for El Cid* (1991).

Fodale, Salvatore. *Comes et Legatus Siciliae: Sul privilegio di Urbano II e la pretesa Apostolica Legazia dei Normanni in Sicilia* (1970).

Freed, John. *Frederick Barbarossa: The Prince and the Myth* (2016).

Fuhrmann, Horst. *Germany in the High Middle Ages c. 1050-1200* (1986).

Gabrieli, Francesco. "Ibn Hawqal e gli Arabi in Sicilia," *L'Islam nella Storia: Saggi di storia e storiografia musulmana* (1966), pages 57-67.

Garufi, Carlo Alberto. "Monete e Conii nella Storia del Diritto Siculo dagli Arabi ai Martini," *Archivio Storico Siciliano* (Palermo 1898), pages 11-171.

Giordano, Nicola. "Nuovo Contributo alla Determinazione dei Rapporti tra Stato e Chiesa in Sicilia al Tempo dei Normanni," *Archivio Storico Siciliano* (Palermo 1916), pages 25-48.

Giunta, Francesco. *Bizanti e Bizantinismo nella Sicilia Normanna* (1950).

Goodman, Jennifer. *Medieval England and Iberia: A Chivalric Relationship* (2007).

Goskar, Tehmina. "Material Worlds: The Shared Cultures of Southern Italy and Its Mediterranean Neighbours in the Tenth to Twelfth Centuries," *Al-Masaq: Journal of the Medieval Mediterranean*, volume 23, issue 3 (London 2011), pages 189-204.

Granara, William. "Ibn Hawqal in Sicily," *Alif: Journal of Comparative Poetics*, number 3, (Cairo, 1983), pages 94-99.

Grassotti, Hilda. "Homenaje de García Ramírez a Alfonso VII dos Documentos Ineditos," *Príncipe de Viana*, volume 25 (number 94-95), 1964, pages 57-66.

Green, Monica. "Medicine in Southern Italy, Twelfth-Fourteenth Centuries: Six Texts," *Medieval Italy: Texts in Translation* (2009), pages 311-327.

Haskins, Charles. "England and Sicily in the Twelfth Century," *English Historical Review*, number 26 (Oxford 1911), pages 641-665.

Herrin, Judith. *Byzantium: The Surprising Life of a Medieval Empire* (2009).
Hill, Barbara. *Imperial Women in Byzantium 1025-1204: Power, Patronage and Idealogy* (1999).
Hilton, Lisa. *England's Medieval Queens* (2010)
Hoffmann, Hartmut. "Die Anfänge der Normannen in Süditalien" *Quellen und Forschungen aus Italienischen Arxhiven un Bibliotheken,* number 49 (Tübingen 1969), pages 95-144.
Hood, Gwenyth, "Falcandus and Fulcaudus Epistola ad Petrum liber de Regno Sicilie: Literary Form and Author's Identity," *Studi Medievali* (June 1999), 3rd Series, XL, pages 1-41.
Houben, Hubert. *Roger II von Sizilien* (1997).
Hoving, Thomas. "A Newly Discovered Reliquary of St Thomas Becket," *Gesta,* volume 4, spring 1965 (New York 1965), pages 28-30.
Hudson, Richard. "The Jusicial Reforms of the Reign of Henry II," *Michigan Law Review,* volume 9, number 5 (Ann Arbor 1911), pages 385-395.
Huesca, Ramon de. *Teatro Historico de las Iglesias del Reyno de Aragón* (1785).
Ingraiti, Gaetano. "Sulla Legittimità della Legazia Apostolica in Sicilia," *Atti del Congresso Internazionale di Studi sulla Sicilia Normanna* (Palermo 1974), pages 460-466.
Jamison, Evelyn. A*dmiral Eugenius of Sicily: His Life and Work and Authorship of the Epistola ad Petrum and the Historia Hugonis Falcandi Siculi* (London 1957).
Jamison, Evelyn. "Alliance of England and Sicily in the Second Half of the Twelfth Century," *Journal of the Warburg and Courtauld Institutes,* volume 6 (London 1943), pages 20-32.
Jamison, Evelyn. "Judex Tarentinus: The Career of Judex Tarentinus *Magne Curie Justiciarius* and the Emergence of the Sicilian *Regalis Magna Curia* under William I and the Regency of Margaret of Navarre, 1156-72," *Proceedings of the British Academy,* volume I, iii (London 1968), pages 289-344.
Jensen, Frede. *The Poetry of the Sicilian School* (1986).
Jimeno Jurío, José María. *¿Dönde fue la batalla de Roncesvalles?* (1974).
Jimeno Jurío, José María. *Historia de Pamplona: Síntesis de una Evolución* (1974).
Johns, Jeremy. *Arabic Administration in Norman Sicily: The Royal Diwan* (2002).
Johns, Jeremy. "The Norman Kings of Sicily and the Fatimid Caliphate," *Anglo-Norman Studies XV* (1995), pages 133-159.
Johns, Susan. *Noblewomen, Aristocracy and Power in the Twelfth-Century Anglo-Norman Realm* (2003).
Joranson, Einar. "The Inception of the Career of the Normans in Italy: Legend and History," *Speculum,* number 23 (July 1948), pages 353-396.
Jordan, Edouard. "La Politique Ecclésiastique de Roger I et les Origines

de la Légation Sicilienne," *Le Moyen Age* (1922), volume 2, pages 237-273.

Jordan, Erin. *Women, Power and Religious Patronage in the Middle Ages* (2006).

Kapitaikin, Lev. "The Daughter of Al-Andalus: Interrelations between Norman Sicily and the Muslim West," *Al-Masaq: Journal of the Medieval Mediterranean*, volume 25, issue 1 (London 2013), pages 113-134.

King, Edmund, et al. *The Anarchy of King Stephen's Reign* (1994).

Kitzinger, Ernst. "The Mosaics of the Cappella Palatina in Palermo," *Art Bulletin*, number 31 (New York 1949), pages 290-319.

Kreutz, Barbara. *Before the Normans: Southern Italy in the Ninth and Tenth Centuries* (1996).

Krönig, Wolfgang. "Sul Significato Storico dell'Arte sotto i Due Guglielmi," *Potere, Società e Popolo nell'Età dei Due Guglielmi* (Bari 1981), pages 292-310.

La Corte, Giorgio. "Appunti di Toponomastica sul Territorio della Chiesa di Monreale nel Secolo XII," *Archivio Storico Siciliano* (Palermo 1902), pages 336-345.

La Mantia, Giuseppe. "Su l'Uso della Registrazione nella Cancelleria del Regno di Sicilia dai Normanni a Federico III d'Aragona 1130-1377," *Archivio Storico Siciliano* (Palermo 1908), pages 197-209.

La Mantia, Giuseppe. "Su gli Studi di Topografia Palermitana del Medio Evo e su la Fonte detta dagli Arabi Ayb-Rum," *Archivio Storico Siciliano* (Palermo 1917), pages 317-357.

Landon, Lionel. *The Itinerary of King Richard I, with Studies on Certain Matters of Interest Connected with his Reign* (1935).

La Via, Mariano. "Le Così Dette 'Colonie Lombarde' in Sicilia," *Archivio Storico Siciliano* (Palermo 1899), pages 1-35.

Lello, Giovanni Luigi. *Descrizione del Real Tempio di Santa Maria Nuova di Monreale* (1702).

Levtzion, Nehemia. "Ibn-Hawqal, the Cheque, and Awdaghust," *Journal of African History*, volume 9, number 2 (Cambridge 1968), pages 223-233.

Lipskey, Glenn Edward. *Chronicle of Alfonso the Emperor*, translation of the *Chronica Adefonsi Imperatoris* (1972).

Loewenthal, Leonard Joseph Alphonse. "For the Biography of Walter Ophamil Archbishop of Palermo," *English Historical Review*, volume 87 (Oxford 1972), pages 75-82.

Loud, Graham. "The Image of the Tyrant in the Work of 'Hugo Falcandus,'" *Nottingham Medieval Studies*, Number 57 (January 2013), pages 1-20.

Loud, Graham. *The Latin Church in Norman Sicily* (2007).

Louda, Jiri and Maclagan, Michael. *Heraldry of the Royal Families of Europe*

(1988). Also published as *Lines of Succession*.

Lourie, Elena. "The Will of Alfonso I 'El Batallador,' King of Aragon and Navarre: A Reassessment," *Speculum*, volume 50, number 4 (October 1975), pages 635-651.

Lupo, Carmelina. "I Normanni di Sicilia di Fronte al Papato," *Archivio Storico Siciliano per la Sicilia Orientale*, volume 20 (Catania 1924), pages 1-74.

Magdalino, Paul. *The Empire of Manuel I Komnenos 1143-1180* (1993).

Makdisi, John. "The Islamic Origins of the Common Law," *North Carolina Law Review*, volume 77, number 5, June 1999, pages 1635-1737.

Mallette Karla. *The Kingdom of Sicily 1100-1250: A Literary History* (2005).

Marongiu, Antonio. "La Legislazione Normanna," *Atti del Congresso Internazionale di Studi sulla Sicilia Normanna* (Palermo 1974), pages 195-212.

Martorana, Pierluigi. *La Monetazione Aurea in Sicilia* (2007).

Massetti, Marco. *Zoologia della Sicilia Araba e Normanna 827-1194* (2016).

Matthew, Donald. *The Norman Kingdom of Sicily* (1992).

Maurici, Ferdinando. *Palermo Araba: Una sintesi dell'evoluzione urbanistica 831-1072* (2015).

Maurolico, Francesco. *Sicanicarum Rerum Compendium* (1562).

McCracken, Peggy. *The Romance of Adultery: Queenship and Sexual Transgression in Old French Literature* (1998).

Mendola, Louis. "English and Italian Legacy of the Norman Knight Figures of Monreale," *The Coat of Arms*, journal of The Heraldry Society, London, edited by John P. Brooke-Little, Norroy and Ulster King of Arms; NS Volume X, Number 166 (London 1994), pages 245-254.

Mendola, Louis. *Sicily's Rebellion against King Charles* (2016).

Menéndez Pidal, Ramón. *Cantar de Mio Cid: Texto, Gramática y Vocabulario* (1908).

Metcalfe, Alexander. *Muslims and Christians in Norman Sicily: Arabic Speakers and the End of Islam* (2011).

Meyendorff, John. *Orthodoxy and Catholicity* (1966).

Millunzi, Gaetano. "Il Mosaicista Mastro Pietro Oddo ossia Restauri e Restauratori del Duomo di Monreale nel Secolo XVI," *Archivio Storico Siciliano* (Palermo 1890), pages 195-251.

Millunzi, Gaetano. *Il Tesoro, la Biblioteca ed il Tabulario della Chiesa di Santa Maria Nuova in Monreale: Studi e Documenti* (1904).

Morso, Salvatore. *Descrizione di Palermo Antico* (1827).

Moshe, Gil. "The Jews in Sicily under Muslim Rule in the Light of Geniza Documents," *Italia Judaica 1* (1983), pages 87-134.

Naro, Massimo. *Gloria di Cristo: I Mosaici del Duomo di Monreale* (2006).

Nef, Annliese. *Conquérir et Gouverner: La Sicile Islamique aux XIe et XIIe Siècles* (2011).

Nelson, Lynn. "Rotrou of Perche and the Aragonese Reconquest," *Traditio*, number 26 (New York 1970), pages 113-133.

Norwich, John Julius. *The Kingdom in the Sun 1130-1194* (London 1970).

Oeillet des Murs, Marc-Athanase. *Historie des Comtes du Perche de la Famille des Rotrou de 943 a 1234* (1856).

Omodei, Filoteo. "La Versione Italiana della Historia di Ugo Falcando," *Archivio Storico Siciliano* (Palermo 1898), pages 465-477.

Orlando, Diego. *Il Feudalismo in Sicilia* (1847).

Palmarocchi, Roberto. "Sul Feudo Normanno," *Studi Storici* (Pavia 1912), pages 349-376.

Paoli, Sebastiano. *Codice Diplomatico del Sacro Militare Ordine Gerosolimitano, oggi di Malta* (1733).

Paratore, Ettore. "Esame delle Varianti dei Codici Vaticano e Cassinense delle Leggi," *Atti del Congresso Internazionale di Studi sulla Sicilia Normanna* (Palermo 1974), pages 477-479.

Parker, John, "The Attempted Byzantine Alliance with the Sicilian Norman Kingdom 1166-1167," *Papers of the British School at Rome* (London 1956).

Parsons, John, et al. *Medieval Queenship* (1993).

Pennington, Kenneth. "The Birth of the Ius Commune: King Roger II's Legislation," *Rivista Internazionale del Diritto Comune*, number 17 (Enna 2006).

Perla, Raffaele. *Le Assise de'Re di Sicilia* (1881).

Perry, Charles. *A Baghdad Cookery Book*. Translation of the *Kitab al-Tabikh* of Muhammad al Baghdadi (2009).

Pirri, Rocco. *Chronologia Regum Penes Quos Siciliae* (1643).

Pirri, Rocco, et al. *Sicilia Sacra Disquisitionibus et Notitiis Illustrata*, 4 volumes (1647).

Poole, Reginald. *Medieval Reckonings of Time* (1918).

Radici, Benedetto. "Il Casale e l'Abbazia di Santa Maria di Maniace," *Archivio Storico Siciliano* (Palermo 1909), pages 1-104.

Re, Edward. "The Roman Contribution to the Common Law," *Fordham Law Review*, number 447 (New York 1961), pages 447-494.

Reilly, Bernard. *The Kingdom of León-Castilla Under King Alfonso VII 1126-1157* (1998).

Riley, Henry. *The Annals of Roger de Hoveden*. English translation in 2 volumes (1853).

Rohlfs, Gerhard. *La Sicilia nei Secoli: Profilo Storico Etnico Linguistico* (1984).

Runciman, Steven. *Byzantine Civilisation* (1933, 1969).

Runciman, Steven. *The Eastern Schism: A Study of the Papacy and the Eastern Churches during the XIth and XIIth Centuries* (1955).

Ruffino, Giovanni, et al. *Lingue e Culture in Sicilia* (2013).

Russo, Rocco. *La Magione di Palermo negli Otto Secoli della Sua Storia* (1975).

San Martino de Spucches, Francesco. *Storia dei Feudi e dei Titoli Nobiliari di Sicilia,* 10 volumes (1927).

Santoro Rodolfo. "Architettura Castellana della Feudalità Siciliana," *Archivio Storico Siciliano,* Series 4, Volume 7 (Palermo 1981), pages 59-113.

Sapio Vitrano, Francesco. *Il Nummarium Islamico e Normanno della Biblioteca Comunale di Palermo* (1975).

Sauer, Michelle. *Gender in Medieval Culture* (2015).

Savagnone, Guglielmo. "Il Diploma di Fondazione della Cappella Palatina di Palermo 1140," *Archivio Storico Siciliano* (Palermo 1901), pages 66-83.

Scaduto, Mario. *Il Monachesimo Basiliano nella Sicilia Medievale: Rinascita e Decadenza* (1947).

Schlunz, Thomas Paul. *Archbishop Rotrou of Rouen 1164-1183: A Career Churchman in the Twelfth Century* (1984).

Sentis, Franz Jacob. *Die Monarchia Sicula* (1869).

Shadis, Miriam. *Berenguela of Castile and Political Women in the High Middle Ages* (2009).

Shepard, Mary, et al. *The Cloisters: Studies in Honor of the Fiftieth Anniversary* (1992), page 226.

Simonsohn, Shlomo. *Between Scylla and Charybdis: The Jews in Sicily* (2011).

Siragusa, Giovanni Battista. *Il Regno di Guglielmo I in Sicilia* (1885, 1929).

Smith, Jennifer. "Women, Land and Law in Occitania 1130-1250," *Medieval Women and the Law* (2000), pages 19-40.

Spahr, Rodolfo, *Le Monete Siciliane dai Bizantini a Carlo I d'Angio 582-1282* and *Le Monete Siciliane dagli Aragonesi ai Borboni 1282-1836* (1959).

Spata, Giuseppe. *Le Pergamene Greche Esistenti nel Grande Archivio di Palermo Tradotte ed Illustrate* (1862).

Stafford, Pauline. *Queens, Concubines and Dowagers: The King's Wife in the Early Middle Ages* (1983).

Stalls, Clay. *Possessing the Land: Aragon's Expansion into Islam's Ebro Frontier under Alfonso the Battler 1104-1134* (1995).

Starrabba, Raffaele. "Del Dotario delle Regine di Sicilia," *Archivio Storico Siciliano* (Palermo 1874), pages 7-25.

Stenton, Doris Mary. "Roger of Howden and Benedict," The *English Historical Review,* volume 68 (Oxford 1953), pages 574-582.

Stephenson, Carl. *Mediaeval Feudalism* (1942).

Stevenson, Joseph. *The Chronicles of Robert de Monte* (1991).

Strauss, Raphael. *Die Juden im Königreich Sizilien unter Normannen und Staufen* (1910).

Takayama, Hiroshi. *The Administration of the Norman Kingdom of Sicily* (1993).

Testa, Francesco. *De Vita, et Rebus Gesti Guilelmi II, Siciliae Regis, Monregalensis Ecclesii Fundatoris,* 4 volumes (1705-1773).

Thompson, Kathleen. "The Lords of Laigle: Ambition and Insecurity on the Borders of Normandy," *Anglo-Norman Studies XVIII* (1996), pages 177-180.

Thompson, Kathleen. *Power and Border Leadership in Medieval France: The County of the Perche 1000-1226* (2002).

Tramontana, Salvatore. "Gestione del Potere, Rivolte e Ceti al Tempo di Stefano di Perche," *Potere, Società e Popolo nell'Età dei Due Guglielmi* (Bari 1981), pages 79-101.

Tramontana, Salvatore. *L'Isola di Allah* (2014).

Travaini, Lucia. "La Monetazione del Regno di Sicilia al Tempo di Tancredi" *Tancredi, Conte di Lecce Re di Sicilia* (2004), pages 193-206.

Treviño, Gloria. *Santa María la Real de Nájera* (2012).

Trindade, Ann. *Berengaria: In Search of Richard the Lionheart's Queen* (1999).

Tronzo, William. *The Cultures of His Kingdom: Roger II and the Cappella Palatina of Palermo* (1997).

Turner, Ralph. *Eleanor of Aquitaine: Queen of France, Queen of England* (2009).

Van Cleave, Rachel, "Rape and Querela Law in Italy: False Protection of Victim Agency," *Michigan Journal of Gender and Law,* volume 13, number 273, January 2007 (Ann Arbor 2007).

Varvaro, Alberto. *Lingua e Storia in Sicilia* (2000).

Venuti, Antonino. *De Agricultura Opusculum* (1516).

Vetere, Benedetto. "Tancredi di Lecce nella Storiografia Medievale," *Tancredi, Conte di Lecce Re di Sicilia* (2004), pages 1-32.

Vitrano, Francesco Sapio. "La Zecca di Palermo dai Primi Insediamenti Fenici al 1836," *Archivio Storico Siciliano,* Series 3, Volume 20 (Palermo 1970), pages 107-202.

White, Lynn Townsend. *Latin Monasticism in Norman Sicily* (1938).

Zecchino, Ortensio. *Le Assise di Ariano: Testo Critico, Traduzione e Note* (1984).

INDEX

Royalty and better known figures are listed by their first names, hence *Benjamin of Tudela*. Others are listed by surname or toponym, so *Aiello, Matthew of* and *Aristippo, Henry*. Entries generally refer to the narrative text and notes rather than appendices. Margaret Jiménez, Queen of Sicily, is treated throughout most of the numbered chapters.

Abbasid dynasty, 66, 264, 330
abbeys. *See* monasteries
Acerenza, Roger of, 427n99
Adelaide Hauteville (daughter of Roger II), 168, 425n77
Adelaide del Vasto (wife of Roger I), 310, 319, 333
Adenolf (chamberlain), 135, 428n112
admiral (and amiratus), 105, 121, 354, 425n84
Adrian IV, Pope, 121, 123, 358, 388, 425n83
Africa. *See* Cairo, Mahdia, Tripoli, etc.
Aghlabids, 100, 105
agriculture, 60, 104-106, 227, 428n105
Agrigento, 215-216, 243
Agrigento, Gentile of. *See* Tuscus, Gentile
Agrò, 210
Ahmed es-Sikeli. *See* Peter, Caïd
Aiello (Ajello), John of, 239, 244, 247, 410, 437n206
Aiello (Ajello), Matthew of, 123, 131, 132, 146, 151, 156, 157, 161, 168, 188, 189, 198, 208, 210, 211, 212, 216, 218, 228, 229, 234, 236, 238, 239, 246, 249, 262, 265, 273, 291, 310, 337, 396, 409, 412
Aigle (l'Aigle). *See* Margaret, Richard, *et al.*
Alexander III, Pope, 123, 131, 183,

186, 198, 216, 243, 247, 248, 256, 257, 258, 264, 274, 293, 295, 297-299, 307, 313, 318

Alexandria (Egypt), 268, 295, 296, 345

Alfonso I of Aragon and Navarre, 77-82 passim, 340

Alfonso VI of León and Castile, 71, 72, 76, 340

Alfonso VII of Castile, 82-83, 91, 114

Alfonso VIII of Castile (nephew of Margaret), 245, 246, 250, 295, 315, 327, 341

Allucingoli, Ubaldo. See Lucius III

Almaric, King of Jerusalem, 295-296

Almohad dynasty, 130, 246, 316, 327

almonds, 104, 106

Almoravid dynasty, 71, 78, 81, 84, 86

amiratus. See admiral *(sic)*

Anarchy (English civil war), 252, 253

Andrew (governor of Messina), 217-219

anointings. See coronations

Ansaldo (castellan), 230-231

Antioch, 77

Antioch, George of, 101, 115, 148, 265

apostolic legateship, 101, 124, 162, 238, 332

Apulia, 110, 121, 122, 130, 135, 144, 156, 158, 190, 268, 271, 290, 291

Aquila, Richard of, 164, 434n170

Aquitaine, 12, 13, 250, 304

Arabic, 7, 27, 62, 68, 100-101, 102, 103, 104, 105, 108, 150, 313, 346, 354, 425

Arabs, xiii, 62, 100, 101, 104-107, 110, 125, 140, 161, 180, 181, 216, 226, 274. *See also* Muslims

Aragon, xi, 6, 12, 13, 46, 61, 63, 67-86 passim, 92, 93, 96, 268, 330

archers, 224, 227, 233, 278, 423n62

architecture. *See* Norman-Arab architecture, Monreale, mosaics, muqarnas, Zisa

archon. *See* familiare

Ariano, Assizes of. *See* Assizes of Ariano

Aristippo, Henry, 137, 138, 144, 145

artichokes, 60, 104

Asclettin (general), 121-123

Assize of Clarendon, 237, 257, 424n67

Assizes of Ariano, xiv, 109, 127, 182, 198, 229, 369-386

astrology, 226, 236, 442n265

Avellino, Roger of, 230, 232, 443n270

Aversa, Richard of, 196-197

Ayyubid dynasty, 264, 295, 296. *See also* Saladin

INDEX

Baghdad, 268, 346, 425n75
Balbano, Richard of, 190, 438n210
Ballarò souk, 105
Barbarossa. *See* Frederick I
Barcelona, xii, 61, 69, 71, 82, 93, 96, 268
Bari, 17, 123, 125, 318
Barletta, 17, 290, 312, 396
baronage (Sicilian) defined, 125-128
Bartholomew of Agrigento (archbishop), 247, 405, 444n298
Basque language. *See* Euskara
Basques, 63-64, 73, 418
Bassonville, Robert of. *See* Loritello, Robert of
Bath, Reginald Fitzjocelin de Bohun of, 307, 350, 365-366
baths. *See* hammam, mikvehs
Beatrice Hohenstaufen (daughter of Frederick I), 292-293, 397, 450n373, 456n442
Beatrice of Rethel, 115, 117, 120, 144, 194, 292, 306, 307, 325
Beauchamp, Hugh of, 304, 401
Bec, Theobald of, 252, 253, 255
Becket, Thomas. *See* Thomas Becket
Bellisina, Robert of, 188-189, 437n207
Benedictines, 82, 101, 114, 148, 194, 201, 274, 297, 301, 309-310, 313, 320, 409. *See also* Cassino, Cava, Monreale
Benevento, 17, 121, 123, 248, 291, 396
Benevento, Treaty of, 130, 358, 426n89
Benjamin of Tudela, 267-269
Bertrand of Perche, 126, 342
betrothals, royal. *See* dowers, marriages
Biblical imagery, 51, 277, 278, 279, 306, 367
Blanca Jiménez (sister of Margaret), 41, 42, 60, 80, 83, 87-89 passim, 92, 93, 96, 114, 124, 150, 245, 341, 342
Blois Massacre, 263
Blois, Peter of, 170, 174, 226, 236, 244, 273, 351, 445n302
Blois, William of, 310, 351, 452n392
Boccaccio, Giovanni, 313, 354
Bohemond of Antioch, xiv, 77, 419n14
Bohemond Hauteville (son of William II), 316, 453n404
Bohemond of Taranto. *See* Bohemond of Antioch
Bonello, Matthew of, 130-141 passim, 143
Boson of Gorron (bishop), 210, 227, 239, 430n128, 444n292
Breakspear, Nicholas. *See* Adrian IV
Brindisi, 16, 17, 122, 295
Bulot, Baldwin, 400, 402
Burgos, 12, 13, 69, 70
Burgundio (justiciar), 216, 441n252

Butera, 18, 122, 442n266
Byzantine Empire, 19, 20, 100, 121, 125, 245, 262, 290, 297, 326, 392
Caccamo, 130, 133, 136, 141, 143, 428n115, 440n251
Cairo, 66, 264, 268, 447n339
Calabria, 3, 16, 17, 122, 130, 201, 203, 219, 227, 239, 244, 305, 312, 325, 349
Calahorra, 12, 14, 114
Calatabiano, Robert of, 147-148, 179-183, 187
Callixtus III (antipope), 298, 313
Calomeno, John, 219, 441n254
Caltanissetta, 168
Camerota, Florio of, 302, 304, 310, 313, 397, 400
Campania. *See* Capua, Naples, Principate, Salerno, *etc.*
Camville, Richard of, 400, 402
canon law, 109, 166, 200
Canterbury, 48, 49, 250, 258, 296, 351, 365
Canterbury, Richard (archbishop) of, 305, 400-401
Canterbury, Thomas of. *See* Thomas Becket
Cantuese, Alduin, 233, 443n277
Capaccio, Arnolf of, 302, 304, 397, 399, 402
caponata, 104
Capua, 16, 17, 164, 292, 312, 320, 423n61, 454n413
Caserta, Robert of, 194-195, 305, 398, 406
Cassino monastery, 274, 320, 349, 351, 454n413
Castile, 12, 13, 67, 68, 69, 70. *See also* Burgos, Toledo, *etc.*
Catalogus Baronum, 127, 144, 426n93
Catalonia, 12, 13, 61, 67, 69, 81, 82, 93, 96, 103. *See also* Barcelona
Catania, 16, 18, 188, 227, 244, 248, 410
Catanzaro, Clementia of, 131, 239, 427n97, 443n277
Catanzaro, Hugh of, 233, 238-239, 406, 443n277, 444n289
Cava monastery, 114, 274
Cefalù, 16, 18, 50, 113, 119, 169, 210, 227, 230, 318, 345, 410
censorship in Italy, 3, 417n1. *See also* historiography
Charlemagne, 63-64
chess, xiii, 90, 113
chickpeas, 104
Cistercians, 201, 309, 452n389
chivalry. *See* knighthood
coats of arms. *See* heraldry
Code of Justinian, 109, 110, 369, 423n64
Codex Vigilanus, 68
coinage, 58, 106, 110, 423n61
common law (in England), 110, 254, 259, 424n67
Constance of Aragon, xi, 343
Constance of Hauteville (daughter

of Roger II), xii, 4, 144, 194, 266, 292, 294, 307, 316, 325-327, 343
Constantine (castellan), 230, 232, 442n269
Constantinople (now Istanbul), 94, 144, 244, 268, 290, 319, 326
Constitutions of Clarendon, 256
Constitutions of Melfi, 355, 423n65, 434n171
Cordoba, 66, 67, 346
Corleone, 274
coronations, 5, 70, 83, 114, 115, 119, 120, 121, 151, 253, 258, 306, 326
Cosenza, 16, 17, 325
Cristina Díaz de Vivar (daughter of El Cid), 72, 76, 80, 341
crowns, 57, 131, 134, 427n103
Crusade, First, 77, 94, 422n44
Crusade, Second, 115
Cuba palace, 22, 24, 107, 313
Cubola pavilion, 22, 24, 107
cuisine, 60, 104-106
dar al-hikma (house of wisdom), 226
Decameron. *See* Boccaccio
Díaz de Vivar, Rodrigo (El Cid). *See* Rodrigo Díaz de Vivar
Diceto, Ralph of, 5, 351, 407-408
divorce laws, 164-166, 434
diwan (treasury), 105, 116, 127, 130, 134, 139, 156, 169, 198, 248, 354
dowers, dowries, 78, 96, 170, 303, 401-407, 419n15

Doxopatrios, Nilos, 101, 422n54
ducat. *See* coinage
dysentery, 2, 151, 389-390
earthquakes, 244, 276, 325, 346, 410, 445n301
Ebro River, 72, 80, 114, 268
Edrisi. *See* Idrisi, Abdullah
Egypt, 66, 264, 268, 295, 296, 345, 447n339. *See also* Cairo, Fatimids, *etc.*
Eire. *See* Ireland
El Cid. *See* Rodrigo Díaz de Vivar
Eleanor of Aquitaine, 129, 154, 246, 301-303, 304, 306, 311, 327, 427n102, 451n375
Eleanor of England (daughter of Henry II), 245, 246, 250, 295, 315, 316
Elvira of Castile, xi, 72, 73, 94, 95, 96, 148, 340, 343
Ely, Geoffrey of, 304, 305, 401
England. *See* Henry II, Thomas Becket, *et al.*
Estella (Lizarra), 92
Etna, Mount, 18, 244, 410
eunuchs, 105, 134, 138, 139, 145, 146, 156, 158, 180, 181, 187, 214, 323
Euskara (Basque language), 7, 61, 418n7
Evreux, Giles of, 304, 305, 401, 402, 403
Faiano, 313
Falcandus, Hugh. *See* Hugh Falcan-

dus

familiare (familiaris) defined, 151, 431n148

familiares, 156-163 passim, 168-175 passim, 181, 188, 189, 192, 198, 209, 210, 213, 228, 230, 237, 238, 239, 247, 262, 291, 358

Fatimid dynasty, 66, 107, 108, 112, 149, 264, 278, 295-296

Favara palace, 107, 149

Fazello, Thomas, 5-6, 349

feminism. *See* women's status

Fernando of León and Castile, 70, 340

feudalism. *See* manorialism

Foliot, Gilbert, 258, 400

follaris. *See* coinage

Fondi, Richard of. *See* Sai, Richard of

food. *See* cuisine

Fragalà monastery, 310

Frankish feudal law, 435n184

Frederick I (Barbarossa), Holy Roman Emperor, 121-124 passim, 161, 186, 198, 208, 248, 257, 290, 292-293, 295, 298, 312, 326, 388, 397

Frederick II, Holy Roman Emperor, 327

furusiyya code, 418n10

Gaeta, Peter of, 243

Galicia (in Spain), 71

gambling, 167, 168, 217, 218, 223, 434n176

gaming. *See* gambling

García Jiménez, 68, 340

García Ramírez (father of Margaret), xv, 6, 59-60, 68-94 passim, 340, 341

García Sánchez I (García I) of Pamplona, 340

García Sánchez II (García II) of Pamplona and Aragon, 340

García Sánchez III of Pamplona and Navarre (García of Nájera), 69-72, 340

gargoyles, 108

Gascony, 12, 13, 61, 68, 84

Genoans, 124, 268, 272, 313, 319, 450n370

Genoard park, viii, 22, 106-107, 111-113, 148, 150, 232

George of Antioch, 101, 115, 148

Gerace (in Calabria), 17, 318, 330

Gerace, Roger of, 227, 237, 441n250

Germany. *See* Holy Roman Empire

Gesualdo, William of, 190, 438n210

Gilbert of Aigle (grandfather of Margaret), 80, 102, 341

Gilbert of Gravina, 126, 131, 135, 144, 145, 157-158, 159-170 passim, 192, 193, 204, 206-211, 238, 342

Gilbert of Perche. *See* Gilbert of Gravina

Glanville, Ranulf of, 254, 424n67, 446n322

INDEX

gold. *See* coinage

grain. *See* rice, wheat

Gravina, 16, 17, 126, 209

Great Schism. *See* Schism of 1054

Greece. *See* Byzantine Empire

Greek Christians. *See* Orthodox Church

Greek language, xv, 27, 28, 30, 31, 99, 100, 102, 148, 194, 218, 224, 277

Guardia. *See* La Guardia

Halkah district (Palermo), 21, 111, 429n120

Hamelin of Warenne, 304, 401

hammam, 108

harems, 105, 134, 138, 144, 145, 146, 214, 303

Hauteville dynasty. *See* Roger I, Roger II, William I, *et al.*

ibn Hawqal, Abdullah (emir), 330

ibn Hawqal, Mohammed (traveler), 317-318, 346, 350

henna, 106

Henry II of England, xii, 5, 154, 174, 226, 245, 247, 248, 250, 251, 253-254, 257, 259, 265, 273, 293, 295, 296-297, 299, 301, 315, 326, 393

Henry VI, Holy Roman Emperor, 326, 327

Henry, Prince of Capua (youngest son of Margaret and William), 4, 125, 289, 290, 291-292, 396

Henry, the Young King (son of Henry II of England), 258, 301, 304, 363-364, 447

Henry of Montescaglioso (Rodrigo Jiménez), 87-88, 89, 167, 168, 190, 203, 205-206, 217, 219-220, 225, 236, 237, 239, 246, 392

heraldry (coats of arms), 277, 278

Hervé the Florid, 232

historiography (historical perspective), xiv, 3, 4, 5, 8, 9, 146, 265, 355, 358, 417n1

Hohenstaufen dynasty of Swabia. *See* Frederick I, Henry VI, *et al.*

Holy Land. *See* Jerusalem, Palestine

Holy Roman Empire, 63, 121, 122, 124, 292, 293, 295, 298, 307, 313, 326, 327, 397

horse breeds, 77, 90, 304

Hospitallers (knights), 81, 86, 326

Howden (Hoveden), Roger of, 5, 51, 399, 402

Huesca, 80

Hugh, Archbishop of Palermo, 123-124, 131, 132, 135

Hugh Falcandus, xviii, 4-5, 32, 87, 131, 353-356

Iberia. *See* Spain

icons, 113, 120, 259, 269, 275, 276-277, 282, 286-287, 306, 319, 390, 410

Idrisi, Abdullah, 104, 116, 125, 349

indigo, 106

Iñigo Arista, 64, 65

Ireland (Eire), 101, 264

Iruña. *See* Pamplona
Islam. *See* Muslims
Italocentrism, 3, 417. *See also* historiography
Jaca, 69
Ja'far al-Kalbi (emir), 107
Jato, 274
Jerusalem, 236, 244, 263, 264, 268, 295, 296, 326, 327
Jews, 2, 25, 26, 27, 63, 66, 78, 84, 95, 100, 109, 198, 201, 263, 267-269, 316
Jiménez dynasty, origins of, 6, 60, 65, 68, 340
Joan Plantagenet. *See* Joanna of England
Joanna of England (wife of William II), 5, 247-250 passim, 293, 298, 301-307, 310, 315, 316, 320, 325, 326, 366, 397-398, 399-408
bin Jubayr, Mohammed, 345-346
Judaism. *See* Jews
Judeo Arabic language, 7, 27, 100, 102
Juliana of Perche, 80, 102, 342
jure uxoris defined, 83, 292
justiciar defined, 198, 431n140
justiciars, 177, 179, 182, 189, 197, 204-206 passim, 216, 298, 302, 312, 438n218
Justinian Code. *See* Code of Justinian
Justus (apothecary), 189

Kala harbor, 147, 232
Kalbid dynasty, 66, 105, 107
kanats, 21, 22, 107, 108, 132
Kasim, Abu'l, 187
Kasr district (Palermo), 21, 230, 232
Kemonia river, 21, 22, 106, 313
al-Kenani. *See* bin Jubayr
Khalesa district (Palermo), 21, 149, 265
Kitab al-Tabikh, 104
knighthood, 64, 65, 126, 127, 418n10
Knights Hospitaller. *See* Hospitallers
Knights Templar. *See* Templars
Koran, 108, 308
La Guardia, 59, 60, 80, 82-83, 93, 114
La Rioja, 59-60, 68, 70, 72-73, 93, 114, 245, 250
Laigle (l'Aigle). *See* Margaret, Richard, *et.al.*
Lateran Council, Second, 200
Lateran Council, Third, 318
Lauro, Robert of. *See* Caserta, Robert of
Lavardin, John of, 211, 230
law. *See* Assizes of Ariano, canon law, divorce, Frankish feudal law, Longobard feudal law, Malaki School, rape law, *etc.*
Lecce, 16, 17, 135
legateship. *See* apostolic legateship

INDEX

Leluce, William of, 441n250

Lentini, 244, 414

León, 68, 70, 71

Leonor Plantagenet. *See* Eleanor of England

Lionheart. *See* Richard I of England

Lizarra. *See* Estella

Logroño, 12, 13, 14, 59, 80, 114

Lombards (Italians in Sicily), 100, 102, 109, 227, 231, 442n266

London, 258, 303, 400

Longobard feudal law, 109, 435n184

Loritello, Robert of, 121, 122, 123, 126, 130, 144, 209-210, 240-241, 248, 388

Louis VII of France, 253, 257, 393

Louis IX of France, 279

Luci, Richard of, 254

Lucius III (Ubaldo Allucingoli), Pope, 166, 318, 319, 320

Lupino, Hugh. *See* Catanzaro, Hugh of

Lusci, Bartholomew of, 207, 439n232

Madonian Mountains, 18, 424n70

Mahdia, 130

Maio of Bari, 116, 121, 123, 125, 129-139 passim, 147-149, 265, 358

Majorca, 96, 319

Malaki School (law), 110

malaria, 2

Malaterra, Godfrey (Geoffrey), 350, 422n49, 442n260

Mallorca. *See* Majorca.

Malta, John of, 236, 237

Mandra, Richard of. *See* Molise, Richard of

Maniace monastery, 272, 275, 278, 294, 301, 310, 411

Manopello, Bohemond of, 191, 208, 233

Manopello, Carbonello of, 233

manorialism (feudalism), 64, 127-128, 176, 308, 435n184

Manuel Comnenus of Constantinople (Byzantine Emperor), 121, 122, 166-167, 262, 290-291, 316, 319, 392

Margaret of Aigle (mother of Margaret Jiménez), 59, 78, 80, 85-88 passim, 92, 341, 342

Margaret Jiménez, Queen of Sicily: ancestry, 59, 80, 341-342; appearance, ix, 97, 365, 367; birth, 60, 75, 82-83; character, 95, 145, 201, 283, 321-324; charters and decrees, 29, 30, 156, 409-415; childhood, 60, 83, 87-89, 92-95; crown, 57; death, 281, 320-321; defamation of, 187; historical legacy, xi, xii, 4, 272, 309-310, 321-324; marriage, 95-97, 145, 388-389; regency, 153-250, 251-266, 389, 391-392

Margaret, Queen of Pamplona. *See* Margaret of Aigle

Margaritus of Brindisi, 326
Maria of Constantinople (daughter of Manuel Comnenus), 166-167, 271, 290-291, 298, 392, 395-396
marriages, royal, 78, 79, 91-94 passim, 96, 110, 166-167, 170, 247-253 passim, 306, 316, 325, 388-389, 397-399, 401-407, 419. *See also* dowers
Martin, Caïd, 145-147 passim, 154, 169, 247, 412, 413
Martorana church, 21, 24, 54, 55, 101, 107, 148, 265, 346, 411
Martorana, Godfrey, 411
Martorano, Roger of, 131
Mary Magdalene churches (Palermo), 129, 148, 149, 279, 318, 320
Matilda, Empress. *See* Maude
Matina monastery, 309-310, 351, 452n392
Maude (mother of Henry II of England), 154, 322, 432n153
Melisende of Jerusalem, 432n153
Messina, 94, 96, 122, 143, 149, 157, 168, 190, 193, 195, 204, 207, 210, 217-220 passim, 221-227, 244, 268, 295, 305
Meulan, Robert of, 231, 233
mihrabs, 108, 318
mikvehs, 21, 24, 25, 108, 269
Milan, 61, 326
Moac, Walter of, 209, 406
Modica (Moac), 244

Molise, Richard of, 159-169 passim, 190, 198, 208, 210, 224, 225, 236-239 passim, 247, 412, 413
Monasteries. *See* Maniace, Monreale, *etc.*
Monopoli, Bohemond of, 131
Monreale Abbey, xv, 259, 271-287, 293-298 passim, 301, 307, 308, 317, 318, 320
Monzón, 59, 72, 73, 76, 78, 79, 81
Moors (Muslim Arabs of Spain), 62, 67, 69, 71, 76, 87, 96, 170
mosaics, 112, 113, 120, 126, 259, 269, 276-279, 281-282, 286-287, 306, 319, 390
Moslems. *See* Muslims
mosques, 63, 95, 108, 111, 112, 148, 317, 318
Mount Cassino. *See* Cassino
Mount Sant'Angelo, 290, 303, 403-405
Muniadona Mayor, 68
muqarnas, 108, 112-113, 276, 317
Muslims, xiii, 62, 63, 65, 66, 67, 71, 77, 78, 79, 84, 95, 101, 104, 105, 106, 110, 126, 139, 140, 145, 146, 180, 181, 187, 199, 201, 263, 268, 308, 316, 345-346. *See also* Moors
Nájera, 60, 65, 68, 69, 70, 72, 73, 93, 114. *See also* Santa María la Real
Naples, 96, 123, 156, 239, 305, 398
Naples, John of, 161-163 passim, 166
Navarra. *See* Navarre

Navarre, xiv, 2, 7, 12, 13, 14, 60-88 passim, 92, 93, 96, 190, 250. *See also* Pamplona, Tudela, *etc.*

Navarro-Aragonese language, 69, 103

Nebrodian fir, 279

Nebrodian Mountains, 18, 144, 194, 272, 294, 319

Neubourg, Robert of, 169

Norman-Arab architecture, 47, 50, 51, 52, 53, 54, 55, 56, 107-108, 272-287

Norman French language, 7, 88, 100, 101, 102, 103, 105, 170, 303

Norman Palace, 51, 52, 97, 111, 112, 133-148 passim, 159, 160, 162, 169, 170, 194, 213, 214, 232. *See also* Palatine Chapel

Normans defined, 93, 94, 99-101

Norwich, John of, 305, 400-402, 407

Noto, 168

Odo of Bayeux, 94, 422n44

Oreto River, 21, 107, 148, 309

Orthodox Church, 8, 62, 101, 210, 276, 277, 346, 410, 422n54, 439n231

Ostia, Ubaldo Allucingoli of. *See* Lucius III

Palatine Chapel (Palermo), 51, 97, 151, 240, 242, 269, 276, 277, 306

Palermo, 18, 21, 22, 23, 24, 93-97 passim, 104-108 passim, 111-120, 169, 180, 183, 186, 210, 215, 230-309 passim, 318, 320

Palermo Cathedral, 53, 129, 123, 149, 151, 183, 212, 243, 247, 272, 277, 307, 319

Palestine, 77, 144, 170, 174, 236, 244, 263, 264, 268, 295, 296, 326, 327

Palmer, Richard. *See* Richard Palmer

Pamplona (city), 4, 6, 12, 13, 14, 61-70 passim, 75, 80-89 passim, 95, 209, 327

Pamplona, Kingdom of. *See* Navarre

Pantocrator, 51, 277, 306

papacy. *See* Adrian IV, Alexander III, *et al.*

Papyrus (Papireto) river, 21, 22, 106, 132, 139

Parisio, Bartholomew of, 164, 203, 209

Pavia, William of, 174

Pedro I of Aragon and Navarre, 340

Peloritan Mountains, 18, 224

Perche family. *See* Rotrou, Stephen, *et al.*

Peter, Caïd (Ahmed es-Sikeli), 156-161 passim, 174, 177, 178-179, 181, 209, 246

Pierleoni, Hugh, 303, 400

Pisa, Bonanno of, 279

Pisan Tower. *See* Norman Palace

Pisans, 319

Plantagenet (Angevin) dynasty. *See*

Henry II, Joanna, Richard I, *et al.*
Poitiers, 304, 401
Poitiers, Simon of, 233
popes. *See* Adrian IV, Alexander III, *et al.*
population: of kingdom, 213, 441n249; of Palermo, 116, 425n75
Primacy of Sicily defined, 124, 175, 193-194
Primates of Sicily. *See* Hugh, Walter (archbishops of Palermo)
Principate, 239
Procida, John of, 313
Puglia. *See* Apulia
Quarrel, Odo, 174, 176, 209-210, 216-219 passim, 221-223
Quran. *See* Koran
Ramiro II of Aragon, 79, 82, 83, 86
Ramiro Sánchez of Monzón (father of García Ramírez), 72, 76, 340, 341
rape laws, 109, 182, 373, 380
Reconquista, 65, 81, 327
redemption tax, 156, 389
Reggio (in Calabria), 16, 17, 209, 219
Regnum Siciliae defined, xiv
religion. *See* Jews, Muslims, *et al.*
revisionism, historical. *See* censorship, historiography, Italocentrism
rex filius defined, 114-116
rice, 104

Richard I (Lionheart) of England, 277, 301, 304, 326, 327, 363-364
Richard of Aigle, 80, 175, 252, 341
Richard, Caïd (chamberlain), 192, 194, 212-213, 218, 234, 236, 237, 247
Richard Palmer, 146, 151, 156, 157, 158, 161-164 passim, 169, 176, 178, 198, 236, 237, 240, 244, 248, 249, 305, 362-363, 389, 398, 405, 406, 412, 413
Rioja. *See* La Rioja
Robert, Prince of Capua (son of Margaret and William), 116, 125, 129, 149
Rochester, Paris of, 400, 401, 402
Rodrigo Díaz de Vivar (El Cid), 69-72, 76, 87, 341
Rodrigo Jiménez. *See* Henry of Montescaglioso
Roger I of Sicily, 310, 319, 343
Roger II of Sicily, xi, 35, 93, 109, 116, 117, 343, 369
Roger, Duke of Apulia (eldest son of Margaret and William), 115, 125, 140, 141, 149
Rome, 123, 162, 183, 248, 268, 276, 298, 326
Rometta, 224
Romuald Guarna of Salerno, 4-5, 33, 87, 116, 123, 130, 151, 175-176, 188-189, 236, 237, 306, 307, 312, 313, 357-358, 387
Rothrud the Great. *See* Rotrou III

INDEX

Rotrou III of Perche, 77-80 passim, 85, 86, 94, 126, 333, 342, 350-351

Rotrou of Perche, Archbishop of Rouen, 169, 242, 302, 303, 342, 400

Rouen, 169, 322, 338

Sai (Say), Richard of, 164-166, 203

Sai (Say), Theodora of, 164-166, 203

Saint Cathaldus church. *See* San Cataldo

Saint-Gilles (city), 304-305, 398, 401, 407, 408

Saint James, Way of, 69

Saint John of the Hermits monastery, 52, 149, 194

Saint Mary of the Latins, 265, 409, 412

Saladin (An-Nasir Salah ad-Din Yusuf ibn Ayyub), 264, 295, 296, 326

Salerno (city), 96, 113, 123, 124, 156, 239, 291, 292, 305, 317, 320

Salerno, Romuald of. *See* Romuald Guarna of Salerno

Salernus (physician), 188-189

San Cataldo church, 54, 101, 148

San Germano (Cassino), 312

San Germano, Richard of, 273, 351

San Giovanni, Robert of, 212, 440n243

San Juan de la Peña, 81

San Marco d'Alunzio, 114, 194, 216, 236, 266, 301, 310

San Severino, William of, 194, 195, 233, 443n277

Sancha of Castile (consort of Sancho VI of Navarre), 124-125, 341

Sancho I of Pamplona (Sancho Garcés I), 65, 68, 340

Sancho II of León and Castile, 70, 71, 340

Sancho II of Pamplona (Sancho Garcés II), 340

Sancho III of Castile (husband of Blanca Jiménez), 114, 245, 341

Sancho III of Pamplona (Sancho Garcés III), 67-70, 340

Sancho IV of Pamplona (Navarre), 72, 340

Sancho IV of Navarre, 72, 340

Sancho VI of Navarre (brother of Margaret Jiménez), 60, 80, 92, 125, 209, 246, 250, 315, 327, 341

Sancho Garcés of Uncastillo, 72, 76, 340

Sancho Ramírez of Aragon and Navarre, 340, 342

Sancho de Rosas, Bishop of Pamplona, 84, 86

Sanchos, War of. *See* Three Sanchos

Sangro, Philip of, 131, 427n99

Santa María la Real (Nájera), 41, 42, 69, 93

Santa Maria delle Scale (Santa Maria della Valle), 210, 410

Santiago, Camino de. *See* Saint James, Way of

Saqaliba district (Palermo), 265, 409, 412

Saracens. *See* Muslims

Saragossa. *See* Zaragoza

sayyid (title) defined, 70

Schism of 1054, 101

Scibene palace, 22, 107, 148

Sclafani, 168

seals, royal, 29, 78, 312, 405, 406, 407, 409, 412, 413, 414

Selby, Robert of, 116

serfdom, 109, 126, 198, 211, 254, 308, 320

sexual defamation, 186-187

Sibylla of Burgundy, 113, 114

Sicilian (language), 7, 102

Sicilian Vespers War, xi, 452n388

Siculo Arabic. *See* Arabic

Siddiq, Caïd, 187

Sienna, Roland of. *See* Alexander III

silver. *See* coinage.

Simon (Hauteville) of Taranto, 135-141 passim, 144

Siracusa. *See* Syracuse

Sorello, Roger, 207, 440n233

souks (suks), 25, 105

Spain. *See* Castile, Navarre, *etc.*

Staufen dynasty. *See* Hohenstaufen

Stephen of Perche, 168-197 passim, 204-219 passim, 227, 228, 230-236 passim, 244, 342

Struma, John of. *See* Callixtus III

synagogues, 25, 26, 92, 95, 269

Syracuse (Siracusa), 16, 18, 25, 26, 100, 108, 124, 149, 244

Tancred of Lecce (later King of Sicily), 135, 136, 137, 139, 140, 144, 294-295, 296, 310, 326, 327, 343

Taormina, 18, 108, 209, 210, 224-225, 244

Taranto, 16, 17, 122, 135, 205, 289, 290, 395, 396

tarì. *See* coinage

Tarsia, Bohemond of. *See* Manopello

Templars, 81, 86, 245

Termini Imerese, 18, 190, 191, 345

Theobald of Monreale (abbot), 310, 405

Theotokos, 277

Thomas Becket, 174, 175, 240, 248, 249, 250, 251-259, 277, 282, 307, 359, 362, 365-366, 392-393

Thomas Brown. *See* Thomas le Brun

Thomas le Brun, 116, 125

Thomas of Canterbury, Saint. *See* Thomas Becket

Three Sanchos, War of, 70, 72

Tiron, Roger of, 212, 233, 440n243

Toledo, 315

Torigni, Robert of, 316

Trani, Barisano of, 280

treasury. *See* diwan

Tricarico, Roger of (son of Robert of Caserta), 131, 427n99

Tripoli (in Africa), 116

INDEX

Troia, Elias of, 302, 304, 397, 399, 400, 402, 405

Tropea, Erveo of, 134, 428n109

Tudela, 63, 78, 83, 85, 87, 170, 267

Tunisia, 100, 264, 279, 316. *See also* Mahdia, *etc.*

Turgisio, 208

Turkey. *See* Byzantine Empire

Tuscus, Gentile, 156, 157, 158, 211, 215-216, 236, 237, 243, 263, 412, 413, 414

Tyre, William of, 348, 445n306, 454n411

Umayyad dynasty, 62, 66

Uncastillo, 72

Urraca of Castile (stepmother of Margaret), 91, 92

Valencia, 71, 76

Venetians, 297

Vespers War. *See* Sicilian Vespers War

Vivar, Cristina. *See* Cristina Díaz de Vivar

Vivar, Rodrigo de (El Cid). *See* Rodrigo Díaz de Vivar

Walter, Archbishop of Palermo, 146, 169, 175, 237, 239, 240, 242-243, 247, 262, 270, 271, 273, 274, 291, 297, 306, 319

Way of Saint James. *See* Saint James, Way of

wheat, 227, 428n105

William I of Sicily (husband of Margaret), 94-97, 112-125 passim, 130-151 passim, 154

William II of Sicily (son of Margaret): accession, 151, 390-391; birth, 121, 426n88; death, 326; education, 146, 174, 199, 213, 240, 273; marriage, 298, 301-308, 366, 397, 399-408; military campaigns, 295-296, 319, 326; obtains age of majority, 269-270; progeny, 316, 325

Winchester, 302, 303, 311, 400

women's status and rights, xii, xiii, xiv, 3-4, 6, 104, 105, 109, 146, 181, 182, 198, 201, 322, 354, 373, 380, 417n1. *See also* dowers, rape laws

Ximenez. *See* Jiménez

Zaragoza, 12, 13, 46, 61, 63, 68, 71, 81-84 passim, 93, 268

Zirid dynasty, 19, 130, 330, 427n95

Zisa palace, 21, 22, 24, 47, 107, 150, 154, 306, 387-388

This book was first printed simultaneously in Italy and in the United States of America in March 2017. The text is set in Garamond, a typeface developed in Paris by the engraver Claude Garamont during the sixteenth century.

www.ingramcontent.com/pod-product-compliance
Lightning Source LLC
Chambersburg PA
CBHW021112300426
44113CB00006B/128